INSIDERS' GUIDE®

W9-CHG-720

FUN WITH THE FAMILY™ SERIES

fun WITH the Family™

NEW YORK

HUNDREDS OF IDEAS FOR DAY TRIPS WITH THE KIDS

MARY LYNN BLANKS

FIFTH EDITION

INSIDERS' GUIDE®

GUILFORD, CONNECTICUT
AN IMPRINT OF THE GLOBE PEQUOT PRESS

The prices, rates, and hours listed in this guidebook were confirmed at press time. We recommend, however, that you call establishments to obtain current information before traveling.

To buy books in quantity for corporate use or incentives, call **(800) 962–0973, ext. 4551,** or e-mail **premiums@GlobePequot.com.**

INSIDERS' GUIDE®

Copyright © 1997, 1999, 2001, 2003, 2005 by The Globe Pequot Press

Insiders' Guide is a registered trademark of The Globe Pequot Press.
Fun with the Family is a trademark of The Globe Pequot Press.

Text design by Nancy Freeborn and Linda Loiewski
Maps by M. A. Dubé
Spot photography throughout © PhotoDisc, Inc. and © Rubberball Productions

ISSN 1542-4189
ISBN 0-7627-3495-7

Manufactured in the United States of America
Fifth Edition/First Printing

Contents

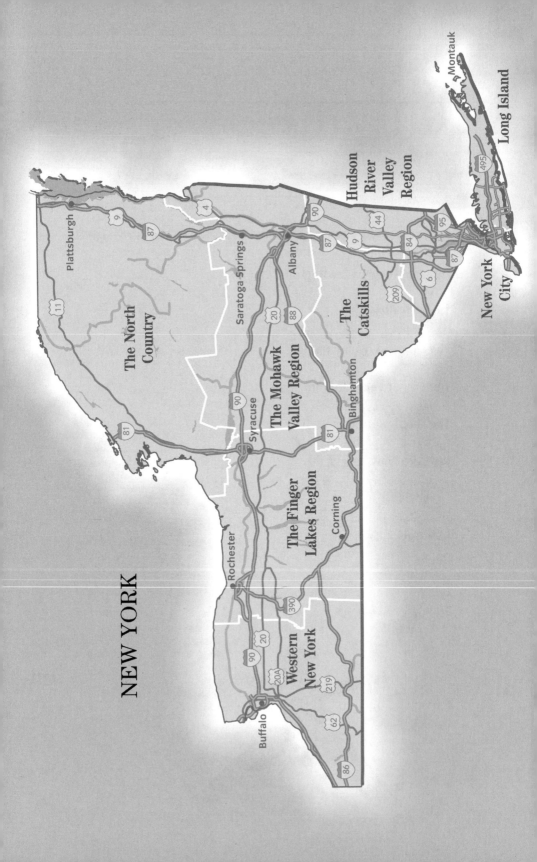

Acknowledgments

Researching the riches of New York would not have been possible without the assistance of the wonderful people at the tourist offices, parks, and attractions throughout the state. Space does not permit the inclusion of the names of all these folks, but you'd be hard-pressed to find a more helpful and enthusiastic group, and I urge you to contact them for more information.

A special thanks to my editors Cheryl McClean and Joan Wheal, who guided me through this adventure with wit, wisdom, and infinite patience. Working with them has been a treasured gift and a tough act to follow.

To all my friends who supported and sustained me through this journey, I am deeply indebted. Their faith in my talent allowed me to believe in myself and find my voice. Thank you with all my heart.

And finally, to my mom and dad, Lola and John Blanks, and my sister, Lisa, all presently touring another dimension, I owe perhaps the most. From London to Leningrad, Istanbul to Indonesia, my parents journeyed with us to just about every Pan-American port of call, encouraging our exploration of new experiences and different cultures. It was their gift of the world when I was young that sparked the fire of adventure and discovery within me and nurtured my sense of wonder. My hope is to pass this gift on to my children and perhaps to yours. Enjoy the trip!

Introduction

L ike a magician's scarf, the glaciers of the last Ice Age grazed across the face of New York, transforming the land into a myriad of geological shapes and spectacular natural beauty. Over half the state is blanketed in thick, verdant forests; bejeweled by thousands of sapphire lakes; laced with ribbons of trout-laden streams; and edged in sugar sand beaches. For the purposes of this book, New York is divided into eight regions, and each area features facets of the state's scenic wonders, rich heritage, and cultural diversity. From the fjords of the Hudson River and the hemlock cathedrals of the Catskills to the Great Camps of the ancient Adirondacks and the homeland of the Haudenosaunee, the legends of Leatherstocking Country, Long Island's Gold Coast, and the grandeur of Niagara Falls have lured visitors from all over the world for generations.

And then there is the apple of my eye, New York City, the capital of the world, a mecca for dreamers and doers, and a place where all is possible. Although time and space don't allow the inclusion of every place of interest, this guide will give you the keys to the original magic kingdom and open a door to the Empire State for you and your family.

Unlike solo travels, where there's a footloose freedom, family travel requires a bit more planning, and everyone should be included in the process. Contact the tourism offices listed via mail, phone, or Web for information packets, money-saving packages, and current event information. As New York is perennially renewing and re-creating itself, things change, so call ahead to confirm hours of operation, admissions, reservations, and to ask about special needs for your family. At the beginning of each chapter is a quick reference map, and each region is threaded in a circular loop, but to open your options and customize your route, you'll want to get a detailed road map. The age recommendations are pretty subjective, but you know your children best. It's a plus if you can tour historical sites relevant to their school studies, especially when festivals or special events are scheduled. Revolutionary War encampments, pioneer days, and powwows can transform a dry history lesson into a virtual-reality time-travel trip worthy of Wishbone and H. G. Wells.

Each chapter has a short list of suggested children's books relevant to that region. While many are fictionalized accounts of the area's history or folklore, they add depth and richness to the tapestry of traveling that a mere guidebook cannot. It's tough to top reading *Rip Van Winkle* by a Catskill campfire or *Last of the Mohicans* from a path in an ancient forest.

As you travel around New York, think of yourselves not as tourists but rather as explorers. As Henry David Thoreau wrote, "The question is not what you look at, but what you see." By sharing the adventure of discovery with your family, you will discover much about each other, as well. These are fleeting years, so get out there, have fun with your family, and collect some treasured memories.

Rates for places to stay and eat, as well as attraction admission prices, are represented with dollar signs and offer a sense of the price ranges at press time. Lodging rates are based on double occupancy and tend to increase seasonally depending on location; many establishments offer family rates and discounts. Places to eat are usually less expensive at lunch than at dinner and may close off-season.

Rates for Attractions

$	up to $5
$$	from $6 to $10
$$$	from $11 to $20
$$$$	more than $20

Rates for Lodging

$	up to $50
$$	from $51 to $75
$$$	from $76 to $99
$$$$	$100 and up

Rates for Restaurants

$	most entrees under $10
$$	most $11 to $15
$$$	most $16 to $20
$$$$	most over $20

Attractions Key

The following is a key to the icons found throughout the text.

SWIMMING		**FOOD**	
BOATING / BOAT TOUR		**LODGING**	
HISTORIC SITE		**CAMPING**	
HIKING / WALKING		**MUSEUMS**	
FISHING		**PERFORMING ARTS**	
BIKING		**SPORTS/ATHLETICS**	
AMUSEMENT PARK		**PICNICKING**	
HORSEBACK RIDING		**PLAYGROUND**	
SKIING/WINTER SPORTS		**SHOPPING**	
PARK		**PLANTS / GARDENS / NATURE TRAILS**	
ANIMAL VIEWING		**FARMS**	

Hudson River Valley Region

D esignated a National Heritage Area by Congress in 1996, the Hudson River valley has enchanted authors and artists for more than three centuries. Its breathtaking scenery cradles a treasure trove of history and culture, and its lore and legends capture the imaginations of young and old alike. Travel back in time as you soar above the lush, rolling hills in a World War I biplane, stroll through the fabulous mansions of millionaires, or speculate on the whereabouts of the buried treasures of Rip Van Winkle and Captain Kidd. Whether your family is interested in castles or country fairs, petroglyphs or planetariums, there is something for everyone here. Long after your visit is over, the Hudson will weave magic in your memories of the adventures shared with your children along these shores.

Driving Tips

West of the Hudson, many of the towns along the river are accessible from U.S. Route 9W or the Palisades Interstate Parkway. Heading southwest from there, use I–84, or Route 17 if heading northwest. Storm King Highway (Route 218) has dramatic views. Seven Lakes Parkway runs through the heart of Harriman, and along the Delaware near Sparrowbush on Route 97 is a wonderfully winding road seen in a lot of car commercials. On the eastern side of the river, U.S. Route 9 is the main artery along the riverbank, but you'll want to check out at least part of the Taconic State Parkway, which runs through some of the prettiest scenery of the valley.

Tarrytown

On Route 9, north of the Tappan Zee Bridge.

Washington Irving said the name of this town came from the local Dutch farmers' tendency to "tarry" at the taverns. Once a small market town and rural port located at one of the Hudson River's widest points, Tarrytown today is a bustling commuter village with several attractions that'll make you want to tarry, too.

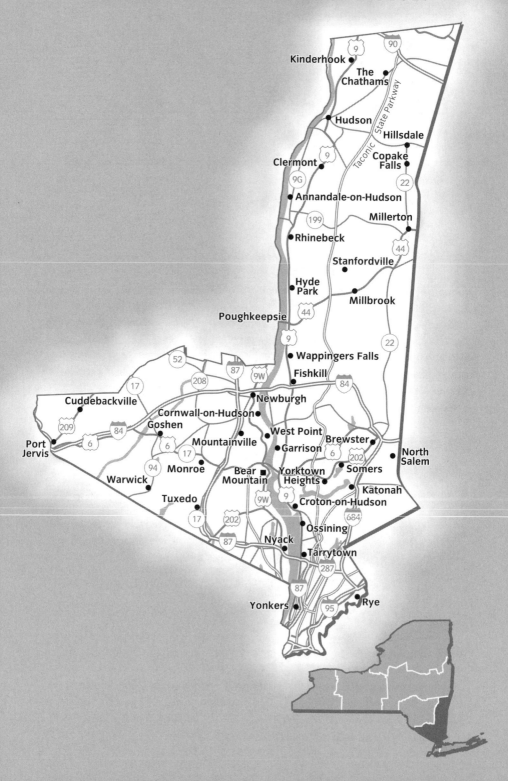

HUDSON RIVER VALLEY REGION

Kinderhook

The Chathams

Hudson

Hillsdale

Clermont

Copake Falls

Annandale-on-Hudson

Millerton

Rhinebeck

Stanfordville

Hyde Park

Millbrook

Poughkeepsie

Wappingers Falls

Fishkill

Cuddebackville

Newburgh

Cornwall-on-Hudson

Goshen

West Point

Brewster

Port Jervis

Mountainville

Garrison

North Salem

Monroe

Bear Mountain

Yorktown Heights

Somers

Warwick

Katonah

Tuxedo

Croton-on-Hudson

Ossining

Nyack

Tarrytown

Yonkers

Rye

Sunnyside 🏛

West Sunnyside Lane, off Route 9; (914) 631–8200; www.hudsonvalley.org. Open daily April through October, except Tuesday, 10:00 A.M. to 5:00 P.M., and November to December, except Tuesday, 10:00 A.M. to 4:00 P.M., weekends only in March. Closed January and February. Adults $$, children 5 through 17 $, under 5 free.

Perhaps the most magical of the Hudson River Estates, Sunnyside was home to Washington Irving, author of *Rip Van Winkle*. Costumed guides offer tours of the charming cottage and grounds, colonial crafts and skills are demonstrated daily, and autumn harvest celebrations culminate with dramatic readings of *The Legend of Sleepy Hollow*.

Lyndhurst 🏛

635 South Broadway; (914) 631–4481; www.lyndhurst.org. Open mid-April through October, Tuesday through Sunday, and holiday Mondays 10:00 A.M. to 5:00 P.M.; open weekends only November 1 through mid-April and holiday Mondays 10:00 A.M. to 4:00 P.M. Adults $$, children under 12 free.

An 1838 Gothic Revival mansion, Lyndhurst was once the home of the notoriously wealthy financier Jay Gould. Many original furnishings are still there, recalling an era of robber barons and pre–income tax wealth. The arboretum includes a historic rose garden, a children's playhouse, and a picnic-perfect landscaped lawn overlooking the river.

Philipsburg Manor 🏛

Route 9, Sleepy Hollow; (914) 631–8200; www.hudsonvalley.org. Open daily April through October, except Tuesday, 10:00 A.M. to 5:00 P.M., and November to December, except Tuesday, 10:00 A.M. to 4:00 P.M., open weekends only in March, closed January and February. Adults $$, children 5 through 17 $, under 5 free.

Carefully restored to its seventeenth-century roots as a farm and gristmill, Philipsburg Manor offers children a chance to check out colonial life firsthand. Help the miller grind grain at the water-powered mill, visit the farm animals, or plan a picnic on the plantation grounds. Across the street from the estate is the Old Dutch Church, believed to be the oldest in New York State. Legend has it that the ghost of a headless Hessian soldier haunts the site, which inspired Washington Irving to write *The Legend of Sleepy Hollow*.

Old Croton Aqueduct State Trailway (all ages)

Many entrances to the trail between Yonkers and Ossining; (914) 693–5259. For a detailed trail map, send SASE plus $5.50 to Friends of Old Croton Aqueduct, 15 Walnut Street, Dobbs Ferry, NY 10522. Free.

Running parallel to the Hudson River is a popular, century-old hiking trail perfect for families. This 26-mile-long linear park is the result of New York City's need for clean water, and the Croton watershed became the chosen source. Considered one of the greatest engineering feats of the nineteenth century, it provides a wide, level, and grassy path that meanders past nineteenth-century estates and historic churches of eleven communities.

Also in **the Area**

Rockefeller State Park Preserve.
Route 117, Pocantico Hills 10591;
(914) 631–1470; www.nysparks
.com/parks. Just off Route 117,
about 1 mile north of Philipsburg
Manor.

The Tarrytown Music Hall. 13
Main Street, Tarrytown 10591;
(914) 631–3390; www.tarry
townmusichall.org.

Where to Eat

Horsefeathers. 94 North Broadway; (914)
631–6606. Hearty homestyle fare and a
kids' menu. $$

Santa Fe. 5 Main Street; (914) 332–4452.
Southwestern cuisine, including taco bas-
kets, fajitas, and homemade desserts, plus
a children's menu. $–$$

Where to Stay

Courtyard by Marriott. 475 White Plains
Road; (914) 631–1122 or (800) 321–2211.
139 rooms, restaurant, and indoor pool.
$$$$

Hampton Inn. 200 Tarrytown Road, Route
119, Elmsford; (914) 592–5680. 156 rooms,
outdoor pool, and continental breakfast.
$$$–$$$$

Boats, Trains, **and Trolleys**

NY Waterways. (800) 53–FERRY or (800) 533–3779; www.nywaterway.com.

Metro North Railroad train tours. (800) 638–7646.

Historic River Towns Trolley. (914) 271–2238.

Empire Boat Tours. Congers; (914) 267–BOAT.

Nyack

Cross the Hudson River via the Tappan Zee Bridge (U.S. 87 and 287) onto Route 9W.

Originally from the area now called Brooklyn, the Native American Nyacks lived here until the Dutch came in the mid-seventeenth century. Memorial Park, down by the river's edge, has wonderful views of the Hudson, and tucked into the steep hills behind you are the spectacular homes of resident artists and celebrities.

Helen Hayes Performing Arts Center (all ages)

117 Main Street; (845) 358–6333; www.hhtco.org. Open year-round. Call for schedule and ticket prices.

This lovely 600-seat center offers a variety of excellent entertainment, including adult and children's theater, magic shows, concerts, dance programs, and lectures.

State Parks **in the Area**

Dotting the western shores along the Hudson River and the Palisades are several terrific parks. While not as large or well known as the vast Bear Mountain and Harriman State Parks, each offers a variety of scenery and recreational facilities to please everyone.

Tallman Mountain State Park. Route 9W, Palisades; (845) 359–0544; www.nysparks.com/parks.

Nyack Beach State Park. Off North Broadway, Upper Nyack; (845) 268–3020; www.nysparks.com/parks.

Hook Mountain State Park. Route 9W, Upper Nyack; (845) 268–3020; www.nysparks.com/parks.

Blauvelt State Park. Highland Avenue, Greenbush Road, Blauvelt; (845) 359–0544; www.nysparks.com/parks.

Rockland Lake State Park. Route 9W between Congers and Valley Cottage, Congers; (845) 268–3020; www.nysparks.com/parks.

High Tor State Park. South Mountain Road, New City; (845) 634–8074; www.nysparks.com/parks.

Buttermilk Falls. Greenbush Road, West Nyack; (845) 364–2670.

Tackamack North and South Park. Clausland Mountain Road, Orangetown; (845) 359–5100.

Where to Eat

Strawberry Place. 72 South Broadway; (845) 358–9511. Great waffles with fruit plus create-your-own omelets. $

Temptations. 80½ Main Street; (845) 353–3355. Family friendly with a kids' menu plus terrific ice cream and desserts. $

Where to Stay

Best Western, Nyack on Hudson. 26 Route 59; (845) 358–8100 or (800) 358–8010; www.bestwestern.com/nyack onhudson. Continental Breakfast. $$–$$$$

Nyack Motor Lodge. 110 Route 303, West Nyack; (845) 358–4100. $$

Tuxedo

Take I–87 west.

The name of the town is believed to come from the Native American word *P'tauk-seet-tough,* which means "place of the bears." Later it was used to describe the attire worn by men of high society from the wealthy enclave of nearby Tuxedo Park.

New York Renaissance Faire (all ages)

600 Route 17A; (845) 351–5174; www.renfair.com/NY. Open rain or shine weekends August to mid-September, 10:30 A.M. to 7:00 P.M. Adults $$$, children 5 to 12 $$, under 5 free. Free parking available, preferred parking $.

Spend a day with a knight, or rescue a damsel in distress . . . it's all part of the fun at this annual festival, the largest of its kind on the East Coast. Spread over sixty-five acres, this re-creation of a sixteenth-century country fair appears on summer weekends like Brigadoon, complete with jousting knights, magicians, mimes, jugglers, acrobats, and a king or queen or two plus craft demonstrations from glassblowing to blacksmithing. For younger kids there are puppet shows, pony rides, and a petting zoo.

Sterling Forest State Park (all ages)

115 Old Forge Road; (845) 351–5907 or (845) 351–5910; www.nysparks.com/parks. Open year-round (avoid hiking during hunting season). Free.

In 1998 New York acquired 15,280 acres of rugged woodland 40 miles northwest of New York City, and it's the largest addition to the state's park system in fifty years. Home to bobcats and bears, dotted with sparkling lakes, Sterling Forest supported a flourishing iron industry in the nineteenth century and years later hosted tulip festivals amid its botanical gardens. Seven miles of the Appalachian Trail wind through here, as well as several other scenic strolls, including walks through the Doris Duke Wildlife Sanctuary. Stop by the information center near the south end of Sterling Lake for current trail conditions.

Horsing **Around**

Nickel-O-Farm. 369 Strawtown Road, West Nyack; (845) 358–8081.

Double D Ranch. 269 North Main Street, New City; (845) 638–0271.

Mountain View Stables. 336 Route 202, Suffern; (845) 354–6666.

Country Lee Farm. 346 Old Route 202, Pomona; (845) 354–0133.

Sterling Forest Ski Center (all ages)

581 Route 17A West; (845) 351–2163; ski school (845) 351–5727; conditions (845) 351–4788; www.skisterlingforest.com. Open daily mid-December to mid-March, 10:00 A.M. to 5:00 P.M., weekends and holidays 9:00 A.M. Night skiing until 10:00 p.m. Wednesday through Saturday, 9:00 P.M. Sunday through Tuesday, January and February. Adults $$$$, children $$$.

Seven slopes to schuss down, with four double chair lifts, lessons, and snowmaking capabilities.

Monroe

North on I–87 to Route 17M.

South of Schunemunk Mountain lies the town of Monroe, birthplace of the notorious Revolutionary War outlaw Claudius Smith and suspected site of his as yet unfound treasure trove.

Museum Village of Old Smith's Clove (all ages)

1010 Route 17M; (845) 782–8247 or (845) 782–8248; www.museumvillage.org. Open June and September through November weekdays 10:00 A.M. to 2:00 P.M., July and August, Tuesday though Sunday 11:00 A.M. to 5:00 P.M.; closed Monday and major holidays. Adults $$, children 4 to 15 $, under 4 free.

Travel back to the nineteenth century at this thirty-five-acre living-history museum. Laid out like a typical crossroads village, forty exhibit and demonstration buildings house more than a quarter million historical artifacts of preindustrial America. Costumed guides answer your questions as you stroll around the village green watching weavers, potters, printers, black-smiths, and bakers busy at work.

Also in **the Area**

94 Pitch & Putt. 1 Hudson Road, Washingtonville; (845) 496–6418.

Arrow Park. Orange Turnpike, Route 19, Monroe; (845) 783–2044.

Goosepond Mountain State Park (all ages)
Route 17M, Chester; (845) 786–2701 (Palisades Interstate Park); www.nysparks.com/parks. Open year-round dawn to dusk. Free.

Undeveloped and wild, the 1,542-acre park's marshes and meadows attract an enormous volume and variety of birds. While most of the trails are not well marked, the two-hour round-trip hike along Lazy Hill Road is pretty easy. Ancient artifacts, including arrowheads and pottery shards dating back to 3500 B.C., have been found in the rock shelters on the mountain and are displayed at Bear Mountain's Trailside Museum. Some say those rock shelters may also have been the hideout of the infamous Claudius Smith and his gang.

Where to Eat

The Barnsider Tavern. 1372 Kings Highway, Sugar Loaf; (845) 469–9810. Chicken fingers, burgers, hot dogs, fries, and dessert. $–$$

Warwick

Head south on Route 5 onto Route 17A west.

The town of Warwick encompasses several nearby villages, including Greenwood Lake, Florida, and Pine Island. The Appalachian Trail passes near here, the hamlets are full of quaint antiques and craft shops, and the valley is famous for its juicy apples and flavorful onions.

New York **Trivia**

New York, the thirtieth-largest state, has a land area of 47,214 square miles.

Farms and Markets **in Warwick**

Warwick Valley Farmers Market. South Street Parking Lot; (845) 986–2720. Open Sunday 9:00 A.M. to 2:00 P.M.

Applewood Orchards. 82 Four Corners Road, County Highway 13; (845) 986–1684.

Masker Orchards. Ball Road; (845) 986–1058.

Wright Family Farm. 325 Kings Highway; (845) 986–1345.

Pennings Orchard Farm Market. 169 Route 94; (845) 986–7080.

Ochs Orchards. Route 94; (845) 986–1591.

Greenwood Lake (all ages)

Parallel to Route 210 (Jersey Avenue). Pontoon boat tours of the lake are available at Long Pond Marina, 634 Jersey Avenue; (845) 477–8425. Departures every hour on weekends 9:00 A.M. to 5:00 P.M., Memorial Day through Labor Day.

Created when a dam was built to power a nearby ironworks, this 10-mile lake is a popular summer resort. Go fishing, boating, skiing, or hiking—there's no shortage of water sports here. For landlubbers, walk a bit of the Appalachian Trail for its scenic vistas of the lake, or check out the 1-mile Mountain Spring Trail off Route 210, south of the village.

Where to Eat

Backyard Grill. 31 Forester Avenue; (845) 987–1822. Burgers, french fries, chicken fingers, salads, and grilled cheese sandwiches. Children's menu. $

Ye Jolly Onion Inn. County Route 1, Pine Island; (845) 258–4277. The onions of Orange County are the star here. Children's menu. $$$

Horse Fun **in Warwick**

Borderland Farm. 340 South Route 94; (845) 986–1704; www.wolfsbane.com/borderland/. Offering lessons and trail rides to children of all abilities. Reservations required.

Crystal Water Farm. 35 Union Corners Road; (845) 986–0100. Horseback rides and lessons.

Also in **the Area**

Warwick Drive-In. Route 94 and Warwick Turnpike; (845) 986–4440. Cinema under the stars! A vanishing bit of America, the drive-in is a classic family adventure.

Mount Peter Ski Area. Old Mount Peter Road, off Route 17A; (845) 986–4940 or (845) 986–4992; www.mtpeter.com. Skiing and snowboarding in winter and hawk-watching in spring and fall.

Where to Stay

Black Bear Campground. 197 Wheeler Road, Florida; (845) 651–7717; www.black bearcampground.com. Campsites, playground, pool, mini-golf and arcade, fishing pond, and summer children's arts and crafts program. $

Warwick Motel. Route 17A; (845) 986–4822 or (888) 8–WARWICK; www .warwickmotel.com. Swimming pool; school playground across the street. $$–$$$

Goshen

Take Route 17A north.

The countryside surrounding Goshen is dotted with many farms, for the black dirt of Orange County is a highly organic soil called "muck," the deposits left by glacial lakes. This area is second only to the Everglades in its concentration of muck, which may be why more than half the crop of New York's most successful vegetable—the onion—is grown here. Pick up a self-guided walking tour map of the town at the chamber of commerce kiosk at Park Place.

Harness Racing Museum and Hall of Fame (ages 6 and up) 🏇
240 Main Street; (845) 294–6330; www.harnessmuseum.com. Open daily 10:00 A.M. to 6:00 P.M.; closed Thanksgiving, Christmas, and New Year's Day. Adults $$, children 6 to 15 $, under 6 free.

Housed in the former Good Time Stables, this museum immortalizes the history of America's pre-baseball passion for trotters and pacers. Visit the Hall of the Immortals with its dozens of small statuettes of famous trainers and drivers, and check out the life-size displays of legendary horses. A 3-D interactive simulator lets you feel what it's like to drive a harnessed horse, judge a race, or visit a breeding farm. Walk next door to Park Place and the Goshen Historic Track, the only sporting arena designated a National Historic Landmark, to watch harness horses training here almost daily, and there's usually a blacksmith at work as well. Ask about behind-the-scenes tours of the track. Racing season runs July 4 through Labor Day (no betting allowed).

Also in **the Area**

Orange Heritage Trail. 182 Greenwich Avenue; (845) 294–8886.

Silent Farm Stables. 35 Axworthy Lane; (845) 294–0846.

The Castle Family Fun Center. Route 17M, Chester; (845) 469–2116; www.thecastlefuncenter.com.

Hill-Hold (all ages)
Route 416, Campbell Hall; (845) 291–2404. Open May through mid-October, Wednesday through Sunday 10:00 A.M. to 4:30 P.M. $

Tour this historic eighteenth-century working farm, complete with a one-room school-house, fragrant herb gardens, and friendly farm fauna.

Where to Eat

Catherine's. 153 West Main Street; (845) 294–8707. Chicken, steak, and pasta specialties. $$$–$$$$

Port Jervis

Take Route 17 north, then I–84 west.

Stephen Crane wrote his famous Civil War novel, *The Red Badge of Courage,* here, but for many, Port Jervis is a doorway to the Delaware. Rent a canoe and paddle on down the lazy river. Landlubbers may opt to walk the 5-mile self-guided Delaware River Heritage Trail through town, from Fort Decker (127 Main Street) to the Tri-State Rock.

New Hope Farms (all ages)
517 Neversink Drive; (845) 856–8384. Open daily year-round. Many events are free. Call for lesson prices and schedule of events.

This is one of the largest equestrian centers in the country, offering lessons at all levels, as well as many events throughout the year.

Gillinder Glass (ages 7 and up)
Corner of Erie and Liberty Streets; (845) 856–5375; www.gillinderglassstore.com. Open year-round except for July. Tours are conducted Monday through Friday at 10:15 A.M., 12:30, and 1:30 P.M. There are some weekend tours throughout the year. Closed holidays. Store: Monday through Friday 9:30 A.M. to 5:30 P.M., Saturday 9:30 A.M. to 4:00 P.M., Sunday noon to 4:00 P.M. $

Watch hot molten masses of glass be formed into crystalline creations at one of the country's oldest glass factories.

West End Beach (all ages)
Water and Pike Streets; (845) 858–4045. Open year-round. Free.

Folks come here to enjoy the swimming, fishing, playground, and softball field.

Where to Eat

Flo-Jean. Route 6 and Route 209; (845) 856–6600. Steaks, seafood, and home-made desserts, plus a children's menu, outdoor deck dining overlooking the Delaware River, and an antique doll and toy collection. $$$

Raft, Canoe, and **Tube Rentals**

Silver Canoe Raft Rentals. 37 South Maple Avenue; (800) 724–8342 or (845) 856–7055; www.silvercanoe.com.

Whitewater Willie's. 17 West Main Street; (800) 233–RAFT or (845) 856–2229; www.whitewaterwillies.com.

Cuddebackville

Head north on Route 209.

In the early nineteenth century, the D&H Canal was built through here, linking the Delaware and Hudson Rivers with a 108-mile-long waterway with which to transport coal from the Pennsylvania mines and bluestone from the Catskills, both destined for New York City. While much smaller than the Erie Canal, it was designed by the same man, and the D&H was considered an engineering wonder.

Delaware and Hudson Canal Park (all ages)
205 Hoag Road, off Route 209; (845) 754–8870 or (845) 457–4900. Museum open April through December, Friday through Sunday noon to 4:00 P.M. and by appointment; park open daily dawn to dusk. $

Housed in the home of a former blacksmith, the **Neversink Valley Area Museum** offers exhibits about the history and people who lived and worked along the D&H Canal. Guided towpath walks offered on Sunday are fun and informative, and special seasonal events and activities for families are offered throughout the year, from nature walks and maple sugaring to ghost stories and silent film festivals.

Area **Camping**

Oakland Valley Campgrounds. 399 Oakland Valley Road; (845) 754–8732. Campsites, playground, swimming pool, recreation hall, video game room, and fishing. $

American Family Campground. 110 Guymard Turnpike, Godeffroy; (800) CAMP–AFC or (845) 754–8388. Campsites, swimming pool, recreation hall, arcade, hayrides, ceramic shop and classes, tube and bike rentals. $

Newburgh

Take Route 209 north, then head east on Route 17K.

Newburgh was once a prosperous whaling center that evolved into a manufacturing town. Today the area has several Revolutionary War sites of interest to older children, as well as festivals, special events, and farmers' markets that will appeal to everyone.

Washington's Headquarters State Historic Park (ages 7 and up)

84 Liberty Street; (845) 562–1195. Open July through August Monday 10:00 A.M. to 5:00 P.M., mid-April through October Wednesday through Saturday 10:00 A.M. to 5:00 P.M., Sunday 1:00 to 5:00 P.M. $, children under 5 free.

This was George's and sometimes Martha's home during the final months of the Revolutionary War. Designated as the nation's first historic site, the Dutch-style farmhouse owned by the Hasbrouck family gave Washington and his aides a good vantage point from which to monitor British troops still encamped in New York City. Adjacent to the house is a museum with videos and exhibits of eighteenth-century military life, along with some of Washington's personal possessions.

Horse Fun **in Northern Orange County**

Denman Farm. 219 Red Mills Road, Pine Bush; (845) 744–7791.

Juckas Stables. Route 302, Bullville; (845) 361–1429; www.juckas stables.com.

Indamora Stables. 70 Coleman Road, Walden; (845) 778–4374.

J&E Ranch. 100 Union School Road, Montgomery; (845) 361–4433.

Farm Markets and **Farm Animals**

Overlook Farm Market. Route 9W, Newburgh; (845) 562–5780 or (800) 291–9137.

Hoeffner Farms. 405 Goodwill Road, Montgomery; (845) 457–3453.

Krisco Farms. Purgatory Road, Campbell Hall; (845) 294–7784.

Kirby Farm. 25 Kinne Lane, Middletown; (845) 355–2718.

Manza Family Farm. 730 Route 211, Montgomery; (845) 692–4364.

Maples Farm. 749 Route 17M, Middletown; (845) 344–0330; www.maples farm.com.

Newburgh Landing (all ages)

City Park, on Front Street, Hudson River; (845) 569–7300 for event schedule. Hudson River Adventures Pride of the Hudson; (845) 220–2120; www.prideofthehudson.com. Departures Wednesday through Sunday, May through October. Call for schedule. $$$, children under 3 free.

This park is the site of numerous special events and festivals designed for children. On Tuesday and Friday from 10:00 A.M. to 6:00 P.M. the Farmers' Market offers an opportunity to stock up on the wide variety of foods grown in the area, and you can also cruise the river aboard the *Pride of the Hudson*.

Where to Eat

Commodore Chocolatier. 482 Broadway; (845) 561–3960. Homemade ice cream and chocolates. $

26 Front Street Restaurant. 26 Front Street; (845) 569–8035. On the waterfront with a great view. $$

Where to Stay

Howard Johnson Inn. 95 Route 17K; (845) 564–4000 or (800) 564–5009. Outdoor pool. $$$–$$$$

Ramada Inn. 1289 Route 300; (845) 564–4500 or (800) 228–2828. Restaurant and outdoor pool on site. $$$

Cornwall-on-Hudson

Head south on Route 9W.

Museum of the Hudson Highlands (all ages)

The Boulevard, off Payson Road; (845) 534–7781; www.museumhudsonhighlands.org. Kenridge Farm, Route 9W south, South Cornwall; (845) 534–5506. The Boulevard facilities open year-round Thursday through Saturday 10:00 A.M. to 4:00 P.M. Kenridge Farm Education Center open Tuesday through Friday 9:00 A.M. to 5:00 P.M. and Sunday noon to 4:00 P.M. Trails open daily from dawn to dusk. Call for prices.

This is one of the oldest environmental education centers in the country, founded by a group of teenagers in 1959 who wanted to display their small collection of plants, animals, and rocks. Natural-history dioramas of regional habitats prepare families for exploring the nature trails on the seventy-acre grounds. Special activities are scheduled throughout the year, from storytelling and dance programs to birdhouse building and raptor watching. The Ogden Gallery at The Boulevard (open Friday and Saturday 10:00 A.M. to 4:00 P.M., Sunday noon to 4:00 P.M.) features nature-inspired artwork and other exhibits. There is also a Nature Shop.

The museum also operates the education center at Kenridge Farm, a wildlife sanctuary that offers programs celebrating the cultural, historical, and natural diversity of the area. Check with the museum for current programs, including the Young Naturalists series. There are single- and multiday programs geared for young children as well as parent/child events; call for prices. Kenridge Farm also has several miles of trails to explore.

New Windsor Cantonment (all ages)

374 Temple Hill Road (Route 300, right side of the road), Vails Gate; (845) 561–1765; www.nysparks.com/hist. Open mid-April through October Wednesday through Saturday 10:00 A.M. to 5:00 P.M., Sunday 1:00 to 5:00 P.M. $, children 4 and under free.

While Washington was settled in at the Hasbrouck house, his 7,000 troops along with about 500 women and children waited out the last months of an eight-year war in log huts, struggling to survive a bitter winter. Today costumed guides demonstrate colonial life—blacksmithing, cooking, or playing musical instruments. The two-story visitor's center is run by the state and offers historical exhibits, including the original Purple Heart medal, and a slide show, with cannons and muskets fired in an artillery demonstration almost every day.

New York **Trivia**

The longest point from north to south in the state is 310 miles.

Hudson Valley **Lighthouses**

Tarrytown Lighthouse. Kingsland Point Park, Palmer Avenue, Sleepy Hollow; (914) 864–7177; www.westchestergov.com/parks.

Esopus Meadows Lighthouse. 13 Monroe Drive, Poughkeepsie; P.O. Box 1290, Port Ewen 12466; (845) 297–1569.

Saugerties Lighthouse. 1 Lighthouse Drive, Saugerties; (845) 247–0656; www.saugertieslighthouse.com.

Hudson Athens Lighthouse. 2 First Street, Riverfront Park, Hudson; (518) 828–5294.

Kingston-Roundout Lighthouse. 1 Roundout Landing, Kingston; (845) 338–0071.

Stony Point Battlefield Lighthouse. Park Road, P.O. Box 182, Stony Point; (845) 786–2521.

The Last Encampment of the Continental Army (all ages)

19 Causeway Road, Route 300, left side of the road, Vails Gate; (845) 561–5073 or (845) 561–0902; www.nationaltemplehill.org. Park open daily during daylight hours; visitor's center open Thursday through Sunday noon to 4:30 P.M. **Free,** donations accepted.

Across the road from the New Windsor Cantonment, this 167-acre site has preserved some of the authentic military huts from the Revolutionary War campground. Walk the Freedom Appreciation Trail, a newer addition, or explore the self-guided Nature Trail and tower.

Also in **the Area**

Kowanese Unique Area at Plum Point. Route 9W, across from Anthony's Pier 9, New Windsor; (845) 457–4900.

Algonquin Powder Mill Park. Powder Mill Road and Route 52, Newburgh; (845) 561–1880.

Stony Point Battlefield State Historic Site. Park Road, off Route 9W, Stony Point; (845) 786–2521.

New York **Firsts**

First school in America (1663)

First potato chips (1925)

First steamboat (1807)

First motion picture (1896)

First telegraph (1831)

First solar-powered battery (1954)

Where to Eat

Painter's. 266 Hudson Street; (845) 534–2109; www.painters-restaurant.com.

Wonderful eclectic cuisine of sandwiches, pasta, salads, and more, plus a special kids' menu. $$

Mountainville

Take Route 32 south.

Storm King Art Center (all ages)
Old Pleasant Hill Road, just off Route 32 North; (845) 534–3115; www.stormking.org. Open April through October Wednesday through Sunday 11:00 A.M. to 5:30 P.M., to November 14 11:00 A.M. to 5:00 P.M. Wednesday through Sunday, May through early September Saturday 11:00 A.M. to 8:00 P.M. Free for children under 5.

It would be hard to find a better place to introduce your children to modern art. The largest sculpture park in the country, this breathtaking 500-acre park and outdoor museum has more than 120 sculptures nestled among rolling foothills and landscaped gardens, backed by the spectacular Shawangunk Mountains. It's an opportunity for everyone in the family to see the works of master sculptors—from Calder and Moore to Nevelson and Noguchi. Pick up a map at the gate and explore! Pack a picnic lunch or eat at the small cafe open on weekends. Call about special events for families.

Storm King **Mountain**

America's environmental consciousness was born at Storm King in 1963, when concerned citizens began a 17-year battle to save the majestic mountain from becoming the site of a massive hydroelectric power plant. Today that spirit of grass-roots environmentalism continues, as people pressure industrial polluters to clean up toxic PCBs dumped in the Hudson River. For more information about area environmental issues and activities, contact:

Scenic Hudson. (845) 473–4440; www.scenichudson.org.

The Riverkeeper. (845) 424–4149 or (800) 21–RIVER; www.riverkeeper.org.

Clearwater. (845) 454–7673; www.clearwater.org.

West Point

Head north on Route 32, then south on Route 9W.

Occupying a strategic bluff overlooking a bend in the Hudson River, West Point was an important American fortification during the Revolutionary War. It was here that Washington ordered a 150-ton iron chain strung across the river in an attempt to block British ships from sailing up the Hudson. This was also the fort that a disgruntled Benedict Arnold tried to betray to the British.

United States Military Academy (ages 6 and up) 🚹🔺
Route 218, Highland Falls; (845) 938–2638 or (845) 938–3614; www.usma.army.mil. Tours, (845) 446–4724; www.westpointtours.com. Museum, (845) 938–3590; www.usma.edu/museum. USMA visitor's center, Building 2107, near Thayer Gate is open daily year-round 9:00 A.M. to 4:45 P.M. Museum open daily 10:30 A.M. to 4:15 P.M. Closed New Year's Day, Thanksgiving, and Christmas. Free. Constitution Island Association, (845) 446–8676; www.constitutionisland.org. Take boat from West Point's South Dock June through September. Tours depart 1:00 and 2:00 P.M. every Wednesday and Thursday. Reservations recommended. $$, children under 5 $.

As cadets, Robert E. Lee, Ulysses S. Grant, Douglas MacArthur, and Norman Schwarzkopf marched here, as did astronauts Buzz Aldrin, Frank Borman, Edward White, and Michael Collins. Tradition and a strong sense of duty, honor, and country are evident everywhere, from the **Cadet Chapel,** with its spectacular stained-glass windows and the largest church organ in the world, to exciting football games and precision parades. Visit the **Military Museum,** where dioramas depict famous battles, galleries highlight the history of war and West Point, and rotating exhibits drawn from more than 15,000 artifacts may include Napoleon's sword, Hitler's pistol, or MacArthur's bathrobe. Stop at Trophy

Point, where some of the 300-pound links of "Washington's watch chain" rest. Nearby are **Battle Monument** and **Fort Putnam,** a partially restored Revolutionary fortification overlooking West Point. For an interesting side trip, take the boat from West Point's South Dock to nearby Constitution Island and explore the Victorian Warner House and gardens.

Hudson Highlands Cruises (all ages)

South Dock, West Point, and Haverstraw Marina; (845) 534–7245; www.commanderboat .com. May through October weekdays and last Saturday of the month. Reservations required. Departs Haverstraw Marina 10:00 A.M. Departs West Point 12:30 P.M. and 2:30 P.M. $$$

Enjoy a narrated Hudson River cruise aboard the historic M/V *Commander.*

Where to Eat

Thayer Hotel. Thayer Road, off Route 218; (845) 446–4731 or (845) 247–5047, fax

(845) 446–0338; www.hotelthayer.com. Dining terrace overlooks the Hudson. $$$$

Bear Mountain

Head south on Route 9W.

Bear Mountain State Park (all ages)

Route 9W; (845) 786–2701; www.nysparks.com/parks. Trailsides Museum and Wildlife Center, (845) 786–2701. Open daily year-round. $ per car; separate admission for pool, ice rink, and museum.

Covering more than 5,000 acres of the Hudson Highlands and adjacent to Harriman State Park in the south, Bear Mountain offers breathtaking views of the Hudson River and, on a clear day, the skyline of Manhattan. Cruise by car to the summit along Perkins Memorial Drive and enjoy the panorama, or visit the Trailsides Museum and Wildlife Center, a refuge for rescued animals of the area. The newest animals in the park are of the carousel kind, carved creatures representing Hudson Valley wildlife circle daily in summer aboard the Bear Mountain merry-go-round. The Appalachian Trail runs through the park, and the nature trails in the area are some of the oldest in the country. Check at the Park Visitor Center for maps and current special events schedules.

Harriman State Park (all ages)

Access via I–87 or Route 17, Palisades Interstate Parkway, Palisades Interstate Park; (845) 786–2701, or Park Visitor Center (845) 786–5003. Sebago Cabins, (845) 351–2360; Beaver Pond Campgrounds, (845) 947–2792; www.nysparks.com/parks. Open daily year-round. $$ per car.

This scenic and historic 46,000-acre preserve, less than an hour from New York City, was created in 1910 from land and cash donated by Mary Harriman and other conservation-minded people. Today the park offers families more than 225 miles of hiking trails, camp-grounds, cabins, lots of wildlife, and numerous lakes in which to swim, fish, or paddle a boat. The surrounding mountains, once more than 12,000 feet high like the Rockies, have eroded to expose Precambrian bedrock, making this one of the oldest land masses in North America.

Lake Sebago is a favorite spot for families with small children because of the shady picnic areas and the playground located near the sandy beach. Lake Welch has one of the largest inland beaches in America, but it can get pretty busy on the weekends, as it's near the Beaver Pond Campground. Rowboat rentals (no gasoline motors allowed) and snacks are available at both lakes in season. Lake Tiorati also has a nice sandy beach and quite a few largemouth bass.

A nature museum is near Lake Kanawauke, and the Silver Mine area has trails and pic-nic grounds. A number of recreational and educational programs are offered throughout the park, from campfire talks to river walks. There are trails to tempt everyone here, including a segment of the Appalachian Trail, but some of the more popular hikes for fami-lies with young children are along the 3-mile-loop trail to Pine Swamp Mine and the 4-mile-loop trail to Pine Meadow Lake. Stop by the Park Visitor Center (located on the Palisades Interstate Parkway) for maps, fishing licenses, and current activities schedules.

Where to Eat

Mount Fuji. 296 Route 17, Hillburn (exit 15A off I–87, then 1 mile north on Route 17); (845) 357–4270; www.mtfuji restaurants.com. This is a great steak-house, Japanese-style. $$

Where to Stay

Bear Mountain Inn. Route 9W South and Palisades Interstate Parkway; (845) 786–2731, fax (845) 786–2543. Built in 1914, this lovely stone and wood lodge has a restaurant, picnic areas, outdoor swim-ming pool, ice skating, boat rentals, and 12-foot fireplaces in the lobby. $$$

Garrison

Cross the Hudson River via the Bear Mountain Bridge, then head north on Route 9D.

When location scouts for *Hello Dolly!* wanted to re-create nineteenth-century Yonkers, Garrison got the part. This picturesque village has a lovely waterfront park, Garrison Land-ing, that offers panoramic views of the Hudson from a gazebo featured in the movie; the Garrison Depot Theatre; the Garrison Arts Center; and numerous children's activities throughout the summer.

Boscobel (ages 4 and up)

1601 Route 9D; (845) 265–3638; www.boscobel.org. Hudson Valley Shakespeare Festival, (845) 265–9575; www.hvshakespeare.org. Open November and December Wednesday through Monday 9:30 A.M. to 4:00 P.M., 9:30 A.M. to 5:00 P.M., except Tuesday, April through October. Closed January, February, March, Thanksgiving, and Christmas. Guided tours every fifteen minutes. House and grounds: adults $$, children under 6 **free.**

Perched on a bluff overlooking the Hudson River, this elegant nineteenth-century Federal mansion once sold for $35 and was scheduled for demolition. Fortunately, concerned citizens raised money to purchase the house and move it to its present location. Restored to its original glory, Boscobel is full of graceful period furnishings. The gardens will captivate the kids, with colorful tulips, fragrant roses, pungent herbs, and an orangerie filled with orchids. In summer the Hudson Valley Shakespeare Festival takes up residence.

Constitution Marsh Sanctuary (all ages)

Indian Brook Road, off Route 9D; (845) 265–2601; www.audubon.org. Grounds are open daily year-round 9:00 A.M. to 5:00 P.M.; Nature Center closed Monday. **Free.**

This 207-acre freshwater tidal marsh, managed by the National Audubon Society, is teeming with wildlife, from snapping turtles and muskrats to more than 194 species of birds. Stop at the visitor's center for directions, then follow a short and easy self-guided nature trail to a boardwalk overlooking the marsh, or follow the path to nearby Indian Brook Falls and wade in the pond at its base. For older children and parents, guided canoe trips are offered daily at high tide.

Manitoga, The Russel Wright Design Center (all ages)

Old Manitou Road and Route 9D; (845) 424–3812; www.russelwrightcenter.org. Open April through October weekdays 9:00 A.M. to 4:00 P.M., weekends 10:00 A.M. to 6:00 P.M. Suggested donation $.

Manitoga is an Algonquin word meaning "place of the spirit," and industrial designer Russel Wright created this center with the intention of bringing the spirits of people and nature together. Three trails wind through the area and connect to the Appalachian Trail. The environmental education center offers guided nature walks, seasonal family programs, and a full-size Native American wigwam. Call in advance to arrange a visit to Wright's cliff home, Dragon Rock, a glass-walled wonder of inspirational architecture.

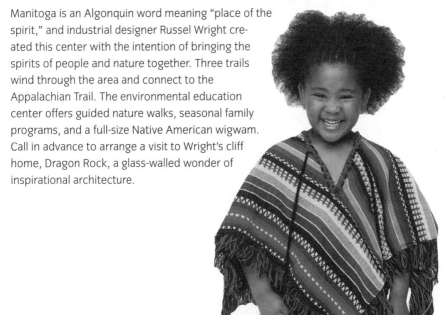

Henry **Hudson**

In 1609, while searching for the fabled northwest passage to the Orient, Henry Hudson sailed his ship *Half Moon* up the river that bears his name. He got as far as Albany before realizing he couldn't get there from here and turned back. He returned in 1611 only to navigate his ship into Hudson Bay, where it became icebound. Hungry, cold, and having serious doubts about their captain's abilities, the crew mutinied. Hudson, his young son, and eight other crew members were put into a small boat in the vast Canadian bay and never seen again.

Clarence Fahnestock State Park (all ages)

Route 301, park office 0.5 mile west on Taconic State Parkway, Kent; (845) 225–7207 or (800) 456–CAMP (campsites); www.nysparks.com/parks. Taconic Outdoor Education Center located at Dennytown Road, Cold Spring. Open daily year-round 9:00 A.M. to dusk. $$

This scenic highlands area once supported numerous farms and a thriving iron industry. Today the popular park comprises more than 10,000 acres of woodlands, streams, and stocked fishing ponds and is laced with a network of easy to moderate hiking trails suitable for families with young children. A favorite hike is the 1.5-mile Pelton Pond Nature Trail. The park's crown jewel is Canopus Lake, with its sandy beach, concession stand, showers, rowboat rentals, and picnic area. In winter the park is open for ice-skating and cross-country skiing. The **Nature Center,** located at the campground, offers guided nature walks, crafts, and interpretive programs; overnight visitors can enjoy family film nights. The larger **Taconic Outdoor Education Center,** west of the main park area, has environmental programs and workshops for all ages, from bird and animal identification to orienteering and star searches (night hikes). If you are a camping novice but want to give your children an extended experience in the great outdoors, the comfortable cabins available here are an easy and inexpensive alternative to roughing it.

Also in **the Area**

Hudson Highlands State Park. Route 9D, Cold Spring; (845) 225–7207; www.nysparks.com/parks.

William Clough Nature Preserve. Farm Market Road, Patterson; (845) 878–6500; www.pattersonny.org.

Patterson Environmental Park. South Street, Patterson; (845) 878–6500; www.pattersonny.org.

Walter G. Merritt County Park. Haviland Hollow Road, Patterson; (845) 878–6500; www.pattersonny.org.

Where to Eat

Cold Spring Depot Restaurant. One Main Street, Cold Spring; (845) 265–5000; www.coldspringdepot.com. Turn-of-the-twentieth-century train station, with outside patio, clam bar, pasta, chicken, burgers, and a Dixieland band on weekends. $$$

Riverview Restaurant. 45 Fair Street, Cold Spring; (845) 265–4778; www.river dining.com. Nice view of Storm King Mountain; brick-oven pizza, pasta, and seafood. $–$$

Fishkill

Head north on Route 9.

The Dutch word for creek is *kill,* hence this town was named for the creek that runs through it. Important strategically during the Revolutionary War, it was briefly the capital for our rebellious young government.

Van Wyck Homestead (ages 7 and up)

Junction of Route 9 and I–84; 1 Snook Road; (845) 896–9560; vanwyckhomestead@ hotmail.com. Open Memorial Day through October Saturday and Sunday 1:00 to 4:00 P.M. or by appointment. $

This Dutch Colonial country farmhouse was built in 1732 by Cornelius Van Wyck and was used as a headquarters, supply depot, and courtroom during the Revolutionary War. Costumed guides conduct tours of the homestead, with its museum of eighteenth-century artifacts, and colonial crafts and skills may be demonstrated during special events.

Splash Down Park (all ages)

2200 Route 9; (845) 896–6606; www.splashdownpark.com. May through September 10:00 A.M. to 7:00 P.M. Adults $$$, children $$.

This small water theme park is a fun way to cool off after a hot hike or a history lesson. Younger folks won't mind being marooned on Ship Wreck Island or left to wallow in Poly Wog Pond. Older children will enjoy three big water slides, water balloon wars, and the 700-foot-long Crocodile Creek Action River. There's also mini-golf, mini-basketball, pirate-themed magic shows, a picnic area, and a snack bar.

Mount Gulian Historic Site (ages 7 and up)

145 Sterling Street, Beacon; (845) 831–8172. Open April through October Wednesday, Friday, and Sunday 1:00 to 5:00 P.M. $

A fourteen-acre restored Dutch Colonial homestead, built in 1730, that was the Revolutionary War headquarters of Gen. Baron Von Steuben.

Also in **the Area**

Sylvan Lake Beach Park. Route 10, East Fishkill; (845) 221–9889; www.gocampingamerica.com/sylvanlake.

Fishkill Ridge. Route 52, Fishkill; (845) 473–4440; www.scenichudson.org.

Mount Beacon. Route 9D to Howland and Wolcott Avenues, Beacon; (845) 473–4440; www.scenichudson.org.

Where to Eat

Hudson's Ribs and Fish. 1099 Route 9; (845) 297–5002. Great barbecue! $$

North Street Grill. 79 Main Street; (845) 896–1000. Casual American. $$–$$$

Where to Stay

Residence Inn by Marriott. 14 Schuyler Boulevard, Route 9, at I–84, exit 13; (845) 896–5210; www.residenceinn.com. All rooms have kitchens. $$$$

Snow Valley Campground. 4 New Road, Route 9; (845) 897–5700. Sixty-acre campground for tents and RVs; nice lake with children's beach. $

Wappingers Falls

Head north from Fishkill on Route 9.

For thousands of years this area was the homeland of the Paleo Indians, and later the Wappingers, long before the Europeans arrived. In 1683, the Wappinger tribal leaders agreed to "sell" to Francis Rombout and his partners Kipp and Ver Planck all the land that Rombout could see. The Wappingers meant, naturally, all the land one could see from ground level and were dismayed when Rombout climbed to the top of nearby South Beacon Mountain and "saw" about 85,000 acres.

Stony Kill Environmental Center (all ages)

Route 9D, about 2 miles north of I–84; (845) 831–8780; www.dec.state.ny.us/website/education/stonykil.html. Open daily year-round dawn to dusk. Visitor's center open weekdays 8:30 A.M. to 4:45 P.M., Saturday 9:30 A.M. to 12:30 P.M., Sunday 1:00 P.M. to 4:00 P.M. Free (fee for materials and some activities).

This 756-acre farm and education center was once part of a large seventeenth-century estate, and today it's a fun place for families to learn about the ecology, agriculture, and natural history of the area. The stone Manor House offers interpretive exhibits, but just about everything else is outdoors. There are three different self-guided trails here, all of them less than 2 miles and easy for children to explore. Family activities and workshops range from building bird feeders to snowshoe hikes to hayrides.

Hudson Valley Renegades (ages 5 and up)

Dutchess Stadium, on Route 9D; (845) 838–0094 or (800) 585–1329 for tickets; www.hv renegades.com. Prices vary by event.

Take everyone out to the ball game! This Class A minor-league club, affiliated with the Tampa Bay Devil Rays, plays mid-June to September.

Fun Central (all ages)

Route 9, 4 miles north of I–84, exit 13; (845) 297–1010; www.fun-central.com. Open year-round Monday through Thursday 3:00 to 9:00 P.M., Friday 3:00 P.M. to midnight, Saturday 10:00 A.M. to midnight, and Sunday 10:00 A.M. to 9:00 P.M. Individual prices for each activity. $

Rain or shine, this popular family amusement park offers activities from batting cages and bumper boats to arcade games, miniature golf, and a virtual-reality indoor roller coaster.

Poughkeepsie

Continue north on Route 9.

Once a thriving nineteenth-century industrial center, Poughkeepsie has several restored historic districts (Academy Street, Garfield Place, and Union Street) that are fun to walk through. Vassar College was founded here in 1861 as a college for women, a concept so radical for the mid-nineteenth century that the main building of the campus was reputedly designed so that if women were found to be uneducable, it could be converted into a brewery.

Mid-Hudson Children's Museum (ages 2 and up)

75 North Water Street; (845) 471–0589; www.mhcm.org. Open Tuesday through Sunday 11:00 A.M. to 5:00 P.M. $$

Hands-on science and art exhibits range from a costume corner to a computer center, with a variety of special programs offered year-round.

Samuel F. B. Morse Historic Site (ages 6 and up)

2683 South Road, Route 9; (845) 454–4500; morsehistoricsite.org. Open daily May through Thanksgiving 10:00 A.M. to 3:00 P.M. Adults $$, children 6 to 18 $.

Locust Grove, the nineteenth-century summer home of telegraph and Morse code inventor Samuel Morse, is an octagonal Tuscan villa chock-full of antiques, art, and historical memorabilia as well as changing exhibits of toys, dolls, and costumes. Morse considered painting his primary career and regarded his inventions as simply a way of paying the bills. Special events include a Civil War Encampment in May. Extensive gardens surround the estate, and the 145-acre **Young Memorial Wildlife Sanctuary** next door offers short hiking trails.

Bardavon Opera House and Children's Theatre (age levels depend on shows offered)

35 Market Street; (845) 473–5288; www.bardavon.org. Performances September through June; tours year-round. Box office open Monday through Friday 11:00 A.M. to 5:00 P.M. Performance times, offerings, and tickets vary; call for current information. $$$

The cultural gem of Poughkeepsie, this performing arts center offers a variety of concerts, puppet shows, ballets, magic shows, and plays for a wide range of ages. Because the emphasis is on learning through entertainment, there are usually opportunities for children to go backstage after the show and meet the performers, and it's a terrific place to introduce your family to the magic of theater.

The Clearwater (all ages)

112 Market Street; (845) 454–7673; www.clearwater.org. Scenic and educational sails, of varying lengths and rates, from mid-April to mid-November. $$–$$$$

This volunteer-built sloop has been sailing the Hudson since 1969, spreading its message of environmental consciousness and sharing love of the river with families everywhere. The *Clearwater* is usually docked at the restored Main Street pier.

Where to Eat

Aloy's Garden Restaurant. 157 Garden Street; (845) 473–8400. Italian-American specialties, burgers, subs, pizza, and kids' menu. $$

River Station. One Water Street; (845) 452–9207. Oldest restaurant in town, with nice river views, serving pasta, steak, and seafood, plus a children's menu. $$$–$$$$

Where to Stay

Holiday Inn Express. 2750 South Road; (845) 473–1151 or (800) HOLIDAY; www.hiexpress.com. Outdoor swimming pool and **free** continental breakfast. $$$

Inn at the Falls. 50 Red Oaks Mill Road; (845) 462–5770; www.innatthefalls.com. Elegant bed-and-breakfast. $$$$

Also in **the Area**

Mid-Hudson Civic Center-McCann Ice Arena. 14 Civic Center Plaza; (845) 454–5800; midhudsonciviccenter.com.

Overlook Golf & Recreation Center. 39 DeGarmo Road; (845) 471–8515.

The *River Rose* Tours & Cruises. Poughkeepsie Dock; (845) 562–1067.

Hyde Park

Continue north on Route 9.

Named after Edward Hyde, Lord Cornbury, an English governor and cousin of Queen Anne, Hyde Park is perhaps best known for the country estates of the Vanderbilts and Roosevelts. That's just as well, for Lord Cornbury, aside from his inclinations toward bribes, bad debts, and booze, had the habit of wearing extravagant women's dresses, much to the annoyance of the colonists.

Franklin D. Roosevelt Home National Historic Site (ages 7 and up)

4079 Albany Post Road (Route 9); (845) 486–7770 or (800) FDR–VISIT; www.fdrlibrary .marist.edu/. Open daily November through April 9:00 A.M. to 5:00 P.M. and May through October 9:00 A.M. to 6:00 P.M. Closed New Year's, Thanksgiving, and Christmas. $$, children under 16 free.

Springwood was the birthplace and lifelong residence of FDR, a former governor of New York and our thirty-second president. It is where he and Eleanor raised their five children, and it is a good place to introduce families to the man who guided America through the Great Depression and World War II. The museum, library, and house are filled with personal memorabilia, and an interactive video game offers older children the chance to make some of the decisions Roosevelt had to make during the war. The grounds surrounding the "Summer White House" are lovely, particularly the rose garden in June, and a nature study center sits on the slightly steep path leading down to the Hudson River.

Eleanor Roosevelt National Historic Site (ages 7 and up)

Route 9G, directly east of FDR home; (845) 229–9115; www .nps.gov/elro. Guided tours Thursday through Monday 9:00 A.M. to 5:00 P.M.; grounds open daily year-round until sunset. Closed Thanksgiving Day, Christmas Day, and New Year's Day. Guided tours $8.00 for adults, children under 16 free. Grounds free.

Eleanor Roosevelt considered Val-Kill to be her only real home. Built as a weekend retreat from the pressures of political life and her domineering mother-in-law, it is striking in its simplicity. Eleanor entertained many heads of state here as well as children from a nearby reform school. After her husband's death, she was enlisted by President Harry Truman as a United Nations delegate, and it was here that Eleanor drafted the Universal Declaration of Human Rights.

Suggested **Reading**

The Legend of Sleepy Hollow by Washington Irving

A Little Maid of Old New York by Alice Turner Curtis

The Lost Treasure of Captain Kidd by Peter Lourie

Eleanor Roosevelt: A Life of Discovery by Russell Freeman

Robert Fulton: From Submarine to Steamboat by Steven Kroll

The Gold Bug by Edgar Allan Poe

Vanderbilt Mansion (all ages)

Route 9; (845) 229–9115; www.nps.gov/vama. Open 9:00 A.M. to 5:00 P.M. daily year-round, closed major holidays. House admission $$, children under 17 free, and admission to grounds free to all.

This fifty-four-room Beaux Arts country palace is filled with European antiques, tapestries, and paintings and cost more than $2.5 million when completed in 1899—at a time when the average annual income was less than $500. The landscaped grounds include formal Italian gardens dotted with fountains and statues, sprawling lawns to run around on, lots of hiking trails winding through the woods, and lovely views of the Hudson River. Pick up a map (at any of the mansions) of the Hyde Park Trail, and explore an 8.5-mile network of easy, well-marked paths that follow the Hudson River between the Vanderbilt and Roosevelt homes.

Where to Eat

Coppola's Italian American Bistro. Albany Post Road (Route 9); (845) 229–9113. Casual Italian; children's menu. $$

Culinary Institute of America. Route 9; (845) 451–1588; ciachef.edu. Legendary chef school with four different award-winning restaurants plus a bakery . . . awesome! $$$

Where to Stay

Golden Manor. Route 9, across the road from FDR home; (845) 229–2157. Some rooms have kitchens; outdoor pool and near to restaurant. $

Village Square, A Country Inn. 531 Albany Post Road (Route 9); (845) 229–7141; www.enjoyhv.com/coppolas. Outdoor pool. $$

Hyde Park **Parks**

Hackett Hill. East Market Street; (845) 229–8086.

Pinewoods Park. Pinewoods Road; (845) 229–8086.

Riverfront Park. West Market Street; (845) 229–8086.

Rhinebeck

Continue north on Route 9.

German immigrants followed the Dutch and English to this area, naming the town in honor of their beloved Rhine River. Today Rhinebeck is a charming village of interesting shops and picturesque Victorian houses, including the oldest inn in America, the Beekman Arms. And yes, George Washington really did sleep here.

Old Rhinebeck Aerodrome (all ages)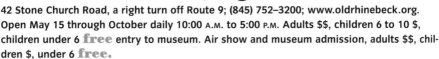
42 Stone Church Road, a right turn off Route 9; (845) 752–3200; www.oldrhinebeck.org. Open May 15 through October daily 10:00 A.M. to 5:00 P.M. Adults $$, children 6 to 10 $, children under 6 free entry to museum. Air show and museum admission, adults $$, children $, under 6 free.

This thrilling aviation museum features dramatic dogfights and spectacular stunts performed by fearless and funny pilots in pre– and post–World War I aircraft. Saturday shows focus on the early history of flight, and on Sunday families can cheer the aerobatic antics of Sir Percy Goodfellow as he battles Der Black Baron. After the show, stroll the grounds and marvel at the amazing collection of antique aircraft and automobiles amassed by museum founder and avid collector Cole Palen, then take to the air aboard a 1929 open-cockpit biplane.

Also in **the Area**

Ferncliff Forest. Mt. Rusten Road and River Road, north of Rhinebeck; (845) 876–3196.

Poets' Walk Park. River Road near Kingston-Rhinecliff Bridge, Red Hook; (845) 473–4440.

Greig Farm. Pitcher Lane, off Route 9, Red Hook; (845) 758–1234 or (845) 758–2020; www.greigfarm.com.

The Southlands Foundation. 5771 Route 9S; (845) 876–4862; www .southlands.org.

Where to Eat

Foster's Coach House Tavern. 6411 Montgomery Street; (845) 876–8052; www.fosterscoachhouse.com. This is a fun equestrian-themed restaurant serving steak, seafood, sandwiches, salads; kids' menu. $$

Village Diner. 7550 North Broadway, Red Hook; (845) 758–6232; www.historic-village-diner.com. Historic art deco family diner, serving great homemade soups, sandwiches, pastries, and daily specials, plus a children's menu. $

Where to Stay

Beekman Arms. 6387 Mill Street; (845) 876–7077. Built in 1766, it has an excellent restaurant with children's menu. $$$$

Interlake Farm Campground. 428 Lake Drive; (845) 266–5387; www.interlake rvpark.com. Lake with ducks; fishing, boating, playground; planned activities for families. $

Whistle Wood Farm. 52 Pells Road; (845) 876–6838; www.whistlewood.com. Working horse farm and bed-and-breakfast. $$$

Annandale-on-Hudson and Clermont

Take Route 9G north, then Route 9.

Montgomery Place (all ages)

River Road, Route 103, Annandale-on-Hudson; (914) 631–8200; www.hudsonvalley.org. Open April through October Wednesday through Monday 10:00 A.M. to 5:00 P.M., weekends November through mid-December 10:00 A.M. to 5:00 P.M. Closed January through March and Thanksgiving. Adults $$, children 5 to 17 $, under 5 free, grounds pass $.

Another of the sites operated by Historic Hudson Valley, this exquisite Federal-style mansion has lovely views of the river and easy trails past manicured gardens, woods, waterfalls, and orchards. Special seasonal activities are scheduled for families.

Clermont (all ages)

1 Clermont Avenue (off Route 9G), Clermont; (518) 537–4240; www.friendsofclermont.org. House and visitor's center open April 1 through October 31 Tuesday through Sunday, plus Monday holidays 11:00 A.M. to 5:00 P.M. Open weekends only November 1 through March 31 11:00 A.M. to 4:00 P.M.; grounds open year-round 8:30 A.M. to sunset. $, children under 5 free.

Home to the illustrious Livingston family for seven generations, Clermont is a restored Georgian-style mansion perched on a breathtaking bluff overlooking the Hudson. Special activities for families occur almost every weekend.

The *Clermont*

In 1686 a royal charter granted Robert Livingston a 162,000-acre tract of land in what later became the southern third of Columbia County. His great-grandson, Robert R. Livingston, signed the Declaration of Independence, administered the oath of office to George Washington, negotiated the Louisiana Purchase, and helped finance Robert Fulton's steamboat, the *Clermont*.

Lake Taghkanic State Park (all ages)

1528 Route 82, Ancram; (845) 851–3631; campground (800) 456–CAMP; www.nysparks.com. Park open daily year-round, campground open May through October. Parking fee $.

This popular park, centered around a lake and nestled among rolling hills and woodlands, has two beaches, several playgrounds, small boat rentals, concession stands, campgrounds, cabins and cottages, ballfields, shady picnic areas, fishing, a nature center, and a 4-mile hiking and biking trail that circles the lake. In winter, equipment rental is available for ice-skating and cross-country skiing.

Where to Eat

West Taghkanic Diner. Route 82, Ancram, off Taconic State Parkway; (518) 851–7117. Diner specialties. $–$$

Where to Stay

Brook-N-Wood Family Campground. 1947 Route 8, Elizaville; (518) 537–6896. Campsites, cabins, playground, pool, recreation hall, and cottage playhouse. $

Taghkanic Motel. 1011 Route 82, Ancram, off Taconic State Parkway; (518) 851–9006. Near state park. $$

Hudson

Continue north on Route 9G.

In the mid-1700s, Nantucket whalers and other fishermen settled in this area, building Hudson into an efficient shipping center that twenty-five schooners called home port. In 1797 the town came within one vote of becoming the state's capital, but by the mid-1800s, the whaling industry was declining, as were the whales. Today a stroll through town reveals a wonderful variety of nineteenth-century New England–style architecture. Warren Street is lined with inviting antiques shops, and 1 block over, Columbia Street (formerly Diamond Street) had the dubious distinction of being the oldest red-light district in the country. Walk down to Front Street and enjoy the river vistas from the Parade or Promenade Hill Park.

American Museum of Firefighting (all ages)

117 Harry Howard Avenue; (518) 828–7695 or (877) 347–3687; www.warrenstreet.com. Open daily year-round 9:00 A.M. to 4:30 P.M. Closed major holidays. Free.

For the fledgling firefighters in your family, this is a fascinating place. The collection, the largest of its kind, includes more than seventy antique and unusual fire engines from 1725 to the present day, as well as firefighting equipment, artwork, and memorabilia from two centuries. Special events throughout the year culminate with the New York State Firefighters Competition and Field Day in July.

Olana (ages 8 and up)

Route 9G, 1 mile south of Rip Van Winkle Bridge; (518) 828–0135; www.olana.org. Guided tours only. House open Tuesday through Sunday 10:00 A.M. to 4:00 P.M., visitor's center 9:30 A.M. to 5:00 P.M. Grounds open daily 8:00 A.M. to sunset year-round. $

Envisioned as a Persian palace by Hudson River School painter Frederick Edwin Church, Olana is his spectacular effort to create a romantic, 3-D landscape work of art. The gilded and tiled mansion was the result of his love of exotic lands. From mixing the vivid paints for the walls himself and filling the rooms with exquisite objects to landscaping the 250-acre grounds overlooking the Hudson River, Church created his vision.

Where to Eat

Columbia Diner. 717 Warren Street; (518) 828–5474. Great home-style food at reasonable prices, plus a children's menu. $

Scali's Pasta and Pizza. 974 Columbia Street; (518) 828–9186. Italian-American specialties. $–$$

Where to Stay

St. Charles Hotel. 16–18 Park Place; (518) 822–9900; www.stcharleshotel.com. Full-service hotel with several large rooms for families. $$$

Sunset Motel. Routes 9 and 23; (518) 851–3721; www.sunsetmoteland suites.com. Rooms and efficiencies and a playground. $$

Kinderhook

Head north on Route 9.

First settled by the Dutch in the 1660s, Kinderhook, or "children's corner," is perhaps best known today as the hometown of Martin Van Buren, our country's eighth president, and, incidentally, the first one to be born a citizen of the United States. Van Buren had several nicknames, among them "the Little Magician" (for his size and political skill) and "the Red Fox" (for his red sideburns), but it was his nickname of "Old Kinderhook" that may have given us the expression "OK."

Martin Van Buren National Historic Site (ages 6 and up) 🏛

1013 Old Post Road, off Route 9H; (518) 758–9689; www.nps.gov/mava. Call for admission and hours of operation.

When Martin Van Buren purchased Lindenwald in 1839, he planned to live there after he retired from politics. His failure to win a second term as president in 1841 (despite his *Amistad* actions) brought about retirement somewhat earlier than expected. A guided tour of the house may be of interest to older children, and special events include a coach and carriage show, a picnic and band concert in period costume, and naturalist-guided nature walks.

Hudson River National Estuarine Research Reserve

Created to protect and manage the biologically diverse Hudson River coastal wetlands, this network of four different ecosystems stretches along 100 miles of the river's estuary and encompasses 4,800 acres. Each of the sites offers frequent public field programs. For more information, call (845) 758–7010, or fax (845) 758–7033; www.dec.state.ny.us/website/hudson/hrnerr.

Iona Island. Route 9W, Bear Mountain.

Piermont Marsh. Route 9W, Piermont.

Tivoli Bays. Route 9, Annandale-on-Hudson.

Stockport Flats. Route 9, Hudson.

Luykas Van Alen House (ages 6 and up)
Route 9H, Lindenwald; (518) 758–9265; www.berk.com/cchsprog_links_sites_1.html. Open Memorial Day through Labor Day Thursday through Saturday 11:00 A.M. to 5:00 P.M., Sunday 1:00 to 4:00 P.M. $, children under 12 free.

Martin Scorsese's film *The Age of Innocence* was filmed in this restored 1737 Dutch Colonial farmhouse. Also on the thirty-acre site is the Ichabod Crane Schoolhouse, named for a local schoolteacher who was the inspiration for the character in Washington Irving's tale *The Legend of Sleepy Hollow.*

Where to Eat

Carolina House. 59 Broad Street (Route 9); (518) 758–1669. Southern cuisine served in a log cabin. $$

Kinderhook Diner. 333 Route 9H, Valatie; (518) 758–1399. Diner delights. $$

Where to Stay

Kinderhook Bed & Breakfast. 67 Broad Street (Route 9); (518) 758–1850. Near the village green; four rooms with feather beds; children welcome. $$$

The Chathams

Take Route 203 south into Chatham, or Route 203 north into North Chatham; Route 295 leads to East Chatham.

German and Dutch farmers settled here in 1758, and by the late nineteenth century the area was a railroad hub. The Chathams—which include the village of Chatham, Chatham Center, East Chatham, North Chatham, and Old Chatham—are spread out over miles of pastoral scenery. If you're in the neighborhood Labor Day weekend, you won't want to miss the Columbia County Fair, the oldest festival of its kind in the country.

Shaker Museum and Library (ages 7 and up)
88 Shaker Museum Road, Old Chatham, off County Road 13; (518) 794–9100; www.shaker museumandlibrary.org/. Open May through October Wednesday through Monday 10:00 A.M. to 5:00 P.M. Adults $$, children $, under 6 free.

Shaker founder Mother Ann Lee was thrown in jail in England for preaching her beliefs in communal living, celibacy, equality, and pacifism, so she and her followers sailed for America in 1774, seeking religious freedom. Children lived apart from the adults, with girls attending school in summer and boys in winter. Older children will appreciate the Shakers' imaginative solutions to everyday problems—the clothespin, circular saw, cut nails, and water-repellent fabric. The museum houses more than 8,500 items in twenty-four galleries—the largest collection of Shaker craftsmanship in the country. You may also want to visit the nearby **Mount Lebanon Shaker Village,** Darrow Road, New Lebanon; (518) 794–9500, the site of the first permanent Shaker community in New York. Open mid-June through mid-October, Friday, Saturday, and Sunday 10:00 A.M. to 5:00 P.M. Adults $$, children $.

Where to Eat

Chatham Bakery and Coffee Shoppe. 1 Church Street, Chatham; (518) 392–3411. Baked goods, burgers, barbecued chicken, an all-you-can-eat fish fry on Friday, and a kids' menu. $

Where to Stay

The Inn at Shaker Mill Farm. 40 Cherry Lane, off Route 22, Canaan; (518) 794–9345; www.shakermill.com. Bed-and-breakfast with a stream and pond to explore. $$

Chatham Travel Lodge. Route 295 and Taconic State Parkway; (518) 392–4066. Twelve rooms. $$

Hillsdale and Copake Falls

Take the Taconic State Parkway south to Route 23. Take Route 23 east to Hillsdale, then Route 22 south to Copake Falls.

These peaceful villages lie along the edge of Taconic State Park and offer a variety of seasonal and scenic outdoor activities.

Catamount Ski Area (ages 2 and up)

Route 23, Hillsdale; (518) 325–3200 or (800) 342–1840 (snow report); www.catamount ski.com. Open weekdays in season 9:00 A.M. to 4:00 P.M., weekends 8:30 A.M. to 4:00 P.M.; night skiing Wednesday through Thursday 5:00 to 9:00 P.M., Friday through Saturday 5:00 P.M. to 10:00 P.M. Adults $$$$, children 7 through 13 $$$. Special ski packages available.

This small, family-oriented ski resort has twenty-seven slopes and trails, seven lifts, snowboarding slopes, and instruction available for snow bunnies age four and up. Baby-sitting is available for children ages two to six.

Taconic State Park—Copake Falls Area (all ages)

Route 344, Copake Falls, off Route 22; (518) 329–3993, camping reservations (800) 456–CAMP (May through October); www.nysparks.com/parks. Summer parking fee $$; camping $.

Nestled in the Taconic Mountains, this is the northern section of a lush 5,000-acre preserve. The Copake Falls area offers swimming, hiking, boat rentals, campsites, picnic areas, playgrounds, and trout fishing. A highlight is spectacular Bash-Bish Falls, and special children's activities are offered throughout the summer.

Where to Eat

Hillsdale House. Anthony Street and Route 22, Hillsdale; (518) 325–7111. Regional American specialties, burgers, chicken fingers, and wood-fired pizza. They'll do half orders for children if you ask. $$$

Random Harvest. Route 23, Craryville; (518) 325–5103. Farm market and gourmet deli shop. $

Where to Stay

Silvanus Lodge. 9350 Route 22, north of Hillsdale; (518) 325–3000. Rooms and one small apartment. $$$–$$$$

Oleana Campground. 2236 route 7 and 7A, Copake; (518) 329–2811. Open year-round, with playground, lake for swimming and fishing, video arcade, basketball, baseball, and hayrides. $

Millerton and Stanfordville

Head south on Route 22 to Millerton, then Route 199 west to Route 82 and south to Stanfordville.

Taconic State Park—Rudd Pond Area (all ages)

Rudd Pond Road, Millerton, off Route 22; (518) 789–3059; www.nysparks.com/parks. Open daily year-round; campgrounds open mid-May through mid-October. Summer parking fee $$; camping $.

The 210-acre Rudd Pond area, the southern part of Taconic State Park, offers swimming, sand beach and bathhouse, a playground, rowboat rentals, fishing, hiking and biking trails, and a nice picnic area, as well as ice-skating, cross-country skiing, and snowmobiling in winter.

Thompson Pond Preserve (all ages)

Lake Road, Pine Plains; turn at the Pine Plains firehouse; (914) 244–3271; www.nature.org. Stissing Mountain Fire Tower, (518) 398–5673. Open daily year-round. Free.

This 372-acre gem lies at the base of Stissing Mountain and is a registered National Natural Landmark. An easy two-hour-loop trail starting from Lake Road will lead you through fields, forests, and swamp, with opportunities for some of the best bird-watching in the Hudson Valley. Scale the fire tower at Stissing Mountain's summit and, on a clear day, you can see all the way to Albany.

Hudson Valley Raptor Center (all ages)

Route 53, South Road, off Route 82, Stanfordville; (845) 758–OWLS (6957). Open April through October Saturday and Sunday 1:00 to 4:00 P.M. Special birds of prey presentation weekends at 2:00 P.M. in July and August. $

The Hudson Valley is an important flyway for migrating raptors. This sanctuary is home to more than a hundred birds of prey from twenty species, including red-tailed hawks, bald eagles, peregrine falcons, and great horned owls.

Wilcox Park (all ages)

Route 199, Stanfordville; (845) 758–6100; www.co.dutchess.ny.us/countygov/departments/ dpw-parks/ppwilcox.htm. Park hours are Memorial Day through Labor Day weekends 9:00 A.M. to 7:00 P.M., weekdays 10:00 A.M. to 7:00 P.M. Labor Day through Memorial Day weekends only 9:00 A.M. to 7:00 P.M. $

This lovely park has a small lake with a sandy beach, paddleboats, miniature golf, a children's playground, bike paths, hiking trails, and campsites.

Where to Stay

Roseland Ranch. North of town on Hunn's Lake Road, Stanfordville; (845) 868–1350 or (800) 431–8292; www.duderanch.com. Open all year. This wonderful family resort, located on 1,000 acres of land hugging a lake, offers horseback riding and lessons, skiing, tennis, indoor and outdoor swimming pools, sauna, petting zoo, paddleboats, children's activities, baby-sitting, and nearby golf. $$$$

Millbrook

Head south on Route 82 to Route 44A.

Wing's Castle (ages 6 and up)

717 Bangall Road, 0.5 mile north of Route 57, northeast of Millbrook; (845) 677–9085; e-mail: wing@idsi.net. Open Memorial Day to September 1 Wednesday through Sunday, September 2 to December 20 Saturday and Sunday noon to 4:30 P.M. $$

Created from recycled and recovered treasures, this whimsical stone castle has been the work and home of Peter and Toni Wing and family for more than two decades. A work in progress, the castle sits atop a hill overlooking the Hudson Valley. Inside are more than 2,000 antiques, oddities, and artifacts. Have a picnic on the grounds, where the Wings built Stonehenge East from 12-foot hand-hewn slabs of rock.

Innisfree Garden (all ages)

Innisfree, Tyrell Road, 1 mile off Route 44 west of Millbrook; (845) 677–8000. Open May through October Wednesday through Friday 10:00 A.M. to 4:00 P.M., weekends and holidays 11:00 A.M. to 5:00 P.M. $, children under 4 free.

Painter Walter Beck and his wife, Marion, created this serene sanctuary using the landscape as their canvas. Although they never visited the Orient, the Becks studied Japanese scroll paintings and sculpted a series of "cup gardens" based on Eastern principles of design. The peaceful 200 acres surrounding a small glacial lake is laced with streams, stones, waterfalls, and terraces connected by carefully laid paths that are wonderful for strolling.

The Institute of Ecosystem Studies
at the Mary Flagler Cary Arboretum (all ages)

Route 44A (off Route 44); (845) 677–5359; www.ecostudies.org. Gifford House Visitor and Education Center, 181 Sharon Turnpike. Open April through December Monday through Saturday 9:00 A.M. to 6:00 P.M., Sunday 1:00 to 6:00 P.M.; closes at 4:00 P.M. October through April. Closed major holidays. Free.

For the budding botanists in your family, this is a combination gardening education center and wetland ecology laboratory. Pick up a permit and map at the Gifford House Visitor and Education Center, then tour the grounds. A tropical greenhouse, unusual plant collections, and a variety of nature trails in and around the 1,900 acres are fun to explore, and fun family workshops are offered.

Trevor Teaching Zoo (all ages)

Located at Millbrook School on School Road off Route 44; (845) 677–3704; www.trevor zoo.org. Open daily 8:00 A.M. to 5:00 P.M. $

This small zoo, founded in 1936 and located on the grounds of a picturesque prep school, is home to more than one hundred exotic and indigenous species of animals, from red-tailed hawks to coati mundis. Care of the creatures is part of the school curriculum in the hopes that familiarity will breed appreciation. A 1.25-mile self-guiding nature trail and a boardwalk overlooking a marsh are both stroller accessible.

Where to Eat

Allyn's Restaurant & Cafe. Route 44, 4 miles east of Millbrook; (845) 677–5888; www.allyns.com. Brunch, lunch, and dinner served in two dining areas. $$$

Millbrook Diner. 224 Franklin Avenue (Route 44); (845) 677–5319. Diner classics. $–$$

Where to Stay

The Cottonwood Motel. 2639 Route 44, 4 miles east of Taconic State Parkway; (845) 677–3283; www.cottonwood motel.com. Eighteen rooms, plus a large cottage with kitchen. $$$$

Sybil Ludington **Statue**

This statue is dedicated to the sixteen-year-old heroine of the American Revolution who rode her horse Star more than 40 dangerous miles to warn the militia of the advancing British troops. The annual Tour de Sybil, a 35-mile bike trip retracing part of her ride, begins at the statue, on Gleneida Avenue in Carmel. Information is available through the Putnam County Tourist Bureau.

Brewster

Head west on Route 44A, then south on the Taconic State Parkway, connecting with I–84 east.

Green Chimneys Farm and Wildlife Conservation Center
(all ages)
Putnam Lake Road; (845) 279–2995. Open weekends year-round 10:00 A.M. to 3:00 P.M. Donation.

Many special events for families are scheduled throughout the year, along with regular self-guided farm tours. Injured wild animals, especially birds of prey, are cared for here.

Southeast Museum (ages 6 and up)
67 Main Street; (845) 279–7500; www.southeastmuseum.org. Open April through December Tuesday through Saturday 10:00 A.M. to 4:00 P.M. Donation.

A small, offbeat museum, located in the lower level of the old Southeast Town Hall, it offers permanent exhibits on Borden's condensed milk factory, the Harlem Railroad, local rocks and minerals, and other interesting oddities.

Putnam Children's Discovery Center (all ages)
Route 6, Mahopac; (845) 276–2076; www.discoveryctr.org. Open Thursday 12:30 to 4:00 P.M. $

This interactive museum has lots of hands-on science exhibits for toddlers to teens, from fantasy play areas and puppet shows to workshops in magic, art, chess, computers, and drama.

Also in **the Area**

Chuang Yen Monastery. Route 301, Kent; (845) 225–1819.

Where to Eat

Carmel Diner and Restaurant. 63 Gleneida Avenue, Carmel; (845) 225–5000. Twenty-four-hour diner with children's menu. $

Red Rooster Restaurant. 1566 Route 22; (845) 279–8046. Fun fast food from fries to franks, with the added bonus of a miniature golf course. $

Where to Stay

Heidi's Inn. Route 22; (845) 279–8011; www.heidisinn.com. Rooms and efficiencies plus a swimming pool. $$

North Salem and Somers

Take Route 121 south, then Route 116.

Once Somers was the center of a booming cattle industry, but in 1810 it became famous as the birthplace of American circus entrepreneurship.

New Hammond Museum and Japanese Stroll Garden (all ages)

28 Deveau Road, off June Road, just north of Route 116, North Salem; (914) 669–5033; www.hammondmuseum.org. Open May through October Wednesday through Saturday noon to 4:00 P.M. Terrace Cafe on grounds. $, children under 12 free.

These graceful Edo-period gardens were designed by Natalie Hays Hammond, daughter of the man who discovered the long-lost King Solomon Mines in Africa. Thirteen small landscapes have been created here, and each component has a special symbolic meaning.

Somers Circus Museum (all ages)

At intersection of Routes 100 and 202, Somers; (914) 277–4977; www.somersmuseum.org. Open Thursday 2:00 to 4:00 P.M., the second and fourth Sunday of every month from 1:00 to 4:00 P.M., or by appointment. Donation.

Hachariah Bailey had a sea captain brother who brought him an elephant from London in 1796. As this was the first elephant seen in America, it caused quite a stir, so Bailey toured "Old Bet" up and down the East Coast. Unfortunately, Old Bet's career as a circus star was cut short one day in Maine, when the pachyderm's passion for potatoes prompted a farmer to shoot her. Still, the folks back in Somers were impressed and soon began rounding up all sorts of exotic creatures for similar road shows.

Katonah

Take I–684 south.

This charming village has dozens of historic homes, many of which were moved from the original town of Katonah 0.5 mile away when the area was flooded at the end of the nineteenth century to create the Cross River Reservoir.

Muscoot Farm (all ages)

Route 100, 1 mile south of Route 35; (914) 864–7282; www.westchestergov.com/parks. Open daily 10:00 A.M. to 4:00 P.M. Families **free,** but donations accepted; groups must make reservations and pay a fee.

The 777-acre working farm at Muscoot was a model of agrarian efficiency when it was built in 1885, and today it's a delightful place for families to experience home on the range. Many activities are scheduled on weekends, from blacksmithing to beekeeping demonstrations, and several acres of nature trails wind through surrounding wetlands and meadows.

Caramoor Center for Music and the Arts (ages 7 and up)

149 Girdle Ridge Road, near intersection of Routes 22 and 35; (914) 232–1252 or (914) 232–5035; www.caramoor.org. Open May through October Wednesday through Friday and Sunday 1:00 to 4:00 P.M., Saturday 1:00 to 5:00 P.M. Adults $$, children 16 and under **free.**

This lavishly romantic mansion was built in the 1930s by financier Walter Rosen to house his fabulous art collection. Each room has a different theme, from alpine cottage to Italian

Free **Natural Attractions**

Hiking trails, petroglyphs, wildlife displays, and family events are all enjoyed **free** of charge at these nature preserves:

Ward Pound Ridge Reservation and Trailside Nature Museum. Route 35 and 121, Cross River; (914) 864–7317; www.westchestergov.com/parks. **Free** admission but $$ parking fee.

Westmoreland Sanctuary. 260 Chestnut Ridge Road (off Route 172), Mount Kisco; (914) 666–8448; www.westmorelandsanctuary.org.

Arthur W. Butler Memorial Sanctuary. Chestnut Ridge Road, Bedford; (914) 244–3271; www.nature.org.

Mianus River Gorge & Botanical Preserve. Mianus River Road, Bedford; (914) 244–3271; www.nature.org.

Renaissance. Entire sections were transplanted from European villas, and walking through the fifty-five rooms is like taking an international architectural tour. Every summer the Caramoor Music Festival offers classical, jazz, and opera concerts in the courtyards, and everyone will enjoy a picnic or a stroll through the statue-studded gardens of this 117-acre estate.

Where to Eat

Blue Dolphin Diner. 175 Katonah Avenue; (914) 232–4791. Homemade pasta, daily specials. $–$$

Where to Stay

Crabtree's Kittle House. 11 Kittle Road, off Route 117, Chappaqua; (914) 666–8044. Two-hundred-year-old inn with twelve rooms and terrific progressive American restaurant. Children welcome. $$$$

Yorktown Heights

Head north on I–684, then take Route 35 west.

Yorktown Museum (all ages)

1974 Commerce Street; (914) 962–2970; www.yorktownmuseum.org. Open year-round Tuesday noon to 4:00 P.M., Thursday 10:00 A.M. to 1:00 P.M., Sunday 1:00 to 4:00 P.M.; closed during lunchtime. Donation.

This small but charming museum has several theme rooms, including the Railroad Room, filled with train memorabilia and a working HO-scale model set; the Small World room, packed with exquisitely furnished dollhouses and miniature displays; and the Woodlands Room, with a Mohican longhouse in which you can learn about the area's original inhabitants.

Also in **the Area**

Osceola Beach. 399 East Main Street, Yorktown; (914) 245–3246; www.osceolabeach.com.

Yorktown Stage. 1974 Commerce Street, Yorktown Heights; (914) 962–0606.

Kitchawan Preserve. Route 134, Yorktown; (914) 864–PARK; www.west chestergov.com/parks.

Franklin D. Roosevelt State Park (all ages)

2957 Crompond Road (entrances off Route 202 and Taconic State Parkway); (914) 245–4434; www.westchestergov.com/parks. Open year-round 8:00 A.M. to dusk. Free.

Rent a boat and fish for perch, bullhead, pickerel, and the elusive largemouth bass in Lake Mohansic, or take a leisurely stroll along a nature trail. Cool off in the swimming pool, then have lunch at the picnic pavilions.

Family Golf Center at Yorktown (all ages)

2710 Lexington Avenue, Mohegan Lake; (914) 526–8337. Open year-round 9:00 A.M. to 9:00 P.M. weekdays and 8:00 A.M. to 9:00 P.M. weekends. $

Miniature golf, plus stalls of practice tees, lessons for all ages, and a snack bar.

Where to Eat

Suen Hai Chinese Restaurant. 2038 Sawmill River Road; (914) 962–7996. Cantonese, Szechuan, and Japanese specialties. $–$$

Croton-on-Hudson and Ossining

Take Route 202 west, then Route 9 south.

Settled by the Italian stonemasons and Irish laborers who constructed the Croton Reservoir in the nineteenth century, Croton-on-Hudson later became a country retreat of bohemian artists and intellectuals from Greenwich Village during and after World War I.

Peekskill **Arts**

Downtown Artists' District. Division Street between Main and South Streets, Peekskill; (914) 737–2780. Guided tours (914) 666–2398. Painters, potters, sculptors, and photographers have revitalized this area, and many offer tours of their studios and galleries on the third Saturday of the month from May to October. It's a wonderful opportunity to see artists at work in a variety of media and perhaps inspire the next generation of the Hudson River School.

Van Cortlandt Manor (ages 7 and up)

5 South Riverside Avenue, off Route 9, Croton-on-Hudson; (914) 631–8200; www.hudson valley.org. Open April through October daily except Tuesday 10:00 A.M. to 5:00 P.M., last tour at 4:00 P.M.; weekends only November and December 10:00 A.M. to 4:00 P.M., last tour at 3:00 P.M. Closed January through March and major holidays. Adults $$, students 6 to 17 $, under 6 free.

A gracious Dutch manor house, Van Cortlandt is filled with a mixture of antiques from several different periods. Demonstrations of colonial crafts, herbal medicine preparation, and cooking take place often, and the eighteenth-century flower and herb gardens are lovely. Legend has it that there are six different ghosts haunting this mansion, from a Redcoat and a Hessian soldier to a laughing girl who arrives by a horse-drawn carriage.

Croton Point Park (all ages)

Croton Point Avenue (off Route 9), Croton-on-Hudson; (914) 862–5290 park information; www.westchestergov.com/parks. Open daily year-round 8:00 A.M. to dusk; nature center open Tuesday through Saturday 9:00 A.M. to 4:00 P.M. Parking fee $$.

Occupying a 500-acre peninsula jutting out into the Hudson, this park has a playground, campground, cabins, a pool, recreation hall, ball fields, miles of hiking and biking trails, and an annual festival.

Teatown Lake Reservation (all ages)

1600 Spring Valley Road, Ossining, off Route 9; (914) 762–2912; www.teatown.org. Grounds open dawn to dusk daily. Interpretive center open Tuesday through Saturday 9:00 A.M. to 5:00 P.M. and Sunday 1:00 to 5:00 P.M. Free.

Long before the Boston Tea Party, there was a similar uprising in this area. Before the Revolution, when King George III tightly controlled and taxed the colonists' favorite beverage, the local women of the settlement heard of a Bronx merchant in the area hoarding a rare stash of tea and stormed his farm demanding a fair share. The women of the merchant's family held the town women at bay until he finally agreed to supply tea for everyone through the black market. Today this 636-acre preserve is laced with 12 miles of trails around a tranquil woodland lake. A small nature museum and wildlife rehabilitation program offer family workshops on weekends, ranging from maple sugaring and wildlife tracking to flower identification.

Boats and **Balloons**

Great Hudson Sailing Center. Dock Street, Kingston; (845) 429–1557; www.greathudsonsailing.com.

North River Cruises. West Strand Park, Broadway, Kingston; (845) 679–8205; www.northrivercruises.com.

Fantasy Balloon Flights. 2 Evergreen Lane, Port Jervis; (845) 856–7103; www.fantasyfliers.com.

Above the Clouds. Randall Airport, Airport Road, Middletown; (845) 692–2556; www.my-balloon.co.

Yonkers

Continue south on Route 9.

Originally named Nappeckamack, this area was a thriving Lenape Indian village before the Europeans arrived. Every town has its ups and downs, but none more so than when inventor Elisha G. Otis introduced his first "perpendicular stairway" here in 1853.

Hudson River Museum (all ages)
511 Warburton Avenue; (914) 963–4550 or (914) 963–2139 (planetarium); www.hrm.org. Open Wednesday to Sunday noon to 5:00 P.M., Friday to 8:00 P.M. Museum $, planetarium $, Friday night planetarium show is free.

Combining science, art, culture, and local history is quite a juggling act, but this museum complex does just that and adds a restaurant with a river view. Next door is the **Andrus Space Transit Planetarium,** home to a state-of-the-art star machine.

Greenburgh Nature Center (all ages)
99 Dromore Road, Scarsdale; (914) 723–3470; www.townlink.com/community-web/gnc. Grounds open daily dawn to dusk. Museum open Monday through Thursday 9:30 A.M. to noon, Saturday and Sunday 1:00 to 4:30 P.M. $

Explore a variety of environments along self-guided trails at this thirty-two-acre nature center. The small museum offers many special events for children.

Also in **the Area**

New Roc City. New Street, Le Count Place, New Rochelle; (914) 637–7575; www.newroccity.com. Entertainment and retail stores.

Where to Eat

Louie and Johnnie's Ristorante.
706–708 Central Park Avenue; (914) 423–3300. Pasta, chicken, steak, and seafood plus a children's menu; takeout and **free** delivery. $$

Where to Stay

Holiday Inn–Yonkers. 125 Tuckahoe Road; (914) 476–3800 or (800) HOLIDAY; www.holiday-inn.com. Outdoor pool, restaurant. $$$$

Royal Regency Hotel. 165 Tuckahoe Road; (914) 476–6200 or (800) 215–3858; www.royalregencyny.com. Comfortable hotel, restaurant. **Free** continental breakfast. $$$$

Rye

Take the Bronx River Parkway to Scarsdale, then I–287 west to Rye.

Settled in the mid-seventeenth century by Connecticut colonials seeking to improve their lives, this suburban seaside town now has lovely tree-lined streets and interesting shops.

Playland (all ages)

Playland Parkway (exit 19 off I–95); (914) 813–7000; Ice Casino (914) 813–7059; www .ryeplayland.org. Open May through Labor Day daily except Monday. Call for hours. No charge to enter park, but ride tickets must be purchased. $$$

This art deco amusement park, built in 1928, was the first family fun park of its kind and is now a National Historic Landmark. Many of the more than forty rides are original, like the wooden Dragon Coaster and painted carousel, but many are new, and younger children will love the toddler-size Kiddy Land. Cool off at the nearby crescent beach with a swim in the Sound. Take a dip in the Olympic-size pool, or go ice-skating. Rent a rowboat on the lake, play a round of miniature golf, or stroll the boardwalk.

The 170-acre **Edith G. Read Natural Park and Wildlife Sanctuary** is right next door if you want to escape the crowds—and Playland can get very crowded on weekends.

Other Things to See and Do in the
Hudson River Valley Region

Highland Lakes State Park. Route 211 East, Middletown; (845) 786–2701; www.nysparks.com/parks.

Norrie Point Environmental Site. Route 9, Staatsburg; (845) 889–4830.

6½ Station Road Sanctuary. 6½ Station Road, Goshen; (845) 744–6047.

Orange County Fair Speedway. 239 Wisner Avenue, Middletown; (845) 342–2573; www.ocfsmotorsports.com.

Wilderstein Preservation. 330 Morton Road, Rhinebeck; (845) 876–4818; www.wilderstein.org.

Foundry School Museum. 63 Chestnut Street, Cold Spring; (845) 265–4010.

Clove Furnace Historic Site. 21 Clove Furnace Drive at Route 17, Arden; (845) 351–4696.

Van Houten Gardens. 241 Little Tor Road, New City; (845) 241–2498.

Dr. Davies Farm. 306 Route 304, Congers; (845) 268–7020.

Van Houten Farms. 12 Sickletown Road, Pearl River; (845) 735–4689.

Orchards of Conklin. 2 South Mountain Road and Route 45, Pomona; (845) 354–0369.

Mills-Norrie State Park. Old Post Road (Route 9), Staatsburg; (845) 889–4646.

Edward Hopper House. 82 North Broadway, Nyack; (845) 358–0774.

Webatuck Craft Village. Route 22 at Route 55, Wingdale; (845) 832–6522; www.huntcountryfurniture.com.

Thomas Paine Museum and Cottage. 983 North Avenue, New Rochelle; (914) 632–5376; www.thomaspaine.org.

Tallix Art Foundry. 310 Fishkill Avenue, Beacon; (845) 838–1111.

Marshlands Conservancy (all ages)

Route 1; (914) 835–4466; www.westchestergov.com/parks. Nature Center open 9:00 A.M. to 5:00 P.M. Wednesday through Sunday. Trails open daily dawn to dusk. Free.

Trails wind through a variety of habitats, from fields and woods to a salt marsh along the shore of Long Island Sound.

Where to Eat

Frankie & Johnnie's Steakhouse. 77 Purchase Street; (914) 925–3900. Pasta, chicken, steak, and seafood. $$$$

Where to Stay

Courtyard by Marriott. 631 Midland Avenue; (914) 921–1110 or (800) 321–2211; www.marriott.com. Indoor pool, restaurant. $$$$

For More Information

Westchester Visitor's Center. (914) 995–8500 or (800) 833–9282; www.westchestergov.com/tourism or www.westchestertourism.com.

Rockland County Tourism. (845) 708–7300 or (800) 295–5723; www.rockland.org.

Orange County Tourism. (845) 291–2136 or (800) 762–8687; www.orangetourism.org.

Putnam County Visitor's Bureau. (845) 225–0381 or (800) 470–4854; www.visitputnam.org.

Dutchess County Tourism. (845) 463–4000 or (800) 445–3131; www.dutchesstourism.com.

Columbia County Tourism. (518) 828–3375 or (800) 724–1846; www.columbiacountyny.com.

The Catskills

Older than the Adirondacks, the Catskills are a delightful dichotomy. Romantically primeval and mysterious, this ancient plateau was once the hunting grounds of the Lenape, who believed the area to be the abode of the Great Spirit. Since the mid-1800s, the paintings of Thomas Cole and Frederick Church, along with the literature of Washington Irving and John Burroughs, have attracted tourists to the region, and resorts sprang up in response. Along with the wilderness and wildlife, there's a wild life of a different nature that exists today. From flume zooming at water parks to fly-fishing on the Willowemoc, there are train trips, petting zoos, putt-putt palaces, and more, all planned to please everyone in the family.

Driving Tips

From the west bank of the Hudson River in Kingston, Route 28 cuts through Ulster County and the Catskill Forest Preserve and Park, a 300,000-acre reserve of public and private land. Continue through the rolling hills of Delaware County or head north near Arkville on Route 30 to intersect with Route 23A. Follow Route 23A through the heart of Greene County and the higher peaks region, all the way to the west bank of the Hudson River in Catskill. Route 30 also follows the east branch of the Delaware River south and connects with Route 17 through the center of Sullivan County and to the scenic Route 98, which winds along the Delaware River. The region is reachable from I–87 on the eastern border and by I–88 on the far western edge.

Kingston

On Route 9W, on the eastern edge of the Catskills, along the Hudson River.

This quiet town was originally named "Wiltwyck" (Wild Place) by the Dutch, who founded a settlement here in 1652, making it the third-oldest city in the state. Later controlled by the British and renamed Kingston, the village was briefly the colonists' state capital during the Revolutionary War. Stop by the Kingston Urban Cultural Park Visitor Center for a guided or self-guided walking tour of the area. Of special interest are the Old Dutch Church, the Sen-

THE CATSKILLS

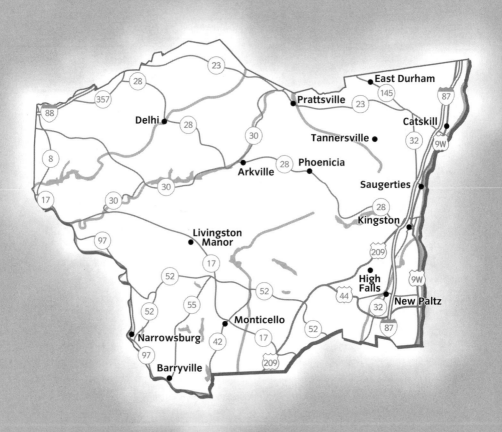

ate House, and the Ulster County Courthouse (where Sojourner Truth won a lawsuit that rescued her son from slavery). Afterward, head down Broadway to the waterfront and Rondout Landing for a stroll around the revitalized river port.

Hudson River Maritime Museum (all ages)

1 Rondout Landing; (845) 338–0071; www.ulster.net/~hrmm. Open daily May through October 11:00 A.M. to 5:00 P.M. Museum and Lighthouse Tour, adults $$, children 6 to 12 $, under 6 free.

This small museum, dedicated to preserving the maritime heritage of the Hudson River, has changing indoor exhibits, as well as several vintage vessels docked outside. Watch craftspeople restoring and rigging wooden ships next door, then hop aboard a boat to tour the biggest beacon on the Hudson, the nearby Rondout Lighthouse.

Trolley Museum (all ages)

89 East Strand, Rondout Landing; (845) 331–3399; www.mhric.org/tmny or www.ci.kingston .ny.us/tourism/museums/html#trolley. Open weekends and holidays Memorial Day to Columbus Day noon to 5:00 P.M. $

Check out subway and rapid transit cars from past to present, then ride the trolley 1.5 miles along the riverfront on original tracks to Kingston Point for a picnic.

Volunteer Fireman's Hall and Museum (ages 4 and up)

266 Fair Street; (845) 331–0866; www.ci.kingston.ny.us/tourism/museums.html. Open April through October Friday 11:00 A.M. to 3:00 P.M. and Saturday 10:00 A.M. to 4:00 P.M.; June through August Wednesday through Friday 11:00 A.M. to 3:00 P.M. and Saturday 10:00 A.M. to 4:00 P.M. Free.

Housed in an 1857 fire station, this small museum has several ornate antique fire engines, artifacts, and other interesting firefighting memorabilia.

Hudson River Cruises (all ages)

Rondout Landing; (845) 340–4700 or (800) 843–7472; www.hudsonrivercruises.com. Operating May, June, September, and October weekends, July and August six days a week, with departures daily at 11:30 A.M. and 2:30 P.M. Adults $$$, children 4 through 11 $$, under 4 free.

Watch the world glide by from aboard the M/V Rip Van Winkle for a two-hour narrated sightseeing voyage.

Jeto's Miniature Golf (all ages)

180 Sawkill Road; (845) 331–2545. Open April through October 10:00 A.M. to 10:00 P.M. daily. $–$$

The lure of the mini-fairway beckons. Putter through eighteen holes, do battle in the batting cages or arcade, or go-kart your way around the racetrack.

Sawkill Family Ski Center (all ages)
167 Hill Road (off Sawkill and Jockey Hill Roads); (845) 336–6977; www.sawkillski.com.

This all-season sports spot offers mini-golf, go-karts, and water slides in summer, and downhill skiing and snowtubing in winter. Hours and prices vary by season and activity; call for details.

Where to Eat

Deising's Bakery and Coffee Shop. 109–117 North Front Street; (845) 338–7503; www.deisings.com. Fresh baked goods, soups, sandwiches, and a children's menu. $

Jane's Home-Made Ice Cream and Restaurant. 305 Wall Street; (845) 338–8315; www.janesicecream.com. Fresh homemade ice cream, soups, sandwiches, and daily specials. $

Where to Stay

Holiday Inn. 503 Washington Avenue; (845) 338–0400. Indoor pool, recreation center, and restaurant. $$$$

Hidden Valley Lake Campground. 290 Whiteport Road; (845) 338–4616 or (866) 338–CAMP; www.gocampingamerica. com/hiddenvalleylake. Campsites, cabins and apartments, boat rentals, hiking trails, nature sanctuary, children's play area. $–$$

Phoenicia

West on Route 28.

Situated on the banks of Esopus Creek, Phoenicia is the tubing capital of the Catskills, if you are twelve years and older. For those under the age limit recommended by the tube-rental shops, the rails are the way to ride.

Catskill Mountain Railroad (all ages)
P.O. Box 46, Route 28, Shokan, about 28 miles west of NYS Thruway exit 19; (845) 688–7400; www.catskillmtrailroad.com. Operating hourly 11:00 A.M. to 5:00 P.M. weekends and holidays Memorial Day to Labor Day and mid-September to mid-October at 11:30 A.M., 1:30, and 3:30 P.M. $$, under 4 free.

Travel by train between the Empire State Railway Museum in Phoenicia and Mount Pleasant, a route that takes you along the scenic banks of Esopus Creek. Special events are scheduled, and the fall foliage rides are spectacular.

Tube **Rentals**

Town Tinker Tube. 10 Bridge Street, Route 28; (845) 688–5553; www.towntinker.com.

FS Tube and Raft. 4 Church Street; (845) 688–7633; or (866) 4FS–TUBE; www.catskillpark.com.

Empire State Railway Museum (all ages)
Route 28, off High Street, Phoenicia Station; (845) 688–7501; www.esrm.com. Open Saturday, Sunday, and holidays Memorial Day through Columbus Day 11:00 A.M. to 4:00 P.M. Donation.

A vintage steam locomotive, a 1913 Pullman dining car, and other exhibits highlighting the history of railroading in the region are displayed in and around the restored 1899 Delaware & Ulster RR station.

Kaatskill Kaleidoscope (ages 4 and up)
5340 Route 28, Mt. Tremper; (845) 688–5800 or (888) 303–3936; www.catskill corners.com/marketplace/kaleidoworld/kworld.htm. Open Sunday through Thursday 10:00 A.M. to 5:00 P.M., Friday through Saturday 10:00 A.M. to 7:00 P.M. $$

At 60 feet tall, this is the world's largest kaleidoscope. Step into the viewing chamber (actually the silo of an 1841 barn) and experience a magical multimedia sound and light show the 'scopes of your childhood could only dream about.

Where to Eat

Sweet Sue's. Main Street; (845) 688–7852. A pancake paradise, with great sandwiches. $

Where to Stay

Phoenicia Motor Village. 5987 Route 28; (845) 688–7772; www.phoeniciamotor village.com; phoeniciamotorvg@aol.com. Five rooms and five efficiency cabins. $$

Woodland Valley Campground. 166 Woodland Valley Road, off Route 28; (845) 256–3099 or (800) 456–CAMP. $

Panther Mountain **Meteor Impact Site**

About 400 million years ago, a huge meteor crashed into what is now the Catskill Mountains. At the time, the area was covered by a shallow sea, and the 6-mile crater was gradually filled in with sediment. Over eons, the layers of rock were pushed upwards, forming Panther Mountain, and the Esopus and Woodland Creeks encircled the site. To explore this scenic geologic formation, head south on Route 47, about 7 miles past Oliverea, to the NYSDEC Giant Ledge trailhead. For more information, check out the Panther Mountain Web site at www.catskillcenter.org/panther.

Arkville and Delhi

Continue west on Route 28.

Native Americans called this area Pakatakan, and at the turn of the twentieth century the town supported a successful artists' colony. Stop by the unusual Round Barn (Route 30, in nearby Halcottsville) to stock the larder at the Pakatakan Farmers Market every Saturday, May through October from 9:00 A.M. to 3:00 P.M. The largest town in Delaware County, Delhi is centered around historic Courthouse Square, where on Wednesday, June through September from 9:30 A.M. to 1:30 P.M., you can purchase produce from local farms and orchards.

Delaware & Ulster Railroad (all ages)

Route 28, D&U Depot, Arkville, halfway between Kingston and Oneonta; (607) 652–2821 or (800) 642–4443; www.durr.org. Open weekends and holidays Memorial Day through October, Wednesday through Sunday July through Labor Day. Departure times vary by date (board fifteen minutes before). Adults $$, children 3 to 12 $, under 3 free.

Ride the DURR, nicknamed the "Up and Down" because of the hilly terrain, aboard old "Doodlebug," a vintage steam train. Special rides are scheduled throughout the season, ranging from railroad robberies to a day out with Thomas the Tank Engine. On weekends mid-September through mid-October, take the train to Belleayre Mountain, where a trolley transports travelers to a chairlift sky ride.

Delaware County Historical Association Museum (ages 8 and up)

Route 10, Delhi, 2 miles north of Delhi; (607) 746–3849; www.dcha-ny.org. Open Memorial Day through October 15 Tuesday through Sunday 11:00 A.M. to 4:00 P.M., October 16 through Memorial Day Monday through Friday 10:00 A.M. to 3:00 P.M. $

This museum has a complex of restored historical buildings and a gallery with changing regional exhibits. On site is the Frisbee house (no, not *that* Frisbee) with rooms decorated in different period styles and a children's room with antique toys. Outside explore the Husted Hollow Schoolhouse, a tollhouse, a gun shop, and an easy nature trail.

Hanford Mills (all ages)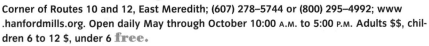

Corner of Routes 10 and 12, East Meredith; (607) 278–5744 or (800) 295–4992; www .hanfordmills.org. Open daily May through October 10:00 A.M. to 5:00 P.M. Adults $$, children 6 to 12 $, under 6 free.

Experience the past at this fully restored water-powered rural industrial complex. This was nineteenth-century one-stop shopping at its best, for farmers had grain ground, builders had lumber cut, creameries had containers made, and homemakers could buy flour here. Fifteen historic structures are spread out on seventy acres, but the heart of the complex is the huge whirring and creaking waterwheel.

Where to Eat

Delhi Diner. 95 Main Street, Delhi; (607) 746–2207. Delicious Delhi deli. $

The Cheese Barrel. Corner of Main and Bridge Streets, Margaretville; (845) 586–4666. Homemade soups and sandwiches, plus gourmet coffee and cheeses. $

Where to Stay

Scott's Oquaga Lake House. Oquaga Lake, Deposit; (607) 467–3094; www.scottsfamilyresort.com. Terrific family-owned 1,100-acre resort with three golf courses, tennis, bowling, water-skiing, live music and dancing, fishing, musical riverboat rides, organized children's activities and playhouse, plus meals and great views. $$$$

Suits-Us Farm Resort. Pink Street, Bovina Center (turn left at Country Store across from church, then go 2.2 miles to the fourth farm on the left); (607) 832–4470 or (607) 832–4369. This wonderful farm resort on 350 acres offers hiking, pony riding, farm animal feeding, brook fishing, pool swimming, tennis, and organized ball games, plus three home-cooked meals and snacks. $$$–$$$$

Delaware County **Farm Tours**

Eastbrook Farms. Eastbrook Road, Walton; (607) 865–7238; www.east brookfarms.com.

Healing Waters Farm. Route 206, 1216 Lower Third Brook Road, Walton; (607) 865–4420 or (888) HWFARMS; www.healingwatersfarms.com.

Stone & Thistle Farm and Kortright Creek Creamery. 1211 Kelso Road, East Meredith; (607) 278–5773; www.stoneandthistlefarm.com.

Skate Creek Farm. 1496 County Highway 12, East Meredith; (607) 278–5602; www.meadowraisedmeats.com.

Ski Spots **in Delaware County**

Bobcat Ski Center. Located 3 miles off Route 28, Andes; information and snow conditions (845) 676–3143; www.bobcatskicenter.com.

Ski Plattekill. Route 30 South (Plattekill Mountain Road), Roxbury; information (607) 326–3500; snow conditions (800) NEED–2–SKI; www.plattekill.com.

Belleayre Mountain. Route 28, Highmount; (845) 254–5600 or (800) 942–6904; www.belleayre.com.

Prattsville

Take Route 10 to Route 23 east.

Zadock Pratt wanted to build the largest tannery in the world in Schoharie Kill. Having accomplished that, he set out to rebuild the entire town. Creating one of the first planned communities in the state (renamed in his honor), Pratt's people planted hundreds of trees along widened streets trimmed with slate sidewalks and constructed dozens of beautiful Greek Revival homes. Textile factories, gristmills, churches, hotels, and schools were built, along with a bank that dispensed currency with Pratt's picture on it.

Zadock Pratt Museum (all ages)

West end of Main Street (Route 23); (518) 299–3395; www.prattmuseum.com. Open Memorial Day through Columbus Day Thursday through Monday 1:00 to 4:30 P.M. or by appointment. $

For all of his civic-minded projects, Zadock Pratt was quite a character. He had a penchant for practical jokes, staged elaborate battle reenactments, and challenged folks to games of skill and strength. His remarkable life is documented inside his former home, in pictures and artifacts, and outside, in the symbolic bas-relief cliffside carvings known as Pratt Rock.

Ski Windham (all ages)

CD Lane, off South Street, Windham; take NYS Thruway (I–87) exit 21 to Route 23 west to Windham; (518) 734–4300; (800) SKI–WINDHAM or (800) 754–9463 for lodging information; (800) SAY–4SNO or (800) 729–4766 for snow reports; www.skiwindham.com. Ask about midweek family rates. $$$$, 6 and under $

More intimate than Hunter, Windham offers thirty-nine trails for all levels, with snowboard, snowtube, and ski lessons in the Children's Learning Center for ages four to twelve and organized activities for nonskiers ages one to seven.

Also in **the Area**

Windham Mountain Ranch. RR1, Box 251, Windham 12496; (518) 734–3364.

Where to Eat

The Victorian Rose Restaurant. Route 23, East Windham, about 6 miles past Ski Windham, on cliffside; (518) 734–3381. Terrific Mediterranean, Southwestern, and American specialties, with family pizza parties. $$$–$$$$

La Griglia Ristorante. Route 296, just off Route 23, Windham; (518) 734–4499. Excellent northern Italian cuisine, steak, and seafood; dinner specials daily, a children's menu, and a bakery. $$–$$$

Where to Stay

Point Lookout Mountain Inn. The Mohican Trail, Route 23, East Windham, about 6 miles past Ski Windham on cliff side of road; (518) 734–3381; www.pointlookout inn.com. Game room, hot tub, two excellent chef-owned restaurants, and views of five states on a clear day. $$

The Winwood Inn. Route 23, in center of Windham; (518) 734–3000; www.winwood inn.com. Rooms and suites next to Ski Windham, with a restaurant, movie theater, tennis court, outdoor pool, recreation center, and nature trail. Children under six **free** anytime, under twelve **free** on a weekday or nonholiday (one child per adult). $$$–$$$$

East Durham

Take Route 23 east to Route 145 north.

Dubbed the Irish Alps, the town of East Durham has been attracting immigrants from the Emerald Isle since the 1880s. Wear green and be seen here Memorial Day weekend for the East Durham Irish Festival, complete with bagpipes, fresh-baked soda bread, and river dancing in the streets.

Zoom Flume (all ages)
Shady Glen Road; off Route 145, 2 miles north of East Durham; (518) 239–4559 or (800) 888–3586; www.zoomflume.com. Open June through Labor Day weekdays 10:00 A.M. to 6:00 P.M., weekends to 7:00 P.M. $$$

The largest water park in the Catskills, Zoom Flume offers a full day of family fun in the sun. Slip-slide down a 300-foot water chute, float around the Lazy River, raft the rapids, or wrestle the Mighty Anaconda. Pelican Pond proffers pint-size thrills, and there are easy nature trails and a playground to explore.

Durham Center Museum (all ages)

Route 145, 2 miles west of East Durham; (518) 239–8461 or (518) 239–4081. Open mid-May through September, Thursday through Sunday 1:00 to 3:00 P.M. $

This volunteer-run museum in an 1825 schoolhouse began as a collection of unusual, historical, or just downright interesting objects amassed by town resident Vernon Haskins. Fossils and minerals, Native American artifacts, pioneer tools, genealogical records, military relics, sculptures, typewriters, toys, and more can be seen here.

Irish American Heritage Museum (all ages)

2267 Route 145, at the center of the village; museum (518) 634–7497; Michael J. Quill Irish Cultural and Sports Centre (518) 634–2286; www.east-durham.org or www.irishamerican heritagemuseum.org. Open Memorial Day through Labor Day Wednesday through Sunday noon to 4:00 P.M., Labor Day through Columbus Day Friday and Saturday 11:00 A.M. to 5:00 P.M. and Sunday noon to 5:00 P.M. Museum $.

Special cultural programs and educational exhibits highlighting the history of the Irish in America are offered at this excellent museum. Next door, the Irish Cultural and Sports Centre offers theater, music, dance, and Gaelic sporting events year-round.

Horsing around **Greene County**

K&K Equestrian Center. Route 67, East Durham; (518) 966–5272.

Baliwick Ranch and Catskill Equestrian Center. 118 Castle Road, Catskill, next to Catskill Game Farm; (518) 678–5665.

Silver Springs Dude Ranch. Route 25, off Route 23A, Haines Falls; (518) 589–5559 or (800) 258–2624.

Tanglewood Ranch. Cornwallville Road, Cornwallville; (518) 622–9531.

Rough Riders Ranch. Route 23C, East Jewett; (518) 589–9159.

Cinema **under the Stars**

Greene County is the home of a memorable but vanishing breed of entertainment–the drive-in movie. Catch a flick at one of the open-air retro movie arenas below for a family-style fifties flashback.

Hi-Way Drive-In. Route 9W, Coxsackie; (518) 731–8672.

Greenville Drive-In. Route 32, Greenville; (518) 966–8990.

Bronck Museum (ages 6 and up)

90 County Road 42, off Route 9W, Coxsackie; (518) 731–6490; www.gchistory.org. Open Memorial Day through mid-October Wednesday through Friday noon to 4:00 P.M., Saturday 10:00 A.M. to 4:00 P.M., and Sunday 1:00 to 4:00 P.M. $, children under 5 free.

Eight generations of the Bronck family worked this farm, a complex of Dutch Colonial homes and nineteenth-century barns filled with period furniture, antiques, spinning wheels, looms, carriages, and other historical artifacts. Out back is the family and slave cemetery, a visual lesson in disparate lifestyles.

Where to Eat

The Shamrock House. Route 145, in the town center; (518) 634–2897 or (888) 634–2897; www.shamrockhouse.com. Shepherd's pie, fish and chips, steak, and chicken. Half orders available for children. (Motel has thirty-six rooms and outdoor pool.) $$

Where to Stay

Blackthorn Guest Ranch. 1 Sunside Road; (518) 634–2541 or (800) 914–ERIN; www.mhonline.net~blacktho/. Dude ranch with rooms and efficiencies, an outdoor pool, lake, mini-golf, horseback riding, go-karts, hayrides, dining, and babysitting. $$–$$$

Hull-O-Farms. 10 Cochrane Road, Durham; (518) 239–6950; www.hull-o.com. Milk a cow, feed the pigs and goats, go fishing in the ponds, pick a pumpkin, and enjoy a barbecue or a hayride. Lodging is in private homes on or next to the 300-acre farm and comes with three home-grown and home-cooked meals a day. $$$–$$$$, children 5 to 14 $$, under 5 $

Also in **the Area**

Supersonic Speedway & Fun Park. Route 145, East Durham; (518) 634–7200.

Catskill

Take Route 67 east to Coxsackie, then head south on Route 385 to Catskill.

The surrounding hillsides sheltered moonshine stills during Prohibition, but the moonshine of the mountains today is of the celestial variety. Folks say Rip Van Winkle slumbered for twenty years here, but there's so much to do in this area that you won't have time for so much as a cat(skill) nap.

Catskill Game Farm (all ages)

Game Farm Road, off Route 32; (518) 678–9595; www.catskillgamefarm.com. Open daily May through October 9:00 A.M. to 5:00 P.M., to 6:00 P.M. weekends July and August. Adults $$$, children 4 through 11 $$, 3 and under free. Additional charges for rides and animal food.

Lions and tigers and bears, oh my—and zebras, giraffes, elephants, llamas, and some 2,000 other exotic animals live here, too. At this well-kept family-owned zoo you can ride a tram through a bird sanctuary, watch an animal show, or visit the nursery and feed baby pigs and lambs a bottle of milk. There's also a small amusement park and playground nearby.

Catskill Area **Campgrounds**

Brookside Campgrounds. 4952 Route 32, Catskill; (518) 678–9729.

Catskill Campground. 79 Castle Road, Catskill; (518) 678–5873.

Earlton Hill Family Campground. Medway-Earlton Road, Earlton; (518) 731–2751.

Devil's Tombstone Campground. Route 214, Hunter; (845) 688–7160, reservations (800) 456–CAMP; www.reserveamerica.com.

Whip-o-will. County Road 31, Round Top; (518) 622–3277.

Doherty's Mountain View Campground. 1077 Joseph Chadderdon Road, Acra; (518) 622–8295.

Family Fun **Centers**

Need to burn off some extra energy? Try bowling, paintball, ATV rentals, and more at these Catskill-area fun centers:

Hoe Bowl Lanes and Family Rec Center. 305 West Bridge Street; (518) 943–4980.

Adventure Machine Rentals. At Baliwick Ranch, 118 Castle Road; (518) 678–5665.

Where to Eat

La Conca D'Oro. 440 Main Street; (518) 943–3549. Excellent pasta, and other Italian specialties, with an extensive children's menu. $$

The Point. 7 Main Street; (518) 943–5352. Steak, seafood, pasta, plus a children's menu; outdoor deck and great views in summer. $$

Where to Stay

Carl's Rip Van Winkle Motor Lodge. 810 Route 23B, Leeds (just west of NYS Thruway exit 21); (518) 943–3303; www.ripvanwinklemotorlodge.com. Rooms and cabins on 160 wooded acres, with outdoor pool, kiddie pool, and playground. $$

Red Ranch Motel. 4555 Route 32; (518) 678–3380 or (800) 962–4560; www.red ranchmotel.com. Rooms and kitchenettes, swimming and kiddie pools, play area, and restaurant. $$

Wolff's Maple Breeze. 360 Cauterskill Road; (518) 943–3648 or (800) 777–WOLF; www.wolffsresort.com. Outdoor pool, three lakes, rowboats, a playground, game room, hayrides, lawn games, supervised children's activities, and restaurant. $$$

Tannersville

West on Route 23A.

During the mid-1800s, the bark from the once abundant hemlock forests of the Catskills provided the necessary tannin for tanning leather, an industry that gave Tannersville its name.

North-South Lakes (all ages)

Route 18, Haines Falls (a few miles east of Tannersville); (518) 589–5058 or (518) 357–2234; campground reservations (800) 456–CAMP or www.reserveamerica.com; www.dec.state .ny.us/website/do/camping/campgrounds/northsouth.html. Open May through October daily 9:00 A.M. to dusk.

Early Native Americans believed the two lakes were the eyes of a fallen giant, and the nearby escarpment was a sacred ground known as "The Great Wall of Manitou." Today this popular area has campsites, a sandy beach, canoe and rowboat rentals, fishing, and some spectacular hiking trails. For an easy and safe hike, head 1 mile east of Haines Falls on Route 23. Leave your car at the parking area and walk carefully along the road to the trailhead on the other side. From there it is a short, easy walk to the base of Kaaterskill Falls, which, at 260 feet, are higher than Niagara Falls.

Hunter Mountain Ski Bowl (all ages)

Route 23A, Hunter, 2 miles west of Tannersville; (518) 263–4223 (information), (800) FOR–SNOW (snow conditions), (888) HUNTER–MTN; www.huntermtn.com. Ski season runs daily from the end of November through April 8:30 A.M. to 4:00 P.M.; summer sky ride weekends July through October 11:00 A.M. to 4:40 P.M. Ask about family package rates and free **ski times for kids. $$$$**

Renowned as the Snowmaking Capital of the World, Hunter offers fifty-three trails and eleven lifts covering three mountains. The new Snowtubing Park has three lifts, 600 tubes, and 1,000-foot chutes to slip-slide down. Programs for children include lessons for ages four to twelve, snowtubing for folks over 42 inches tall, free ski for those under age six, and child care for ages six months to six years.

Where to Eat

Last Chance Antiques and Cheese Café. 602 Main Street; (518) 589–6424. Gourmet cafe and takeout featuring soups, sandwiches, salads, steaks, burgers, ribs, fondues, homemade pastries and desserts, more than 300 beers, and a children's menu. Everything, including the table, is for sale. $$

Where to Stay

Catskill Mountain Lodge. 334 Route 32A, about 7 miles north of NYS Thruway exit 20, between 32 and 23A, Palenville; (518) 678–3101 or (800) MTN–LODGE; www.catskillmtnlodge.com. Forty-two rooms and cottages, playground, outdoor heated pool, kiddie pool, game room, and a microbrew pub on the premises. $$$

Silver Springs Dude Ranch. 111 County Road 25, Haines Falls; (518) 589–5559 or (800) 258–2624. Motel and hotel, with year-round horseback riding. $$$$

Also in **the Area**

Bear Creek Landing Family Sport Complex. Routes 23A and 214, Hunter; (518) 263–3839; www.bearcreeklanding.com.

Tannersville Lake. South Main Street, Tannersville; (518) 589–5850.

Saugerties

Take Route 23 east to Route 9W south.

Opus 40 and Quarryman's Museum (all ages)

7480 Fite Road, High Woods; (845) 246–3400; www.opus40.org. Open Memorial Day through October Friday through Sunday, plus Monday holidays, noon to 5:00 P.M. Adults $$, children $, under 5 free but must be supervised.

This is a six-acre environmental sculpture chiseled from an abandoned bluestone quarry by one man, Harvey Fite. Fun to explore and marvel at, Opus 40 is especially enchanting during the regularly scheduled sunset concerts, so plan for a picnic dinner on the grounds.

Puttin' Plus (all ages)

455 Washington Avenue; (845) 246–4501. Open June through August Monday through Thursday 11:00 A.M. to 10:00 P.M., Friday through Saturday to 11:00 P.M., Sunday to 8:00 P.M.; September through May Monday through Saturday 3:00 to 7:30 P.M. $

Tired of driving? Let your kids take the wheel at this figure-eight monster go-kart race-track. Putter away the day's pressures with eighteen-hole mini-golf or do battle in the baseball or softball batting cages.

Where to Eat

Ann Marie's Bistro. 216 Main Street; (845) 246–5542. Casual gourmet cafe serving great omelet wraps, buttermilk pancakes, ice cream, and takeout available. $$

Emiliani Ristorante. 147 Ulster Avenue; (845) 246–6169. Fresh homemade pasta and wonderful northern Italian favorites, with half orders available for children and special children's menu. $$

Krause's Homemade Candy. 41 South Partition Street; (845) 246–8377. Freshly made buttercrunch, peanut brittle, caramels, and fudge. $

Where to Stay

Bed by the Stream. 9 George Sickle Road; (845) 246–2979. Three rooms, a stream to explore, and an outdoor pool. Children welcome. $$$

Saugerties Lighthouse Bed and Breakfast. 168 Lighthouse Drive, at Coast Guard Station, off Main Street; (845) 247–0656 or (845) 246–4380; www.saugertieslighthouse.com. Two rooms with terrific views for a night to remember, plus breakfast. $$$$

Horsing around **Ulster County**

Saddle Up. 22 Kinsey Road, Phoenicia; (845) 688–7336.

Coyote Ridge Stables. 376 Route 32, New Paltz; (845) 255–3077; www.coyoteridgestables.com.

High Falls

South on I–87, then west on Route 213.

D&H Canal Museum (all ages)
Mohonk Road, off Route 213; (845) 687–9311; www.canalmuseum.org. Open May through October Monday and Thursday through Saturday 11:00 A.M. to 5:00 P.M., Sunday 1:00 to 5:00 P.M. $

With dioramas, artifacts, and photographs, this museum highlights the history of the Delaware and Hudson Canal. Take the self-guided Five Locks Walk past one of the four aqueducts built by Brooklyn Bridge builder John Roebling, several original canal locks, and the Central Hudson Canal Park for views of the town waterfalls.

Pinegrove Resort Ranch (all ages)
30 Cherrytown Road, Kerhonkson; (845) 626–7345 or (800) 926–6520; www.pinegrove-ranch.com. Reservations required. $$$$, children 4 to 14 25 to 50% off, under 4 free.

For city slickers seeking the "best of the West in the East," this is a terrific all-inclusive, award-winning dude ranch resort. Trail rides, nature hikes, hayrides, pro golf and mini-golf, tennis, swimming, archery, a video arcade, cookouts, and many more activities are offered. For younger rustlers there's the Lil' Maverick Day Camp and the Belle Star Nursery.

Rails to Trails in **Ulster County**

Catskill Scenic Trail. P.O. Box 310, Railroad Avenue, Stamford 12167; (607) 652–2821 or (800) 225–4132; www.durr.org.

Hudson Valley Rail Trail. Highland; (845) 483–0428, (845) 691–8666, or (800) DIAL–UCO; www.ulstertourism.info.

Wallkill Valley Rail Trail. P.O. Box 1048, New Paltz 12561; www.gorailtrail.org.

New Paltz

Head east on Route 213 to Route 32 south.

Nestled between the spectacular Shawangunks and the Hudson River, New Paltz was settled in the seventeenth century by French Huguenot Protestants seeking religious freedom. Several of their 300-year-old stone houses are still there to explore on Huguenot Street, the "oldest street in America."

Mohonk Mountain House (all ages)

Take exit 18 off I-87 and head west on Route 299 through town about 6 miles, and watch for signs of turnoff to the right. Lake Mohonk; (845) 255-1000 or (800) 772-6646; fax (845) 256-2161; www.mohonk.com. Open daily year-round. $$$$ (meals included), day passes $$.

A Victorian castle perched on the edge of a glacial lake, Mohonk Mountain House is magical. Built by the Smiley family in 1870, when mountain resorts were all the rage, Mohonk Mountain House and the nearby Mohonk Preserve encompass more than 8,000 acres of forest and rock, laced with a variety of trails and dotted with more than a hundred picturesque gazebos. Day passes are available until mid-afternoon for hiking the grounds, and Sunday brunch is available with reservations, but if time and budget allow, book a room and enjoy more than forty theme programs offered throughout the year, many specifically designed for families. Call for a schedule and ask about special times when children stay **free.**

Minnewaska State Park Preserve (all ages)

P.O. Box 893, New Paltz 12561; (845) 256-0579; www.nysparks.com/parks. Take Route 299 west to Route 44/55, then turn right about 4.5 miles. Open daily 9:00 A.M. to dusk. $

Once the site of two grand Catskill hotels, the preserve's 11,630 acres, cradled by the Shawangunks, include two crystal clear lakes framed by white conglomerate cliffs and many miles of wide carriage paths that lead to numerous scenic overlooks. Swimming is allowed near the sandy beach at Lake Minnewaska, but if you're willing and able to hike a few miles farther into the woods, you'll find Lake Awosting a bit more primeval and private.

Sam's Point Dwarf Pine Ridge Preserve (all ages)

Sam's Point Road, off Route 52, Cragsmoor; (845) 647-7989. Open daily dawn to dusk. $ parking, call to arrange group visits.

This spectacular 4,600-acre National Natural Landmark, home to almost forty rare plant and animal species, has been designated one of Earth's "Last Great Places" by the Nature Conservancy. Several trails wind through the rugged rock formations and scenic canyons of the Shawangunks, and on a clear day, you can see breathtaking views of the Hudson Valley and Catskills.

Auction **Adventures**

Catskill country auctions are almost as legendary as the mountains themselves. Bidding is spirited, you never know what will be put on the block, and bargains abound. Check local newspapers for current information, and come early, because seats fill up fast.

Liberty Antique Warehouse Auctions. Liberty; (845) 292–7450.

Roberts' Auction. Fleischmanns; (845) 254–4490.

McIntosh Auction Service. Bovina Center; (607) 832–4241 or (607) 832–4829; www.mcintoshauction.com.

Where to Eat

Main Course. 232 Main Street; (845) 255–2600 or (845) 255–2650; www.main courserestaurant.com. Homemade pastas, grilled seafood, and spa specialties. $

Main Street Bistro. 59 Main Street; (845) 255–7766; www.mainstreetbistro.com. American and vegetarian cuisine, breakfast, lunch, and dinner. $

Where to Stay

Econo Lodge. 530 Main Street; (845) 255–6200 or (800) 424–4777; www.econolodge.com. Swimming pool. Free continental breakfast. $$

Nevele Grand. Nevele Road, off Route 209, Ellenville; (845) 647–6000 or (800) 647–6000; www.nevele.com. This 1,000-acre megaresort has pools, eighteen tennis courts, an ice rink, pro golf and mini-golf courses, horseback and pony riding, boating, and a day camp for kids. Meals are included, and special family packages are available. $$$$

Rocking Horse Ranch. 600 Route 44/55, Highland; (845) 691–2927 or (800) 647–2624; www.rhranch.com. This all-inclusive family dude ranch resort offers trail rides, hayrides, water-skiing and boating, pools, mini-golf, and a day camp and nursery. $$$$

Monticello

Take Route 299 west to Route 55 west, then Route 209 into Ellenville and Route 52 west to Route 42 south.

Nicknamed the buckle of the "Borscht Belt," Monticello and the surrounding towns of Liberty, Fallsburg, and Kiamesha Lake are home to several family-owned megaresorts, where legendary comedians Jerry Lewis, Joan Rivers, Milton Berle, Mel Brooks, Jerry Seinfeld, and others springboarded to stardom.

Holiday Mountain (all ages)

99 Holiday Mountain Road; (845) 796–3161 for snow conditions; www.holidaymtn.com. Off NYS Thruway exit 16, or take exit 107 off Route 17. Open late November through April weekdays noon to 9:00 P.M., Saturday 9:00 A.M. to 9:00 P.M., Sunday 9:00 A.M. to 4:30 P.M. $$$$

This family-oriented ski spot, with fifteen trails, six lifts, and a vertical drop of 400 feet, offers an expanded children's program and ski school for all levels.

Where to Eat

Carpenito's Restaurant. 145 State Route 17B; (845) 791–6000. Elegant Italian dining, plus a children's menu. $$

Miss Monticello Diner and Restaurant. 199 Broadway; (845) 791–8934. Early American home-style cooking; children's menu. $–$$

Where to Stay

All Seasons Campsite on Autumn Lake. Fraser Road, off Route 42, Kiamesha; (845) 794–0133 or (845) 794–1698. On 375 acres with campsites, lake swimming, fishing and boating, pool table, video games, and a small playground. $

The Inn at Lake Joseph. 400 Saint Joseph Road, off Route 42, Forestburgh; (845) 791–9506; www.lakejoseph.com. This 130-year-old lakeside Victorian mansion offers swimming, fishing, hiking, and full breakfast. $$$

Kutsher's Country Club. Kutsher Road, off Route 42; (845) 794–6000 or (800) 431–1273; www.kutshers.com. Wonderful, friendly megaresort with nonstop activities, including pro golf and mini-golf, boating, swimming (indoor and outdoor pools), indoor ice-skating, tennis and bocce courts, and nightly entertainment. Horse-drawn sleigh rides and snowtubing are offered in winter, and nursery and toddler care, a day camp, and a teen program are offered year-round. $$$$

Also in **the Area**

Birdies of Mongaup Valley. Route 17B, Mongaup Valley; (845) 583–6652.

Pizza the Rock. 345 Rock Hill Drive, Rock Hill; (845) 796–3900.

Skater's World Roller Rink. Old Route 17, Ferndale, 2 miles off exit 102; (845) 292–3288.

Lake Superior State Park. Dr. Duggan Road, Bethel; (845) 794–3000, ext. 3006; www.nysparks.com/parks.

Livingston Manor

Take Route 17 north.

A river runs through it, and between here and Roscoe, the American art of fly-fishing was born. This is trout territory, big time, and somewhere in the Willowemoc or the nearby Beaverkill, there's a fish with your name on it.

Catskill Fly-Fishing Center and Museum (ages 8 and up)
1031 Old Route 17; (845) 439–4810; www.cffcm.org. Open April through October daily 10:00 A.M. to 4:00 P.M.; November through March Saturday 10:00 a.m. to 4:00 P.M., Tuesday through Friday to 1:00 P.M. except holidays. $

Learn about the lore, legends, and lures of the Catskill creeks at this charming museum honoring famous fisher folk and their fly-tying folk art. Special fly-fishing programs for kids eight and older are offered in July and August, and nature trails meander over thirty-five lush acres along a catch-and-release section of the Willowemoc.

Horsing around **Sullivan County**

Hadley Riding Stables. 1074 Old Liberty Road, Monticello; (845) 434–9254.

RR Stables. 2 Sullivan Street, Wurtsboro; (845) 888–2210.

Arrowhead Ranch. Cooley Road, Parksville; (845) 292–6267.

New York State Fish Hatchery (all ages)

402 Mongaup Road; (845) 439–4328. Three miles north of DeBruce, off Route 17, exit 96. Open July through September, Monday through Friday 8:00 A.M. to 4:00 P.M. Saturday, Sunday, and holidays 8:00 A.M. to noon. October through June weekends 8:30 A.M. to 4:00 P.M. Free.

More than a million rainbow, brown, brook, and lake trout are raised here every year to be released in rivers and lakes throughout the state. Every angler older than age sixteen needs a fishing license, easily obtainable at local tackle shops.

Roscoe O&W Railway Museum (ages 3 and up)

Railroad Avenue, at junction of Route 17 and Route 206, Roscoe; (607) 498–4346 or (607) 498–5289; www.nyow.org/museum.html. Open Memorial Day weekend to mid-October Saturday and Sunday 11:00 A.M. to 3:00 P.M. Free.

Artifacts and memorabilia from the Ontario and Western Railway are displayed here, from a Beaverkill Trout car to a red caboose.

Apple Pond Farming Center (all ages)

80 Hahn Road, Callicoon Center; (845) 482–4764; www.applepondfarm.com. Open year-round with a pre-reserved guided tour only, minimum of five people per tour. $$

Learn about pioneer-style agronomy on this horse-powered organic farm, where you may be allowed to milk the goats or help drive the horses. Hayrides and wagon and carriage rides are offered in summer, sleigh rides in winter, and a variety of victuals are for sale at the farm's roadside stand.

A Jeffersonville **Jaunt**

Western Sullivan County has an eclectic assortment of attractions, with the lovely Victorian village of Jeffersonville at the center. See www.jefferson villechamber.org.

WJFF Radio Catskill. Route 52, Jeffersonville; (845) 482–4141; www .wjffradio.org. Open house first Saturday of every month 1:30 to 3:30 P.M., but visitors welcome anytime between 9:00 A.M. and 5:00 P.M. Free.

Stone Arch Bridge Historic Park. Junction of Routes 52 and 52A, Kenoza Lake; www.co.sullivan.ny.us. Open year-round, 8:00 A.M. to dusk. Free.

The Bridges of Sullivan County

Sullivan County has several scenic covered bridges, all reachable on an afternoon drive.

Livingston Manor Covered Bridge.
Town Road 39, Livingston Manor.

Beaverkill Covered Bridge.
Town Road 29, Beaverkill.

Willowemoc Covered Bridge.
Town Road 18, DeBruce.

Halls Mills Covered Bridge.
County Road 19, Grahamsville.

Chestnut Creek Covered Bridge.
Off Route 55, Grahamsville.

Where to Eat

Catskill Morning Farm. 87 DeBruce Road; (845) 439–4900; www.morning farm.com. Lunch and weekend brunch in a garden cafe. $–$$

The New Robin Hood Diner. Old Route 17, exit 96; (845) 439–4404. European and American home-style specialties. $

Where to Stay

Frost Valley YMCA. 2000 Frost Valley Road, Claryville; (845) 985–2291; www.frostvalley.org. More than 5,000 acres to explore, with cross-country skiing, snowshoeing, tubing, tobogganing, and ice fishing in winter, and seasonal nature activities and arts and crafts for families on weekends throughout the year. Variety of cabins and lodge rooms available, plus meals. Ask about family rates. $$$

Twin Island Campsite. 3199 Old Route 17, Roscoe (off exit 94); (607) 498–5326; www.twinislands.com. Private camp-ground stretched along the Beaverkill River, but ask about renting a treehouse or camp cabin. A full playground and recreation hall with video games and pool table, and a hand-built replica of an O&W train. $

Willowemoc Motel. 1 DeBruce Road, off Route 17, exit 96; (845) 439–4220. On the Willowemoc River. $$

Narrowsburg

Head south on scenic Route 97.

Located at a strategic bend in the Delaware, the town of Narrowsburg is another favorite place to be sent down the river *with* a paddle.

Fort Delaware Museum of Colonial History (all ages)
Route 97, just north of town; (845) 252–6660 or (845) 794–3000, ext. 3066; www.co
.sullivan.ny.us/DPW/parks. Open weekends September through June 10:00 A.M. to 5:30 P.M.,
Wednesday through Sunday July and August 10:00 A.M. to 5:30 P.M. $, children under 6
free when accompanied by two adults.

This authentic rustic re-creation gives kids the chance to experience family life pioneer style, as costumed guides demonstrate the skills and crafts necessary for survival in the New York frontier.

Delaware River **Canoe Trips and Rentals**

Catskill Mountain Canoe and Jon Boat Rentals. Hankins; (845) 887–6743.

Lander's River Trips. Route 97, Narrowsburg; (800) 252–3925; www
.landersrivertrips.com.

Kittatinny Canoes and Rafts. Barryville; (800) FLOAT–KC or (800)
356–2852; www.kittatinny.com.

Indian Head Canoes and Campground. Barryville; (845) 557–8777 or (800)
874–BOAT; www.indianheadcanoes.com.

Wild and Scenic River Tours and Rentals. 166 Route 97, Barryville; (845)
252–3925 or (800) 836–0366; www.landersrivertrips.com.

Cedar Rapids Kayak and Canoe Outfitters. Barryville; (845) 557–6158;
www.cedarrapidsrafting.com.

Jerry's Three River Canoe Corp. Pond Eddy; (845) 557–6078.

Silver Canoe Rentals. Pond Eddy; (845) 856–7055 or (800) 724–8342.

Where to Eat

Narrowsburg Inn. 182 North Bridge Street (Route 52); (845) 252–3998. Built in 1840, this is the third-oldest inn in the country, with eight rooms and a restaurant (closed in winter) serving steaks, burgers, chicken, and seafood. $$

The Whistle Stop Cafe. 117 Kirk Road; (845) 252–3355. Family-friendly breakfast, lunch, and dinner with children's menu. $

Where to Stay

Lander's Campground. Route 97; (800) 252–3925; www.landersrivertrips.com. Riverfront campsites. $

Lander's Ten Mile River Lodge. Route 97; (800) 252–3925; www.landers rivertrips.com. Motel and efficiencies, restaurant, swimming pool, and package deals. $$$

Barryville

Continue south on Route 97.

The gateway to a particularly pretty part of the Delaware River, Barryville has numerous outfitters supplying a variety of vessels to float your family.

Eldred Preserve and Audubon Nature Center (all ages)
1040 Route 55, Eldred (5 miles north of Barryville); (845) 557–8316 or (800) 557–3474, Nature Center (845) 557–8316; www.eldredpreserve.com. Open year-round 8:00 A.M. to 6:00 P.M. $

If you're hankering to hook a fish or the big one got away, head for the trout ponds at this private resort. You're almost guaranteed to catch something, and your charge is calculated by the weight of the catch. Nature trails lace through 3,000 acres of woodland and wetland, and the Audubon Society operates a small museum.

Suggested **Reading**

Rip Van Winkle by Washington Irving

The Red Badge of Courage by Stephen Crane

The Matchlock Gun by Walter D. Edmonds

The Deerslayer by James Fenimore Cooper

My Side of the Mountain by Jean Craighead George

Eagle **Eyeing**

Bald eagles like to vacation in the Catskills, too. From December through March, southern Sullivan County attracts the largest population of migrating eagles in the Northeast. The Eagle Institute sponsors seasonal festivals featuring eagle dances, art projects, workshops, and watches. Child-size binoculars and telescopes are provided at these recommended spotting sites:

Mongaup Falls Reservoir, Observation Hut, Forestburgh.

Rio Reservoir, Forestburgh.

Basha Kill Wildlife Management Area, Wurtsboro.

Rondout Reservoir, Grahamsville.

Delaware River, Hawks Nest to Narrowsburg, Route 97.

For more information, contact the institute at P.O. Box 182, Barryville 12719; (845) 557–6162 or (570) 685–5960; www.eagleinstitute.org; the D.E.C. Endangered Species Unit at (518) 439–7365; or the Upper Delaware Scenic and Recreational River National Park Service at (570) 729–8251.

Minisink Battleground Park (all ages)
City Road 168, off Route 98, Minisink Ford; (845) 794–3000, ext. 3066; www.co.sullivan.ny.us. Open daily mid-May to mid-October 8:00 A.M. to dusk. **Free.**

The Battle of Minisink was one of the bloodiest battles of the Revolutionary War and the only one fought in this area. Colonial Americans were defeated by Iroquois working for the British, and the area was so remote it was nearly fifty years before the bodies were discovered and buried. Pick up a map at the interpretive center and explore some of the easy hiking trails that meander through this historic fifty-six-acre wooded wetland park.

Where to Stay

All Breeze Guest House. 227 Haring Road; (845) 557–6485. Three rooms at this friendly bed-and-breakfast with low rates for children and groups. $

Washington Lake Resort. 172 Airport Road, Yulan; (845) 557–0140 or (917) 376–1831; www.wlretreat.com. Rooms, suites, and cottages with lake swimming, boating. $$$

Other Things to See and Do
in the Catskills

Erpf House. Route 28, Arkville; (845) 586–2611; www.catskillcenter.org.

Hudson River Islands State Park. c/o John Boyd Thatcher State Park, 1 Hailes Cave Road, Voorheesville; (518) 872–1237; www.nysparks.com/parks.

Forestburgh Playhouse. 39 Forestburgh Road, Forestburgh; (845) 794–1194; www.fbplayhouse.com.

Slabsides. Floyd Ackert Road, off Route 9W, West Park; (845) 384–6320, (845) 255–5077, or (845) 679–2642.

Byrdcliffe Art Colony Historic District. 34 Tinker Street, Woodstock; (845) 679–2079; www.woodstockguild.org.

Canal Forge. Route 6 and Towpath Road, Alligerville; (845) 687–7130.

Esopus Meadows Environmental Center. 275 River Road, Ulster Park; (845) 331–5771, (845) 454–7673, or (845) 473–4440; www.clearwater.org.

Widmark Honey Farms. Route 44/55, Gardiner; (845) 255–6400.

Arrowhead Maple Syrup Farm Tour. 5941 Route 209, Kerhonkson; (845) 626–7293.

Lyonsville Sugarhouse and Farm. 591 County Route 2, Kripplebush-Krumville Road, Accord; (845) 687–2518.

Tibetan Buddhist Monastery. Karma Triyana Dharmachakra, 352 Meads Mountain Road, Woodstock; (845) 679–5906; www.kagyu.org.

Armstrong's Elk Farm. 936 Hervey Sunside Road, Cornwallville; (518) 622–8452.

Round Barn. Route 30, Halcottsville; (845) 586–3326.

Catskill Mountain Wolf Center. Route 32, Catskill; (518) 696–3318; www.cmwc.org.

Rams Horn–Livingston Sanctuary. Grandview Avenue, Catskill; (845) 473–4440, ext. 270; www.scenichudson.org.

Bear Spring Mountain. East Trout Brook Road, Walton; (607) 865–6989.

Headless Horseman Hayrides. 778 Broadway (Route 9W), Ulster Park; (845) 339–2666; www.headlesshorseman.com.

John Burroughs Woodchuck Lodge and Memorial Field. Roxbury; (607) 326–7641; www.roxburyny.com.

For More Information

General Information. (800) NYS–CATS.
Delaware County Chamber of Commerce. (607) 746–2281 or (800) 642–4443; www.delawarecounty.org.
Greene County Promotion Department. (518) 943–3223 or (800) 355–CATS; www.greene-ny.com.
Sullivan County Tourism. (845) 794–3000 or (800) 882–CATS; www.scva.net.

Ulster County. (845) 340–3566 or (800) 342–5826; www.ulstertourism.info.

The Mohawk Valley Region

Home to the Iroquois for thousands of years, the Mohawk Valley was an important route between the Great Lakes and the Atlantic Ocean and the easiest path through the Appalachians. The Dutch and the English were drawn here by the lucrative fur trade at the beginning of the seventeenth century, many of the battles that won America's independence were fought here, and the Erie Canal transformed the Mohawk into an industrial and transportation mecca. The mystery, romance, and passion of James Fenimore Cooper's stories still reside in the breathtaking scenery and enchanting villages of this ancient river plateau. Whether your family seeks carousels or crystal caverns, history of times gone by or history in the making, baseball diamonds or Herkimer diamonds, there is something here to please children of all ages.

Driving Tips

After the Revolutionary War, settlers headed across the Mohawk Valley toward the Great Lakes area by way of the Great Western Turnpike, now known as Route 20. Running parallel to that and the Mohawk River is I–90, the New York State Thruway. Cutting diagonally from Albany to Binghamton is I–88, while I–81 and Route 12 run north and south across the valley.

New York **Trivia**

The most popular apple varieties grown in New York are McIntosh, Empire, Red Delicious, Cortland, Golden Delicious, Red Rome, Idared, Crispin, Paula Red, and Gala. For more information, check out www.nyapplecountry.com.

THE MOHAWK VALLEY REGION

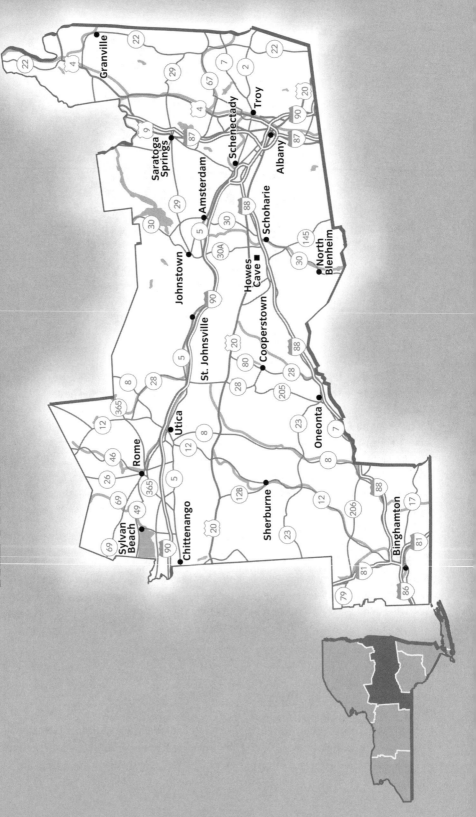

Albany

Accessible via I–87, I–787, and I–90.

Known as Fort Orange when it was a seventeenth-century Dutch trading post, Albany is New York's capital and its oldest city. While the theme here is business, politics are the lifeblood of the city, and the roots are still very Dutch. Visit in springtime, when the tulips are in bloom and the town transforms itself into a Dutch village at Pinksterfest.

Albany Heritage Area Visitors Center (all ages)

25 Quackenbush Square, at intersection of Broadway and Clinton Avenues; (518) 434–0405 or (800) 258–3582; www.albany.org. Open year-round Monday through Friday 9:00 A.M. to 4:00 P.M., Saturday and Sunday 10:00 A.M. to 4:00 P.M. Free.

Make this your first stop upon arriving in Albany, for along with an orientation show, the center offers seasonal guided walking or trolley tours, **free** self-guided walking tour maps, and audiotape guides.

Henry Hudson Planetarium (all ages)

25 Quackenbush Square, next to visitor center; (518) 434–0405 or (800) 258–3582; www.albany.org. Open daily 10:00 A.M. to 4:00 P.M. $

For a tour of the celestial sort, special children's star shows are on Saturday.

Empire State Plaza (all ages)

Located between Madison Avenue and State Street, and Swan and Eagle Streets. Plaza Visitor's Center and Capitol Tours, Concourse Level, Room 106 (518) 474–2418; www.ogs.state.ny.us. Capitol tours offered hourly weekdays 9:00 A.M. to 4:00 P.M., Saturday and Sunday 10:00 A.M. to noon and 2:00 to 4:00 P.M. The Egg box office (518) 473–1845 or (518) 473–1061; www.theegg.org. New York State Museum, 3140 Cultural Education Center; (518) 474–5877; www.nysm.nysed.gov. Museum open daily year-round 9:30 A.M. to 5:00 P.M., closed major holidays. Corning Tower observation deck (518) 474–2418. Free.

A vast complex of eleven buildings covering almost one hundred acres, this is the heart of the city. Take a **free** tour of the **State Capitol,** designed by five different architects, where you can view the senate chambers and the "Million Dollar Staircase." At the opposite end of the plaza is the **New York State Museum,** the largest and oldest state museum in the country. Chock-full of interesting artifacts and specimens, it features exhibits highlighting New York's culture, history, and environment. While at the museum, stop by Discovery Place, a special area designed just for kids. Also nearby is the **Plaza Art Collection,** featuring work from "New York School" artists. But the building that really grabs your attention is **The Egg,** a futuristic performing-arts arena that hosts many special events for families. Then stop by the

Albany's **Parks and Preserves**

Albany isn't all architecture and government. The Capital City has several lovely green spaces to explore, too. Call the Albany Department of Parks and Recreation (518–434–5699) for more information.

Academy Park. Eagle Street.

Erastus Corning Riverfront Preserve. West Bank of Hudson.

Washington Park. State and Willett Streets, Madison and Lake Avenues.

Lincoln Park. Delaware, Morton, and Park Avenues.

Six Mile Waterworks. Fuller Road.

Swinburne Park. Clinton Avenue and Manning Boulevard.

NATURE CONSERVANCY PRESERVES

For more information, call the New York Regional Office at (518) 463–6133; www.nature.org.

Bear Swamp Preserve. County Road 404, Westerlo.

Limestone Rise. County Road 252, Knox.

Christman Sanctuary. County Road 2D, Duanesburg.

Lake Julia Preserve. Lake Julia Road, Remsen.

Corning Tower and take the elevator to the observation deck for a bird's-eye view of the area.

Dutch Apple Cruises (all ages)

137 Broadway; (518) 463–0220; www.dutchapplecruises.com. Sailing daily 11:00 A.M. to 10:00 P.M. April through October. $$$$

Choose a cruise on the Hudson, from the brunch, lunch, locks, and sunset and moonlight sightseeing itineraries offered.

Family **Fun Parks**

Jeepers! Crossgate Commons, 161 Washington Avenue Extension, Albany; (800) JEEPERS.

Hoffman's Playland. Route 9, Latham; (518) 785–3842.

John Boyd Thatcher State Park (all ages)
Route 157 (off Route 85), Voorheesville; (518) 872–1237; www.nysparks.com/parks. Open daily year-round 8:00 A.M. to dusk. Summer parking fee $$.

This 2,300-acre park features rich fossil-bearing limestone cliffs and panoramic views of the Mohawk-Hudson Valley. Explore the 0.5-mile Indian Ladder Trail, the Escarpment Trail, or the Nature Trail. Be sure to hold little folks by the hand on narrow footpaths around the ledges. Afterward, cool off with a swim in the Olympic-size pool.

Five Rivers Environmental Education Center (all ages)
56 Game Farm Road, Delmar; (518) 475–0291; www.dec.state.ny.us. Located about 5 miles south of Albany off Route 443. Grounds open year-round sunrise to sunset; interpretive center open Monday through Saturday 9:00 A.M. to 4:30 P.M., Sunday 1:00 to 5:00 P.M. Free.

Take a self-guided nature walk past ponds and through forests at this interesting preserve, or stop by the interpretive center and check out the regional flora, fauna, and ecology exhibits.

Hollyhock Hollow Sanctuary (all ages)
46 Rarick Road, Selkirk, off NYS Thruway exit 22; (518) 767–9051; www.audubonintl.org. Open daily dawn to dusk year-round. Free.

Managed by the Audubon Society, this is a wonderful place to explore with your family. Of the six trails, a favorite with children is the Water Trail. Winding along a creek down to a

Albany Athletics

Albany River Rats. American Hockey League, Pepsi Arena, 51 South Pearl Street; (518) 487–2244 or (877) YES–RATS; www.albanyriverrats.com.

Albany Conquest. Arena Football 2 League (AF2), Pepsi Arena, 51 South Pearl Street; (518) 487–2222; www.albanyconquest.com.

small pond, the trail passes ten workstations designed to help kids appreciate nature. Wear long pants and sleeves, bring the insect repellent, and you'll have a great time.

Where to Eat

Grandma's Country Restaurant. 1273 Central Avenue; (518) 459–4585 or (888) 595–4726; www.grandmascc.com. Home-cooked favorites, from chicken with biscuits to meat loaf, roast chicken, and lasagna, plus Grandma's pies for dessert. $

Miss Albany Diner. 893 Broadway; (518) 465–9148; www.missalbanydiner.com. A real classic, featured in the movie *Ironweed*, serving excellent diner favorites and an interesting brunch. $

Where to Stay

Clarion Hotel of Albany. 1–3 Watervliet Avenue; (518) 438–8431; www.quality inn.com/hotel/ny058. Indoor and outdoor pools, restaurant. $$$

Ramada Inn Downtown. 300 Broadway; (518) 434–4111 or (800) 272–6232; www.ramada.com. Outdoor pool, complimentary continental breakfast, restaurant. $$$

Troy

Head north on I–787.

Once the country's leading producer of brushes, bells, stoves, surveying instruments, horseshoes, and collars and shirts, Troy now focuses on services and education.

Riverspark Troy Visitor Center (all ages)

251 River Street at Broadway; (518) 270–8667; www.troyvisitorcenter.org. Open year-round May through September Tuesday through Saturday 10:00 A.M. to 5:00 P.M.; October through May Tuesday through Saturday 11:00 A.M. to 5:00 P.M., some Fridays to 8:00 P.M. Free.

Stop at this great information center first to get oriented. A film of historical highlights, electronic map printouts, and labor and industry exhibits will help you explore the area.

Junior Museum (all ages)

The Winslow Building, 105 Eighth Street; (518) 235–2120; www.juniormuseum.org. Open July through Labor Day Monday through Saturday 10:00 A.M. to 5:00 P.M. September through June Thursday 10:00 A.M. to 2:00 P.M., Friday through Sunday 10:00 A.M. to 5:00 P.M. $$, children under 3 free.

Investigate an Iroquois longhouse, spy stars in the planetarium, or try your hand at colonial crafts at this children's museum, housed in an old brick firehouse. There are live reptiles and other small creatures to see, a lot of hands-on exhibits, and special workshops for children throughout the year.

Crailo State Historic Site (all ages)

9½ Riverside Avenue, Rensselaer; (518) 463–8738; www.nysparks.com/hist. Open mid-April through October Wednesday through Saturday 10:00 A.M. to 5:00 P.M. Closed holidays except summer; guided tours on the hour and half hour until 4:00 P.M. $

Built in 1704, the Crailo mansion is the home of the Museum of Hudson Valley Dutch Culture and is furnished with antiques and historical artifacts. The song "Yankee Doodle" was reportedly written here. Outside are fragrant herb gardens, and in summer concerts are held on the grounds.

Grafton Lakes State Park (all ages)

Long Pond Road, Box 163, Route 2, Grafton 12082; (518) 279–1155; www.nysparks.com/parks. Open daily year-round 8:00 A.M. to dusk. Free, except for parking fee in summer $ and boat rentals $$.

This popular 2,357-acre park has four small lakes (some with beavers), a large sandy beach, snack bar, rowboat rentals, fishing, a nature center, a twelve-station nature trail, ball fields, and a playground. In winter the activities shift to ice-skating, sledding, cross-country skiing, and ice fishing.

Empire State **Officials**

State Bird—red-breasted bluebird

State Flower—rose

State Fruit—apple

State Gem—garnet

State Tree—sugar maple

State Fish—brook trout

State Animal—beaver

State Insect—lady bug

State Fossil—Eurypterus remipes (sea scorpion)

State Beverage—milk

State Motto—Excelsior (Ever Upward)

State Muffin—apple muffin

Berkshire Bird Paradise (all ages)

43 Red Pond Road, Petersburg, off Route 2 (3 miles past Grafton Lakes); (518) 279–3801 or (800) 349–7150; www.birdparadise.com or www.birdparadise.org. Open daily mid-May through October 9:00 A.M. to 5:00 P.M. Donation.

From emu to eagle, more than 2,000 birds from more than one hundred species live in this sanctuary for injured or adopted birds. Visitors can walk through an evergreen and hardwood forest seeking spotted owls or snowy egrets. Guided tours are also offered.

Dyken Pond Environmental Education Center (all ages)

475 Dyken Pond Road, Cropsyville; (518) 658–2055; www.dykenpond.org. About 14 miles east of Troy. Open daily year-round during daylight hours. $

This lovely preserve has nature trails excellent for bird-watching and offers owl prowls and other activities and workshops.

Where to Eat

Uncle Sam Brewery. 417–419 River Street; (518) 273–2337; www.troypub .com. Riverfront Park place that brews its own soda and beer. $$

Holmes and Watson, Ltd. 450 Broadway; (518) 273–8526. Historic British pub with Sherlock Holmes theme and a children's menu. $

Where to Stay

Best Western Rensselaer Inn. 1800 Sixth Avenue; (518) 274–3210. Pool, restaurant. $$$

Fairfield Inn. 124 Troy Road, East Green-bush; (518) 477–7984. Pool, restaurant, coin laundry, and free continental break-fast. $$

Also in **the Area**

Oasis Park Miniature Golf. 97 North Greenbush Road, Troy; (518) 283–3646.

Funplex Mystic Lagoon. 589 Colonial Turnpike, East Greenbush; (518) 477–2651; www.funplexfunpark.com.

Gardener's Ice Cream & Miniature Golf. Route 22, Stephentown; (518) 733–6700.

Tri-City Valley Cats. The Class A affiliate of the Houston Astros, and member of the New York–Penn League; Vandenburg Drive, Troy; (518) 629–2287; www.tcvalleycats.com.

Rolling on **the River**

Captain J. P. Cruise Line. 278–280 River Street; (518) 270–1901.

Granville

Head north on Route 40 to Route 149.

Settled by Quakers in the late eighteenth century, the town's chief resource was its abundance of blue, green, and maroon slate, thereby earning it the nickname of the Colored Slate Capital of the World.

Pember Museum of Natural History (all ages)

33 West Main Street, Route 149; (518) 642–1515; www.pembermuseum.com. Open year-round Tuesday through Friday 1:00 to 5:00 P.M., Saturday 10:00 A.M. to 3:00 P.M. $

Franklin T. Pember and his wife, Ellen, wanted to build a library and museum for their town. In 1909, the Pembers amassed a collection of more than 10,000 regional and exotic natural-history objects, from bears and butterflies to fossils and frogs. Children will enjoy the "Please Touch" naturalist's cabinets, with all sorts of shells, bones, and pelts to examine. Special programs may include nature hikes and scavenger hunts.

Pember Nature Preserve (all ages)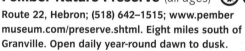

Route 22, Hebron; (518) 642–1515; www.pember museum.com/preserve.shtml. Eight miles south of Granville. Open daily year-round dawn to dusk.

Affiliated with the Pember Museum, this is a great place to explore a variety of natural habitats with children. Seven easy nature trails lace through this 125-acre preserve, and an observation deck offers the chance to spot the waterfowl, beavers, muskrats, and deer that reside here. Nature hikes, owl prowls, and other activities are offered throughout the year.

More to Do **around Granville**

Granville Recreational Center. 1142 County Road 24, Granville; (518) 642–9855; www.granvillelanes.com.

Battenkill Rambler. Broad Street and West Main Street, Route 372, Cambridge; (518) 692–2191.

Log Village Grist Mill. Route 30, East Hartford; (518) 632–5237. Two miles east of Route 40.

Skenesborough Museum & Urban Cultural Park Center. Skenesborough Drive, Whitehall; (518) 499–0716. Off Route 4.

Slate Valley Museum. 17 Water Street, Granville; (518) 642–1417; www.slate valleymuseum.org.

Hillbilly Fun Park. Fort Ann; (518) 792–5239.

Where to Eat

Rathbun's Maple Sugar House. Hatchhill Road, off Route 22, North Granville; (518) 642–1799. Fabulous breakfasts, plus springtime maple-sugaring demonstrations. $

The Schoolhouse Restaurant. Route 149, South Granville Road; (518) 642–0679. Steak, seafood, Italian specialties, and Saturday night buffet. $–$$

Where to Stay

Finch & Chubb Inn, Restaurant, and Marina. 82 North Williams Street, Whitehall; (518) 499–2049; www.visitwhitehall .com. Located on the water at Lock 12, Finch & Chubb has a swimming pool, playground, small boat rentals, and picnic area. $$$–$$$$

Panorama Motel. 2227 Route 22A, Hampton (6 miles north of Granville); (518) 282–9648 or (888) 423–9648; www .panoramamotelny.com. Twelve rooms, set on a hillside, with nice views. $

Saratoga Springs

South on Route 22 to Route 29 west.

Whether you come to take the waters at the "Queen of Spas" or visit the racetrack to watch the "Sport of Kings," Saratoga Springs will reward your family royally with a treasury of fun things to see and do.

Saratoga Springs Urban Heritage Area & Visitor Center (all ages)
297 Broadway; (518) 587–3241. Open daily year-round 9:00 A.M. to 4:00 P.M.; closed Sunday December through March. Free.

To start your exploration of Saratoga, stop here for self-guided tour maps and a schedule of special events, then cross the street to Congress Park, one of the oldest parks in the country, and sample the fabled mineral waters of Saratoga Springs.

Children's Museum at Saratoga Springs (all ages)
69 Caroline Street; (518) 584–5540; www.childrensmuseumatsaratoga.org. Open Labor Day to end of June Tuesday through Saturday 9:30 A.M. to 4:30 P.M., Sunday noon to 4:30 P.M.; July through Labor Day also open Monday, closed Sunday. $

Walk through a toddler-size cityscape, climb aboard a fire truck, create giant bubbles, or construct a Lego village at this interactive museum.

Petrified Sea Gardens (all ages)
42 Petrified Sea Gardens Road; (518) 584–7102; www.petrifiedseagardens.org. Hours vary by season. $, children under 6 free.

Stroll among the stromatolites, or Cambrian sea cabbage fossils, formed when Saratoga Springs was at the bottom of the ocean. There are two trails and a sundial garden to explore, a small rock and mineral museum, and Native American activities and workshops for children.

Fun for **Horse Lovers**

Take in a summer horse race at the oldest racetrack in the country, watch the horses work out, take a tram tour of the paddock area, then head to a couple of museums sure to delight horse lovers of all ages.

Saratoga Race Course. Exit 14 off I–87, Union Avenue; (518) 584–6200 or (888) 285–5961; www.nyra.com/saratoga.

National Museum of Racing and Hall of Fame. 191 Union Avenue; (518) 584–0400 or (800) JOCKEY–4; www.racingmuseum.org.

Saratoga Harness Hall of Fame and Equine Sports Center. 352 Jefferson Street; (518) 587–4210.

Saratoga Polo. Whitney and Bostwick Fields; (518) 584–8108; www .saratogapolo.com.

Saratoga Spa State Park (all ages)

19 Roosevelt Drive (between Routes 9 and 50); (518) 584–2000 or (518) 584–2535; www.nys parks.com. Lincoln Mineral Baths (518) 583–2880; www.gideonputnam.com. Open daily year-round 9:00 A.M. to 4:00 P.M. $

Pamper yourselves with a stop at the spas for a mineral bath, or take the kids swimming at the ornately tiled Victoria Pool or the larger Peerless Pool. This lushly manicured 2,200-acre park also has two golf courses, six tennis courts, the grand Gideon Putnam Hotel, the Spa Little Theatre, and the Saratoga Performing Arts Center to keep you entertained in high style.

Saratoga National Historic Park (all ages)

648 Route 32 (at Route 4), Stillwater; (518) 664–9821, ext. 224; www.nps.gov/sara. Open year-round 9:00 A.M. to dusk; visitor center closes at 5:00 P.M. $

Possibly the most decisive battles of the American Revolution were fought here in the autumn of 1777. Led by generals Horatio Gates and Benedict Arnold, the American troops routed British general John Burgoyne's army in two savage assaults, effectively bringing about the beginning of the end of British rule in America. The visitor center offers interpretive exhibits, an orientation film, and a ten-stop auto tour map of the battlefields.

Brookside Saratoga County History Center (all ages)

6 Charlton Street (off Route 50), Ballston Spa; (518) 885–4000; www.brooksidemuseum.org. Open year-round Tuesday through Friday 10:00 A.M. to 4:00 P.M., Saturday 10:00 A.M. to 2:00 P.M. $

This interesting museum offers permanent and changing exhibits of cultural and social history, with a hands-on history room, a costume display, and interactive computers.

More Fun in **Saratoga Springs**

National Museum of Dance. 99 South Broadway; (518) 584–2225.

Bog Meadow Nature Trail. Route 29; (518) 587–5554; www.openspaceproject.org.

Saratoga Mini Golf. Route 50; (518) 581–0852.

Tee Shot Golf. Weibel Avenue; (518) 505–4653.

Where to Eat

Lillian's. 408 Broadway; (518) 587–7766. Fresh seafood, prime rib, pasta, vegetarian entrees, and a children's menu. $$

Saratoga Diner. 153 South Broadway; (518) 584–4044. Open twenty-four hours, serving diner classics. $

Where to Stay

Gideon Putnam Hotel. 24 Gideon Putnam Road; (518) 584–3000 or (800) 732–1560; www.gideonputnam.com. A grand hotel located inside Saratoga Spa State Park, with 132 rooms and suites, outdoor pool, restaurant, lawn games, and mineral spa. $$$$

Saratoga Lake Motel. 1192 Route 9P; (518) 584–7438; www.saratoga.org/lake motel. Eight rooms, overlooking Saratoga Lake. $$

Schenectady

South on Route 50.

Schenectady, the site of the earliest European settlement in the Mohawk Valley, was once referred to as The City that Lights and Hauls the World. The theme here is still labor and industry, but it's probably the historical aspects of the downtown area that will interest kids the most.

Schenectady Museum and Planetarium (all ages)

15 Nott Terrace Heights; (518) 382–7890; www.schenectadymuseum.org. Open year-round Tuesday through Friday 10:00 A.M. to 4:30 P.M., Saturday and Sunday noon to 5:00 P.M. Planetarium shows Saturday and Sunday at 1:00, 2:00, and 3:00 P.M. Adults $$, children $

Pilot a space shuttle, make a flat bubble, or create lightning in a globe. This museum, located next door to the Schenectady Heritage Area Visitor's Center, offers many interactive science and industry exhibits as well as an extensive costume collection and weekend sky shows inside a 30-foot planetarium.

The Stockade (all ages)

32 Washington Avenue; (518) 374–0263; www.schist.org or www.historicstockade.com. Historical Society Museum open year-round Tuesday through Friday 1:00 to 5:00 P.M., Saturday 10:00 A.M. to 4:00 P.M. $

Named for the succession of wooden stockades built in the seventeenth century to protect the early Dutch settlers, this is the oldest section of Schenectady. Pick up a map of the district at the Historical Society Museum, located at the southern end on Washington Street. Children will enjoy the museum's antique dolls and toys.

Empire State Aerospace Museum (all ages)

250 Rudy Chase Drive, Glenville; (518) 377–2191; www.esam.org. Open year-round Thursday through Saturday 10:00 A.M. to 4:00 P.M., Wednesday and Sunday noon to 4:00 P.M. $

If you ever dreamed of being a rocket scientist or an ace fighter pilot or astronaut, here's your chance. There are many hands-on aviation activities offered, from rocket building to model flying, and new aircraft are added all the time. In the Restoration Center you can watch vintage planes being rebuilt.

Vischer Ferry Nature Preserve (all ages)

Riverview Road, Clifton Park; (518) 371–6667. Adjacent to Mohawk River. Open daily dawn to dusk. **Free.**

Old double lock 19, a historic section of the Erie Canal, can be seen here, and hiking trails lead to some great bird-watching.

Where to Eat

Canali's Restaurant. 126 Mariaville Road; (518) 355–5323. Terrific pasta, Italian specialties, and a children's menu. $$

Jumpin' Jack's Drive-In. 5 Schonowee Avenue, Scotia; (518) 393–6101. Great burgers, chicken fingers, and fries. $

Where to Stay

Residence Inn by Marriott. 1 Residence Inn Drive, Latham; (518) 783–0600; www.marriott.com. Outdoor pool, tennis and basketball courts, hot and cold buffet breakfast, and all rooms are suites with full kitchens. $$$$

Amsterdam

Head west along Route 5.

This river valley was home to the Mohawks for thousands of years before Dutch and German settlers arrived in the early eighteenth century.

Walter Elwood Museum (all ages)

300 Guy Park Avenue; (518) 843–5151. Open July and August Monday through Thursday 10:00 A.M. to 3:00 P.M., September through June Monday through Friday 10:00 A.M. to 3:00 P.M. Closed legal holidays. Donation.

One of only two public school museums in the state, this museum emphasizes the lives of children of the Mohawk Valley. Exhibits range from animal displays and labor-saving inventions to historical dioramas.

National Shrine of North American Martyrs (ages 7 and up) 🏛

136 Shrine Road, Auriesville; (518) 853–3033; www.martyrshrine.org. Open May through October daily 10:00 A.M. to 4:00 P.M. **Free.**

In the 1640s, Father Issac Joques and seven other Jesuit missionaries were martyred by the Mohawks. This shrine was erected in 1885 as a monument to these first American saints.

Where to Eat

Clay's Food Emporium. Minaville Road; (518) 842–8679. Good burgers, chicken, fries, and Italian specialties. $

Raindancer Steak Parlour. 4582 Route 30; (518) 842–2606. Rustic steak and seafood restaurant with salad bar, early-bird specials, and children's menu. $$

Where to Stay

Best Western. 10 Market Street; (518) 843–5760. Indoor pool, restaurant, and children under eighteen stay **free.** $$

Super 8 Motel. At junction of I–90, exit 27 and Route 30 South; (518) 843–5888. Complimentary continental breakfast, and children under twelve stay **free.** $$

Johnstown

Continue west on Route 5, then north on Route 30A.

This was the birthplace of suffragette Elizabeth Cady Stanton and was once, along with nearby Gloversville, the center of a thriving leather- and glove-manufacturing industry.

Johnson Hall State Historic Site (ages 7 and up) 🏛

Hall Avenue (between Johnson Avenue and West State Street); (518) 762–8712; www.nys parks.com/hist. Open May through October Wednesday through Monday 10:00 A.M. to 5:00 P.M., Sunday 1:00 to 5:00 P.M. $

The former home of Sir William Johnson, brother-in-law of Iroquois leader Joseph Brant, is now a museum that offers interesting exhibits on the French and Indian War.

Johnstown Historical Society Museum (ages 8 and up) 🦽

17 North William Street; (518) 762–7419. Call for hours of operation. **Free,** donations appreciated.

This restored eighteenth-century cottage houses artifacts from Johnstown's Revolutionary and Civil War past, as well as an exhibit on town native and pioneer for women's rights, Elizabeth Cady Stanton.

Adirondack Animal Land (all ages)

3554 Route 30, Gloversville; (518) 883–5748; www.adirondackanimalland.com. Open daily mid-May through Labor Day 10:00 A.M. to 5:00 P.M. $$

Spread over seventy-five acres, this wildlife park is home to hundreds of regional and exotic birds and animals. Visit the nursery and petting zoo, then wander through a wild west frontier village.

Fonda National Kateri Tekakwitha Shrine and Mohawk-Caughnawaga Museum (ages 7 and up)

Route 5 (about .25 mile west of I–90 exit 28), Fonda; (518) 853–3646; www.katerishrine .com. Open daily 9:00 A.M. to 6:00 P.M. Free.

Known as "the Lily of the Mohawks," Kateri, born in 1656, was the daughter of an Algonquin mother and a Mohawk chief. Orphaned at three, then stricken with smallpox at four, she suffered failing eyesight and was given the name Tekakwitha. Baptized at age twenty, she was known for her courage and compassion for others and is said to have performed many miracles. The museum houses an excellent collection of ancient and modern Native American art, as well as artifacts from the excavated Iroquois village on the grounds.

Where to Eat

Dick and Peg's Northward Inn Restaurant. Route 29A, northwest of Gloversville; (518) 725–6440. This family-owned place specializes in steaks and seafood. See if you can spot the hidden owls while you're waiting. $$$

Where to Stay

Johnstown Holiday Inn. 308 North Comrie Avenue (Route 30A); (518) 762–4686; www.holiday-inn.com/johnstownny. Heated outdoor pool, restaurant, children under twelve stay and eat free. $$$

Peck's Lake Park and Campground. 180 Peck's Lake Road, Gloversville; (518) 725–1294 or (518) 725–3996. Family fishing resort with cottages, campsites, and boat rentals. $

Native Americans of **New York**

The earliest known humans to settle in the New York region were the "mound people," about 7000 B.C. Later, probably 6,000 to 8,000 years ago, came the tribes of the Lenape (Munsee, Unami, Renneiu, Unalatchtigo, and Esopus), Poospapuck, Delaware, Mohican, Nanticoke, and Wappinger, along with the thirteen tribes of Long Island (Montauk, Shinnecock, Unquachaug, Secatogue, Massapequa, Merrick, Rockaway, Canarsie, Matinecock, Nissequogue, Setaukets, Corchaug, and Manhanset), linked by the similarities of their Algonquin language, and the Iroquois, comprised of the Mohawk, Oneida, Onondaga, Cayuga, Seneca, and, later, the Tuscarora. Most lived in communal homes, called longhouses, made from saplings and bark (some as long as a football field). While many of the Algonquin tribes were wiped out by exposure to European diseases such as smallpox and measles, the Iroquois prospered, mostly due to the fur trade. The more powerful Iroquois tribes formed a confederacy of Six Nations, with rules of social order and government meant to promote peaceful relations. Allied with the Susquehanna, Abenaki, Erie, and Huron to the west, the Iroquois aided the British during the French and Indian War and were a major factor in France's defeat. During the Revolutionary War most of the Native Americans sided with the British again. After that defeat, and the attack Gen. George Washington unleashed on the Iroquois in 1779, the Native American way of life was changed forever.

St. Johnsville

South on Route 30A, then Route 5 west.

Once a major stop on seventeenth- and eighteenth-century fur trade routes, St. Johnsville later became an important mill town.

Fort Klock (all ages)
Route 5 (between Routes 67 and 10); (518) 568–7779; www.fortklock.com. Open May through October Tuesday through Sunday 9:00 A.M. to 5:00 P.M. $

Built in 1750, this fortified stone house was a fur trading post along the Mohawk River. Several other buildings—including a schoolhouse, a blacksmith shop, and a Dutch barn—have been added to the complex.

Canajoharie Wintergreen Park and Gorge (all ages)

Wintergreen Park Road, Canajoharie, near exit 29 off I–90; (518) 673–5508. Open Memorial Day weekend through Labor Day daily 9:00 A.M. to 9:30 P.M. $

Canajoharie is the Iroquois word for "the pot that washes itself," and a spectacular waterfall rushing over geological potholes does just that. Follow nature trails past this unusual phenomenon.

Herkimer County Historical Society Museum (all ages)

400 North Main Street, Herkimer; (315) 866–6413; www.rootsweb.com/~nyhchs. Open year-round Monday through Friday 10:00 A.M. to 4:00 P.M.; also Saturday from July through August 10:00 A.M. to 3:00 P.M. Free.

A restored 1834 jail and a wonderful collection of dollhouses and miniatures grace this 1884 Queen Anne house.

Dig for **Diamonds**

The diamonds, called "Herkimer Diamonds," are actually eighteen-faceted, double-terminated quartz crystals formed half a million years ago in pockets of dolomite.

Herkimer Diamond Mines. Route 28, Middleville, 7 miles north of Herkimer; (315) 891–7355 or (800) 562–0897; www.herkimerdiamond.com. Open daily April through early November 9:00 A.M. to 5:00 P.M. Adults $$, children $.

Ace of Diamonds Mine. Route 28, Middleville, 8 miles north of I–90, exit 30; (315) 891–3855; www.herkimerdiamond.com. Open April through October 9:00 A.M. to 5:00 P.M. Adults $$, children $.

Crystal Grove Diamond Mine. 161 County Highway 114, St. Johnsville; (518) 568–2914; www.crystalgrove.com. Open April 15 through October 15 daily 8:00 A.M. to 8:00 P.M. Adults $$, children $.

Diamond Acres. 1716 Stone Arabia Road, Mohawk; (518) 762–7960. Open daily sunup to sundown, weather permitting. Adults $, children under 13 free.

Where to Eat

Parkside Drive-In. 7485 Route 5; (518) 568–2802. Classic drive-in delights. $

Where to Stay

Herkimer Diamond KOA. 7 miles north of Herkimer on Route 28; (315) 891–7355; www.herkimerdiamond.com. Cabins, cottages, RV and tent sites, restaurant and cafe. $–$$$$

Herkimer Motel. 100 Marginal Road; (315) 866–0490. Rooms and efficiencies, heated outdoor pool, coin laundry, restaurant, children under thirteen stay **free.** $$–$$$$

Utica

Continue west on Route 5.

Home to the Oneida Nation for centuries, Utica evolved into a major trading and manufacturing center after the Dutch and English came to trade and never left. Woolworth opened his first five-and-dime store here in 1879.

Children's Museum (all ages)

311 Main Street; (315) 724–6129; www.museum4kids.net. Open year-round Monday through Tuesday and Thursday through Saturday 9:45 A.M. to 3:45 P.M. Closed Wednesday, Sunday, Thanksgiving, Christmas, and New Year's. $

Considered one of the best children's museums in the Northeast, it offers wonderful interactive and hands-on exhibits, ranging from Native American displays to a dinosaur discovery zone. Arts and crafts projects are offered daily for all ages, and your kids will probably bug you to take them to the insect zoo on the third floor.

Adirondack Scenic Railroad (all ages)

Union Station, Main and Railroad Streets, Thendara; (315) 724–0700 or (315) 369–6290; www.adirondackrr.com. Operates May through October; call for schedule and special events. Adults $$$$, children $$.

Make tracks to this rustic railroad for a ride aboard vintage coaches and open-air cars, traveling from Utica to Old Forge and back. Special excursions range from train robberies to a Santa Express, and the fall foliage rides are spectacular. Trips also originate from the Thendara Station in Old Forge.

Saranac Brewery (all ages)

Court and Varick Streets; (315) 624–2434 or (800) 765–6288; www.saranac.com. Saranac Brewery tours offered post–Memorial Day through Labor Day Monday through Saturday 1:00 to 4:00 P.M. every hour on the hour and Sunday at 1:00, 2:00, and 3:00 P.M.; September through May (reservations recommended), Friday and Saturday at 1:00 and 3:00 P.M. Special holiday hours. $

Tour this fascinating brewery, founded in 1888 and one of the oldest in America, with the help of Victorian-costumed guides, then take a trolley to the tavern for a complimentary mug of the best brew or a frosty root beer.

Where to Eat

Babe's Macaroni Grill & Bar. 80 North Genesee Street; (315) 735–0777. Sports-theme atmosphere with early-bird specials and a children's menu. $

Tiny's Grill. 1014 State Street; (315) 732–9497. American cuisine, with entertainment. $

Where to Stay

Best Western Gateway Adirondack Motor Inn. 175 North Genesee Street; (315) 732–4121. Game room, complimentary continental breakfast, and children under twelve stay **free.** $$$–$$$$

Radisson Hotel. 200 Genesee Street; (315) 797–8010 or (800) 333–3333; www.radisson.com. Indoor pool, Jacuzzi, restaurant, game room, some refrigerators. $$$$

Fifteen Miles **on the Erie Canal**

Cruise the waterways of the 524-mile New York State Canal System for a voyage through history and time. Linking more than 2,500 recreational facilities and attractions, the Erie, Champlain, Oswego, and Cayuga-Seneca Canals offer a scenic slice of life not available to landlubbers. For more information, contact the New York State Canal System at P.O. Box 189, Albany 12201; (800) 4–CANAL–4; www.canals.state .ny.us.

Rome

From Utica, take Route 49.

Called De-O-Wain-Sta by local Native Americans, this was an important portage point for travel between the Great Lakes and the Atlantic Ocean. During the Revolutionary War, the Stars and Stripes were first flown in battle here, and the settlement was renamed Rome when the British were defeated. The Erie Canal and the railroads that followed soon transformed the town into a major transportation hub.

Fort Rickey Children's Discovery Zoo (all ages)

5135 Rome–New London Road, 3 miles west of Rome on Routes 49 and 46; (315) 336–1930; www.fortrickey.com. Open mid-May through mid-June weekdays 10:00 A.M. to 2:00 P.M., weekends 10:00 A.M. to 4:00 P.M., mid- to late June weekdays 10:00 A.M. to 4:00 P.M., weekends 10:00 A.M. to 5:00 P.M., July to Labor Day daily 10:00 A.M. to 5:00 P.M. $$

This wonderful wildlife park encourages children to explore, investigate, and interact with a wide variety of animals, from antelopes and eagles to reindeer and reptiles. A large petting area with goats, sheep, and deer offers daily pony rides and animal shows. A playland features geysers and waterfalls, tunnels, slides, and a clubhouse.

Fort Stanwix National Monument (all ages)

112 East Park Street; (315) 336–2090; www.nps.gov/fost. Open April through December 9:00 A.M. to 5:00 P.M. Closed Thanksgiving and Christmas. Free.

This reconstructed log-and-earth fort was strategically important during the Revolutionary War. Costumed guides explain life lived behind these logs, and a small museum contains interesting artifacts.

Erie Canal Village (all ages)

Route 49W, 5789 New London Road; (315) 337–3999 or (888) 374–3226; www.eriecanal village.net. Open Memorial Day through Labor Day Wednesday through Saturday 10:00 A.M. to 5:00 P.M., Sunday noon to 5:00 P.M., weekends only Labor Day through Columbus Day. $$

Take a ride back in time aboard a mule-drawn packet boat on the Erie Canal. This nineteenth-century village has been re-created on the spot where the first shovelful of earth was turned for the canal in 1817.

Where to Eat

Fric & Frac's Flying Food Factory. 601 West Dominick Street; (315) 339–3742. Pizza, buffalo wings, salads, more than twenty kinds of sandwiches, plus a children's menu. $

Savoy Restaurant. 255 East Dominick Street; (315) 339–3166. Family owned, featuring American and Italian cuisine and homemade pasta, plus a children's menu. $

Where to Stay

The Beeches. Route 26N; (315) 336–1776 or (800) 765–7251; www.thebeeches.com.

Located on a fifty-two-acre estate, with great outdoor swimming pool, restaurant, lawn games, pond, and children under twelve stay **free.** $$$

Sylvan Beach

On the shores of Oneida Lake; take Route 49 west to Route 13 south.

This is a popular family resort area, where you can ride a in a horse-drawn carriage or a roller coaster, reel in a fat bass, or paddle a canoe.

Sylvan Beach Amusement Park (all ages)

112 Bridge Street, Route 13; (315) 762–5212. Open late April through Labor Day Friday at 6:00 P.M., Saturday and Sunday at 1:00 P.M. Free entrance, $ for rides.

Twenty-one classic rides rock and roll here each summer, from the tilt-a-whirl to the scrambler, and there's skee ball for all at the arcade. Beyond the midway, explore the 4 miles of cottage-lined beach.

Verona Beach State Park (all ages)

Route 13, Verona Beach; (315) 762–4463; www.nysparks.com/parks. Off Route 13, 2 miles south of Sylvan Beach. Open year-round; campground open May through mid-October. Vehicle fee $.

The best of both worlds, this 1,735-acre park is part sandy beach and part forest. Sixteen miles of hiking trails wind around a peaceful pond, where wildlife is abundant, and there are ball fields and courts, picnic areas, a playground, and a concession stand near the campgrounds.

Also in **the Area**

Shako:wi Cultural Center. 5 Territory Road, Oneida; (315) 829–8801.

Peter Paul Recreation Park. Rome–New London Road, Route 49W; (315) 339–2666.

Where to Eat

Cinderella's Ice Cream and Cafe. 1208 Main Street; (315) 762–4280; www .cinderellarestaurant.com/sleephome.htm. Casual family dining with an extensive menu, freshly baked pastries, and more than thirty flavors of ice cream. $

Yesterday's Royal. 13 Canal Street; (315) 762–4677. Casual place featuring American cuisine, homemade ice cream and desserts, early-bird specials, and a children's menu. $$

Where to Stay

Dwarf Line Motel and Cottages. 6550 Lake Shore Road North, Verona Beach; (315) 762–4645; www.sylvan beach.org/dwarfline. Six rooms. $$$

Sunset Cottages North & South. 801 Park Avenue; (315) 762–4093. Twenty-eight cottages, cable TV, and restaurant. $$$$

Chittenango

Continue south on Route 13.

Follow the yellow brick road, and you will come to Chittenango, the birthplace of L. Frank Baum, author of *The Wizard of Oz*. Every May the town honors its favorite native son by hosting the Oz Festival and parade, with guest appearances by some of the original Munchkins.

Chittenango Landing Canal Boat Museum (all ages)

7010 Lakeport Road; (315) 687–3801; www.chittenangolandingcanalboatmuseum.com. Open weekends May, June, September, and October 1:00 to 4:00 P.M., July through August daily 10:00 A.M. to 4:00 P.M. $, children under 5 free. Ask about deals for families.

This is an archeological work in progress, with an interpretive center offering hands-on activities and exhibits, a blacksmith shop, and a restored sawmill. The 36-mile towpath of the Old Erie Canal Park runs through here and serves as an easy hiking and biking path.

Chittenango Falls State Park (all ages)

2300 Rathbun Road; (315) 655–9620; www.nysparks.com/parks. Off Route 13, 6 miles south of town. Open year-round; campground open mid-May through mid-October. Vehicle fee $.

Higher than Niagara at 167 feet, the cascades of Chittenango Falls are breathtaking. Hike along the scenic trails of this 192-acre park, formed when the last glaciers retreated about 10,000 years ago.

Also in **the Area**

Stone Quarry Hill Art Park. Route 20, Cazenovia; (315) 655–3196.

Great Swamp Conservancy. Pine Ridge Road, Canastota; (315) 697–2950.

Muller Hill State Forest. Muller Hill Road, Georgetown; (607) 674–4036.

Nichols Pond Park. Oxbow Road, Canastota; (315) 366–2376.

Oxbow Falls Park. Oxbow Road, Canastota; (315) 366–2376.

Nelson Swamp Unique Area. Stone Quarry Road, Cazenovia; (607) 674–4036.

Where to Eat

Auntie Em's Restaurant. 262 Genesee Street; (315) 687–5704. Like walking into Oz . . . don't miss it! $$

Oz Cream Parlor. 277 Genesee Street; (315) 687–5504. All the soda fountain classics. $

Where to Stay

Canastota Days Inn. Route 13, off exit 34 of NYS Thruway, Canastota; (315) 697–3309 or (800) 325–2525. Sixty rooms. $$$

Cazenovia Motel. 2392 Route 20 E, Cazenovia; (315) 655–9101. Restaurant onsite. $$$

Sherburne

Take Route 13 south to Route 80.

Roger Environmental Education Center (all ages)

2721 Route 80; (607) 674–4017; www.dec.state.ny.us/website/education. Grounds open year-round dawn to dusk; center open weekdays 8:30 A.M. to 4:45 P.M., Saturday (and Sunday in June through August) 1:00 to 4:45 P.M. Closed state holidays. Free.

The nature museum houses exhibits on native plants and animals, and there are a number of trails meandering through the 571 acres of woodlands. A good choice for families is the 2-mile trail dotted with eco-educational stations.

New York **Trivia**

There are nine major rivers in New York: Hudson, Mohawk, Genesee, Oswego, Delaware, Susquehanna, Allegheny, East, and Chemung.

Bowman Lake State Park (all ages)

745 Bliven Sherman Road, Oxford; (607) 334–2718 or (800) 456–CAMP; www.nysparks
.com/parks. Eight miles northwest of Oxford off Route 220. Open year-round; campgrounds
open May through mid-October. $

There are several easy but sometimes soggy trails to explore over 660 acres of beautiful
hardwood forest, with swimming, rowboating, and fishing opportunities at the thirty-five-
acre artificial lake, and 103 species of birds to spot.

Where to Eat

D&D Diner. 47 North Main Street; (607)
674–9697. Diner fare served breakfast,
lunch, and dinner. $

Where to Stay

Sherburne Motel. 63 Main Street; (607)
674–5511. Eleven rooms. $

Wampum

Wampum was made of tiny white and purple beads carved from
whelk and oyster shells, drilled with stone awls, and woven
into belts using hemp or deer sinew. Designs were incorpo-
rated in the beadwork to record treaties or documents,
and it was used for barter among Native Americans
for at least four thousand years before the
Europeans arrived. It wasn't that
the material wampum was made
from was rare—in fact, shells were
abundant everywhere. Rather, the
value of wampum came from the document itself as
well as the labor and craftsmanship put into its creation. When the Dutch traders introduced steel awls
to the Algonquins, the beads became easier to make,
and wampum was devalued as a currency.

Binghamton

South on Route 12.

The Industrial Revolution boosted Binghamton's fortunes, but it was the paternalistic pride of George F. Johnson, founder of Endicott-Johnson, that really transformed the city. Long before it was required, or even fashionable, Johnson treated his employees like family and provided health care, an eight-hour work day, and company-sponsored picnics and ballgames.

Roberson Museum and Science Center (all ages)

30 Front Street; (888) 269–5325; www.roberson.org. Open Tuesday through Friday 10:30 A.M. to 4:30 P.M., Thursday to 8:00 P.M., Saturday 10:00 A.M. to 4:30 P.M., Sunday noon to 4:30 P.M. $. Heritage Center open Monday through Friday 10:30 A.M. to 4:30 P.M., Thursday to 8:00 P.M., Saturday 10:00 A.M. to 5:00 P.M., Sunday noon to 5:00 P.M. Free.

This complex offers a wonderful blend of regional art and history as well as a science wing, planetarium, and children's center with interactive and hands-on exhibits. The Susquehanna Heritage Center is a good place to pick up self-guided tour maps of the town.

Discovery Center of the Southern Tier (all ages)

60 Morgan Road; (607) 773–8661; www.thediscoverycenter.org. Open year-round Tuesday through Friday 10:00 A.M. to 4:00 P.M., Saturday 10:00 A.M. to 5:00 P.M., Sunday noon to 5:00 P.M. $

Pilot a jet, drive a fire truck, make monster bubbles, or shop till you drop at a kid-size grocery store. Fantasy play is big here, and kids will love exploring all the options.

Ross Park Zoo (all ages)

60 Morgan Road; (607) 724–5461; www.rossparkzoo.com. Open April through November daily 10:00 A.M. to 5:00 P.M. $

Built in the late nineteenth century, this is the fifth-oldest zoo in the country, with more than 150 animals in residence, including big cats, bears, and wolves. The Carousel Museum, next door, houses one of Binghamton's prettiest carousels.

Chenango Valley State Park (all ages)

153 State Park Road (off Route 369, 12 miles northeast of town), Chenango Forks; (607) 648–5251; www.nysparks.com/parks. Park open year-round; campgrounds and cabins open May through mid-October. $$

This 1,075-acre park offers swimming at a sand beach, rowboat rentals, fishing from two lakes and a river, nature trails, and an eighteen-hole golf course.

The Carousels of **Broome County**

When George F. Johnson was a boy, he couldn't afford a ticket to ride a carousel. He decided that if he ever became rich, he would make sure no one would be deprived of that joy. Years later, as owner of twenty-two shoe factories, he made good on his promise and commissioned six county fair–style carousels complete with calliopes. The price of a ticket now, as it was then, is one piece of litter, and if you ride all six you'll receive a special button. Call for hours of operation. See www.binghamtoncvb.com.

Ross Park. Morgan Road, Binghamton; (607) 724–5461.

Recreation Park. Beethoven Street, Binghamton; (607) 722–9166 or (607) 772–7017.

George W. Johnson Park. Oak Hill Avenue, Endicott; (607) 757–2427.

West Endicott Park. Page Avenue, Endicott; (607) 786–2970.

C. Fred Johnson Park. C. F. J. Boulevard, Johnson City; (607) 797–9098.

Highland Park. Hooper Road, Endwell; (607) 786–2970.

Where to Eat

The Copper Cricket Cafe. 266 Main Street; (607) 729–5620. Full menu and great homemade desserts. $$

Number 5. 33 South Washington; (607) 723–0555. Steak, seafood, chicken specialties, served in a former 1897 fire station. Lots of fire memorabilia, early-bird specials, and a children's menu. $$$$

Where to Stay

Days Inn. 1000 Front Street; (607) 724–3297 or (800) 469–7009; www.daysinn.com. Pool, game room, picnic area with grills, complimentary continental breakfast, and children under eighteen stay **free.** $$$

Quality Inn and Suites. 1156 Front Street; (607) 722–5353 or (800) 424–6423; www.choicehotels.com. Rooms and kitchen suites with complimentary continental breakfast; children under eighteen stay **free.** $$

Also in **the Area**

Game It Family Fun Center. 225 Harrison Avenue, Endicott; (607) 785–7612.

Conklin Sports Park. 942 Conklin Road, Conklin; (607) 771–7526.

New Image Roller Dome. Kelly Street, Endwell, off Watson Boulevard; (607) 785–5012.

Skate Estate. 3401 Old Vestal Road, Vestal; (607) 797–6278.

Polar Cap Ice Rink. Katelville and River Roads, Chenango Bridge; (607) 648–9888.

Family Sports Complex. 333 Grand Avenue, Johnson City; (607) 217–0947.

Binghamton Municipal Baseball Park. 211 Henry Street, Binghamton; (607) 723–METS.

Northgate Speedway. 1250 Upper Front Street, Binghamton; (607) 723–1362.

Oneonta

From Binghamton head north along I–88.

Oneonta was a huge railroad town in its day, and the world's largest roundhouse was at the center of it all.

Science Discovery Center (all ages)

I–88, exit 15, SUNY College, College at Oneonta, Physical Science Building, Ravine Parkway; (607) 436–2011; www.organizations.oneonta.edu/sdc. Open September through June Thursday through Saturday noon to 4:00 P.M., July and August Monday through Saturday. Closed major holidays. **Free.**

This interactive science museum has more than seventy exhibits kids can get their hands on, ranging from electrical experiments and optical illusions to matter and motion models.

Also in **the Area**

Cooperstown & Charlotte Valley Railroad. Leatherstocking Railway Historical Society, P.O. Box 681, Oneonta 13820; (607) 432–2429; www.lrhs.com.

Sports in **Oneonta**

National Soccer Hall of Fame and Museum. Wright Soccer Campus, 18 Stadium Circle; (607) 432–3351; www.soccerhall.org.

Oneonta Tigers. 95 River Street, Damaschke Field, Neawha Park; (607) 432–6326.

Oneonta Sports Park. Route 18 (exit 16, I–88); (607) 432–0624.

Gilbert Lake State Park (all ages)
County Road 12, off Route 205, Laurens; (607) 432–2114; www.nysparks.com/parks. Park open year-round; campground open May through mid-October. Summer parking fee $$.

This popular park 10 miles north of town offers hiking, small boat rentals, swimming, a nature center, ball fields, cabins, and campgrounds.

Where to Eat

Christopher's Restaurant and Country Lodge. I–88, exit 15, Route 23, Southside Oneonta; (607) 432–2444. Steaks, seafood, burgers, pizza, great desserts, and a children's menu, with carved bears and a talking moose in residence. $$$

The Farmhouse Restaurant. I–88, exit 16, Route 1; (607) 432–7374. Steak, chicken, pasta, and vegetarian specialties, with peel-and-eat shrimp and a salad bar. $$–$$$$

Where to Stay

Christopher's Lodge and Country Restaurant. I–88, exit 15, Route 23, Southside Oneonta; (607) 432–2444. Unique Adirondack-style lodge rooms; great restaurant with children's menu. $$$$

Cooperstown

Northeast on I–88, then Route 28 north.

James Fenimore Cooper's Leatherstocking tales immortalized his Glimmerglass Country, but today it's probably best known for its passion for baseball.

National Baseball Hall of Fame (ages 5 and up)
25 Main Street; (607) 547–7200 or (888) HALL–OF–FAME; www.baseballhalloffame.org. Open daily year-round, May through September 9:00 A.M. to 9:00 P.M., October through April 9:00 A.M. to 5:00 P.M. Closed Thanksgiving, Christmas, and New Year's. Adults $$, children 7 to 12 $, children under 7 **free;** ask about combination tickets.

In 1839 Abner Doubleday chased the cows out of his neighbor's pasture and invented the national pastime of baseball. That's the local legend, anyway, and there's no shortage of legends at this excellent museum. Gloves, bats, uniforms, trading cards, and other memorabilia, with media presentations and interesting exhibits on the "Negro leagues" and women in baseball.

Doubleday Field and Batting Range (all ages)
Doubleday Field, Main Street (between Pioneer and Chestnut); (607) 547–2270. Season runs May through Labor Day. $

The oldest baseball diamond in the world, this is the original field of dreams. The outstanding semi-pro Otsego Macs play here on Saturday in season, but in August the dream teams arrive for the Hall of Fame's All-Star and Old Timer's games. Just in case the scouts are looking for a midseason replacement, polish your skills at the batting cages next door.

American Baseball Experience (ages 5 and up)
99 Main Street; (607) 547–1273; www.cooperstown.com/aba/aba.html. Open mid-June through Labor Day 9:00 A.M. to 9:00 P.M.; after Labor Day 10:00 A.M. to 6:00 P.M. Adults $$, children $.

A block from the Baseball Hall of Fame is this fun museum, featuring virtual-reality entertainment, more than a thousand autographed items, and a wax museum re-creating great moments in baseball history.

Farmers' Museum (all ages)
1 mile north of town on Lake Road (Route 80); (607) 547–1450 or (888) 547–1450; www.farmersmuseum.org. Open daily mid-May through mid-October 10:00 A.M. to 5:00 P.M. Call for fall and spring hours. Ask about combination tickets. $$, children under 7 free.

Founded in 1943, this was one of the first living-history museums in the country. Stroll past a dozen restored buildings at the Village Crossroads as costumed guides demonstrate nineteenth-century skills and crafts, from spinning and weaving to baking and blacksmithing.

Fenimore Art Museum (all ages)
1 mile north of town on Lake Road (Route 80); (888) 547–1450; www.fenimoreartmuseum.org. Open daily mid-May through mid-October 10:00 A.M. to 5:00 P.M. Call for fall and spring hours. Ask about combination tickets. $$, children under 7 free.

Possibly the finest folk art collection in the state is housed here, and with the recent addition of the Thaw Collection of American Indian Art, this museum is a national treasure. Hudson River School paintings here include Thomas Cole's *Last of the Mohicans*. The landscaped grounds are lovely, and a cafe serves light refreshments.

Also in **the Area**

Cooperstown Fun Park. Route 28, Hyde Park, Cooperstown, 3 miles south of town; (607) 547–2767; www.cooperstownfunpark.com.

Cooperstown Dreamscape. Corner of East Lake Road and Briar Hill Road, Cooperstown; (607) 264–3394; www.cooperstownchamber.org/dtee.

Cooperstown Bat Company. 118 Main Street, Cooperstown; Factory, 6106 Route 28, Fly Creek; (888) 547–2415; www.cooperstownbat.com.

Fly Creek Cider Mill. 288 Goose Street, Fly Creek; (607) 547–9692; www.fly creekcidermill.com.

Hogs Hollow Farm. Basswood Road, off Route 51 north, Burlington Flats; (607) 965–8555.

Lollypop Farm and Petting Zoo. 230 Petkewec, Cooperstown, off Route 11, southwest of town; (607) 293–7766.

Brass Ring Farm. 4015 Route 28, Milford; (607) 286–9333.

Royal Llamas Ltd. 515 Old Stone Robbie Road, Oneonta; (607) 432–5827.

Petrified Creatures Museum (all ages)

Routes 20 and 80 (12 miles north of Cooperstown), Richfield Springs; (315) 858–2868 or (315) 627–6399; www.cooperstownchamber.org/pcm. Open mid-May through mid-September 9:00 A.M. to 5:00 P.M. $$

This is the oldest museum in central New York, founded in 1934, but the petrified Devonian sea creatures found here beat that by about 300 million years. Tools are provided for excavating these tiny critters, and you can keep what you find. Kids will definitely enjoy the life-size dinosaur replicas poised to pounce along the nature paths and the hands-on discovery center.

Where to Eat

Cafe Milano. 161 Main Street; (607) 544–1222. Upscale Italian, steak, seafood, homemade desserts, and a children's menu. $$

Pepper Mill. Route 28 South; (607) 547–8550. This family-owned seasonal restaurant specializes in chicken, ribs, game fowl; children's menu. $$

Where to Stay

The Cooper Inn. 16 Chestnut Street; (607) 547–2567 or (800) 348–6222; www.cooper inn.com. Built in 1812, this is a historic classic inn, with twenty rooms, complimentary continental breakfast and afternoon tea, and guests may use the sports facilities of the Otesaga Resort. $$$$

Lake View Motel & Cottages. Lake Road, Route 80; (607) 547–9740 or (888) 452–5384; www.cooperstown vacations.com. Overlooking Lake Otsego, with **free** boating, swimming, and fishing. $$–$$$$

North Blenheim

Take Route 28 south toward Oneonta, Route 23 east to Grand Gorge, then Route 30 north.

The longest single-span covered bridge in the country crosses Schoharie Creek here, and the same road (Route 30) will afford great views and access to the natural landmark known as Vroman's Nose.

Blenheim-Gilboa Power Project (ages 4 and up)
Route 30, 20 miles south of I–88; (518) 827–6121 or (800) 724–0309; www.nypa.gov. Visitor's center open daily 10:00 A.M. to 5:00 P.M., closed major holidays. Reservations must be made for tours of power plant. Free.

The dynamics of hydropower are demonstrated here, New York's largest energy storage plant, with hands-on activities and historic displays. With advance reservations, families can venture underground to view giant turbine generators that, by recycling the water between the Blenheim and Gilboa reservoirs, generate 1.6 billion kilowatt hours of electricity a year.

Mine Kill State Park (all ages)
Next door to the Power Project, Route 30; (518) 827–6111; www.nysparks.com/parks. Open year-round; summer parking fee $.

Overlooking the reservoir, this popular 500-acre park offers a nature trail, three swimming pools, ball fields and courts, boating, fishing, picnic areas, and a scenic overlook of Mine Kill Falls.

Gilboa Fossil Forest (all ages)
Route 990V, near the dam, south of Gilboa; (607) 652–3316. Free.

Eons ago a fern forest grew here, along the shores of an ancient Devonian Sea. Discovered in the 1920s, these are the fossilized remains of some of the oldest trees in the world.

Where to Eat

Waterfall House. Route 990V, Gilboa;
(607) 588–9891. Steaks, seafood, chicken,
and kid-friendly appetizers. $–$$

Where to Stay

Country Roads Campgrounds. Kingsley
Road, off Route 990V, Gilboa; (518)
827–6397. Scenic hilltop location, with
pool, Jacuzzi, playground, laundry, game
room, and hayrides. $

Twin Oaks Campground. 142 Twin Oaks
Lane, Middleburgh; (518) 827–5641.
Seven-acre lake, 125 campsites, laun-
derette. $

Schoharie

Continue north on Route 30.

Old Stone Fort (all ages)

**145 Fort Road; (518) 295–7192; www.theoldstonefort.org. Open Tuesday through Saturday
May through October 10:00 A.M. to 5:00 P.M., Sunday noon to 5:00 P.M. Closed Monday
except in July and August. $, free for children under 5.**

A former church built in 1772, the Stone Fort was unsuccessfully attacked during the
largest British raid in the area by Chief Joseph Brant. An interesting collection of artifacts,
automobiles, fossils, and firearms are exhibited, and the complex of buildings on the site
includes several restored barns and a schoolhouse.

Suggested **Reading**

Drums Along the Mohawk by Walter D. Edmonds

The Pioneers by James Fenimore Cooper

Saratoga Secret by Betsy Sterman

Guns for General Washington by Seymour Reit

Little Maid of Mohawk Valley by Alice Turner Curtis

Howes Cave

Continue north on Route 30 to Route 30A north, then connect with Route 7 west.

One hot summer day in 1842, local farmer Lester Howe became curious as to why his cows were standing in the middle of the pasture instead of under the shade of nearby trees. Upon investigation, he discovered a small crevice in the ground with a cool breeze rushing up from it. Lowering himself by ropes, he explored more than a mile of the subterranean cavern, and a short time later he opened the caves to the public.

Howe Caverns (all ages)

Caverns Road, off Route 7; (518) 296–8900; www.howecaverns.com. Open daily September through June 9:00 A.M. to 6:00 P.M., July through Labor Day 8:00 A.M. to 8:00 P.M., closed major holidays. Adults $$$, children $$.

Descend 156 feet, via elevator, to the heart of Howe Caverns, central New York's oldest tourist attraction. Formed millions of years ago, the one-and-a-half-hour guided tour takes you past shimmering stalactites and stalagmites and ends with a boat ride on the enchanting underground Lake Venus.

Secret Caverns (all ages)

Caverns Road, between Routes 7 and 20; (518) 296–8558; www.secretcaverns.com. Open September, October, November, April, and May daily 10:00 A.M. to 4:30 P.M., June through September daily 9:00 A.M. to 6:30 P.M. Adults $$, children $.

Left in a natural state, these caverns retain much of their "wild" character. Guided forty-five-minute tours are offered, gleaming flow stone and stalactites and stalagmites bloom everywhere, and a 100-foot underground waterfall cascades down the wall at the far end.

Iroquois Indian Museum (all ages)

Caverns Road, 3 miles from I–88; (518) 296–8949; www.IroquoisMuseum.org. Open Labor Day through December and April through June Tuesday through Saturday 10:00 A.M. to 5:00 P.M., Sunday noon to 5:00 P.M.; July through Labor Day weekend, Monday through Saturday 10:00 A.M. to 5:00 P.M., Sunday noon to 5:00 P.M.; closed January through March and major holidays. Adults $$, children 5 to 12 $, under 5 free.

The art and artifacts of the Iroquois people, from past to present, are displayed in this

New York **Trivia**

People of the Iroquois Confederacy were matrilineal, with each household headed by the family's oldest woman. In peacetime these women chose the clan chiefs, but during war the men appointed their own leaders.

wonderful longhouse museum. The Children's Museum downstairs offers activities from beading bracelets to making music and programs featuring native dances, stories, crafts, and nature walks.

Where to Eat

Bulls Head Inn. 2 Park Place, Cobleskill; (518) 234–3591. Dine in a historic building; specializing in steak, prime rib, seafood, pasta, and sandwiches. $$$

Historic Throop Drug Store & Soda Fountain. Main Street, Schoharie; (518) 295–7300. Old-fashioned ice cream parlor, plus homemade soups and baked goods. $

Where to Stay

Gables Bed and Breakfast Inn. 436 West Main Street, Cobleskill; (518) 234–4467; http://nyinn.com. Children welcome at fuelingthefun.com participating property; $25 in **free** gas with two-night stay. $$$–$$$$

Howe Caverns Motel. Caverns Road, off Route 7; (518) 296–8950; www.howe caverns.com. Twenty-one rooms; swimming pool and restaurant; next door to the Howe Caverns. $$

Schoharie **County Bounty**

Barber's Farm Greenhouses. Route 30, Fultonham Road, Middleburgh; (518) 827–5452.

Borhinger's Fruit Farm. Routes 30 and 145, Middleburgh; (518) 827–5783.

Pick-A-Pumpkin Patch. Creek Road, Central Bridge; (518) 868–4893.

The Carrot Barn at Schoharie Valley Farms. Route 30, Schoharie; (518) 295–7139.

Other Things to See and Do
in the Mohawk Valley Region

Cherry Plain State Park. Off Route 22, Berlin; (518) 733–5400 or (518) 279–1155; www.nysparks.com/parks.

Flag Acres Zoo. 2 Rowley Road, Hoosick Falls; (518) 686–3159.

Sherman's Park. Routes 10 and 29, Caroga Lake; (518) 835–4110.

International Boxing Hall of Fame. 1 Hall of Fame Drive, Canastota; (315) 697–7095; www.ibhof.com.

Easter Egg Museum. Route 30 and 443, Schoharie; (518) 295–8696.

Delta Lake State Park. 8797 SR 46, Rome; (315) 337–4670; www.nysparks .com/parks.

Utica Zoo. 99 Steel Hill Road, Utica; (315) 738–0472.

Munson-Williams-Proctor Institute. 310 Genesee Street, Utica; (315) 797–0000, ext. 2170; www.mwpi.edu.

Eagle Mills Cider Company. Eagle Mills Road, Route 138, Broadalbin; (518) 883–8700; www.eaglemillsfun.com.

Yaddo Gardens. 312 Union Avenue, Saratoga Springs; (518) 584–0746; www.yaddo.org.

Albany Pine Bush Preserve. Off Karner Road, Albany; (518) 785–1800.

Albany Institute of History & Art. 125 Washington Avenue, Albany; (518) 463–4478; www.albanyinstitute.org.

Clark's Broadalbin Heritage & Photographic Museum. 141 Midline Road (141 Extension South Second Avenue), Amsterdam; (518) 883–3357.

Fulton County Historical Society Museum. 237 Kingsboro Avenue, Gloversville; (518) 725–2203.

Schuyler Mansion State Historic Site. 32 Catherine Street, Albany; (518) 434–0834; www.nysparks.com/hist.

Dakota Ridge Llama Farm. 189 East High Street, Ballston Spa; (518) 885–0756; www.llamaweb.com.

Pixley Falls State Park. 11430 Route 46, Boonville; (315) 942–4713 or (800) 456–CAMP; www.nysparks.com.

Northeast Classic Car Museum. 24 Rexford Street, Route 23, Norwich; (607) 334–AUTO; www.classiccarmuseum.org.

Roland B. Hill Museum of Indian Archeology. 361 Main Street, Otego; (607) 988–2229.

Royal Mountain Ski Center. Route 10, Caroga Lake; (518) 835–6445.

Reineman Wildlife Sanctuary. 155 Wyman Road, Dolgeville; (518) 568–7101.

For More Information

Regional Information. (518) 434–1217 or (800) 732–8259.

Albany County Convention and Visitor's Bureau. (518) 434–1217 or (800) 258–3582; www.albany.org.

Fulton County Chamber of Commerce. (518) 725–0641 or (800) 676–3858; www.fultoncountyny.org.

Rensselaer County Tourism. (518) 274–7020; www.renscochamber.com.

Saratoga County Chamber of Commerce. (518) 584–3255 or (800) 526–8970; www.saratoga.org.

Schenectady County Chamber of Commerce. (518) 372–5656 or (800) 962–8007; www.schenectadychamber.org.

Washington County Tourism. (518) 746–2294 or (888) 203–8622; www.washingtoncounty.org.

Leatherstocking Country. (315) 866–1500 or (800) 233–8778; www.leather stockingny.org.

Broome County Convention and Visitors Bureau. (607) 772–8860 or (800) 836–6740; www.binghamtoncvb.com.

Chenango County Chamber of Commerce. (607) 334–1400 or (800) 556–8596; www.chenangocounty.org.

Herkimer Chamber of Commerce. (315) 866–7820 or (877) 984–4636; www .herkimercountychamber.com.

Madison County Tourism Committee. (315) 684–7320 or (800) 684–7320; www.madisontourism.com.

Montgomery County Chamber of Commerce. (518) 842–8200 or (800) 743–7337; www.montgomerycountyny.com.

Oneida County Convention and Visitors Bureau. (315) 724–7221 or (800) 426–3132; www.oneidacountycvb.com.

Otsego County Chamber of Commerce. (607) 643–0059 or (800) 843–3394; www.cooperstown-otsego.com.

Schoharie County Chamber of Commerce. (518) 295–7033, (800) 418–4748, or (800) 41VISIT; www.schoharie chamber.com.

The Finger Lakes Region

Slender strands of sapphire water sparkle amid pastoral farmlands and craggy gorges, a glacier's good-bye caress during the last couple of ice ages. The Haudenosaunee believed the lakes were formed when the Great Spirit reached down to bless the land, leaving behind two handprints. Whatever version you believe, the Finger Lakes have undoubtedly been graced with the spirit of such great men and women as Samuel Clemens, Harriet Tubman, Tahgahjute, George Eastman, and Susan B. Anthony. This was the heart of the Iroquois Confederacy until 1779, when George Washington ordered the destruction of all Native American settlements in the region. The Industrial Revolution spurred factory growth, and country crossroads blossomed into major industrial hubs with the opening of the Erie Canal. The fertile farmlands fed the nation until the mid-nineteenth century, when the focus shifted to fruit orchards and vineyards. Today more than seventy wineries dot the glacial lake slopes, and the region is second only to California in domestic wine production.

Driving Tips

Running south from Syracuse, I–81 forms the eastern edge of this region, hemmed in the south by Route 17, in the west by I–390, and in the north by I–90, with Routes 14 and 89 cutting through the center, hugging the shores of the two largest Finger Lakes, Seneca and Cayuga.

THE FINGER LAKES REGION

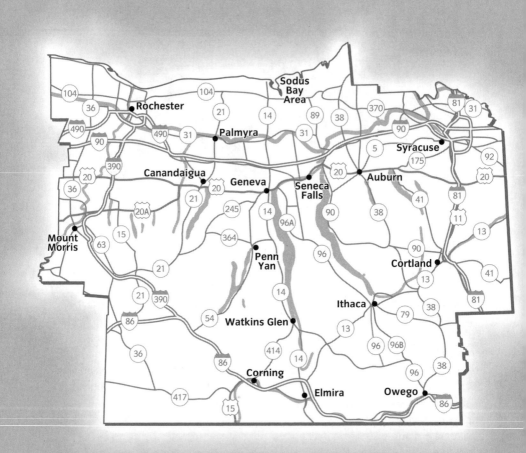

Syracuse

Syracuse is easily reached via I–481, I–81, I–90, and Routes 5 and 11.

Sprinkled with salt springs, this area was home to the Onondaga for thousands of years. With the opening of the Erie Canal, the town transformed into a major transportation and manufacturing hub. Incidentally, Syracuse was named after a Sicilian city that was also built around salt springs.

Erie Canal Museum (all ages)

318 Erie Boulevard (Route 5), at Montgomery Street; (315) 471–0593; www.eriecanal museum.org. Open Tuesday through Saturday 10:00 A.M. to 5:00 P.M., Sunday 10:00 A.M. to 3:00 P.M. Closed major holidays. Free, exception: guided tours $2.50. Donations accepted.

Housed in a former canal boat weighing station, this is also the area's Urban Cultural Park Visitor Center and a great place to learn about the world's most successful canal. Step aboard a 65-foot passenger cargo boat, check out the interactive exhibits in the Education Gallery, and view a film highlighting the adventurous history of Syracuse. Then pick up a free walking tour map and begin your adventure.

Rubenstein Museum of Science and Technology (MOST) (all ages)

500 South Franklin Street; (315) 425–9068; www.most.org. IMAX information (315) 473–IMAX. Open Wednesday through Sunday 11:00 A.M. to 5:00 P.M. Museum $, IMAX $$.

Hundreds of hands-on exhibits and activities fill three levels of this "most" fun science center. Create giant bubbles, freeze your shadow, explore ecosystems, or star search at the planetarium. Then head to the Bristol Omnitheatre to "Feel the Reel" at the IMAX dome theater.

The Rosamond Gifford Zoo at Burnet Park (all ages)

1 Conservation Place (off South Wilbur Avenue); (315) 435–8511; www.rosamondgifford zoo.org. Open year-round daily 10:00 A.M. to 4:30 P.M. Closed major holidays. Adults $$, children 3 to 15 $, under 3 free.

From sharks and sheep to snow leopards and Siberian tigers, there are hundreds of wild and domestic animals residing in naturalistic habitats at this thirty-two-acre zoo.

Beaver Lake Nature Center (all ages)

8477 East Mud Lake Road, Baldwinsville; (315) 638–2519; www.co.onondaga.ny.us. Open year-round from 7:30 A.M. to dusk. $

Eight marked trails, ranging from 0.25 to 3 miles in length, wrap around a 200-acre wilderness lake and meander through a variety of habitats. The visitor center offers a lot of hands-on exhibits and interpretive programs, including arts and crafts workshops, guided nature walks, and canoe tours.

More Syracuse **Area Museums**

Salt Museum. Route 370, Onondaga Lake Park, Onondaga Lake Parkway, Liverpool; (315) 453–6712 or (315) 453–6715; www.ongov.net. Free.

Sainte Marie Among the Iroquois. Route 370, Onondaga Lake Park, Onondaga Lake Parkway, Liverpool; (315) 451–7275; www.ongov.net. $

Everson Museum of Art. 401 Harrison Street, Syracuse, at State Street; (315) 474–6064; www.everson.org. $

Onondaga Historical Association Museum. 321 Montgomery Street, Syracuse; (315) 428–1864; www.cnyhistory.org. Free.

Wilcox Octagon House. 5420 West Genesee Street, Camillus; (315) 488–7800. Donation.

Where to Eat

Dinosaur Bar-B-Que. 246 West Willow Street; (315) 476–4937. Fun honky-tonk rib joint serving the best barbecue north of the Mason-Dixon line. $–$$

Doc's Little Gem Diner. 832 Spencer Street; (315) 422–1686. Classic '50s diner delights. $

Where to Stay

Embassy Suites. 6646 Old Collamer Road; (315) 446–3200 or (800) EMBASSY; www.embassy-suites.com. Kitchen suites, indoor pool, coin laundry, complimentary full breakfast. $$$$

Fairfield Inn by Marriott. 6611 Old Collamer Road; (315) 432–9333 or (800) 228–2800; www.marriott.com/fairfieldinn. Pool, adjacent restaurant, complimentary continental breakfast, and children under eighteen stay free. $$

Unusual Excursions in **Onondaga County**

Go behind the scenes of forests, farms, fish, furniture, and more, aboard boats, trains, and horse-drawn sleighs.

Cedarvale Maple Syrup Co. 3769 Pleasant Valley Road, Syracuse; (315) 469–6422; www.com-site.com/cedarvale.

Agway Farm Research Center. 6978 Route 80, Tully; (315) 683–5380.

Highland Forest Park. Highland Park Road, Fabius; (315) 683–5550; www.ongov.net.

L. & J. G. Stickley Furniture Factory. P.O. Box 480, Manlius; (315) 682–5500; www.stickley.com.

Mid-Lakes Navigation Company. 11 Jordan Street, Skaneateles; (315) 685–8500 or (800) 545–4318; www.midlakesnav.com.

Carrier Dome. 900 Irving Avenue, Syracuse; (315) 443–2121, or (888) DOMETIX; carrierdome.syr.edu.

OnTrack. 269 West Jefferson Street, Syracuse; (315) 424–1212 or (800) FOR–TRAIN.

The *Post-Standard*. 1 Clinton Square, Syracuse; (315) 470–2121.

Carpenter's Brook Fish Hatchery. P.O. Box 269, Elbridge 13060; (315) 689–9367.

The Museum of Automobile History. 321 North Clinton Street, Syracuse; (315) 478–9552.

Syracuse **Area Parks**

Camillus Erie Canal Park, Sims Store, and Lock Tender's Shanty. 5750 DeVoe Road, Camillus; (315) 488–3409 or (315) 672–5110; www.eriecanal camillus.com.

Old Erie Canal State Park. Andrus Road, DeWitt; (315) 687–7821; www.nys parks.com/parks.

Green Lakes State Park. 7900 Green Lakes Road, Route 5, Fayetteville; (315) 637–6111; www.nysparks.com/parks.

Baltimore Woods Nature Preserve. 4007 Bishop Hill Road, Marcellus; (315) 673–1350; www.takeahike.org.

Cortland

South on I–81.

Cortland is the ski capital of central New York, with three ski centers surrounded by fertile farmland.

1890 House Museum (ages 7 and up)
37 Tompkins Street; (607) 756–7551 or (607) 756–7552. Open May through December Tuesday through Sunday 1:00 to 4:00 P.M., January through April 1:00 P.M. to 3:00 P.M. Closed Monday and most major holidays. $, children under 12 free.

Located in the historic district, this restored Victorian chateau has thirty rooms full of antiques, stained-glass windows, and beautiful hand-carved woodwork.

Cortland's Country Music Park & Campground (all ages)
1804 Truxton Road, Route 13; (607) 753–0377; www .cortlandcountrymusicpark.com. Open daily year-round. $–$$$

Nicknamed the "Nashville of the East," this is the home of the New York State Country Music Hall of Fame. Kick up your heels to live music or line dance on one of New York's largest dance floors. Miniature golf and paddleboats are available when you're too tuckered to two-step.

Cortland County **Skiing**

Greek Peak. 2000 Route 392, Virgil; (607) 835–6111 or (800) 955–2754; www.greekpeak.net.

Labrador Mountain. 6935 North Road, Route 91, Truxton; (607) 842–6204 or (800) 446–9559; www.labradormtn.com.

Song Mountain. P.O. Box 149, Song Mountain Road, Tully 13141; (315) 696–5711 or (800) 677–SONG; www.songmountain.com.

Lime Hollow Nature Center (all ages)

3091 Gracie Road; (607) 758–5462; www.limehollow.org. Open daily year-round; trails open daylight hours, nature center open daily 9:00 A.M. to 4:30 P.M. Free.

Educational exhibits and a variety of nature trails offer opportunities to enjoy an interesting ecosystem.

Suggett House Museum (ages 6 and up)

25 Homer Avenue; (607) 756–6071; www.cortland.org. Open Tuesday through Saturday 1:00 to 4:00 P.M. Closed major holidays. $

Home of the Cortland County Historical Society, this nineteenth-century Italianate house offers exhibits on the home arts, military history, and a charming children's room complete with antique dolls and toys.

Where to Eat

Frank & Mary's Diner. 10 Port Watson Street; (607) 756–2014. Open twenty-four hours for home-style cooking. $

The Red Dragon. 222 Tompkins Street; (607) 753–7746. Rustic restaurant serving pizza, subs, chicken wings, and salads. $–$$

Where to Stay

Comfort Inn. 2 1/2 Locust Avenue; (607) 753–7721 or (800) 228–5150. Complimentary continental breakfast, twenty-four-hour adjacent restaurant. $$$–$$$$

Econolodge. 10 Church Street; (607) 756–2856 or (800) 800–0301. Restaurant nearby. $–$$$$

New York **Trivia**

The eleven Finger Lakes are Seneca, Cayuga, Canandaigua, Keuka, Hemlock, Honeoye, Owasco, Otisco, Canadice, Coneses, and Skaneateles.

Owego

Take Route 13 south to Route 38 south.

Located on the Susquehanna River, Owego was the home of Belva Lockwood, who, in 1884, became the first woman to run for the presidency of the United States.

Tioga County Historical Museum (ages 8 and up)
110 Front Street; (607) 687–2460; www.tiogahistory.org. Open year-round Tuesday through Saturday 10:00 A.M. to 4:00 P.M. Donation.

Native American artifacts, pioneer crafts and folk art, and local history exhibits can be found at this county museum and research library.

Tioga Scenic Railroad (all ages)
25 Delphine Street; (607) 687–6786; www.tiogascenicrailroad.com. Operating weekends July through October. Also dinner theater and holiday rides. $$–$$$

Ride the rails aboard a vintage train for an excursion to Newark Valley and the Bement/Billings Farmstead. Costumed guides welcome you at this nineteenth-century living-history museum, offering demonstrations of what life was like more than 150 years ago.

Tioga Gardens (all ages)
2217 Route 17C East; (607) 687–2940 or (800) 649–0494; www.tiogagardens.com. Summer: Monday through Friday 8:30 A.M. to 7:00 P.M., Saturday 8:30 A.M. to 5:00 P.M., Sunday 10:00 A.M. to 5:00 P.M. Winter: Monday through Friday 8:30 A.M. to 6:00 P.M., Saturday and Sunday 8:30 A.M. to 5:00 P.M. Free.

A two-acre water garden, a solar dome conservatory filled with rare and unusual plants, and a Japanese garden are featured at this lush tropical oasis.

Also in **the Area**

Bement Billings Farmstead. Route 38, Newark Valley; (607) 642–9516; www.tier.net/nvhistory/farm.htm.

The Newark Valley Depot Museum. Depot Street, Newark Valley; (607) 642–9516; www.tier.net/nvhistory/depot.htm.

Metro's Miniature Golf. Route 96, Owego; (607) 687–3080.

The New Owego Bowl. 1404 Taylor Road, Owego; (607) 687–5631.

New York **Trivia**

New York has more than 8,000 lakes, including Lake Champlain and Lake George.

Waterman Center (all ages)
403 Hilton Road, Apalachin; (607) 625–2221; www.watermancenter.org. Open daily Monday to Saturday 10:00 A.M. to 4:00 P.M., Sunday noon to 4:00 P.M. Free.

This nature museum offers interesting hands-on exhibits on the ecosystems of four wildlife refuges along the Susquehanna River and trail information for some fauna-filled nature hikes.

Where to Eat

Awakenings Coffeehouse. 208 Front Street; (607) 687–1336. Good brunch, lunch, desserts, and cappuccino. $$

Where to Stay

Owego Treadway Inn and Suites. 1100 New York 17C; (607) 687–4500; www.owegotreadway.com. Indoor pool and restaurant, located on river, and children under sixteen stay **free.** $$–$$$$

Sunrise Motel. 3778 Waverly Road; (607) 687–5666. Coffee shop and nearby swimming, fishing, and golf. $

Animal Agritainment in **Tioga County**

Crocker Creek Buffalo Farm. 3145 Dutchtown Road, Endicott; (607) 786–0571; www.angelfire.com/ny3/frontierdays.

Fallow Hollow Deer Farm. 125 Williams Road, Candor; (607) 659–4635; www.fallowhollow.com.

Mini Mounts Miniature Horse Farm. 195 Swartlick Road, Owego; (607) 687–4065.

Side Hill Acres Goat Farm. 79 Spencer Road, Candor; (607) 659–4121 or (888) 743–3445; www.sidehillacres.bizland.com.

Iron Kettle Farm. Route 96, Candor; (607) 659–7707; www.ironkettlefarm.com.

Ithaca

Head north on Route 96 to intersect with Route 96B.

Once the site of a thriving Cayuga community, Ithaca is situated at the southern shore of Cayuga Lake and surrounded by steep slopes and sparkling waterfalls. Stroll through the Commons, a lovely pedestrian mall where State and Tioga Streets meet, then walk north up Cayuga Street to see the cascades of Ithaca Falls, located off Falls Street.

Cornell **University**

The 745-acre dramatically beautiful campus of Cornell, an internationally acclaimed teaching and research university in Ithaca, includes more than 250 major buildings and a variety of natural areas, some open to the public. Below are several interesting places to explore **free** of charge, a real bargain in these days of tuition increases.

Cornell Plantations. One Plantation Road; (607) 255–2400; www .plantations.cornell.edu.

Sapsucker Woods Bird Sanctuary. 159 Sapsucker Woods Road; (607) 254–BIRD or (800) 843–BIRD; www.birds.cornell.edu.

Wilder Brain Collection. Uris Hall, 2nd floor, at East Avenue and Tower Road; (607) 255–6394 or (607) 254–INFO.

Herbert F. Johnson Museum of Art. University Avenue; (607) 255–6464; www.museum.cornell.edu.

Sagan **Planet Walk**

Billions and billions of stars twinkle over Ithaca every evening, but to get a closer view of the planets you'll have to take a walk. Stretching 1,200 meters from the Ithaca Commons to the Sciencenter is the Sagan Planet Walk, named for astronomer Carl Sagan. On a scale of one to five billion, the sun and nine planets are accurately sized and spaced and marked by monuments displaying fascinating facts and photos. Pick up a "Passport to the Solar System" at the Sciencenter or various other locations for $2.00 and get it stamped at each planet, and you'll receive a souvenir button and one free admission to the Sciencenter. (607) 272–0600; www.sciencenter.org/saganpw/.

Buttermilk Falls State Park (all ages)

Located 6 miles south of town off Route 13S; (607) 273–5761, (607) 273–3440, or (800) 456–CAMP; www.nysparks.com/parks. Park open year-round; campground open mid-May through October. $$

Cascading more than 500 feet down a series of ten waterfalls into a natural swimming pool at its base, this is a great place to cool off on a hot summer day. A scenic trail leads to Pinnacle Rock and Lake Treman, and there are ball fields, a playground, picnic areas, good creek and lake fishing, and campsites and cabins available.

The Sciencenter (all ages)

601 First Street at Franklin Street; (607) 272–0600; www.sciencenter.org. Open year-round Tuesday through Saturday 10:00 A.M. to 5:00 P.M., Sunday noon to 5:00 P.M., and holiday Mondays. Closed New Year's Day, Thanksgiving, and Christmas. Adults $$, seniors and children 3 to 17 $, children under 3 free.

This nationally acclaimed museum has more than a hundred hands-on interactive exhibits that offer families the opportunity to experience the excitement of science.

Robert H. Treman State Park (all ages)

Route 327, off Route 13S; (607) 273–3440; www.nysparks.com/parks. Park open year-round; campground open mid-May through October. $

Traverse the trails and craggy gorges of the Devil's Kitchen and Lucifer Falls, then revel in the rustic beauty of scenic Enfield Glen.

Performing **Arts of Ithaca**

The arts are alive in Ithaca, as evidenced by the vast array of venues for live self-expression. Below is a partial list of places to amuse the muse in your child. Call for performance schedules or stop by the Ticket Center in the lobby of the **Clinton House** (116 North Cayuga Street; 607–273–4497 or 800–28–ITHACA; www.ithacaevents.com) for one-stop ticket shopping.

Hangar Theatre. (607) 273–8588 or (800) 28–ITHACA; www.hangartheatre.org.

Kitchen Theatre. (607) 272–0403, (607) 273–4497, or (800) 28–ITHACA; www.kitchentheatre.com.

Ithaca College Theatre. (607) 274–3224.

Ithaca Ballet. (607) 277–1967.

The Schwartz Center for Performing Arts. (607) 254–2700; www.arts .cornell.edu/theatrearts.

Cayuga Chamber Orchestra. (607) 273–8981; www.cayugachamber orchestra.org.

Tompkins County Museum (ages 7 and up)

401 East State Street; (607) 273–8284; www.tompkinscountyhistory.org. Open year-round Tuesday, Thursday, and Saturday 11:00 A.M. to 5:00 P.M. Donation.

This excellent local museum highlights the history of the area. Drawing on a collection of thousands of artifacts and photographs, the exhibits focus on Ithaca's fascinating film heritage, industrial achievements, and regional arts.

Cayuga Nature Center (all ages)

1420 Taughannock Boulevard (Route 89); (607) 273–6260; www.cayuganaturecenter.org. Trails open year-round daily dawn to dusk. Free.

Five miles of marked nature trails lace through 135 miles of forests, fields, gorges, and waterfalls at this environmental education center. Live farm animals, a land lab, and forestry and agricultural exhibits are located at the farmstead, and a variety of nature programs and seasonal festivals are scheduled on weekends.

Ithaca **Boat Trips**

Cruise the Cayuga aboard a variety of vessels sure to satisfy the skippers and seadogs in your crew.

M/V Manhattan. (607) 256–0898; www.cayugalakecruises.com.

Loon-A-Sea Charters. (607) 387–5474.

Alcyone II Sailing Charter. (607) 272–7963; www.14850.com/web/alcyone.

Allen Treman State Marine Park. (607) 272–1460.

Cayuga Boat Rentals & Ferry. (607) 277–5072.

Puddle Dockers Kayak Shop. (607) 273–0096.

Paleontological Research Institution (all ages)

1259 Trumansburg Road; (607) 273–6623; www.priweb.org. Open Memorial Day through Labor Day daily 10:00 A.M. to 5:00 P.M. and Labor Day through Memorial Day Monday and Wednesday through Saturday 10:00 A.M. to 5:00 P.M., Sunday noon to 4:00 P.M. Call to confirm hours. Adults $$, children $.

Founded in 1932, this is one of the largest fossil collections in the country. A Tyrannosaurus rex cast and the world's largest sea scorpion fossil are on display, along with exhibits on New York's geology and unusual fossil finds.

Taughannock Falls State Park (all ages)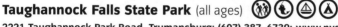

2221 Taughannock Park Road, Trumansburg; (607) 387–6739; www.nysparks.com/parks. Park open year-round; campground open April through mid-October. $

Possibly one of the prettiest falls in the state and 30 feet higher than Niagara, the Taughannock Creek plunges 215 feet down, past a dramatic steep stone amphitheater. The 783-acre park offers campsites, cabins, hiking trails, swimming, fishing, rowboat rentals, a picnic and playground area, recreation programs, and a summer concert series.

Also in **the Area**

Greater Ithaca Art Trail. Community Arts Partnership of Tompkins County, The Clinton House, 116 North Cayuga Street, Ithaca; (607) 273–5072, ext. 2; www.arttrail.com.

Ithaca Farmers' Market. P.O. Box 6575, Ithaca 14851; (607) 273–6952; www.ithacamarket.com.

Deere Haven Museum (all ages)
County Road 141, between Routes 89 and 96, Interlacken; (607) 532–4288. Open year-round, but call for hours. **Free.**

Dick Bauer's wonderful collection of children's antique toys, pedal cars, and rare farm implements housed in a replica of a 1775 Dutch barn, with more than eighty antique farm machines parked outside.

Where to Eat

The Station Restaurant. 806 West Buffalo Street; (607) 272–2609; www.ithaca station.com. Located in a real train station, complete with train, serving Italian-American specialties, plus a children's menu. $$–$$$

Taughannock Farms Inn. 2030 Gorge Road, across from Taughannock Falls State Park, Trumansburg; (607) 387–7711; www.t-farms.com. Three-course steak, seafood, chicken, or pasta dinners, with child's portions available. $$$$

Horses, Skates, Cars, and
Carousels in the Ithaca Area

Patchwork Therapeutic Riding Center. 90 Old Peruville Road, Groton; (607) 898–3808; e-mail: Patchwork2@hotmail.com.

Cass Park Rink and Pool. 701 Taughannock Boulevard, Ithaca; (607) 273–9211.

The Rink. 1767 East Shore Drive, off Route 34, Ithaca; (607) 277–RINK.

Ringwood Raceway. Ringwood Road, off Route 13, Freeville; (607) 347–4198.

Stewart Park and Carousel. Corner of Routes 13 and 34, Ithaca; (607) 273–8364.

Freebrook Farms. 39 Fall Creek Road, Freeville; (607) 844–8754.

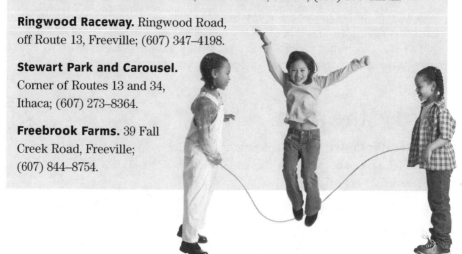

Where to Stay

Clarion University Hotel. 1 Sheraton Drive; (607) 257–2000; www.clarion hotel.com. Rooms and suites, with indoor pool, restaurant, and children under eighteen stay **free.** $$$$

Statler Hotel. 11 East Avenue; (607) 257–2500 or (800) 541–2501; www.hotelschool.cornell.edu/statler. Located on Cornell campus, with restaurant, room service, and pool, golf, and tennis privileges at university facilities. $$$$

Auburn

Head north on Route 34B to Route 34 north.

Located north of Lake Owasco, this is the birthplace of Abner Doubleday, the inventor of baseball; Tahgahjute (Logan), the great Cayuga orator; Millard Fillmore, U.S. president; and T. E. Case, the inventor of sound movies.

Emerson Park (all ages)

6879 East Lake Road, Route 38A; (315) 253–5611; www.co.cayuga.ny.us/parks/emerson. Merry-Go-Round Playhouse (315) 255–1785, (315) 255–1305, or (800) 457–8897; www.merry-go-round.com. Agricultural Museum (315) 252–7644. Open dawn to dusk. Parking fee $; donations requested for museums.

Located on the northern shore of Owasco Lake, Emerson Park has something for everyone in the family. Swimming, fishing, and boat rentals are available for lake lovers, and a huge playground area includes classic swings and slides with a carousel, roller coaster, and other kiddie rides. The Merry-Go-Round Playhouse stages five professional musicals every summer. The Ward O'Hara Agricultural Museum features farm tools and tractors, a 1900 farm kitchen, creamery, blacksmithery, woodshop, vet's office, general store, and herb garden. The Cayuga Museum Iroquois Center highlights the history and heritage of the prehistoric Owasco and present-day Cayuga cultures.

Auburn **Amusements**

Reese's Dairy Bar & Miniature Golf. Routes 5 and 20; (315) 252–7323.

Arnold Palmer Miniature Golf. Gates Road, off Route 5; (315) 253–8072.

Finger Lakes Drive-In. Routes 5 and 20; (315) 252–3969.

Reva Rollerdrome. 357 West Genesee Street; (315) 252–8225.

Other Parks **in the Area**

Fillmore Glen State Park. RD 3, Box 26 (off Route 38), Moravia; (315) 497–0130; www.nysparks.com/parks.

Long Point State Park. Lake Road (off Route 90), Aurora; (315) 497–0130; www.nysparks.com/parks.

Casey Park. 120 North Division Street, Auburn; (315) 255–4120; www.auburn ny.virtualtownhall.net.

Bear Swamp State Forest. 1285 Fisher Avenue, Cortland; (607) 753–3095 or (800) 388–8244.

Howland Island Wildlife Management Area. Howland Island Road, Port Byron; (607) 753–3095 or (800) 388–8244, ext. 247.

Harriett Tubman Home (all ages)

180 South Street; (315) 252–2081; www.harriettubmanhome.org. **Open February through October Tuesday through Friday 11:00 A.M. to 4:00 P.M., Saturday 10:00 A.M. to 3:00 P.M. $**

Born a slave in 1821, Harriet Tubman escaped to freedom in the North in 1849. Known as the "Moses of her people," she made nineteen dangerous trips south in eleven years, risking her life to deliver more than 300 slaves to freedom via the Underground Railroad. She also served as a nurse, scout, and spy for the Union Army.

Seward House (all ages)

33 South Street; (315) 252–1283; www.sewardhouse.org. **Open February through June and mid-October through December Tuesday through Saturday 1:00 to 4:00 P.M.; July through mid-October Tuesday through Saturday 10:00 A.M. to 4:00 P.M., Sunday 1:00 to 4:00 P.M. $**

Home for more than fifty years to William Henry Seward, who was governor of New York, a U.S. senator, secretary of state to Abraham Lincoln, and promoter of the purchase of that Russian property, Alaska. Take a guided tour of the seventeen-room Federal-style house, once a stop on the Underground Railroad, and you will see an amazing collection of rare and unusual souvenirs from Seward's travels and career.

Cayuga Museum and Case Research Lab (ages 7 and up)

203 West Genesee Street; (315) 253–8051; www.cayuganet.org/cayugamuseum. **Open Tuesday through Friday 10:00 A.M. to 5:00 P.M., Saturday and Sunday noon to 5:00 P.M. Closed Thanksgiving, Christmas, and New Year's Day. Free.**

Permanent and changing exhibits highlighting the history of Cayuga County can be found in this Greek Revival mansion, from Native American culture to Civil War relics. In a building behind the Willard Case Mansion is the research laboratory of Theodore W. Case, where, in 1923, the "talkies" were born.

Horses, Ponies, and Sheep, **Oh My!**

Fans of farm animals will find a flock of furry fauna in Cayuga County.

Moravia Downs. VFW Fairgrounds, off Route 38, Moravia; (607) 539–7440.

Moses Mountain Horseback Riding. 1504 Lick Street, Moravia; (315) 497–3412.

Daly's Equestrian Center. 1912 Townline Road, Union Spring; (315) 253–9274.

Auburn Doubledays (all ages)

103 North Division Street; (315) 255–2489; www.auburndoubledays.com. Season runs June through September. $

Named for baseball founder Abner Doubleday, this single A farm team for the Houston Astros has been playing in the New York–Penn League for more than forty years. Take everyone out to the ballgame some summer night for half the cost of a movie, and twice as many memories.

Roadster Rooters, **Rejoice!**

Weedsport is the speed sport capital of Cayuga County. Around this town wheels rule, so rally the crew and race over to:

DIRT Motorsport Hall of Fame and Classic Car Museum. Route 31, Cayuga County Fairgrounds, Weedsport; (315) 834–6667; www.dirt motorsports.com.

Weedsport Speedway and Rolling Wheels. 1 Speedway Drive, Cayuga County Fairgrounds, Weedsport; (315) 834–6606 or (315) 689–7809; www.dirtmotorsports.com.

Agritainment

The bounty of the county is a beauty to behold. Tour these friendly farms for an up close and personal look at an important link in the food chain.

Hillcrest Dairy. West Cayuga Street, Moravia; (315) 497–0659.

Grisamore Farms. Route 90, Locke; (315) 497–1347.

Joyful Acres. 1020 Howell Road, Port Byron; (315) 776–4548.

Where to Eat

Auburn Family Restaurant. 161 Genesee Street; (315) 253–2274. Home cooking. $

Lasca's. 252 Grant Avenue; (315) 253–4885. Seafood, steak, chicken, and pasta specialties, with a children's menu. $$$

Where to Stay

Springside Inn. 6141 West Lake Road (Route 38S); (315) 252–7247; www .springsideinn.com. Restored nineteenth-century inn, formerly a boys' school, with seven rooms, complimentary continental breakfast, and a terrific restaurant. $$

Whispering Winds Motel. 4233 East Genesee Street, Route 20; (315) 685–6056; www.skaneateles.com/whisperingwinds. Twelve rooms and a pool. $$

Seneca Falls

From Auburn, take Routes 5 and 20 west to Seneca Falls.

"We hold these truths to be self-evident; that all men and women are created equal." So began the Declaration of Sentiments, written in 1848 in Seneca Falls, the birthplace of the women's rights movement in America.

Seneca Falls Heritage Center (all ages)

115 Fall Street; (315) 568–2703; www.senecafallsheritage.com. Open year-round Monday through Saturday 10:00 A.M. to 4:00 P.M., Sunday noon to 4:00 P.M. Free.

This interpretive center explores the area's history of industry and transportation and its heritage of social reform.

Seneca Falls Historical Society (all ages)

55 Cayuga Street; (315) 568–8412; www.welcome.to/sfhs. Open year-round weekdays noon to 5:00 P.M. and Saturday and Sunday (July through September) 1:00 to 5:00 P.M. Closed holidays. $

A variety of permanent and changing exhibits can be found in this lovely twenty-five-room 1880 Queen Anne mansion. Children will especially enjoy the colorful collection of costumes and the unusual circus toys found in the playroom.

National Women's Hall of Fame (ages 6 and up)

76 Fall Street; (315) 568–8060; www.greatwomen.org. Open May through September Monday through Saturday 10:00 A.M. to 4:00 P.M., Sunday noon to 4:00 P.M.; October through April Wednesday through Saturday 10:00 A.M. to 4:00 P.M. Closed major holidays and January. $

This museum and education center offers exhibits and displays honoring the achievements of American women.

Women's Rights National Historical Park and Visitor's Center (ages 6 and up)

136 Fall Street; (315) 568–2991; www.nps.gov/wori/. Open daily year-round 9:00 A.M. to 5:00 P.M. Closed major holidays except Memorial Day, July 4, and Labor Day. Adults $, under 17 free.

Located across the street from the ruins of the Wesleyan Chapel and site of the first Women's Rights Convention, this center offers an orientation film, interactive videos, exhibits on political issues ranging from women's employment and sports to fashion and marriage, and ranger-conducted tours.

Elizabeth Cady Stanton House (ages 6 and up)

32 Washington Street; (315) 568–2991; www.nps.gov/wori/. Open daily 9:00 A.M. to 5:00 P.M. $

In the mid-nineteenth century, women in America were not allowed to own property or money, be legal guardians of their own children, or vote. Exhibits highlight Stanton's life and times in the restored Greek Revival home where she raised her family and the nation's consciousness.

Montezuma National Wildlife Refuge (all ages)

3395 Routes 5 and 20 East; (315) 568–5987; www.fws.gov/r5mnwr. Open year-round dawn to dusk. Free.

This 7,000-acre haven is a terrific place to observe more than 300 species of migrating birds and other wetlands wildlife. A popular and easy nature hike for families is the 2-mile Esker Brook Trail.

Seneca **County Bounty**

Lively Run Goat Dairy. 8978 Country Road 142, Interlaken; (607) 532–4647.

Schuster Farms. 1883 Route 89, Seneca Falls; (315) 568–9337.

The Luce Farm. 7381 Hall Road, Ovid; (607) 532–9475.

Sampson State Park (all ages)

6096 Route 96A, Romulus; (315) 585–6392. Museum (315) 585–6203; www.nysparks
.com/parks. Park open daily year-round. Museum open Memorial Day weekend through
Labor Day Wednesday through Sunday 10:00 A.M. to 4:00 P.M., Labor Day through Columbus
Day weekends only. **Free,** vehicle fee $$.

On the shores of Seneca Lake, this 1,852-acre park is the home of the Sampson Memorial
Naval Museum. The park offers hiking and nature trails, ball fields and courts, a play-
ground and picnic area, swimming with a sand beach, lake fishing, bicycling, a recreation
program, and great terrain for winter sledding, cross-country skiing, and snowshoeing.

Where to Eat

Abigail's Restaurant. 1978 Routes 5 and
20, between Seneca Falls and Waterloo;
(315) 539–9300. All-you-can-eat luncheon
buffet, on a deck overlooking Seneca-
Cayuga canal. $–$$

Mac's Drive-In. 511 Routes 5 and 20,
Waterloo; (315) 539–3064. Carhop service
at the area's largest drive-in, serving
chicken, shrimp, burgers, hot dogs, root
beer, and ice cream. $

Also in **the Area**

Memorial Day Museum. 35 East Main Street, Waterloo; (315) 539–0533.

Scythe Tree. Routes 5 and 20, 2 miles west of Waterloo; (315) 568–2906 or
(800) SEC–1848; www.seneca.org.

Cayuga Lake State Park. 2678 Lower Lake Road, Seneca Falls; (315)
568–5163; www.nysparks.com/parks.

Terwilliger Museum. 31 East Williams Street, Waterloo; (315) 539–0533.

Erie Canal Cruise Lines. 5 Water Street, Seneca Falls; (800) 962–1771.

Where to Stay

Inland Motel. 984 Waterloo-Geneva Road, Waterloo; (315) 539–0604. Ten rooms, located on Cayuga-Seneca canal. $

Tillinghast Manor Bed and Breakfast. 7246 South Main Street, Ovid; (607) 869–3584. An 1873 Victorian home with four rooms, family-style full breakfast, and children are welcome. $$–$$$

Geneva

Take Routes 5 and 20 west.

Known as Kanadesaga by the Seneca who lived here until the eighteenth century, Geneva is also where Elizabeth Blackwell became the first woman in America to earn her medical diploma.

Prouty-Chew House (ages 7 and up)

543 South Main Street; (315) 789–5151; www.fingerlakes.org. Open year-round Tuesday through Friday 9:30 A.M. to 4:30 P.M., Saturday 1:30 to 4:30 P.M., plus Sunday 1:30 to 4:30 P.M. in July and August. Closed holidays. Free.

This nineteenth-century Federal-style mansion is the home of the Geneva Historical Society, and there are several interesting exhibits on the area's history and culture. Walking and driving tour maps are available here as well.

Rose Hill Mansion (ages 7 and up)

East Lake Road, Route 96A; (315) 789–3848. Open May through November Monday through Saturday 10:00 A.M. to 4:00 P.M., Sunday 1:00 to 5:00 P.M. $

Overlooking Seneca Lake, this beautiful 1838 Greek Revival estate is a National Historic Landmark with twenty-one period rooms filled with elegant Empire-style furniture.

Seneca Lake State Park (all ages)

100 Waterloo/Geneva Road, Routes 5 and 20; (315) 789–2331; www.nysparks.com/parks. Open year-round daily sunrise to sunset. Vehicle fee $.

A favorite place for swimming and fishing, this park also features a marina, picnic area, and playground.

Also in **the Area**

Seneca Cruise Company. 212 High Street; (315) 789–1822 or (800) 756–7269.

Where to Eat

Emile's. East North Street, 3 miles east on Routes 5 and 20; (315) 789–2775. Continental cuisine, featuring prime rib, baby back ribs, seafood, salad bar, and a children's menu. $–$$$

Pasta Only's Cobblestone Restaurant. 258 Hamilton Street, 1 mile west on Routes 5 and 20; (315) 789–8498; www.pastaonlyscobblestone.com. Classic wood-fired-grill cooking, featuring fresh pasta, chicken, seafood, and Italian specialties. $$$

Where to Stay

Belhurst Castle. Box 609, Lochland Road, on Route 14 South; (315) 781–0201; www.belhurstcastle.com. Fourteen rooms in a century-old Romanesque stone castle full of antiques and stained glass, sitting in a twenty-acre park overlooking Seneca Lake, with a great restaurant. $$$$

Chanticleer Motor Inn. 473 Hamilton Street; (315) 789–7600 or (800) 441–5227; www.chanticleerlodge.com. Rooms, some with kitchens; complimentary continental breakfast. $

Geneva-on-the-Lake. 1001 Lochland Road, Route 14 South; (315) 789–7190 or (800) 3–GENEVA; www.GenevaOnThe-Lake.com. Kitchen suites in an Italianate villa with private lakefront, sailing, tennis, golf privileges, swimming pool, and a restaurant with terrace. $$$$

Lake **Drums**

For centuries local folks have spoken of unusual rumbling sounds coming from the middle of Seneca Lake. Native Americans thought the eerie noises were the drums of their gods or ancestors, but scientists today believe the booms may be the result of methane gas bubbling up from cracks in the lake bed. Some still summer night, sit by Seneca Lake and see if you can spot some of the pure-white deer said to wander the eastern shore, and listen carefully for the music of the "lake drums."

Penn Yan

Take Route 14 south to Route 54 south.

Located on the northern tip of slingshot-shaped Keuka Lake, this peaceful village was named for the Pennsylvanians and Yankees who settled here in the early nineteenth century.

The Outlet Trail (all ages)

A convenient access point, next to a playground, is at the Public Boat Launch near the corner of Water and Keuka Streets; (315) 536–3111, (315) 536–8895, or (800) 868–9283; www.yatesny.com. For complete trail assistance stop at the visitor center at 2375 Route 14A, south of the village. Free.

This 7-mile linear trail follows an abandoned railroad bed along the Keuka Outlet, which links Keuka and Seneca Lakes. Although the trail descends nearly 300 feet, it's an easy and scenic hike past woods, wildlife, waterfalls, and old abandoned mill towns.

Keuka Lake State Park (all ages)

3370 Pepper Road, Bluff Point; (315) 536–3666; www.nysparks.com/parks. Park open year-round; campground open mid-May through mid-October. Vehicle fee $.

Located 6 miles southwest of Penn Yan, this 621-acre park along the shores of Keuka Lake offers swimming with a gravel beach, good fishing, docks and a boat launch, a playground, picnic area, hiking trails, and 150 campsites.

Glenn H. Curtiss Museum (ages 5 and up)

8419 Route 54, Hammondsport; (607) 569–2160; www.linkny.com/curtissmuseum. Open May through October Monday through Saturday 9:00 A.M. to 5:00 P.M., Sunday 11:00 A.M. to 5:00 P.M.; November through April Monday through Saturday 10:00 A.M. to 4:00 P.M., Sunday noon to 5:00 P.M. Adults $$, children 7 to 18 $, under 7 free.

A motorcycle, airplane, and dirigible daredevil, Curtiss made the world's first preannounced airplane flight, developed the world's first amphibian plane, opened the first flight school in this country, and was awarded the first U.S. pilot's license. Historical aircraft and a great collection of vintage motorcycles are here, and visitors can watch a 1913 flying boat being constructed.

C. E. K. Mees Observatory (ages 6 and up)

6586 Gannett Hill Road, Naples; (585) 275–4385. Call for summer tours, available with reservations, Friday and Saturday evenings. Free.

Do a bit of star searching with this observatory's 24-inch telescope on a clear summer night.

Cruising on **Keuka Lake**

Viking Spirit **Cruise Ship.** Route 54, 680 East Lake Road, Penn Yan; (315) 536–7061; www.vikingresort.com.

Keuka Maid **Dinner Boat.** Route 54, Champlain Beach, Hammondsport; (607) 569–BOAT (2628).

Where to Eat

Miller's Essenhaus. 1300 Route 14A, Benton Center; (315) 531–8260. Amish cuisine, famous for whoopie and shoo-fly pie and barbecue sandwiches. $–$$

Where to Stay

ABC's Rentals. 295 West Lake Road; (315) 536–6623. Variety of two- to five-bedroom houses for rent, located on lake, with swimming, fishing, and boating. $$$–$$$$

Flint Creek Campground. 1455 Phelps Road; (585) 554–3567 or (800) 914–3550. Playground, mini-golf, laundry, hayrides, hiking trails, fishing pond, and children's activities. $

Viking Resort. 680 East Lake Road, Route 54; (315) 536–7061; www.viking resort.com. Rooms, apartments, suites, and efficiencies, with outdoor pool, private lakeshore, fishing, boating, and cruises on the Keuka Lake aboard the Viking Spirit. $–$$$$

Also in **the Area**

Keuka Karts Go Kart Track. 98 Westlake Road, Penn Yan; (315) 536–4833 or (315) 595–6613; e-mail: Kkarts@eznet.net.

Star View Bowling Lanes. Route 14A, Penn Yan; (315) 536–9595.

Sugar Shack Blueberry Farm. 824 East Swamp Road, Penn Yan; (585) 526–5442.

The Windmill Farm & Craft Market. 3900 Route 14A, Penn Yan; (315) 536–3032; www.thewindmill.com.

Black Rock Speedway. Route 14A South, Dundee; (607) 243–8686; www.blackrockspeedway.com.

Agricultural Memories Museum. 1110 Townline Road, Penn Yan; (315) 536–1206.

Other Parks **in the Area**

Red Jacket Park. Lake Street, Route 54, Penn Yan; (315) 536–3015.

Indian Pines Park. Route 54A, Penn Yan; (315) 536–3015.

High Tor Wildlife Area. Route 245, at Canandaigua Lake, Naples; (585) 226–2466.

Cumming Nature Center. 6472 Gulick Road, Naples; (585) 374–6160; www.rmsc.org.

Watkins Glen

Take Route 54 east to Route 14 south.

Situated on the southern shore of Seneca Lake, this is the home of American road racing and the site of some seriously spectacular waterfalls.

Watkins Glen State Park (ages 5 and up)
North Franklin Street, junction of Routes 14 and 414; (607) 535–4511; www.nys parks.com/parks. Open daily mid-May through late October 8:00 A.M. to dusk. Free. Timespell (607) 535–8888 or (800) 853–SPELL. $$

Running through the heart of this park is a dramatic gorge bejeweled by nineteen waterfalls and creek-carved crags. Hike the 1.5-mile Gorge Trail, nature's version of the Stairmaster, up 832 stone steps through tunnels and over bridges to the top, where you can hop a shuttle bus or walk back to the entrance. The park also offers an Olympic-size swimming pool, ball fields, a playground and picnic area, recreation programs, 305 campsites, and the popular Finger Lakes Hiking Trail and the North Country National Scenic Trail. When darkness descends, Timespell takes visitors on a sound, light, and laser journey through the creation of this 550-million-year-old gift from the glaciers.

Farm Sanctuary (all ages)
3100 Aikens Road, off Route 23, next door to Sugar Hill State Forest, 8 miles west of town; (607) 583–2225; www.farmsanctuary.org. Guided tours on the hour 11:00 A.M. to 3:00 P.M. Wednesday through Sunday from June through August, weekends in May, September, and October. $

Guided tours of the barns, along with an educational visitor center, gift shop, and vegetarian snack shop are offered, with bed-and-breakfast cabins available for overnight guests.

Speedsters and **Sailors**

Watkins Glen International Raceway. County Road 16; (607) 535–2486; www.theglen.com. Off Route 14/414, 4 miles south of Watkins Glen.

Seneca Daysails. Public Fishing Pier; (607) 535–LAKE; www.seneca daysails.com.

Captain Bill's Seneca Lake Cruises (all ages)

1 1/2 North Franklin Street; (607) 535–4541. Cruises May through October, daily 10:00 A.M. to 8:00 P.M. $$–$$$

Take a 10-mile one-hour scenic voyage on Seneca Lake, or dine on deck during an evening dinner cruise.

Where to Eat

Curly's Family Restaurant. 2780 Route 14; (607) 535–4383. Good breakfasts as well as steak, seafood, vegetarian and Italian specialties, and a children's menu. $

Savard's Family Restaurant. Corner of Franklin and Sixth Streets; (607) 535–4538. Extensive menu and friendly service. $

Where to Stay

Hawaii on the Lake. Junction of Routes 14 and 14A; (607) 535–4232. Rooms, efficiencies, and cabins, on a forty-acre site, with picnic areas and nice views of Seneca Lake. $–$$$$

Seneca Lodge. Route 329, off Route 14, at south entrance to Watkins Glen State Park; (607) 535–2014. Main lodge, motel rooms, cabins, and A-frames, with restaurant, pool, and hiking trails. $$

More Parks around **Watkins Glen**

Finger Lakes National Forest. 5218 Route 414, Logan Road, Hector; (607) 546–4470; www.fs.fed.us/.

Havana Glen Park. 135 Havana Glen Road, Montour Falls; (607) 535–9476.

Catherine Valley Marsh. Off Route 14, Montour Falls; (607) 535–4300 or (800) 607–4552.

New York **Trivia**

The Iroquois Confederacy's Great Law of Peace proposed the rights of freedom of speech, equal representation, and impeachment and served as a framework for the U.S. Constitution.

Elmira

Continue south on Route 14.

Known as the Soaring Capital of America and Mark Twain's town, Elmira also has the largest concentration of Victorian-era architecture in the state. Take the trolley for a terrific $2.00 tour of historical highlights, departing hourly in summer from the Riverview Holiday Inn.

Mark Twain's Study (ages 6 and up)
**One Park Place; Elmira College Campus, off Route 14; (607) 735–1941; www.elmira.edu\
academic/ar_marktwain.shtml. Open June through Labor Day Monday through Saturday
9:00 A.M. to 5:00 P.M. Free.**

Tom Sawyer and Huckleberry Finn were born here, sprung from the imaginative mind of Samuel Clemens, better known as Mark Twain.

Harris Hill Park & National Soaring Museum (all ages)
**51 Soaring Hill Drive (off Route 352), Harris Hill; (607) 734–0641 or (607) 796–2988;
www.soaringmuseum.org. Harris Hill Park (607) 737–2843; www.harrishillsoaring.org. Open
daily year-round 10:00 A.M. to 5:00 P.M. Closed some major holidays. Adults $$, children $
(sailplane rides $$$$).**

More than a dozen vintage sailplanes are hangared here, the largest collection of its kind in the world. During regattas and festivals, the gliders take to the skies like flocks of silent pterodactyls. Although rides may not be recommended for young children, the view from the blue is spectacular. Inside the museum are scale models of gliders, from 1833 to today, that will appeal to professional and pretend pilots alike. The park also features miniature golf, go-karts, driving range, swimming pool, and small amusement rides.

Science and Discovery Center (all ages)

Arnot Mall, 3300 Chambers Road, Horseheads; (607) 739–5297; www.sciencenter.org. Open year-round Monday through Saturday 10:00 A.M. to 6:00 P.M., Sunday 11:00 A.M. to 6:00 P.M. $

Hands-on interactive science displays and exhibits.

Tanglewood Nature Center (all ages)

246 West Hill Road; (607) 732–6060; www.tangle-wood.org. Trails open year-round dawn to dusk; center open May through October Monday through Saturday 9:00 A.M. to 5:00 P.M., Sunday 11:00 A.M. to 5:00 P.M.; November through April closes at 4:00 P.M. Monday through Saturday and 3:00 P.M. Sunday. $

Marked nature trails perfect for families to explore the local flora and fauna.

Park Station Recreation Area (all ages)

2 West Beaver Pond Road, Erin; (607) 739–9164. Open daily 8:00 A.M. to sunset; campground opens in March. Summer weekends $$.

Hiking, swimming, boating, and camping at this artificial lake.

Newtown Battlefield Park (all ages)

Lowman Road, off Route 17; (607) 737–2843 (before Memorial Day), (607) 732–6067 (after Memorial Day). Open Memorial Day through Columbus Day. Free.

The site of Gen. John Sullivan's victory over the Iroquois during the Revolutionary War is now a 330-acre county park offering camping, hiking, and picnicking.

Where to Eat

Maple Lawn Dairy Family Restaurant. 3162 Lower Maple Avenue; (607) 733–0519. Homemade ice cream; breakfast, lunch, and dinner; special fish-fry nights. $

Where to Stay

Gardner Hill Campground. 1451 Norway Road, Lowman; (607) 732–9827. Campsites, three cabins, a swimming pool, and a restaurant nearby. $

Mark Twain Motor Inn. 1996 Lake Street; (607) 733–9144. Restaurant nearby. $

Red Jacket Motel. 489 Route 17; (607) 734–1616 or (800) 562–5808. Pool and coin laundry on the premises. $$

Also in **the Area**

Elmira Pioneers Baseball Team. Dunn Field Stadium, 546 Luce Street; (607) 734–1270; www.elmirapioneers.com.

Other Museums **in Elmira**

Chemung Valley History Museum. 415 East Water Street, Elmira; (607) 734–4167; www.chemungvalleymuseum.org. **Free.**

Arnot Museum. 235 Lake Street, Elmira; (607) 734–3697; www.arnotart museum.org. $

National Warplane Museum. 17 Aviation Drive, Horseheads; (607) 739–8200; www.wingsofeagles.com. $

Corning

Take Route 17 west.

Take a walk down the Crystal City's Market Street, a restored nineteenth-century historic district with boutiques, museums, and glass studios all along the brick-paved sidewalks and tree-lined streets.

Corning Museum of Glass (all ages)
1 Museum Way; (607) 974–2000, (607) 937–5371, or (800) 732–6845; www.cmog.org. Open daily year-round 9:00 A.M. to 5:00 P.M.; to 8:00 P.M. in July and August. Closed major holidays. $$, children under 17 free.

Gaze at 3,500 years of glittering glass, gleaned from the museum's collection of more than 35,000 priceless objects displayed in the Art and History and the Sculpture Galleries. Glass you can touch, bend, and play with can be found at the **Glass Innovation Center,** with a variety of interesting interactive tech and manufacturing exhibits. The amazing **Hot Glass Show,** where artisans craft crystalline creations, is not to be missed! Finally, tour the **Steuben Factory**, the only place in the world to see Steuben glass being melted, molded, cut, polished, and engraved.

Rockwell Museum of Western Art (all ages)
111 Cedar Street; (607) 937–5386; www.rockwellmuseum.org. Open Monday through Sunday 10:00 A.M. to 4:00 P.M. year-round; May, June, September, and October 9:00 A.M. to 5:00 P.M.; July through Labor Day 9:00 A.M. to 8:00 P.M. Closed major holidays. Adults $$, children under 18 free.

Housed in the historic Old City Hall, this is considered to be the most comprehensive collection of art of the American West in the East. Upstairs are more than 2,000 objects of Steuben glass designed by Frederick Carder. Of special interest is the collection of antique toys, with a hands-on activity area just for children.

Also in **the Area**

Nasser Civic Center Ice Rink. At Pearl and Denison Streets, Corning; (607) 962–8146.

Birdseye Hollow Park and State Forest. 7291 Coon Road, Bath; (607) 776–2165.

Mossy Bank Park and Nature Center. Mossy Bank Park Road, Bath; (607) 776–3811.

Pinnacle State Park. 1904 Pinnacle Road, Addison; (607) 359–2767; www.nysparks.com/parks.

Vitrix Hot Glass Studio. 77 West Market Street, Corning; (607) 936–8707; www.vitrixhotglass.com.

Hands-on Glass. 124 Crystal Lane, Corning; (607) 962–3044; www.handson glass.com.

Patterson Inn Museum Complex (all ages)
59 West Pulteney Street; (607) 937–5281; www.corningny.com/bpinn. Open mid-March through mid-December weekdays 10:00 A.M. to 4:00 P.M. Closed major holidays. $

Costumed guides bring nineteenth-century America to life at this complex of historic buildings that include a settler's cabin, schoolhouse, tavern, blacksmith shop, and agricultural exhibits.

Spencer Crest Nature Center (all ages)
Powder House Road, 2 miles south up the hill; (607) 962–2169. Trails open daily dawn to dusk year-round. Nature center open Monday through Saturday 9:00 A.M. to 3:00 P.M. Free, $ for programs.

Wander 7 miles of nature trails winding through 250 acres of woods, or take in a variety of educational programs for families.

New York State Fish Hatchery (all ages)
7169 Fish Hatchery Road, Bath; (607) 776–7087. Open daily 8:00 A.M. to 3:45 P.M. Call for weekend hours. Free.

Nearly a million fish, from fry to a foot long.

Where to Eat

Spencer's Restaurant and Mercantile.
359 East Market Street; (607) 936–9196.
Largest menu in the area, serving homemade soups, steaks, seafood, pasta, daily
fish fry, and children's meals. $$–$$$$

Three Birds Restaurant. 73–75 East His-
toric Market Street; (607) 936–TUNA;

www.threebirdsrestaurant.com. Steak and
seafood specialties. $$–$$$$

Where to Stay

Holiday Inn. 304 South Hamilton Street,
Painted Post; (607) 962–5021; www
.holiday-inn.com/corningny. Swimming
pool and wading pool, restaurant, coin
laundry. $$$–$$$$

Mount Morris

Take Route 17 west to I–390.

The largest dam east of the Mississippi is here, causing folks to say this is the "Best Town
by a Damsite."

Letchworth State Park (all ages)

**Off Route 36 (exit 7 off I–390), 6 miles south of Mount Morris, and One Letchworth State
Park, Castile; (585) 493–3600 or (800) 456–2267; www.nysparks.com/parks. Park open year-
round, campground open mid-May through October. Vehicle fee $ mid-May through mid-
October.**

Stretching for 14,350 acres along the Genesee River, this vast park has a variety of activi-
ties for families. Perhaps one of the prettiest sights in the state is the 17-mile scenic Letch-
worth Gorge, the river's work in progress for thousands of years, nicknamed the "Grand
Canyon of the East." The three waterfalls that glisten through the gorge were saved from
hydroelectric power plant destruction by William P. Letchworth, who deeded much of this
area to the people of New York in 1910. Pool swimming, fishing, hiking, bicycling, boating,
and cross-country skiing are favorite activities, and there are picnic and playground areas,
campsites, and cabins available.

William Pryor Letchworth Museum (all ages)

**One Letchworth State Park, Castile; (585) 493–2760; www.nysparks.com/parks. Open daily
mid-May through October 10:00 A.M. to 5:00 P.M., November and December weekends only
10:00 A.M. to 3:00 P.M. Donation.**

Within the park and near Middle Falls, the Letchworth Museum houses a collection of
Seneca and settler artifacts, along with regional, natural history, and archaeological dis-
plays. Of particular interest to children is the exhibit on Mary Jemison, known as the
"White Woman of the Genesee," an Irish immigrant girl captured by a Shawnee war party
in 1758 when she was fifteen years old and adopted by the Seneca. She remained with
the Seneca for the rest of her life, raised seven children, and became a respected leader.
Her grave is near the museum.

The Finger **Lakes Trail**

Stretching 559 miles across the state, this trail system is part of the official North Country National Scenic Trail, which when completed will extend 4,200 miles from eastern New York to North Dakota. Mountain bikes, motorized vehicles, and horses are prohibited along this ribbon of wilderness, and the scenery is spectacular. If biking is your preference, pedal along Bike Route 17 (follow small green oval road signs with a bicycle), a 435-mile path from the Hudson River to the Erie Canal. For more information: www.fingerlakes .net/trailsystem or (585) 658–9320.

Mount Morris Dam (all ages)

1 Mount Morris Dam, off Route 408; (585) 658–4790 or (585) 658–4791; www.lrb.usace.army.mil/brochure/mmd.html. Visitor center open daily in May and Labor Day through mid-November from 8:00 A.M. to 4:00 P.M., Memorial Day through Labor Day to 5:00 P.M. Call for winter hours. Guided dam tours at 10:00 A.M. and 2:00 P.M. **Free.**

Stop by the William B. Hoyt II Visitor Center for a tour given by the U.S. Army Corps of Engineers of the largest dam east of the Mississippi.

Also in **the Area**

Mount Morris Lanes. 9–11 Erie Street, Mount Morris; (585) 658–2540 or (585) 658–2310.

Livingston Lanes and Restaurant. Route 20A, Geneseo; (585) 243–1760.

Silver Lake Drive-In Theatre & Family Arcade. 73–7 Chapman Road, Perry, between Perry and Castile; (585) 237–5270.

Balloons Over Letchworth. 6645 Denton Corners Road, Castile; (585) 493–3340.

Minnehan's Family Entertainment Center. 5601 Big Tree Road, Lakeville; (585) 346–6167.

Wolcott Farms. 3820 Hermitage Road, Warsaw; (585) 786–3504.

Valley Outfitters. 8259 Dudley Road, Nunda; (585) 468–2499.

Mills Mansion (ages 7 and up)

14 Main Street; (585) 658–3292 or (585) 658–3132 to schedule a tour. Open June through Labor Day Friday through Sunday noon to 4:00 P.M. Donation.

Home of the founder of the town, Gen. William Mills, this fourteen-room Federal-style mansion, built in 1838, is furnished in Greek Revival decor.

Stony Brook State Park (all ages)

10820 Route 36 South, Dansville; (585) 335–8111; www.nysparks.com/parks. Park open year-round, campground open mid-May through mid-October. $

Swim in two stream-fed gorge pools, hike the Gorge Trail, enjoy the picnic area, playground, baseball fields, and tennis courts, and camp out at one of the 125 sites on 577 wooded acres.

Where to Eat

The Big Tree Inn. 46 Main Street, Geneseo; (585) 243–5220; www.bigtreeinn.com. Casual dining in an 1833 building, with a children's menu; early-bird specials and takeout available. $–$$

Bob's Dugout. 39 Mill Street; (585) 658–2880. Char-broiled burgers and ice cream. $$$–$$$$

Where to Stay

Avon Inn. 55 East Main Street, Avon; (585) 226–8181. Rooms and suites, complimentary continental breakfast. $$–$$$$

Glen Iris Inn. Inside Letchworth State Park, Castile; (585) 493–2622. Inn rooms efficiencies, and cottages; restaurant, playground, and picnic area overlooking waterfall. $$$–$$$$

Canandaigua

Take I–390 north to Routes 5 and 20.

Sonnenberg Gardens and Mansion (all ages)

151 Charlotte Street; (585) 394–4922; www.sonnenberg.org. Open daily May through October 9:30 A.M. to 4:00 P.M., open to 5:30 P.M. May 31 through September 6. Adults $$, children $, under 12 free.

Perhaps the finest Victorian gardens in America are here, spread over fifty lush acres and landscaped in a variety of themes. Nine different styles of horticultural artistry can be explored on a self-guided tour of the Japanese, Italian, Colonial, Rose, and Rock Gardens. There's also a thirteen-room conservatory, Butterfly House, a very long greenhouse to stroll through, and the ornately furnished 1887 stone mansion.

Family Recreation **in Canandaigua**

Bristol Mountain Sky Rides. 5662 Route 64; (585) 374–6000; www .bristolmountain.com.

Canandaigua Speedway. Ontario County Fairgrounds, 10 Townline Road; (315) 834–6606; www.dirtmotorsports.com/canandaigua.

Roseland Bowl Family Fun & Recreation Center. 4357 Recreation Drive; (585) 394–5050; www.roselandbowl.com.

Sutter's Canandaigua Marina. 808 South Main Street, City Pier; (585) 394–0918.

Roseland Waterpark. 250 Eastern Boulevard, Routes 5 and 20; (585) 396–2000; www.roselandwaterpark.com.

Granger Homestead and Carriage Museum (all ages)

295 North Main Street; (585) 394–1472; www.grangerhomestead.org. Open late May through mid-October Tuesday through Friday 1:00 to 5:00 P.M., June through August Tuesday through Sunday 1:00 to 5:00 P.M. Closed holidays. $

The Carriage Museum, out back, with a collection of more than fifty nineteenth-century vehicles, will amaze you and delight your kids. Carriages, coaches, sleighs, wagons, and even a hearse have been restored to their gleaming glory.

Ontario County Historical Museum (all ages)

55 North Main Street; (585) 394–4975; www.ochs.org. Open year-round Tuesday through Saturday 10:00 A.M. to 4:30 P.M., Wednesday evenings till 9:00 P.M. Closed holidays. $

In 1794, the Senecas and the pioneer settlers signed the Pickering Treaty, granting the latter the right to settle the Great Lakes Basin. An original copy of this important treaty can be seen here, along with a life mask of Abraham Lincoln, local history displays, and a discovery room with hands-on activities for children.

Cruising **Canandaigua Lake**

Captain Gray's Boat Tours. Inn on the Lake, 770 South Main Street; (585) 394–5270; www.captgrays.com.

The *Canandaigua Lady* Paddle Wheel. 169 Lakeshore Drive; (585) 396–7350 or (866) 9–ANCHOR; www.steamboatlandingonline.com.

Ontario County Courthouse (ages 7 and up)
27 North Main Street; (585) 396–4239. Open year-round Monday through Friday 8:30 A.M. to 5:00 P.M. **Free.**

Legend has it that when Susan B. Anthony was brought here to be tried for the heinous crime of attempting to vote in the national election in Rochester, the arm of Lady Justice, perched atop the courthouse, fell to the ground when the suffragette was fined $100.

Kershaw Park (all ages)
Located at southern end of Main Street, Lakeshore Drive; (585) 396–5082. Open daily Memorial Day through Labor Day 9:00 A.M. to 9:00 P.M. $

Seven acres along the north shore of Canandaigua Lake offer opportunities for swimming, sailboarding, volleyball, and picnicking.

Onanda Park (all ages)
West Lake Road; (585) 394–1120 or (585) 396–2518. Open year-round dawn to dusk. $

Enjoy fishing, swimming, and hiking along more than 2 miles of scenic interpretive trails at this park, with picnic areas, a playground, children's programs, and cabin and lodge rentals available.

Ganondagan State Historic Site (all ages)
1488 State Route 444 (off County Road 41), Boughton Hill Road, Victor; (585) 742–1690; www.ganondagan.org. Trails open year-round, visitor's center open mid-May through October Tuesday through Sunday 9:00 A.M. to 5:00 P.M. $

This was once the site of a thriving Seneca settlement of more than 4,500 people. Destroyed by the French in 1687 to cut down on the competition for the fur industry, today the area offers interpretive trails and exhibits that recount the history of the Senecas, the destruction of their village, and the native plants they prized.

Also in **the Area**

Valentown Museum. 7370 Valentown Square, Fishers; (585) 924–2645.

Antique Wireless Association Museum. 8 South Avenue, Bloomfield; (585) 657–6260.

Wizard of Clay Pottery. 7851 Route 20A, Bristol; (585) 229–2980; www .wizardofclay.com.

Copper Creek Farm. 5041 Shortsville Road, Shortsville; (585) 289–4441.

Willow Pond Aqua Farm. 3581 Swamp Road, Canandaigua; (585) 394–5890 or (888) 854–8945; www.willowpondaquafarms.com.

Where to Eat

Kellogg's Pan-Tree Inn. 130 Lakeshore Drive; (585) 394–3909 or (585) 394–7343; www.stegalls.com/kelloggs. Great breakfasts, chicken pie, and children's meals; overlooking the lake. $

Lincoln Hill Inn. 3365 East Lake Road; (585) 394–8254. Alfresco dining on covered decks and porches, serving seafood, chicken, steak, and a children's menu. $$$

Manetti's. Parkway Plaza, Routes 5 and 20; (585) 394–1915. Steak, seafood, chicken, and Italian entrees, with salad bar and children's menu. $$

Where to Stay

Canandaigua Inn On the Lake. 770 South Main Street; (585) 394–7800 or (800) 228–2801. Rooms and suites, heated pool, restaurant; located on the lake; children under seventeen stay **free.** $$$$

Finger Lakes Inn. 4343 Routes 5 and 20; (585) 394–2800 or (800) 727–2775; www.fingerlakesinn.com. Located on eight landscaped acres, with a family activity center, heated pool, sundeck, picnic area, gas grills, complimentary continental breakfast; more than twenty-five restaurants nearby. $$

Palmyra

Take Route 21 north.

The Erie Canal brought prosperity to Palmyra, making the town an important agricultural and industrial distribution center.

Alling Coverlet Museum (ages 6 and up)
122 William Street; (315) 597–6737; www.palmyrany.com. Open daily June through September 1:00 to 4:00 P.M. Free.

More than 200 nineteenth-century handwoven coverlets are displayed here, the largest collection of its kind in the country.

Palmyra Historical Museum (ages 6 and up)

132 Market Street; (315) 597–6981; www.palmyrany.com/historicpal/index.htm. Open Tuesday through Thursday and Saturday 1:00 to 4:00 P.M. **Free.**

The town's history is highlighted here, with exhibits of elegant furniture, household articles, local memorabilia, and a collection of antique toys.

William Phelps General Store Museum (all ages)

140 Market Street; (315) 597–6981 or (315) 597–4173; www.palmyrany.com. Open Wednesday, Thursday, and Saturday June through September 1:00 to 4:00 P.M., Saturdays only in October. **Free.**

As if frozen in time, this nineteenth-century store contains much of its original merchandise, and the upstairs residence has been left as if the owners just stepped out.

The Amazing Maize Maze (all ages)

Long Acre Farms, 1342 Eddy Road, Macedon; (315) 986–9821; www.longacrefarms.com. Open late July through early September Thursday to Sunday 10:00 A.M. to 6:00 P.M., mid-September through October weekends 10:00 A.M. to 4:00 P.M. Adults $$, children $, 4 and under **free.**

This is a field of dreams you could get lost in . . . literally. But since that's the general idea, your family will have some seriously un-cornditional fun. Maze masters are around to give "Kernels of Knowledge" to the hopelessly lost, and special events include evening Moonlight Maze runs and a Fall Family Fun Fest.

Also in **the Area**

Sportsworks Family Fun Park. 180 Route 31, Macedon; (315) 986–4245. $–$$

Doug Kent's Rose Bowl Lanes. 725 West Miller Street, Newark; (315) 331–2007. $

Hoffman Clock Museum. Newark Public Library, 121 High Street, Newark; (315) 331–4370. **Free.**

Wayne County Historical Museum. 21 Butternut Street, Lyons; (315) 946–4943. $

Joseph Smith Home and Sacred Grove. 830 Stafford Road, Palmyra; (315) 597–4383.

Spinners Family Skate Center. 280 Route 31, Macedon; (315) 986–7755 or (315) 986–7709; www.spinnersfuncenter.com. $$

Where to Eat

Athenia Restaurant. 606 East Main Street; (315) 597–4287. Hearty breakfasts begin at 5:30 A.M. seven days a week; daily and seasonal specials for lunch and dinner. $

Where to Stay

Nor-Win Farm & Campsite. 2921 Pilgrim-port Road, Lyons; (315) 946–4436 or (315) 946–6248. More than 200 campsites, swimming pool, paddleboats, children's area, recreation activities, and camp store. $

Sodus Bay Area

Take Route 21 north, then turn east onto Route 104.

The Lighthouse at Sodus Bay—Maritime Museum (all ages)

7606 North Ontario Street, Sodus Point; (315) 483–4936; peachey.com/soduslight. Open May and October Tuesday through Sunday 10:00 A.M. to 4:00 P.M., June through September to 5:00 P.M. Donation.

Built in 1870, this lighthouse is now a maritime museum with ship models, dioramas, and other memorabilia reminiscent of life on Lake Ontario.

Fair Haven Beach State Park (all ages)

Route 104A, Fair Haven; (315) 947–5205; www.nysparks.com/parks. Park open year-round, campground open April through October. $$

The steep bluffs and white-sand beaches of this 862-acre park are beautiful, and the nearby marshlands are home to a wide variety of birds. Hiking and nature trails wind through wetlands. There is swimming with a sand beach; fishing in a pond, bay, or lake; a playground and picnic area; boat rentals; recreation programs; and campsites and cabins.

Chimney Bluffs State Park (all ages)

8105 Garner Road, Wolcott; (315) 947–5205 or (800) 527–6510; www.tourism.co.wayne .ny.us. Summer vehicle fee $$.

If you haven't booked a ticket to the moon or Mars lately, this place is the next best thing. Ice Age glaciers deposited drumlins along the shore of Lake Ontario, and the eroded result is an eerie and surreal landscape of chimney-shaped rocks, ridges, and spires. Towering over the lake, with names like Dragon's Back and Castle Spire, this place is New York's version of the Badlands. Be extra careful on the trails in this undeveloped park, however, for they do skirt steep edges of the cliffs.

Alasa Farms (all ages)

6450 Shaker Road, Alton; (315) 483–6321 or (800) 645–4251; www.alasafarms.com. Open June through October. $

Seasonal farm activities, from apple picking to sheepshearing, on the site of a former nineteenth-century Shaker community.

More Sodus Bay **Area Parks**

Phillips Park. Route 104A, Fair Haven; (315) 947–5112; co.cayuga.ny.us/fairhaven.

West Barrier Bar Park. West side of Fair Haven Bay, Fair Haven; (315) 253–5611; www.tourcayuga.com.

Blue Cut Nature Center. 7210 Route 31W, Lyons; (315) 946–5836.

Sterling Lake Shore Park and Nature Center. 15730 Jensvold Road, off 104A, Sterling; (315) 947–6143; www.cayuganet.org/sterlingpark.

Where to Eat

Orbaker's Drive-In. 4793 Route 104, Williamson; (315) 589–9701. Cheeseburgers, hot dogs, ice cream, and old-fashioned milk shakes. $

Papa Joe's. 8506 Greig Street, Sodus Point; (315) 483–6372. Deck dining, featuring prime rib, steaks, seafood, pasta, chicken, plus a children's menu. $$

Where to Stay

Bartucca's Rentals. 2288 Route 88, Newark; (800) 244–0886; www.lakeontario cottagerentals.com. Two-bedroom cottage on a sandbar (1 mile off shore), with boat provided; also a three-bedroom cottage in downtown Sodus Bay. $$

Joanne's Cottages. Sprongs Bluff, Sodus; (315) 524–4411; www.waynecounty tourism.org. (Contact J. Scozzarri, 4568 Ontario Center Road, Walworth 14568.) Each cottage sleeps six, with porch facing lake and beach, and fishing charters available. Must provide own linens. $$$–$$$$

Rochester

Head west on Route 104.

Known as the Lilac City because of its gorgeous gardens, Rochester is also the place that gave us cameras, contact lenses, and copiers.

Rochester Heritage Area and High Falls Visitor Center (all ages)
60 Brown's Race; (585) 325–2030; www.centerathighfalls.org. Open year-round; call for hours. Extended hours during laser season. Laser shows Friday and Saturday night. **Free.**

Before roaming Rochester, stop here for maps and current information about area events. The center has several interesting interactive exhibits, as well as the Triphammer Forge excavation, the Pont de Rennes pedestrian bridge to High Falls, and **free** nighttime summer sound and light shows presented on the gorge walls.

Strong Museum (all ages)
1 Manhattan Square; (585) 263–2700 or (585) 263–2702; www.strongmuseum.org. Open Monday through Thursday 10:00 A.M. to 5:00 P.M., Friday 10:00 A.M. to 8:00 P.M., Saturday 10:00 A.M. to 5:00 P.M., and Sunday noon to 5:00 P.M. Adults $$, children $.

Margaret Strong was an avid collector. From early childhood she collected anything and everything that interested her, and she had eclectic taste. From toys to tea sets, paperweights to parasols, Margaret accumulated more than 300,000 objects all by herself by 1969. Three decades later the collection has grown to half a million items, and the doll collection, numbering nearly 30,000, is the largest in the world.

Cruising around **Rochester**

A variety of tour boats ply the waters around town, with mini-voyages on the Erie Canal, the Genesee River, or Lake Ontario. Call for current sailing schedules.

Spirit of Rochester. (585) 865–4930 or (585) 663–0088.

Sam Patch Tour Boat. (585) 262–5661; www.sampatch.org.

Colonial Belle. (585) 223–9470; www.colonialbelle.com.

Discover the River. (585) 288–1680 or (585) 288–1684.

Oak Orchard Canoe Experts. (585) 288–5550; www.oakorchardcanoe.com.

Suggested **Reading**

The Story of Harriet Tubman by Kate McMullan

Sweet Clara and the Freedom Quilt by Deborah Hopkinson

The First Woman Doctor by Rachel Baker

A Brilliant Streak: The Making of Mark Twain by Kathryn Lasky

Follow the Drinking Gourd by Jeanette Winter

Indian Captive: The Story of Mary Jemison by Lois Lenski

Rochester Museum and Science Center & Strasenburgh Planetarium (all ages)

657 East Avenue; (585) 271–4320 or (585) 271–1880; www.rmsc.org. Open Monday through Saturday 9:00 A.M. to 5:00 P.M., Sunday noon to 5:00 P.M. Closed Thanksgiving and Christmas. $–$$

Excellent exhibits on science and technology, anthropology, geology, regional history, women's cultural heritage, and the Seneca Nation can be found here. The planetarium schedules regular laser and sky shows.

Susan B. Anthony House and Visitors Center (ages 7 and up)

17 Madison Street; (585) 235–6124; www.susanbanthonyhouse.org. Open Memorial Day through Labor Day Tuesday through Sunday 11:00 A.M. to 5:00 P.M. and Labor Day through Memorial Day Wednesday through Sunday 11:00 A.M. to 4:00 P.M. Closed holidays. Adults $$, children $.

Writing the *History of Women's Suffrage* in her third-floor attic, Susan B. Anthony led the revolution for women's rights from her residence here from 1866 to 1906. Police arrested her here for the crime of voting, and her home became a hotbed of social reform as she met with Frederick Douglass, Elizabeth Cady Stanton, and other revolutionaries of her day.

George Eastman House (ages 8 and up)

900 East Avenue; (585) 271–3361; www.eastman.org. Open year-round Tuesday through Saturday 10:00 A.M. to 5:00 P.M. (to 8:00 P.M. Thursday), Sunday 1:00 to 5:00 P.M.; in May open daily 10:00 A.M. to 5:00 P.M. Closed major holidays. Adults $$, children $.

Dropping out of school at age thirteen to work and support his mother, George was gifted with an insatiable curiosity. At age twenty-three he bought a camera and experimented with ways to simplify film development. Working in his mother's kitchen, he invented a dry plate machine, and several years later he created a camera with rolled film. He became a multimillionaire, sharing his wealth with Rochester and the world. Of all his beneficent acts, my favorite is the time he gave a free Kodak camera to every thirteen-year-old child in America. Tours are available of his fifty-room mansion and gardens and of the world's largest collection of cameras, photographs, and historic films.

Memorial Art Gallery (all ages)

500 University Avenue; (585) 473–7720; www.mag.rochester.edu. Open year-round Wednesday through Friday 10:00 A.M. to 4:00 P.M., Thursday to 9:00 P.M., Saturday 10:00 A.M. to 5:00 P.M., Sunday noon to 5:00 P.M., Tuesday noon to 9:00 P.M. Closed Monday and major holidays. Adults $$, children $.

Journey through 5,000 years of art history at this excellent teaching museum. Be sure to visit the Looking Laboratory at the Dorothy McBride Gill Education Center, an interactive hands-on discovery room where families can explore new ways of looking at art.

Seneca Park Zoo (all ages)

2222 Saint Paul Street; (585) 467–WILD; www.senecaparkzoo.org. Open daily year-round 10:00 A.M. to 4:00 P.M., until 5:00 P.M. Memorial Day through Labor Day. $

Climb a giant spider web on the Genesee Trail, interact with the web of life at the Discovery Center, or watch the underwater antics of penguins, polar bears, and sea lions.

Seabreeze Park (all ages)

4600 Culver Road; (585) 323–1900 or (800) 395–2500; www.seabreeze.com. Open Memorial Day through Labor Day Sunday; call for hours. $$$

Opened in 1879, this is the fourth-oldest amusement park in America. Seventy-five rides are offered, including four roller coasters, and there are magic shows, video arcades, water slides, and a Looney Lagoon for the little guys.

Ontario Beach Park (all ages)

1 Beach Avenue; (585) 256–4950. Park open daily year-round, carousel operates June through Labor Day. $

One of the oldest carousels in the country still spins at this lakeside beach, a 0.5-mile ribbon of sand with a long fishing pier to stroll.

Animal Watching **around Rochester**

Humane Society at Lollypop Farm. 99 Victor Road, off Route 31 East, Fairport; (585) 223–1330; www.lollypop.org.

New York State Fish Hatchery. Route 36, 16 North Street, Caledonia; (585) 538–6300; www.dec.state.ny.us.

Springdale Farm. 696 Colby Street, Spencerport; (585) 352–5320.

Other Rochester **Area Museums**

Rochester and Genesee Valley Railroad Museum. 6393 East River Road, West Henrietta; (585) 533–1431; www.rochnrhs.org/rgvrrm.html.

Stone-Tolan House Museum. 2370 East Avenue, Rochester; (716) 546–7029; www.landmarksociety.org.

Charlotte-Genesee Lighthouse. 70 Lighthouse Street, Rochester; (716) 621–6179; www.frontiernet.net/~mikemay.

Genesee Country Village and Museum (all ages)

1410 Flint Hill Road, off Route 36, Mumford; (585) 538–6822; www.gcv.org. **Open May through October Tuesday through Friday 10:00 A.M. to 4:00 P.M., Saturday, Sunday, and holidays to 5:00 P.M., July through Labor Day to 5:00 P.M. Nature center open year-round Tuesday through Friday 10:00 A.M. to 4:00 P.M., to 5:00 P.M. on weekends; closed Monday. $$**

Travel back in time at this living-history museum, where costumed interpreters and craftspeople bring the nineteenth century to life. A complex of fifty-seven restored and fully furnished buildings, the third-largest collection of its kind in the country, it offers families the opportunity to experience American country life of the 1800s. The Nature Center offers 5 miles of interpreted nature trails, with family nature walks and programs and children's nature classes.

Where to Eat

Charlie's Frog Pond. 652 Park Avenue; (585) 271–1970. Upscale diner serving seafood, steak, pasta, and gourmet specials. $–$$

Dinosaur Bar-B-Q. 99 Court Street; (585) 325–7090; www.dinosaurbarbque.com. Genuine pit barbecue, Cajun and Cuban specialties, and live blues. $–$$

Where to Stay

Days Inn Downtown. 384 East Avenue at Alexander Street; (585) 325–5010 or (800) 329–7466; www.daysinn.com. Located in the Preservation District, convenient to area attractions; **free** continental breakfast. $$$$

Residence Inn by Marriott. 1300 Jefferson Road; (585) 272–8850. Kitchen suites, outdoor pool, complimentary continental breakfast, nearby restaurant (Monday through Thursday **free** social hour dinner), coin laundry, and picnic area; children under twelve stay **free.** $$$$

Other Things to See and Do
in the Finger Lakes Region

Tired Iron Tractor Museum. Route 20A, Leicester; (585) 382–3110.

Homeville Museum. 49 Clinton Street, Route 41, Homer; (607) 749–3105.

International Speedway. 3011 Route 104, Williamson; (315) 589–3018.

Victorian Doll Museum. 4332 Buffalo Road, North Chili; (585) 247–0130; www.museumsfirst.com.

Big Flats Historical Museum. 258 Hibbard Road, Big Flats; (607) 562–7460.

Stone Barn Castle. 737 Stone Barn Road, off Route 49, Cleveland; (315) 675–3602.

Genoa Historical Association's Rural Life Museum. Route 34B, King Ferry; (315) 364–8202.

Little Red Schoolhouse Museum. 1290 Route 104A, Sterling; (315) 564–6189.

Clark Reservation State Park. Jamesville Road, Route 173W, Jamesville; (315) 492–1590.

Hammond Hill State Forest. Hammond Hill Road, Dryden; (607) 753–3095; www.dec.state.ny.us.

1941 Historical Aircraft Group. Geneseo Airport, Big Tree Lane, Geneseo; (585) 243–2100; www.1941hag.org.

Hamlin Beach State Park. 1 Camp Road, Hamlin; (585) 964–2462 or (800) 456–CAMP; www.nysparks.com/parks.

For More Information

Finger Lakes Association. (315) 536–7488 or (800) KIT4FUN; www.finger lakes.org.

Cayuga County Office of Tourism. (315) 255–1658 or (800) 499–9615; www.tour cayuga.com.

Chemung County Chamber of Commerce. (607) 734–5137 or (800) 627–5892; www.chemungchamber.org.

Cortland County Convention & Visitors Bureau. (607) 753–8463 or (800) 859–2227; www.cortlandtourism.com.

Livingston County Tourism. (585) 243–2222 or (800) 538–7365; www.livchamber.com or www.finger lakeswest.com.

Ontario County Tourism. (585) 394–3915 or (877) FUN–IN–NY; www.visitfingerlakes.com.

Greater Rochester Visitors Association. (585) 546–3070 or (800) 677–7282; visit rochester.com.

Schuyler County Chamber of Commerce. (607) 535–4300 or (800) 607–4552; www.schuylerny.com.

Seneca County Tourism. (315) 539–1752 or (800) 732–1848; www.visitsenecany.net.

Steuben County Convention and Visitors Bureau. (607) 936–6544 or (866) 946–3386; www.corningfingerlakes.com.

Syracuse/Onondaga County Convention and Visitors Bureau. (315) 470–1910 or (800) 234–4SYR; www.visitsyracuse.org.

Tioga County Chamber of Commerce. (607) 687–2020 or (800) 671–7772; www.tiogachamber.com.

Tompkins/Ithaca Convention and Visitors Bureau. (607) 272–1313 or (800) 284–8422; www.visitithaca.com.

Wayne County Office of Tourism. (315) 946–5469 or (800) 527–6510; www.tourism.co.wayne.ny.us.

Yates County Chamber of Commerce. (315) 536–3111 or (800) 868–YATES; www.yatesny.com.

The North Country

Most folks agree the North Country begins at the Canadian border and runs all the way to the Mohawk River, embraced in the east by Lake Champlain and in the west by the Saint Lawrence River. Within that region is the largest wilderness area in the lower forty-eight states, the six million acres of Adirondack Park. This vast expanse is larger than all our continental national parks put together, dotted with several thousand glistening lakes and ponds; more than 30,000 miles of pristine brooks, streams, and rivers; more than forty mountains topping 4,000 feet; and more than 2,000 miles of scenic hiking trails. There are more trees here than people, and the breathtaking primeval forests beckon exploration. But there are plenty of other attractions for families, too. From a multitude of miniature golf courses and amusement parks to historical reenactments, cool runs on a bobsled, or cruising a crystal clear lake in an antique boat, the activities are endless. Whatever you choose to do, you will discover that the haunting call of the loon, the dazzling glow of the Northern Lights, and the pristine beauty of the wilderness will stay with your family for generations.

Driving Tips

There are more miles of hiking trails in the Adirondacks than there are roads, which means for drivers it's pretty hard to get lost, but sometimes it can be difficult or time-consuming to get where you want to go. Still, the scenery is spectacular, so just take your time, and watch out for the wildlife. In general, the section of I–87 (also known as the Adirondack Northway) that runs from Queensbury to Ausable Chasm is particularly scenic, and it parallels Route 9N, which hugs the western shore of Lake George. Route 30 bisects the mountains down the center, from the Canadian border in the north to the Mohawk River

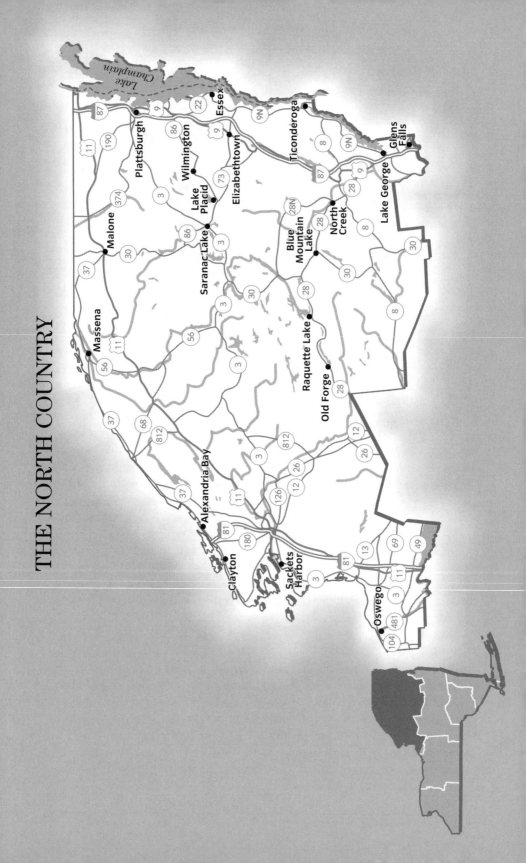

THE NORTH COUNTRY

in the south. Going east to west, Route 8 cuts through the southern Adirondacks, scenic Route 28 snakes through the central region, and dramatic Route 3 winds from Platts- burgh, on the shores of Lake Champlain across the northern peaks, all the way to Lake Ontario. The Seaway Trail, comprised of several roads, follows the coastline of Lake Ontario and the Saint Lawrence River and is one of the most beautiful byways in the country.

Glens Falls

Take exit 18 or 19 off I–87.

Glens Falls was called Chepontuc by the Iroquois and Wing's Falls in 1763 by sawmill entre- preneur Abraham Wing. Apparently a high roller, Wing gambled the town away to Col. Johannes Glen in a card game, and the town's name changed again to honor the victor.

World Awareness Children's Museum (all ages)

227 Glen Street, Suite 3A; (518) 793–2773; www.worldchildrensmuseum.org. Hours and days of operation vary; call for details.

Children's art from around the world and interesting interactive displays are offered here, along with many hands-on activities for families.

Family Fun Centers in
Glens Falls and Queensbury

Skateland Family Fun Center and Aqua Adventure Water Slide.
1035 Route 9, Glens Falls; (518) 792–8989; www.lakegeorgefun.com.

Adventure Racing and Family Fun Center.
1079 Route 9, Queensbury; (518) 798–7860; www.adventure racinglg.com.

Adirondack Billiards and Video Games.
197 Glens Falls; (518) 798–5406.

Tilt Arcade. Aviation Mall, Queensbury; (518) 792–2180.

Rocksport Indoor Climbing. 138 Quaker Road, Queensbury; (518) 793–4626.

Glen Drive-In Cinema. Route 9, Queensbury; (518) 792–0023.

Hyde Collection (all ages)

161 Warren Street; (518) 792–1761; www.hydeartmuseum.org. Open year-round Tuesday through Saturday 10:00 A.M. to 5:00 P.M., Sunday noon to 5:00 P.M. Closed Monday and national holidays. Donation.

This is an excellent museum featuring an important collection of Old Masters and American works of art from the fifteenth through the twentieth centuries, displayed in the Italian Renaissance villa of the original collector. Rembrandt, Rubens, Degas, van Gogh, Picasso, and other masters are represented here, along with a variety of changing exhibits.

Glens Falls Feeder Canal (all ages)

9 miles long, with easy access on Richardson Street and at the Feeder Dam, located in Haviland's Cove Park, off Shermantown Road; (518) 792–5363; www.adirondack.net/orgs/ feedercanal. Open dawn to dusk year-round. Free.

This was an important link for loggers during the nineteenth century. Families can walk and bike along the towpath trail or canoe in the canal.

Crandall Park International Trail System (all ages)

Route 9; (518) 761–3813. Open daily dawn to dusk year-round. Free.

Easy nature trails lace through here, and there's good fishing from a stocked pond. Also on-site are ball fields, basketball and tennis courts, and a picnic area.

Pack Demonstration Forest (all ages)

Routes 9 and 28, Warrensburg; (518) 623–9679.

This 2,500-acre environmental demonstration forest, an outdoor campus of SUNY's Forestry College, features the easy 1-mile Grandmother's Tree Nature Trail, as well as canoeing, fishing, and mountain biking.

Drive-In Dining **in the Area**

A & W Root Beer Drive-In. Route 9, Lake George; (518) 668–4681.

The Loft Drive-In. Routes 9 and 149, Queensbury; (518) 793–2296.

Quaker Road Restaurant and Jimmy's Diner. 384 Quaker Road, Queensbury; (518) 792–7305.

New York **Trivia**

The highest point in the state is Mt. Marcy, in Essex County (5,344 feet).

Hovey Pond (all ages)

Lafayette Street, Queensbury; (518) 761–8216. Open year-round dawn to dusk. Free.

Fish from a stocked pond, cycle along the Warren County Bikeway that runs through here, or go ice-skating in winter.

West Mountain (all ages)

59 West Mountain Road, Queensbury; (518) 793–6606; www.skiwestmountain.com. Snow conditions determine season opening; Monday through Friday 10:00 A.M. to 10:00 P.M., Saturday and Sunday 8:30 A.M. to 6:00 P.M. $$$–$$$$

This family ski scene has twenty-two trails for all skiing levels, a ski school, night skiing, a snowboard park, and a snowtubing park.

Empire East Aviation (all ages)

Floyd Bennett Memorial Airport, 443 Queensbury Avenue, Queensbury; (518) 798–3091. Call for appointment. Daily year-round. Half hour $75, one hour $150 for up to three people.

For a bird's-eye view, slip the surly bonds of Earth and soar on silver wings in a scenic area airplane ride.

Where to Eat

Boston Candy Kitchen. 21 Elm Street; (518) 792–1069. Lunch and breakfast specials and homemade candy. $

Peter's Diner. 36 South Street; (518) 792–9772. Home cooking, with fresh homemade doughnuts. $

Where to Stay

Brown's Welcome Inn. 932 State Route 9, Queensbury; (518) 792–9576 or (800) 379–0246; www.brownswelcomeinn.com. Outdoor heated pool and playground. $$–$$$$

Canoe Island Lodge. 3820 Lake Shore Drive, P.O. Box 144, Diamond Point; (518) 668–5592; www.canoeislandlodge.com. Family resort with cottages, houses, villas, and chalets, with private beach, plus children's activities. $$$$

Lake George

Take Route 9 north.

An interesting dichotomy of spectacular natural beauty and kitschy amusements, Lake George offers families a wide variety of activities to choose from.

Fort William Henry (all ages)
Beach Road, off Canada Street (Route 9); (518) 668–5471; www.fortwilliamhenry.com. Open May through October daily 9:00 A.M. to 6:00 P.M. Adults $$$, children $$.

For fans of James Fenimore Cooper's classic The Last of the Mohicans, this is the fort featured in his story, based on an incident that occurred in 1757 during the French and Indian War. Completely restored, this colonial fortress offers a window to eighteenth-century frontier life, with living-history demonstrations of musket and cannon firing by costumed guides, audiovisual displays, and artifacts uncovered on-site.

Lake George Historical Museum (ages 5 and up)
Canada and Amherst Streets; (518) 668–5044; www.lakegeorgehistorical.org. Open mid-May through June weekends 11:00 A.M. to 4:00 P.M.; July through September Friday through Sunday 11:00 A.M. to 4:00 P.M.; Wednesday through Thursday 3:00 to 8:00 P.M. in July and August; weekends only in early October 11:00 A.M. to 4:00 P.M. $

Located in the Old County Courthouse, this local museum has interesting artifacts, historical maps, and prints recalling the history of the area. But the nineteenth-century jail cells will really fascinate the kids as they imagine what sort of desperados were detained here a hundred years ago.

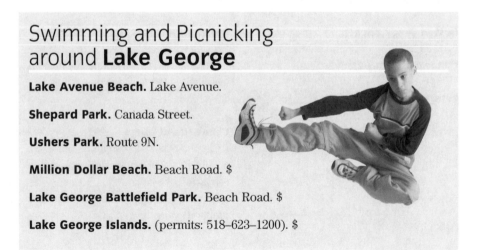

Swimming and Picnicking around **Lake George**

Lake Avenue Beach. Lake Avenue.

Shepard Park. Canada Street.

Ushers Park. Route 9N.

Million Dollar Beach. Beach Road. $

Lake George Battlefield Park. Beach Road. $

Lake George Islands. (permits: 518–623–1200). $

Miniature Golf at **Lake George**

Around the World and Around the U.S. in 18 Holes. Beach Road; (518) 668–2531.

Fort Mini-Golf. Fort William Henry Commons; (518) 668–5471.

Gooney Golf/Haunted Castle. Routes 9/9N; (518) 668–2589.

Indoor Miniature Golf. 275 Canada Street; (518) 668–3777.

Lumber Jack Pass. Routes 9 and 149; (518) 793–7141.

Pirates Cove Adventure Golf. 1089 Route 9; (518) 745–1887.

Putts N Prizes. Canada Street and Beach Road; (518) 668–9500.

Pirates Cove Lake George. 2115 Route 9; (518) 668–0493.

Prospect Mountain Veteran's Memorial Highway (all ages)

Route 9, south of Lake George Village; (518) 668–5198. Open daily late May to mid-October. Vehicle fee $.

Drive this 5.5-mile road to the parking area for panoramic 100-mile views of Vermont's Green Mountains, New Hampshire's White Mountains, the Adirondack high peaks region, and the Laurentian Mountains of Canada. Then take the "viewmobile" to the 2,030-foot summit for even more spectacular views.

House of Frankenstein Wax Museum (ages 10 and up)

213 Canada Street; (518) 668–3377; www.frankensteinwaxmuseum.com. Open April through June Friday noon to 10:00 P.M., Saturday open at 10:00 A.M., Sunday through Thursday 10:00 A.M. to 6:00 P.M. (weekdays starting mid-May); June through early September open daily 9:00 A.M. to 11:00 P.M.; early September through Halloween open Friday and Saturday 10:00 A.M. to 10:00 P.M., Sunday to 6:00 P.M. Adults $$, children $.

Not for young children or the fainthearted; this may appeal to the Goosebumps crowd.

The Great Escape and Splashwater Kingdom Fun Park (all ages)

Route 9, between exits 19 and 20; (518) 792–3500; www.thegreatescape.com. Open daily Memorial Day through Labor Day 10:00 A.M. to 6:00 P.M., with extended hours in summer. Adults $$$$, children under 48 inches $$$.

This is New York's largest theme park, with one admission price for over 125 wet and dry rides (including five roller coasters), shows, and attractions, including high-diving shows, ice shows, and the Red Garter Saloon Revue. Toddlers love Storytown, Noah's Lark, and Noah's Sprayground.

Transportation in the **Lake George Area**

Lake George Steamboat Company. Steel Pier, Lake George; (518) 668–5777 or (800) 553–BOAT; www.lakegeorgesteamboat.com.

Lake George Shoreline Cruise. 2 Kurosaka Lane, Lake George; (518) 668–4644 OR (888) 542–6287; www.lakegeorgeshoreline.com.

Trolley Rides. Route 9, Lake George; (518) 792–1085.

Lake George Carriage Rides. Beach Road, Lake George; (518) 668–4958; www.lakegeorge-saratoga.com/carriage/.

Pony Express Carriage Company. Mountain Road, Lake George; (518) 696–6100.

Indian Pipes Passage Co. At the Sagamore Resort, Bolton Landing; (518) 644–2979 or (518) 644–9400, ext. 6040; www.lakegeorgenewyork.com/indianpipes.

The Morgan. At the Sagamore Resort, Bolton Landing; (518) 644–9400, ext. 6110.

A Beautiful Balloon. 47 Assembly Point Road, Lake George; (973) 335–9799; www.Balloon-Rides.com.

Adirondack Balloon Flights. Aviation Road, Glens Falls; (518) 793–6342; www.adirondackballoonflights.com.

Para-sailing Adventures. Shoreline Cruise Dock, Lake George Village; (518) 668–4644; www.lakegeorgeshoreline.com.

Sun Sports Para-Sail Rides. Chic's Marina, Route 9N, Bolton Landing; (518) 644–3470.

Up Yonda Farm (all ages)

5239 Lake Shore Drive, Bolton Landing; (518) 644–9767 www.upyondafarm.com. Open July through Labor Day daily 8:00 A.M. to 5:00 P.M. and Labor Day through June daily 8:00 A.M. to 4:00 P.M.; closed weekends November through February. $

This environmental education center features a variety of nature programs, a tour of the farm, nature trails to explore, bird and bat houses dotting the woods, a butterfly garden, and special activities for children.

Hudson River Recreation Area (all ages)

River Road, Lake Luzerne; (518) 623–1200. Open daily year-round. Free.

More Family Fun Centers
around Lake George

Magic Forest. Route 9; (518) 668–2448; www.magicforestpark.com.

Water Slide World. Routes 9 and 9L South; (518) 668–4407; www
.adirondack.net/tour/waterslideworld.

Lake George Bowl and Billiards. Route 9; (518) 668–5741.

Fun World. 127 Canada Street; (518) 668–2708.

Playland Arcade North. 227 Canada Street; (518) 668–5255.

Wild West Ranch and Western Town. Bloody Pond Road, off Route 9;
(518) 668–2121; www.wildwestranch.com.

Alien Encounter. 255 Canada Street; (518) 668–5910; www.scaryfaces.com.

Spread over 1,132 acres, this wooded park has several easy, marked hiking trails that follow old logging roads. Follow the Ferguson Brook Trail for great views of Hudson River, or trek to Buttermilk Falls by way of the Bear Slide Trail.

Warren County Fish Hatchery (all ages)
Echo Lake Road, off Hudson Street, Warrensburg; (518) 623–5576. Usually open daily 8:00 A.M. to 4:00 P.M. year-round. Free.

This hatchery is home to the yearling brown, rainbow, and tiger trout that stock the rivers and lakes of the area. Families can stop by the visitor's center, watch a fish film, learn some fish facts, then tour the trout tanks.

Warren County Nature Trail System (all ages)
Located off Hudson Avenue, north of town beyond the golf course, Warrensburg; (518) 623–5576. Open daily year-round. Free.

Adjacent to the Hudson River, this area has several easy to moderate trails leading to a nice vista and features unusual rock formations at the water's edge. Pick up a brochure at the trailhead parking area.

Hickory Ski Center (ages 4 and up)
43 Hickory Hill Road, off Route 418, Warrensburg; (518) 623–2825; www.skihickory.com. Season depends on snowfall; open weekends and holidays 9:00 A.M. to 4:00 P.M. Adults $$$$, children $$$.

This alpine spot offers a 1,200-foot vertical drop, a ski school, and eighteen trails for all levels of skill.

Where to Eat

The Barnsider Smoke House Restaurant. Route 9 South; (518) 668–5268; www.barnsider.com. Great barbecue, outdoor deck, very family friendly. $$

Log Jam Restaurant. 1484 Route 9, at Route 149; (518) 798–1155; www.logjam restaurant.com. Wonderful Adirondack decor, salad bar, steak, chicken, seafood, and a children's menu. $$–$$$

Where to Stay

O'Connor's Resort Cottages. 3454 Lake Shore Drive; (518) 668–3367; www .lakegeorgenewyork.com/cottages. Cottages, family rates, playground, restaurant, mini-golf, paddleboats and rowboats, private beach, lawn games, and picnic area. $$$

Roaring Brook Ranch & Tennis Resort. Luzerne Road, 1 mile west of I–87 exit 21; (518) 668–5767 OR (800) 882–7665; www.roaringbrookranch.com. Family rates, three pools, summer cookouts, restaurant, tennis courts, lawn games, game and rec rooms, and free supervised children's activities. $$$$

The Sagamore Resort. 110 Sagamore Road, Bolton Landing; (518) 644–9400 or (800) 358–3585; www.thesagamore.com. This is one of the all-time great resorts, with rooms and suites, an indoor heated pool, tennis, golf, horse-drawn carriages, a private beach, boat rentals, sightseeing boats, a nature trail, playground, supervised children's activities, and five restaurants. $$$$

Horsing around **Warren County**

Saddle Up Stables. 3513 Lake Shore Drive, Lake George; (518) 668–4801; www.ridingstables.com.

Bennett's Riding Stables. Route 9N, Lake Luzerne; (518) 696–4444; www.lakegeorgenewyork.com/horses.

Bailey's Horses. Route 9N, Lake Luzerne; (518) 696–4541.

Bit 'n Bridle Ranch. 184 Tucker Road, Stony Creek; (518) 696–2776.

Circle B Ranch. Friends Lake Road, Chestertown; (518) 494–4888.

1000 Acres Ranch Resort. 465 Warrensburg Road, Stony Creek; (518) 696–2444 or (800) 458–7311; www.1000acres.com.

Stirrups & Spurs Stables. 111 Roaring Branch Road, Stony Creek; (518) 696–4406.

Loon Lake Riding Stables. Route 8, Loon Lake, Chestertown; (518) 494–5168.

U-Drive **Boat Rentals**

For the more adventurous, there are numerous marinas dotting the lake offering families the chance to be captains of their own destiny, or at least captain a variety of watercraft ranging from rowboats and canoes to motorboats and sailboats. Here's a partial list:

Lake George Boat Rental. Lower Amherst Street, Lake George; (518) 668–4828.

U-Drive Boat Rental. Kurosaka Lane, Lake George; (518) 668–4644; www.commercial.com/shoreline.

Beckley's Boat Rentals. 5824 Lake Shore Drive, Diamond Point; (518) 668–2651; www.beckleysboats.com.

Gilchrist Marina. 3686 Lake Shore Drive, Diamond Point; (518) 668–5848.

Chic's Marina. Route 9N, Lake Shore Drive, Bolton Landing; (518) 644–2170.

Water's Edge Marina. Sagamore Road, Bolton Landing; (518) 644–2511.

Werner's Boat Rentals. Route 9N, Lake Shore Drive, Silver Bay; (518) 543–8866; www.wernersboatrentals.com.

F. R. Smith & Sons. Sagamore Road, Bolton Landing; (518) 644–5181.

Dockside Landing Marina. 9130 Lake Shore Drive, Hague; (518) 543–8888 or (518) 668–4300; www.lakegeorgeboats.com.

Ticonderoga

Head north on Route 9N.

Strategically located between Lake Champlain and Lake George, Ticonderoga is steeped in the military history of three countries and two wars. Today Ticonderoga is also known for its popular fishing derbies, scenic boat tours, and the birthplace of the first commercial pencil and school supply essential, the #2 Ticonderoga. Farther north, near Crown Point, is the reported lair of Lake Champlain's Champ, a prehistoric sea monster known to the Iroquois for hundreds of years. There have been more than 300 sightings of Champ since the seventeenth century, mostly in the area around Bulwagga Bay, a favorite local beach. To the west is scenic Schroon Lake, as well as more than seventy other sparkling lakes and ponds. For a picturesque drive, follow Boreas Road (Route 2) as it winds from North Hudson past many spectacular natural wonders, including the lovely Blue Ridge Falls.

Fort Ticonderoga (all ages)

Fort Road, off Route 74; (518) 585–2821; www.fort-ticonderoga.org. Open daily May through October 9:00 A.M. to 5:00 P.M. $$, children under 7 **free.**

This restored colonial fort, erected by the French in 1755 to protect their southern frontier, was called the "Key to the Continent." Captured by the British in 1759 during the French and Indian War, the fort was captured sixteen years later by Ethan Allen and his Green Mountain Boys during the Revolutionary War. The military museum houses some interesting artifacts, including a lock of George Washington's hair.

Ticonderoga Heritage Museum (ages 5 and up)

East end of village on Montcalm Street at Bicentennial Park; (518) 585–2696. Open daily June through Labor Day 10:00 A.M. to 4:00 P.M. Donation.

Everything you ever wanted to know about mills, be they of the saw, grist, graphite, iron, cotton, wool, or paper variety, can be gleaned here, along with other historical and regional lore.

Schroon Lake Boat Tours (ages 7 and up)

c/o Schroon Lake Chamber of Commerce, P.O. Box 726, Schroon Lake 12870; (518) 532–7675 or (888) SCHROON. Operating July and August Tuesday 2:00 P.M. and Saturday 7:00 P.M. Adults $$, juniors $, children under 6 not allowed on board.

Cruise the lake for an hour, catch up on the area's facts and folklore, and drink in the serene beauty of this 9-mile lake.

Natural Stone Bridge and Caves (all ages)

535 Stone Bridge Road, off Route 9, Pottersville; (518) 494–2283; www.stonebridgeand caves.com. Open daily Memorial Day to Labor Day 9:00 A.M. to 7:00 P.M., Labor Day to Columbus Day 10:00 A.M. to 6:00 P.M. Adults $$, children 5 through 12 $.

Take a self-guided tour of the caves, grottos, gorge, underground river, and waterfall of this unique geological formation or fish in the trout-laden pools, hike the easy nature trails, pan for pretty rocks in an enriched sluiceway, or gaze at the gems and geodes inside the rock shop and museum.

Crown Point State Historic Site (all ages)

Route 910L, 4 miles east of Route 9N/22 at Champlain Bridge, Crown Point; (518) 597–3666; www.nysparks.com/hist. Park open 9:00 A.M. to dusk, museum open to dusk May through October Wednesday through Monday. Grounds **free,** museum $, vehicle fee $.

Fort Saint Frederic was built in 1734 by the French in an effort to control the narrows of Lake Champlain. In 1759, The British wrested control and built Fort Crown Point. Today you can walk among the windswept ruins of two lost empires and imagine life on the front lines of the frontier.

Animals of the **Adirondacks**

The Adirondacks are alive with animals! Aside from the numerous wildlife parks, petting zoos, ranches, and farms that dot the area, the North Country is the habitat for 55 species of mammals, 218 species of birds, 86 species of fish, and 35 species of reptiles and amphibians. White-tail deer, black bear, lynx, red foxes, porcupines, beavers, and moose live here, as well as bald eagles, peregrine falcons, osprey, and wild turkeys.

Essex County Fish Hatchery (all ages)
Fish Hatchery Road, Crown Point; (518) 597–3844. Open daily year-round 8:00 A.M. to 4:00 P.M. $

At this indoor and outdoor trout farm, coin-operated feeding stations are part of the circle of life, from fry fish to fish fry.

Penfield Homestead Museum (ages 8 and up)
Ironville Road, Crown Point; (518) 597–3804; www.penfieldmuseum.org. Open June through October Thursday through Sunday 11:00 A.M. to 4:00 P.M. $

This local museum features exhibits on nineteenth-century inventor and industrialist Allen Penfield, as well as the area's iron industry and Civil War history.

Where to Eat

Hot Biscuit Diner. 528 Montcalm Street; (518) 585–3483. Diner specials include meat loaf, pot roast, freshly baked biscuits, home cooked desserts, and nightly specials Monday to Saturday. $

Where to Stay

Circle Court Motel. 6 Montcalm Street; (518) 585–7660. Fourteen rooms. $$

Elk Lake Lodge. Elk Lake Road, off Blue Ridge Road, north of North Hudson; (518) 532–7616 or (518) 942–0028. Breathtaking, peaceful retreat located on private lake, inside a 12,000-acre preserve laced with hiking trails. $$$$

Elizabethtown, Essex, and Plattsburgh

Take Route 9N/22 north along Lake Champlain to Westport, then turn left onto Route 9N to Elizabethtown, or continue north toward Essex on Route 22 into Plattsburgh.

Stroll the shore of the Saranac, through Plattsburgh's historic area, along RiverWalk Park. The Heritage Trail, a self-guided walking tour, originates here as well and winds past many of the town's architectural gems. The nearby villages of Elizabethtown and Essex also have a wealth of beautifully preserved historic districts, and both are surrounded by lush scenery. In Elizabethtown, walk around the Hand-Hale neighborhood or plan a picnic at Lincoln Pond. Essex boasts 160 structures built between the 1790s and 1860s, and the whole town is listed on the National Register of Historic Places.

Clinton County Historical Museum (all ages)

3 Cumberland Avenue, Plattsburgh; (518) 561–0340. Open year-round Tuesday through Friday noon to 4:00 P.M., Saturday 1:00 to 4:00 P.M. Closed holidays. $, children free.

This interesting museum has textiles, cannons, rifles from after the War of 1812, and the Redford Glass exhibit, as well as many archaeological artifacts discovered beneath the lake's surface.

Point au Roche State Park (all ages)

19 Camp Red Cloud Road, Plattsburgh; (518) 563–0369; www.nysparks.com/parks. $

Formerly farmland near the northwestern shore of Lake Champlain, this park offers a nature center, swimming at a sandy beach, and hiking trails through diverse habitats.

Cumberland Bay State Park (all ages)

152 Cumberland Road, Plattsburgh; (518) 563–5240; www.nysparks.com/parks. Open daily May through October 8:00 A.M. to 8:00 P.M. $

Encompassing 319 acres, this park and campground has a long sand beach, a playground, basketball and volleyball courts, a recreation room, camp store, biking and hiking trails, fishing, and campsites.

New York **Trivia**

The record low temperature in the state is –52°F, which was recorded in Old Forge on February 18, 1979.

Ausable Chasm (all ages)

2144 Route 9, off exit 34 of I–87, Ausable Chasm; (518) 834–7454 or (800) 537–1211; www.ausablechasm.com. Open daily mid-May through mid-October 9:30 A.M. to 4:00 P.M., to 5:00 P.M. July and August. Adults $$$, children 5 to 17 $$, under 5 free.

One of the oldest tourist attractions in the country and the only natural water park in the East, this dramatic gorge is the Ausable River's 500-million-year-old work in progress. Walk past unusual rock formations named Jacob's Ladder, the Punch Bowl, and the Elephant's Head, then board a twelve-person rubber raft for a flume adventure along a 2-mile stretch of gentle white water.

Adirondack Center Museum (all ages)

Court Street (Route 9), Elizabethtown; (518) 873–6466. Open Memorial Day through Columbus Day Monday through Saturday 9:00 A.M. to 5:00 P.M., Sunday 1:00 to 5:00 P.M. $

Eleven exhibit areas, housed in a former schoolhouse, examine pioneer life, wilderness exploration, mining, lumbering, transportation, and the area's Native American heritage. A Champlain Valley sound and light show offers a multimedia presentation of the French and Indian War, and there's also an extensive doll collection, garden, and colonial observation tower to explore.

Where to Eat

The Deer's Head Inn. Court Street, Elizabethtown; (518) 873–9903. Excellent casual and fancy food, served in oldest inn in the Adirondack Park. $$–$$$$

Where to Stay

Marine Village Cottages. 82 Dickson Point Road, Plattsburgh; (518) 563–5698. Three-bedroom cottages; with beach, playground, and boat docks. $$

Stonehelm Lodge. 72 Spellman Road, exit 40 off I–87, Plattsburgh; (518) 563–4800. With picnic area and nature trails. $$

Stony Water Cottage. Roscoe Road, Elizabethtown; (518) 873–9125. Two-story, two-bedroom house with fieldstone fireplace, situated on eighty-seven acres with little swimming brook, hiking trails, and gardens. $$$

Lake Placid and Wilmington

Take I–87 south to Route 9N west to Route 86 southwest.

Centered in the heart of the High Peaks region, Lake Placid has always possessed spectacular scenery. But after hosting the 1980 Olympics, it captured the heart of American winter sports, as well. Nearby Wilmington sits snugly at the feet of the fifth-highest peak in New York, majestic Whiteface Mountain. Iroquois legend tells the tale of the Great White Stag, whose death by magic arrows transformed the mountain's surface to white.

Olympic Center Ice Arenas (all ages)

218 Main Street, Lake Placid; (518) 523–1655 or (800) 462–6236; www.orda.org. Open daily year-round. Museum open daily 10:00 A.M. to 5:00 P.M.; self-guided audio tour $. Public skate hours mid-June through August 8:00 to 9:30 P.M. Center free, except for special events; museum and skating $.

With four ice rinks, this is where the pros practice, and the U.S. Hockey Team and figure skating champions train year-round. A small museum houses exhibits from the Lake Placid Olympics of 1932 and 1980, and for a brief period on summer nights families can skate the site of our hockey team's 1980 "Miracle on Ice."

MacKenzie-Interval Olympic Ski Jump Complex (all ages)

Route 73, Lake Placid; (518) 523–2202 or (800) 462–6236; www.orda.org/skijump.htm. Seven miles southeast of Lake Placid. Open daily year-round 9:00 A.M. to 4:00 P.M. Closed Thanksgiving and Christmas. $

Take a ride on the chairlift elevator to the 120-meter ski jump tower used in Olympic and World Cup events. In summer and fall, visitors can watch the U.S. freestyle aerial team train, as plastic mats on the jumps sub for snow.

Verizon Sports Complex (all ages)

Route 73 (south of the ski complex at Olympic Sports Complex), Lake Placid; (518) 523–1655 or (800) 462–6236; www.orda.org/verizoncomplex.htm. Open daily year-round 9:00 A.M. to 4:00 P.M., closed Monday December through March. $–$$$$

Cool running on the bobsleds is offered year-round, with luge rides available in winter at this Olympic event site. A mellower means of movement is a trolley ride to the top in summer. The nearby Cross-Country Center has 31 miles of groomed trails to explore.

Adirondack Craft Center (all ages)

93 Saranac Avenue, Lake Placid; (518) 523–2062; www.adirondackcraftcenter.com. Open daily year-round 10:00 A.M. to 5:00 P.M., to 6:00 P.M. in summer. Closed Thanksgiving and Christmas.

The folk art of the North Country—from the twiglike Adirondack furniture and intricately woven baskets to the lifelike hand-carved decoys—is gracefully rustic, and there is always a chance to watch artisans at work.

John Brown Farm State Historic Site (ages 5 and up)

2 John Brown Road, off Route 73, Lake Placid; (518) 523–3900. Open May through late October Monday and Wednesday through Sunday 10:00 A.M. to 5:00 P.M. $ guided tour.

This is the home and final resting place of John Brown, the famous abolitionist. He was executed in 1859 after attempting to seize the U.S. Arsenal at Harpers Ferry, West Virginia. Outside, winding through Brown's farm, is an easy nature trail to explore.

Whiteface Mountain Visitor Center (all ages)

Box 277, Route 86, Wilmington; (518) 946–2255 or (888) WHITEFACE; www.whiteface region.com. Open daily 9:00 A.M. to 1:00 P.M. in winter, to 4:00 P.M. in summer. Free.

Stop here for friendly information about area events, then step outside and fish for famously titanic trout along a 5-mile catch-and-release section of the west branch of the Ausable River.

Whiteface Mountain Ski Center and Gondola (all ages)

Route 86, Wilmington; (518) 946–2223 or (800) 462–6236 (snow info.), www.orda.org and www.whiteface.com. Ski season runs late November through April. Gondola rides mid-June through mid-October and Thanksgiving weekend through mid-April. Skiing $$$$, gondola $$.

This is the largest ski resort in New York and the only one of the High Peaks reachable by car. With the highest vertical drop in the East (3,216 feet), this was the site of the 1980 Winter Olympics downhill competitions. The wide variety of trails provides fun for all skill levels, and families will appreciate the Whiteface Kids Kampus, with ski and snowboard instruction. Ride the gondola to the summit of Little Whiteface, then hike back to base lodge along the scenic Stag Brook Falls nature trail.

High Falls Gorge (all ages)

Route 86, Wilmington Notch; (518) 946–2278; www.highfallsgorge.com. Open daily May through October 9:00 A.M. to 5:30 P.M., to 5:00 P.M. May, June, September, and October. Call for winter hours. $$

Follow a self-guided nature walk alongside the rushing Ausable River, with three waterfalls that plunge past ancient granite cliffs.

Take Me to **the Water**

Lake Placid Marina. Mirror Lake Drive, Lake Placid; (518) 523–9704.

Adirondack Rafting Co. Main Street, Indian Lake; (518) 523–1635.

Middle Earth Expeditions. Route 73, Lake Placid; (518) 523–7172.

Blue Heron Drive-It-Yourself Boating Vacations. 88 Main Street, Whitehall; (914) 668–1040.

Lake Placid Olympic Site Passport and
Gold Medal Adventure

Lake Placid/Wilmington region; (518) 523–1655 or (800) 462–6236; www.orda.org. Tour June through mid-October. Times vary with site. Tickets may be purchased at any Olympic attraction, the Center box office, and many local hotels and campgrounds. Passport $19 per person, children under 7 free. Gold Medal Adventure available June through September Tuesday through Friday 10:00 A.M. to 3:00 P.M. Reservations required June and September, suggested July and August. Gold Medal Adventure $65 per person per day.

Sponsored by Eastman Kodak, this self-guided motor tour simplifies sightseeing the sports centers. The money-saving package includes one-time admission to the Ski Jump Complex, Verizon Sports Complex, Olympic Museum, Whiteface Mountain, plus discounts at many other area attractions. A new attraction for children ages seven and up is the Gold Medal Adventure. Kids can choose a one- to four-day combo of Olympic winter sport activities, such as sledding, luge, and freestyle jumping, led by international coaches and athletes.

Where to Eat

Goldberries. 137 Main Street, Lake Placid; (518) 523–1799. Outdoor dining, serving breakfast, lunch, and dinner, prime rib buffets, plus a children's menu and toy room. $$

Hungry Trout Restaurant. Route 86, 2 miles southwest from Wilmington; (518) 946–2217 or (800) 766–9137; www .hungrytrout.com. Serving a variety of trout to titillate your tastebuds; as well as steak, wild game, and pasta dishes; a children's menu; and great views overlooking the Ausable River. $$$

Mini-Golf in the
Lake Placid Area

Putt-N-Play Mini Golf. Route 86, Wilmington; (518) 946–7733 or (800) 245–0228.

Mount Marcy

The highest peak of the High Peaks region and all of New York is Mount Marcy, towering over the Adirondacks at 5,344 feet. It's also the origin of the Hudson River, flowing from Lake Tear of the Clouds, a mile from the summit. So remote was this area that the source of the Nile River was discovered long before the source of the Hudson. While the trek to the top is a popular one, the grade is a bit steep for younger children, and it can get very crowded in summer. For more information, contact the Department of Environmental Conservation at (518) 897–1200; www.americasroof.com/ny.html, or the Adirondack Mountain Club at (518) 523–3441.

Where to Stay

Adirondak Loj. Adirondak Loj Road, off Route 73, 8 miles south of Lake Placid; (518) 523–3441; www.adk.org. Private rooms, family rooms, and campsites, with many nature workshops for families. $–$$$$

Mirror Lake Inn. 5 Mirror Lake Drive; (518) 523–2544; www.mirrorlakeinn.com. Casual elegance, indoor and outdoor pools, beach, afternoon tea, paddleboats and rowboats, and children "stay and eat **free**" packages. $$$$

Natural Attractions

The Adirondack Nature Conservancy preserves seven sanctuaries within the North Country. Each is unique and is home to unusual or rare plants or animals. For more information about these gems of nature, contact the ANC at P.O. Box 65, Route 73, Keene Valley 12943; (518) 576–2082; www.tnc.org.

Silver Lake Preserve, Black Brook

Clintonville Pine Barrens, Clintonville

Whiteface Mountain, Wilmington

Spring Pond Bog, Altamont

Everton Falls Preserve, Santa Clara

Gadway Sandstone Pavement Barrens, Mooers

Coon Mountain Preserve, Wadhams

Saranac Lake

Take Route 86 west.

When Dr. Edward Livingston Trudeau was diagnosed with tuberculosis in 1876, he decided to come to the Adirondacks to die. Instead, the fresh mountain air and friendly people restored his health and inspired him in 1884 to open the first successful tuberculosis clinic in the country at Saranac Lake.

Robert Louis Stevenson Memorial Cottage (ages 7 and up)
11 Stevenson Lane (off junction of Routes 3 and 86); (518) 891–1462 or (800) 347–1992; www.adirondacks.com/robertlstevenson.html. Open July through mid-September Tuesday through Sunday 9:30 A.M. to 4:30 P.M.; closed Mondays. $

Calling Saranac Lake his "Switzerland in the Adirondacks," the author of *Treasure Island* and other memorable children's classics used this as his mountain retreat. The cottage is full of Stevenson's personal items.

Dewey Mountain (all ages)
State Road, off Route 3; (518) 891–2697 or (800) 347–1992; www.saranaclake.com/dewey. Season and trails open when snow conditions permit. Open daily noon to 5:00 P.M., to 8:00 P.M. on Tuesday. Free.

This family-friendly Nordic-style ski center offers groomed cross-country ski trails for beginners to advanced, plus lighted trails for night ski adventures, lessons, and tours.

Adirondack Park Visitor Interpretive Center (all ages)
Route 30, Paul Smiths, 1 mile north of Paul Smith's College; (518) 327–3000; www.north net.org/adirondackvic/. Open daily year-round 9:00 A.M. to 5:00 P.M. Closed Thanksgiving and Christmas. Free.

This center offers interesting exhibits on the area's logging camps and the effects of acid rain. Touch-screen computers with free printouts provide hiking and canoe trail information, and park rangers are available to answer your questions. Take a walk through the butterfly house out back, then explore one of the nature trails that meander through a sixty-acre marsh.

Area **Campgrounds**

For camping reservations, call (800) 456–CAMP, or log on to www.reserve america.com.

Fish Creek Pond State Public Campground. (518) 891–4560. $

Rollins Pond State Public Campground. (518) 891–3239. $

Suggested **Reading**

The Last of the Mohicans by James Fenimore Cooper

Farmer Boy by Laura Ingalls Wilder

The Iroquois by Craig A. Doherty & Katherine M. Doherty

The Arrow Over the Door by Joseph Bruchac

Shoo-Fly and Other Folktales from Upstate by Donald J. Sawyer

The Mystery of the Lake Monster by Gertrude Chandler Warner

White Pine Camp (all ages)
At the end of White Pine Road (off intersection of Route 86 and Route 30), Paul Smiths; (518) 327–3030 or (518) 834–9328; www.whitepinecamp.com. Open for public tours every Saturday from July through Labor Day weekend at 10:00 A.M. and 1:30 P.M. Adults \$\$, children \$.

Built in 1907 and overlooking secluded Osgood Pond, this is a classic Adirondack "Great Camp." The summer White House for President Calvin Coolidge in 1926, the recently restored site encompasses more than twenty buildings, including an indoor bowling alley and a Japanese teahouse.

Six Nations Indian Museum (ages 4 and up)
Roakdale Road, Route 30 (8 miles from Gabriels off Route 86), Onchiota; (518) 891–2299; e-mail: redmaple@northnet.org. Open July through Labor Day daily except Monday 10:00 A.M. to 5:00 P.M. \$

Founded by schoolteacher Ray Fadden, this museum houses hundreds of historical and contemporary artifacts of the Iroquois Confederacy. Of special interest to children are the pictographs used to tell the stories of the Mohawk, Seneca, Oneida, Onondaga, Cayuga, and Tuscarora tribes.

Other Equestrian Excitement **in the Area**

Emerald Springs Ranch. Lake Clear Road, Saranac Lake; (518) 891–3727; www.emerald-springs.com.

Cold River Ranch. Corey's Road, Tupper Lake; (518) 359–7559.

Also in **the Area**

Mount Pisgah Ski Center. (518) 891–0970 or (518) 891–4150.

Saint Regis Canoe Area (ages 8 and up)

Access points include Little Clear Pond and Paul Smith's College. For equipment rental, supplies, maps, advice, and guides, stop at St. Regis Canoe Outfitters on Floodwood Road, Lake Clear, about 4 miles off Route 30; (518) 891–1838 or (888) 775–2925; www.canoe outfitters.com. Canoe area free; rentals $$$$.

The biggest wilderness canoe area in the Northeast, this 20,000-acre expanse is dotted with dozens of ponds, lakes, and streams perfect for exploring by canoe and kayak, most with minimal or no portages.

Adirondack Fish Hatchery (all ages)

Route 30, Saranac Inn, Lake Clear; (518) 891–3358. Open 8:00 A.M. to 4:30 P.M. daily, including weekends. Free.

See schools of salmon swim, future inhabitants of nearby lakes and rivers swim in rearing ponds.

Where to Eat

Tail O' the Pup. Route 86, Ray Brook; (518) 891–0777. Eat inside, under a tent, or be served by a carhop as you feast on ribs, onion rings, waffle fries, and seafood. $–$$

Wawbeek on Upper Saranac Lake. 553 Panther Mountain Road, off Route 30, Upper Saranac Lake; (518) 359–2656 or (800) 953–2656; www.wawbeek.com. Classic Adirondack cuisine, with daily specials and Monday-night buffet. $$$$

Where to Stay

Hotel Saranac of Paul Smith's College. 101 Main Street; (518) 891–2200 or (800) 937–0211; www.hotelsaranac.com. The lobby is a reproduction of the foyer in the Florentine Danvanzati Palace, Lydia's restaurant is terrific, and children under eighteen stay free. $$$

Pine Terrace Motel & Resort. 94 Moody Road, Tupper Lake; (518) 359–9258. Rooms, cabins, and cottages; pool and kids' wading pool, tennis courts, lawn games, and boat rentals. $$$

Malone

Head north on Route 30.

Every August for nearly 150 years, the Franklin County Fair has materialized in Malone. From livestock shows and cooking contests to the magic of the midway, this is a wonderful slice of North Country good-time fun.

Malone Memorial Recreation Area (all ages)

Duane Street; summer (518) 483–3550, winter (518) 483–0680; www.adirondacklakes .com/attract.cfm. **Open daily Memorial Day to Labor Day 9:00 A.M. to 8:00 P.M. Free.**

A major migration stop for thousands of Canada geese in their trek southward each fall, this park has a large playground, **free** paddleboats, supervised swimming, tennis courts, picnic pavilions, and special children's programs.

Titus Mountain (all ages)

Johnson Road, off County Route 25; (518) 483–3740; (800) 848–8766 for ski conditions; www.titusmountain.com. **Season depends on snow conditions but usually runs Thanksgiving to just before Easter. Open Sunday through Tuesday 9:00 A.M. to 4:00 P.M., Wednesday through Saturday 9:00 A.M. to 10:00 P.M. Adults $$$$; children $$$; under 5, skiing with an adult, free.**

This family ski resort offers twenty-seven trails, seven lifts, night skiing, snowtubing, a ski school, two lodges, a cafeteria, and special children's races and programs on weekends and holidays.

Franklin County **Fishing Fun**

For young fisherfolk who prefer angling with an advantage, several stocked pond preserves almost guarantee you'll catch a good-size trout or salmon quickly. Because these are privately owned ponds, you don't need a license, you pay between $3.00 to $5.00 per pound of live weight, and cleaning the catch is often included.

Hinchinbrooke Fish Hatchery. Box 1010, Earlville Road, Chateaugay 12920; (518) 497–6505.

Restful Ponds. Route 374, Brainardsville; (518) 425–3319.

Also in **the Area**

Wood's Sugar Bush Tours. Burke County Road, Chateaugay; (518) 497–6387/6956.

Franklin Historical Museum. 51 Milwaukee Street, Malone; (518) 483–2750.

High Falls Park (all ages)

One mile south of Route 11, Chateaugay; (518) 497–3156. Open mid-May to mid-October 9:00 A.M. to 9:00 P.M. $, under 5 free.

Formed more than 12,000 years ago by retreating glaciers, these 120-foot cascades create a lovely fishing spot, and there's a scenic nature trail to explore.

Almanzo Wilder Homestead (all ages)

Burke Road, off Route 11, Burke; (518) 483–FARM or (518) 483–1207; www.almanzowilder farm.com. Open Memorial Day to Labor Day Monday through Saturday 11:00 A.M. to 4:00 P.M., Sunday 1:00 to 4:00 P.M. Adults $$, children $.

For fans of the Little House on the Prairie series, this restored farmhouse was the boyhood home of author Laura Ingalls Wilder's husband, Almanzo. Recollections of his childhood here were the inspiration for her book *Farmer Boy.*

Where to Eat

Villa Fiori Italian Restaurant. 18 East Main Street; (518) 481–6557. Italian favorites, with half orders available for children. $$

Where to Stay

Crossroads. Box 239, Moira, 11 miles west on Route 11; (518) 529–7372 or (800) 433–XRDS; www.crossroadsmoira.com. Pool, restaurant, and children under twelve stay free. $–$$

Four Seasons Motel. 236 West Main Street; (518) 483–3490 or (877) 299–3448; www.fsmotel.com. Pool. $$

Blue Mountain Lake

Head south on Route 30.

This azure jewel sparkles in the center of the Adirondacks, surrounded by thick forests of birch, oak, and pine.

Adirondack Museum (all ages)

Route 28N and Route 30; (518) 352–7311; www.adirondackmuseum.org. Open daily Memorial Day through mid-October 10:00 A.M. to 5:00 P.M. Adults $$$, children 6 to 12 $$, under 6 free.

Called the "Smithsonian of the Adirondacks" by *National Geographic,* this is a must-see museum. Take a self-guided tour of twenty-two terrific exhibit areas that explore the land and the lives of the Adirondackers.

Adirondack Lakes Center for the Arts (all ages)

Routes 28 and 30 (next to the post office); (518) 352–7715; www.adk-arts.org. Open year-round Monday through Friday 10:00 A.M. to 4:00 P.M.; in July and August also Saturday 10:00 A.M. to 4:00 P.M., Sunday noon to 4:00 P.M. Free, but $$–$$$ for evening events.

This community center offers a seasonal schedule of concerts, theater, and artist workshops, as well as an excellent arts and crafts shop.

Adirondack Park Visitor Interpretive Center (all ages)

Box 101, Route 28N, Newcomb 12852, 14 miles east of Long Lake; (518) 582–2000; www.northnet.org/adirondackvic. Open daily 9:00 A.M. to 5:00 P.M. Closed Thanksgiving and Christmas. Free.

This is a good place to learn about the natural history of this six-million-acre park. The multimedia presentations and interpretive exhibits are informative, and computer printouts of canoe and hiking trails are available. Take a self-guided or naturalist-led trail walk along the 3.5-mile trail system, past dense woods and beaver ponds.

Where to Eat

Oak Barrel Restaurant. Routes 28 and 30, Indian Lake; (518) 648–5115. Steak, seafood, chicken, pasta, pizza, and burgers, amid Adirondack decor. $$

Also in **the Area**

Natural History Museum of the Adirondacks. P.O. Box 897, Tupper Lake 12986; (518) 359–7800; www.adknature.org.

Marinas in **the Area**

Scenic boat trips and rentals for fun on the water.

Blue Mountain Lake Boat Livery. Indian Lake; (518) 352–7351.

Camp Hilary Marina. Deerland Road, Long Lake; (518) 624–2233; www .camphilary.com.

Lake Eaton State Public Campground. Route 30, Long Lake; (518) 624–2641.

Clark's Indian Lake Marina. Sabael; (518) 648–5459.

Long Lake Marina. Box 146, Route 30, Long Lake 12847; (518) 624–2266.

Where to Stay

Burke's Cottages. Route 28, Lake Shore Road, Sabael, Indian Lake; (518) 648–5258. Six cottages, each with view of Indian Lake; private swimming beach, dock, and hiking trails. $$$$

Curry's Cottages. Route 28; (518) 352–7354 or (518) 352–7355. Ten cottages and a shallow sandy beach great for small fry. $$–$$$$

Timberlock. Off Route 30, Sabael, Indian Lake; (518) 648–5494 or (802) 453–2540. Rustic resort with cottages and cabins, woodstoves, screened porches, sandy beach, boats, tennis courts, hiking trails, horseback riding, a wide range of nature-related activities and programs for all ages, and three meals a day. $$$$

North Creek

Take Route 28 east.

Some of the best white water in the East flows through this area's dramatic Hudson River Gorge, and while the high water of spring is best left to the pros, summer is family-friendly.

Gore Mountain (all ages)
Peaceful Valley Road, off Route 28; (518) 251–2411; ski conditions (800) 342–1234; www.goremountain.com. Open daily mid-November to late April 8:00 A.M. to 4:30 P.M. $$$$

This is the second-largest ski resort in New York, with a 2,100-foot vertical drop, forty-four trails, and eight lifts. There are also excellent cross-country trails, a ski school, a ski patrol, special children's programs, and a nursery. If you're here in the fall, take the gondola ride to the top to see seriously spectacular foliage.

Barton Garnet Mines (ages 5 and up)

Barton Mines Road (5 miles from Route 28); (518) 251–2706. Open late June through Labor Day Monday through Saturday 9:30 A.M. to 5:00 P.M., Sunday 11:00 A.M. to 5:00 P.M., weekends only Labor Day through Columbus Day. $, plus fee for rocks collected ($1.00 a pound).

The garnet has garnered the honor of being New York's state stone. This is one of the largest garnet mines in the world and produces much of the world's industrial garnet.

Where to Eat

The Copperfield Inn Dining Room. 307 Main Street; (518) 251–2500 or (800) 424–9910; www.copperfieldinn.com. Excellent American cuisine, plus a children's menu. $–$$$

Where to Stay

Black Mountain Ski Lodge and Motel. Route 8, 4 miles west of Route 28; (518) 251–2800 or (888) 846–4858; www.black mountainskilodge.com. Pool, playground, restaurant, with family rates and sports packages. $$

Garnet Hill. At top of Thirteenth Lake Road, off Route 28, North River; (518) 251–2444 or (800) 497–4207; www.garnet-hill.com. Wonderful rustic lodge and cottages with private beach, stocked lake, nature trails, cross-country ski trails, mountain bikes, game room, a great restaurant, and canoe, rowboat, and sailboat rentals. $$$–$$$$

White **Water!** (ages 10 and up)

Hudson River Rafting Co. 1 Main Street; (518) 251–3215, (518) 696–2964, or (800) 888–RAFT; www.hudsonriverrafting.com.

Whitewater Challengers. Route 28; (570) 443–9727 or (800) 443–RAFT; www.wc-rafting.com.

Whitewater World. 307 Main Street; (800) WHITEWATER; www.white waterrafting.com.

Old Forge and Raquette Lake

West on Route 28.

The Fulton Chain, a necklace of eight lakes strung along Route 28, links Old Forge to Raquette Lake. Many of the Great Camps were built here, and today the area's beauty attracts hikers, canoeists, mountain bikers, white-water rafters, and snowmobilers.

Adirondack Scenic Railroad (all ages)

Thendara Station, Route 28, Old Forge; (315) 369–6290; www.adirondackrr.com. Canoe & Rail (315) 369–6286. Operating May through October, five departures daily in season. $$–$$$$

Ride the rails aboard vintage coaches for an hour-long excursion past lush forests and the lovely Moose River. Special events include train robberies in summer and fall foliage and Halloween spook trains in autumn. A canoe and rail combo allows folks to canoe the Moose, then return by train, or try the two-hour trip aboard air-conditioned coaches to historic Union Station in Utica.

Arts Center (all ages)

Route 28, P.O. Box 1144, Old Forge 13420; (315) 369–6411; www.artscenteroldforge.org. Open daily year-round 10:00 A.M. to 4:00 P.M., Sunday noon to 4:00 P.M. Closed major holidays. Free; events $–$$.

This is the oldest multiarts center in the Adirondacks, with a gallery of permanent and changing exhibits, special workshops and programs for families, and seasonal concerts and guided nature hikes.

Forest Industries Exhibit Hall (ages 5 and up)

3311 Route 28, Old Forge; (315) 369–3078; e-mail: nela@northernlogger.com. Open Memorial Day through October Monday and Wednesday through Saturday 10:00 A.M. to 5:00 P.M., Sunday noon to 5:00 P.M.; September and October weekends only. Free.

Exhibits, dioramas, and scale models of forest and wildlife management are on display here, explaining the history of logging and the future need for forestry management.

Great Camp Sagamore (all ages)

Sagamore Road, 4 miles south of Route 28, Raquette Lake; (315) 354–5311; www .sagamore.org. Open daily July through Labor Day and weekends only Labor Day to Columbus Day. Guided tours 10:00 A.M. and 1:30 P.M. Spring and fall tours weekends at 1:30 P.M. Adults $$$, children $$.

Built in 1897, this was Alfred Vanderbilt Sr.'s wilderness retreat and hunting lodge. The classic Great Camp, Sagamore hospitality was extended to movie stars, moguls, and the elite of the gaming crowd.

Cross-Country Skiing **in the Adirondacks**

For the quintessential Adirondack experience, it's hard to beat cross-country skiing. There are ski centers throughout the region, but the area around Speculator and Lake Pleasant, known as Big Country, is laced with hundreds of miles of groomed trails surrounded by the West Canada Lake, Silver Lake, and Siamese Ponds Wilderness Areas. The following are some popular cross-country ski centers in the Adirondacks:

Lapland Lake Cross-Country Ski Center. 139 Lapland Lake Road, Northville; (518) 863–4974 or (800) 453–SNOW; www.laplandlake.com.

Garnet Hill Cross-Country Ski Center. Thirteenth Lake Road, North River; (518) 251–2821.

Cunningham's Ski Barn. 1 Main Street, North Creek; (518) 251–3215 or (800) 888–RAFT.

Friends Lake Inn Nordic Ski Center. Friends Lake Road, Chestertown; (518) 494–4751; www.friendslake.com.

Adirondack Woodcraft Ski Touring Center. Rondaxe Road, Old Forge; (315) 369–6031.

Ausable Chasm Cross-Country Ski Center. Route 9, Ausable Chasm; (518) 834–9990.

Cascade Cross-Country Ski Center. Cascade Road, Lake Placid; (518) 523–9605.

Lake Placid Nordic Center. Route 86, Lake Placid; (518) 523–7888 or (800) 422–6757.

T & M Equestrian Center (ages 4 and up)
Route 28, Inlet; (315) 357–3594. Open daily 9:00 A.M. to 6:00 P.M. mid-June through Columbus Day. $$$

Pony rides and horse trail rides.

Water **Excursions**

Cool off with a cruise, canoe, seaplane, or tubing trip through the center of the Adirondacks.

Old Forge Lake Cruises. Main Street Dock, Route 28, Old Forge; (315) 369–6473; www.oldforgecruises.com.

Adirondack River Outfitters. Main Street, Old Forge; (800) 525–7238; www.aroadventures.com.

Raquette Lake Navigation Company. Off Route 28, Raquette Lake; (315) 354–5532; www.raquettelakenavigation.com.

Tickner's Moose River Canoe Trips. Main Street, Old Forge; (315) 369–6286.

Burke's Marina. Route 28, Raquette Lake; (315) 354–4623.

Rivett's Marine. Waterfront of Old Forge; (315) 369–3123.

Clark's Boat Rentals. Fourth Lake, Eagle Bay; (315) 357–3231.

Dunn's Boat Rentals. Big Moose Road, Big Moose Lake, Eagle Bay; (315) 357–3532.

Bird's Seaplane Service. Route 28, Inlet; (315) 357–3631; www.inletny.com.

The Stillwater Shop. Box 243, Star Route, Lowville 13367; (315) 376–2110; www.stillwaterreservoir.com.

Whitewater Challengers. Route 28, Okara Lakes, Old Forge; (570) 443–9532 or (800) 443–RAFT; www.wcrafting.com.

Old Forge **Family Fun Centers**

When the kids have maxed out on nature's scenic sights, head for these Adirondack amusements:

Enchanted Forest/Water Safari. 3181 Route 28, Old Forge; (315) 369–6145; www.watersafari.com.

Calypso Cove. Route 28, next to Enchanted Forest, Old Forge; (315) 369–2222.

Where to Eat

The Farm Restaurant. Route 28, Thendara; (315) 369–6199. Great breakfasts and lunches, soups, sandwiches, and salads, served surrounded by hundreds of farm tools, with a children's play area outside. $

Trails End Restaurant. North Street, Old Forge; (315) 369–2632. Everything from pizza and burgers to pasta, chicken, seafood, and steak, with a six-lane bowling alley attached. $$

Where to Stay

Brynilsen's Viking Village. South shore of Fourth Lake, north of Old Forge; (315) 357–3150. Cottages with a Viking motif; sandy beach, and children's programs. $$$$

Holl's Inn. South Shore Road, Fourth Lake, Inlet; (315) 357–2941; www.hollsinn.com. Family summer resort on Fourth Lake, with sand beach, tennis, boating, golf, and lakeside dining; meals included. $$$–$$$$

The Kenmore. Off Route 28, on north shore of Fourth Lake, 8 miles northeast of Old Forge; (315) 357–5285; www.kenmore cottages.com. All-weather cottages, most with lake view; private sandy beach, playground, picnic area, rowboats and canoes, and volleyball court. $$

Oswego

Go south on Route 28 to Route 12 to connect with I–90 toward Syracuse, then head north on Route 481.

The first freshwater port in the country, Oswego today is an angler's paradise and a good place to embark upon the Seaway Trail.

Roadster Rooters, **Rejoice!**

Oswego Speedway. 300 East Albany Street, Oswego; (315) 342–0646; www.oswegospeedway.com.

Brewerton Speedway. Route 11, Brewerton; (315) 668–RACE or (315) 668–6906; www.brewerton-speedway.com.

Fulton Speedway. Route 57S, Fulton; (315) 593–6531; www.fulton speedway.com.

H. Lee White Marine Museum (all ages)

In front of West First Street Pier; (315) 342–0480; www.hleewhitemarinemuseum.com. Hours and days of operation vary by season; call for details.

Exhibits on shipwrecks, archaeological artifacts, and the legendary lake monsters of the region are displayed in this charming museum. Kids can explore a World War II tugboat and derrick barge docked outside.

Fort Ontario (all ages)

1 East Fourth Street; (315) 343–4711; www.co.oswego.ny.us/. Open mid-May through October Wednesday through Saturday 10:00 A.M. to 5:00 P.M., Sunday 1:00 to 4:30 P.M. $, children under 4 free.

Costumed guides take you on a tour of this restored nineteenth-century fort, with cannon and musket firings daily and exhibits on life lived behind the logs. This is also the site of the only refugee camp for Holocaust survivors during World War II.

Selkirk Shores State Park (all ages)

7101 State Route 3, Pulaski; (315) 298–5737 or (800) 456–CAMP; www.nysparks.com/parks. Park open daily year-round, campgrounds open May through October. $

Sandwiched between Lake Ontario and the Salmon River, this 980-acre park has a sand beach, hiking trails, a playground, lake and river fishing, a recreation program and hall, cabins, and campsites.

Where to Eat

Vona's. West Tenth and Utica Streets; (315) 343–8710. Homemade pasta, Italian specialties, and children's menu. $$

Where to Stay

Best Western Captain's Quarters. 26 East First Street; (315) 342–4040 or (800) 528–1234. Rooms and suites, indoor pool, restaurant, view of the river, and children under twelve stay **free.** $$$–$$$$

Oswego Inn. 180 East Tenth Street; (315) 342–6200 or (800) 721–7341. Complimentary continental breakfast, and children under twelve stay **free.** $$

More **Oswego County Fun**

Midway Drive-In Theater. West River Road (Route 48), Minetto; (315) 343–0211 or (315) 593–0699.

Sandy Island Beach. County Road 15, Sandy Creek; (315) 387–2657 or (800) 596–3200.

Rice Creek Field Station. Thompson Road, State University of New York at Oswego; (315) 312–7961.

Salmon River Fish Hatchery. 2133 Route 22, Altmar; (315) 298–5051.

Oneida Lake Fish Cultural Station. Route 49, Constantia; (315) 623–7311.

Thunder Island Amusement Complex. Wilcox Road and Route 48, Fulton; (315) 598–8016; www.thunder-island.com.

Grandpa Bob's Animal Park. Valley Road, Mexico; (315) 298–2347.

Tri-R Karts & Super Golf. Route 3, Pulaski; (315) 298–RACE.

Fort Brewerton & Block House Museum. Route 11, Brewerton; (315) 668–8801.

John D. Murray Firefighters Museum. East Side Firestation, East Cayuga Street, Oswego; (315) 343–0999.

The Thousand **Islands**

This is the longest navigable inland passage in the world, stretching for 2,300 miles and dotted with 1,864 islands. Iroquois legend tells the tale of the Great Spirit's gift of a magical garden, called Manitonna, given to the tribes on the condition they play nice. When the tribes broke their word and started quarreling among themselves, the Great Spirit picked up the paradise and headed home. Somehow, however, the garden slipped from the Spirit's hands, and the Eden of the Iroquois fell into the Saint Lawrence River, shattering into the islands we see today. Follow the 454-mile Seaway Trail, a National Historic Motor and Water Byway, where the best scenery and most attractions are located. There are forty-five New York and Canadian parks in this region, so bring the camping gear. For maps and information, call (315) 646–1000 or (800) SEAWAY–T, log on to www.seawaytrail.com, or visit the Seaway Trail Discovery Center at Ray and West Main Streets in Sackets Harbor. Open year-round daily May through October, Monday through Saturday November through April, from 10:00 A.M. to 5:00 P.M. $.

Sackets Harbor

Follow the Seaway Trail along Route 3 north.

In 1804, Augustus Sacket acquired at auction enough land on the shores of Lake Ontario to build a village. His primary interest was to trade with Canada, less than 30 miles away. Unfortunately, the U.S. Embargo Act of 1808 shut down operations, and Sackets Harbor became the major military stronghold of America's northern frontier in the War of 1812. Today the charming town offers families a strong historical and architectural heritage, as well as waterfront concerts, festivals, and fireworks on the Fourth of July.

Sackets Harbor Heritage Area Visitors Center (all ages)

301 West Main Street; (315) 646–2321; www.sacketsharborny.com. Open Memorial Day through Columbus Day daily 10:00 A.M. to 5:00 P.M. and by appointment Columbus Day through Memorial Day. Free.

Stop here first for Seaway Trail information, a good multimedia introduction to the area, and special events.

Sackets Harbor Battlefield State Historic Site (all ages)

505 West Washington Street; (315) 646–3634; www.nysegov.com. Open Memorial Day through Labor Day Tuesday through Saturday 10:00 A.M. to 5:00 P.M., Sunday 11:00 A.M. to 5:00 P.M. Grounds open year-round 8:00 A.M. to sunset. $

Every summer the Battle of Sackets Harbor, a major battle of the War of 1812, is reenacted at this state historic site. There's also a museum at the Navy Yard featuring artifacts from that war and a hands-on battle station.

Old McDonald's Farm (all ages)

North Harbor Road; (315) 583–5737; www.1000islands.com./mcfarm. Open daily at 10:00 A.M. May through October. $

There's a plethora of petting animals as well as pony rides at this farm-theme children's village, with a nice mini-golf course next door.

Thompson Park and New York State Living Museum (all ages)

1 Thompson Park, off State Street, Watertown; (315) 782–6180; www.nyslivingmuseum.org. Open daily year-round 10:00 A.M. to 4:00 P.M. Adults $$, children $.

This 355-acre park and zoo has pleasant panoramic lookouts and naturalistic exhibits featuring black bear, eagle, cougar, lynx, wolf, and elk. For those who wish to get up close and personal, there's a petting zoo and camel and donkey rides. There's also a swimming pool, a playground, walking trails, and a picnic area.

Sci-Tech Center (all ages)

154 Stone Street, Watertown; (315) 788–1340. Open year-round Tuesday through Saturday 10:00 A.M. to 4:00 P.M. Closed major holidays. $

This wonderful interactive museum of science and technology offers more than forty hands-on science exhibits.

Alex T. Duffy Fairgrounds (all ages)

Coffeen Street, Watertown; (315) 785–7775; Watertown Wizards (315) 782–4006; Watertown Red & Black (315) 779–8646; www.eteamz.com/watertownredandblack. Park free, events $–$$.

Home of the Jefferson County Fair, the oldest continuously operating fair in the United States, this is also home to the Wizards, a collegiate baseball team. For football fans, this is also home to the Red & Blacks, the oldest semi-pro football team in the country. Available to the public are the athletic fields, an indoor sports center (315–768–4625), picnic areas, swimming, and fishing.

Horseback Riding **in the Area**

Artisan Well Stables. Spencer Road, off Sulphur Springs Road, Watertown; (315) 782–6221.

Parks Near **Sackets Harbor**

Waterworks Park. Huntington Street, Watertown; (315) 785–8870.

Westcott Beach State Park. Route 3 West, Sackets Harbor; (315) 646–2239 or (800) 456–CAMP; www.nysparks.com/parks.

Southwick Beach State Park. 8119 Southwicks Place, Woodville; (315) 846–5338 or (800) 456–CAMP; www.nysparks.com/parks.

Long Point State Park. 7495 State Park Road, off Route 12E, Three Mile Bay; (315) 649–5258 or (800) 456–CAMP; www.nysparks.com/parks.

Behling's Spookhill Farms (all ages)
12139 Route 11, Adams Center; (315) 583–6181. Open mid-September through December; call for hours. $

Kids will enjoy walking through a corn tunnel to fields dotted with pumpkins and Indian popcorn, and there's a seasonal spookhouse for the braver souls.

Where to Eat

Partridge Berry Inn. 26561 Route 3, Watertown; (315) 788–4610. Rustic decor with continental cuisine and children's menu. $$$

Where to Stay

Davidson's. 26177 Route 3, Watertown; (315) 782–3861. Pool, picnic area, nature walk near beaver pond. Children under twelve stay **free.** $$

Tug Hill **Plateau**

The snowiest place east of the Rockies, yet similar to a Scottish moor, Tug Hill Plateau is a unique landscape of limestone and shale, thick forests, misty swamps, and spectacular river gorges. Black bears, bobcats, moose, and migratory songbirds populate the place, and the cross-country skiing and canoeing are excellent. In 2002, New York State and The Nature Conservancy crafted a deal to protect 44,650 acres from development, making it the largest land preservation pact outside Adirondack Park. For more information, visit www.northernforestalliance.org or www.tnc.org.

Clayton

Travel north on Route 180 to Route 12E north.

Where the Saint Lawrence River meets Lake Ontario, Cape Vincent is the village Napoleon wanted to retire to after Waterloo, had he been able to escape the arms of St. Helena. Today it remains a picturesque place full of charming old houses on tree-lined streets. It's also the only place you can ride a car ferry across the Saint Lawrence to Canada. Farther north along the Seaway Trail is the town of Clayton, settled in 1822, famous for its fine shipbuilding. Much later, the town was a popular port for smugglers and rumrunners during Prohibition. Today, area anglers are lured by the giant muskellunge, and the arts and crafts community is flourishing.

Antique Boat Museum (all ages)

750 Mary Street; (315) 686–4104; www.abm.org. Open daily 9:00 A.M. to 5:00 P.M. Museum closed for the winter, Haxall Building exhibits **free** Monday through Saturday 9:00 A.M. to 5:00 P.M. Boat rides every hour 10:00 A.M. to 4:00 P.M. $$, children $.

The largest collection of antique freshwater recreational boats in the country is on display here, along with several hundred engines and about 12,000 other articles of nautical memorabilia. Head outside for a whirl around the waterways aboard the *Seagull,* a 1935 40-foot antique cruiser, or a 1929 Hacker Craft speedboat.

Thousand Islands Museum of Clayton (ages 6 and up)

403 Riverside Drive; (315) 686–5794; www.timuseum.org. Open Memorial Day through Labor Day 9:00 A.M. to 5:00 P.M. $

Browse through artifacts and photos from the golden years of the Thousand Islands region. A replica of the largest muskellunge ever caught is mounted at the Muskie Hall of Fame, and duck fans will be delighted by the Decoy Hall of Fame.

American Handweaving Museum & Thousand Island Craft School

(ages 7 and up)

314 John Street; (315) 686–4123; www.hm-ac.org. Open September through December Monday through Friday 9:00 A.M. to 4:30 P.M., Saturday 10:00 A.M. to 4:00 P.M. September and October only. Call for spring-summer hours. Donation.

Gallery exhibits of handwoven textiles are the focus at this museum, and workshops in pottery and weaving are offered to the public.

Parks of **Clayton**

Cedar Point State Park. 36661 Cedar Point Park Drive; (315) 654–2522 or (800) 456–CAMP; www.nysparks.com/parks.

Clayton Village Park. Mary Street; (315) 686–5552.

Frink Park. 510 Riverside Drive; (315) 686–3771.

Clayton Recreation Park & Arena. 600 East Line Road; (315) 686–4310.

Grass Point State Park. Off Route 12; (315) 686–4472 or (800) 456–CAMP; www.nysparks.com/parks.

Cape Vincent Fisheries Station and Aquarium (all ages)

541 East Broadway, Cape Vincent; (315) 654–2147. **Fishery open daily 8:00 A.M. to 5:00 P.M. Aquarium open June through October 9:00 A.M. to 4:30 P.M. Free.**

Five large aquariums stocked with Lake Ontario and Saint Lawrence River fish can be seen here, as well as other aquatic displays and exhibits.

Horne's Ferry (all ages)

At the foot of Saint James Street, Cape Vincent; (613) 385–2402, (315) 783–0638, or (613) 385–2262; www.wolfeisland.com. **Operates daily May through mid-October 8:00 A.M. to 7:30 P.M. Crossing time: ten minutes. Car and driver $$.**

New York State's only international auto/passenger ferry crosses the Saint Lawrence River by way of Wolfe Island to Kingston, Ontario.

Where to Eat

Riverside Cafe. 506 Riverside Drive; (315) 686–2940. Italian cuisine and more, with river views. $$

Thousand Islands Inn. 335 Riverside Drive; (315) 686–3030 or (800) 544–4241; www.1000-islands.com. Steak, seafood, homemade pasta, and home of the original "Thousand Island Salad Dressing." $$$

Where to Stay

Remar Houseboat Rentals. 510 Theresa Street; (315) 686–3579 or (315) 686–4170; www.thousandislands.com/remar. A terrific way to see the Thousand Islands! No experience necessary, but you must make reservations. $$$$

West Winds. 38267 Route 12E; (315) 686–3352, (607) 625–2963, or (888) WESTWND; www.thousandislands .com/westwinds. Rooms, cabins, and cottages; heated pool; lawn games; game room; dock; boats; picnic area; and gazebo, on five acres. $$

Alexandria Bay

Head north on Route 12.

The stomping grounds of millionaires around the turn of the twentieth century, the area now has a variety of mainstream attractions for families. Stroll down Sisson Street to Scenic View Park for a picnic, a concert, or swimming at the sand beach. Or meander down Market Street to Cornwall Brother's Store for a piece of penny candy and a flashback to Alex Bay's golden days.

Boldt Castle (all ages)

Heart Island; (315) 482–2501 or (800) 847–5263; www.BoldtCastle.com. Open daily mid-May through mid-October daily 10:00 A.M. to 6:30 P.M., July and August to 7:30 P.M. Adults $$, children $.

George Boldt rose from humble beginnings to become, among other things, the owner of New York's Waldorf-Astoria Hotel. Wealthy and passionately in love with his wife, Louise, he ordered a 120-room, six-story Rhineland-style castle to be built as a summer home. The finest craftspeople in the world were called in, hearts were carved and painted everywhere, and the island itself was even shaped into a heart. Then one day in 1904 a telegram arrived, telling the workers to stop construction. Louise had died suddenly, and George was so heartbroken he never returned to his fairy-tale island again. Restoration was begun in 1977. The Boldt Yacht House, with three antique boats, has been completely restored and is accessible by a **free** shuttle service. The main island can be reached by tour boats and water taxis.

Alex Bay **Area Fun**

Mazeland Gardens. Route 12; (315) 482–2186.

Bonnie Castle Greens Miniature Golf Course. 43672 Route 12; (315) 482–5128 or (800) 955–4511; Recreation Center (315) 482–5122; www.bonnie castle.com.

Alex Bay 500 Go-Karts. 46772 Route 12; (315) 482–2021; www.1000islands.com/alexbay500.

Bay Drive-In Theater. Route 26; (315) 482–3874.

Boating around **Alexandria Bay**

Uncle Sam Boat Tours. 47 James Street; (315) 482–2611, (800) ALEXBAY, or (800) 253–9229; www.usboattours.com.

O'Brien's Boats. 51 Walton Street, (315) 482–9548.

River Queen Charters & Rental. (613) 659–3310 or (877) 659–3310; www.1000islandhouseboating.com.

Empire Boat Lines. Upper Harbor; (315) 482–TOUR or (888) 449–ALEX.

Aqua Zoo (all ages)

43681 Route 12; (315) 482–5771; www.abay.com/aquazoo. Open daily May through September 10:00 A.M. to 8:00 P.M. Call for winter hours. $

Feed a piranha, pet an alligator, or stare at the sharks at this water world's fourteen naturalistic exhibits of fish and sea creatures from all over the world, swimming in 9,000 gallons of water. There are touch tanks to explore, and guided educational tours are offered.

Wellesley Island State Park (all ages)

44927 Cross Island Road (exit 51 off I–81), Wellesley Island; (315) 482–2722; camping reservations (800) 456–CAMP; nature center (315) 482–2479; www.nysparks.com/parks. Open daily year-round; nature center open Monday through Saturday 8:30 A.M. to 8:00 P.M., to 4:00 P.M. Sunday in summer. $$ in summer.

This 2,636-acre park is laced with hiking trails and offers swimming beaches, a playground, nice river views, a nine-hole golf course, mini-golf, campsites, and cabins. The Minna Anthony Common Nature Center, a 600-acre portion of Wellesley State Park, has nature trails, a museum with live local animals, a working beehive, excellent bird-watching, and guided nature hikes.

More State Parks **in the Area**

Keewaydin State Park. 43165 Route 12, Alexandria Bay; (315) 482–3331 or (800) 456–CAMP; www.nysparks.com/parks.

Dewolf Point State Park. 45920 Route 191, Wellesley Island; (315) 482–2012 or (800) 456–CAMP; www.nysparks.com/parks.

Kring Point State Park. 25950 Kring Point Road, Redwood; (315) 482–2444 or (800) 456–CAMP; www.nysparks.com/parks.

Where to Eat

Admiral's Inn. 33 James Street; (315) 482–2781. Prime rib, fresh seafood, sandwiches, salads, and a children's menu. $$–$$$

Cavallario's Steak and Seafood House. 24 Church Street; (315) 482–9867. Medieval motif; serving prime rib, seafood, pasta, plus a children's menu. $$$

Where to Stay

Bonnie Castle Resort. Holland Street; (315) 482–4511 or (800) 955–4511; www.bonniecastle.net. Built in 1875, it offers two swimming pools, restaurant, room service, and mini-golf, and children under twelve stay **free.** $$$$

Captain Thomson's Motel. 1 James Street; (315) 482–9961; www.capt thomsons.com. On the seaway, with swimming and wading pools, dock, restaurant, and children under twelve stay **free.** $$$–$$$$

Massena

Head north along the Seaway Trail on Route 12 to Route 37 north.

The Seaway International Bridge is the gateway from East Ontario and Quebec, connecting Cornwall, Ontario, with Massena, New York.

Robert Moses State Park (all ages)

19 Robinson Bay Road (4 miles northeast of town off Route 37); (315) 769–8663 or (800) 456–CAMP; www.nysparks.com/parks. Open daily year-round; beach open late June through Labor Day. $–$$

Located on the Saint Lawrence River, between the Seaway Shipping Channel and the Robert Moses Power Dam, this 2,232-acre park offers hiking and nature trails that start at the nature center, swimming at a sand beach, lake and river fishing, a playground, boat rentals, campsites, and cabins.

Saint Lawrence-FDR Power Project (all ages)

Route 131, Barnhart Island; (315) 764–0226 or (800) 262–NYPA; www.stl.nypa.gov. Visitor center is currently closed except for school groups or by reservation. Free.

For an electrifying outing, visit this power plant on the Saint Lawrence River for hands-on energy-related exhibits, working models, computerized exhibits, a multimedia show on power development, murals painted by Thomas Hart Benton, and views from the 116-foot observation deck overlooking the Moses-Saunders Power Dam and Canadian border.

Other Things to See and Do
in the North Country

Uihlein Sugar Maple Field Station. 60 Bear Cub Road, Lake Placid; (518) 523–9337.

Adirondack Flying Service. Route 73, Lake Placid; (518) 523–2473; www.flyanywhere.com.

Lake Placid North Elba Historical Society Museum. P.O. Box 189, Averyville Road, Lake Placid 12946; (518) 523–1608.

McCauley Mountain Ski Area. 300 McAuley Road, Old Forge; (315) 369–3225; www.oldforgeny.com.

Jacques Cartier State Park. 251 Old Mills Road, off Route 12, Morristown; (315) 375–6371 or (800) 456–CAMP; www.nysparks.com/parks.

Frederic Remington Art Museum. 303 Washington Street, Ogdensburg; (315) 393–2425; www.fredericremington.org.

Coles Creek State Park. 13003 Route 37, Chippewa Bay; (315) 388–5636 or (800) 456–CAMP; www.nysparks.com/parks.

TAUNY Art Museum. 2 West Main Street, Canton; (315) 386–4289.

American Maple Museum. Main Street, Route 812, Croghan; (315) 346–1107.

Burrville Cider Mill. 18176 Route 156, Watertown; (315) 788–7292 or (866) 612–1980; www.burrvillecidermill.com.

Whetstone Gulf State Park. RD #2, Lowville; (315) 376–6630 or (800) 456–CAMP; www.nysparks.com/parks.

Fiddlers Hall of Fame & Museum. Route 13, Comins Road, Osceola; (315) 599–7009.

Clements Iroquois Farm. 10951 Route 37, Lisbon; (315) 393–6252 or (877) 575–9128.

Colonial Village Fun Park. Route 11B, Potsdam; (315) 265–PARK; www.colonialvillagefunpark.com.

Dwight D. Eisenhower Lock (all ages)

Route 131 (2 miles north of Route 37); (315) 769–2049 or (315) 764–3208. Call (315) 769–2422 for ships' origins and expected locking times. Open daily 9:00 A.M. to 9:00 P.M. Memorial Day through Labor Day. $

Visit the viewing deck to watch huge ships lifted and lowered 42 feet inside the lock chamber, with an interpretive center and films to explain the process.

Akwesasne Museum (all ages)

321 Route 37, Hogansburg, about 10 miles east from Massena, inside the St. Regis Mohawk Reservation; (518) 358–2461. Open year-round Monday through Friday 8:30 A.M. to 4:30 P.M., Saturday 11:00 A.M. to 3:00 P.M., closed Saturday in July and August. $, children under 5 **free.**

This Mohawk cultural center and museum has a wonderful collection of art and artifacts, from beadwork and wampum belts to sweetgrass baskets, masks, and photographs.

Where to Eat

Baurenstraube Restaurant. 15054 Route 37; (315) 764–0246. German and American cuisine, with all-you-can-eat haddock on Friday. $$

Where to Stay

Econo Lodge Meadow View. 15054 Route 37; (315) 764–0246. Restaurant, and children under eighteen stay **free.** $$$

Stone Fence Motel. Route 37 south, Riverside Drive, Ogdensburg; (315) 393–1545 or (800) 253–1545; www.stone fenceresort.com. Motel and hotel rooms and townhouses on twelve acres along the Saint Lawrence River, with sandy beach, pool, boat rentals, fishing, and restaurant. $$–$$$$

For More Information

Adirondacks.com. (518) 891–3745; www.adirondacks.com.

Adirondack Mountain Club's Info Centers. (518) 668–4447 or (800) 395–8080, Lake Placid (518) 523–3441; www.adk.org.

Adirondack Regional Tourism Council. (518) 846–8016 or (800) 487–6867; www.adk.com.

NYS Gateway Information Center. (518) 846–8016 or (800) 487–6867.

Central Adirondack Association. (315) 369–6983; www.caany.org.

Franklin County Tourism. (518) 483–9470 or (800) 709–4895; www .adirondacklakes.org.

Hamilton County Tourism. (518) 648–5239 or (800) 648–5239; www .hamiltoncounty.com.

Indian Lake Chamber of Commerce. (518) 648–5112 or (800) 328–LAKE; www.indian-lake.com.

Schroon Lake Chamber of Commerce. (518) 532–7675 or (888) SCHROON; www.schroonlake.org.

Lake Placid/Essex County Visitors Bureau. (518) 523–2455 , (800) 44–PLACID, or (800) 447–5224; www.lake placid.com.

Lewis County Chamber of Commerce. (315) 376–2213 or (800) 724–0242; www.lewiscountychamber.org.

Champlain Shores Visitors and Convention Bureau. (518) 563–1000; www.go adirondack.com.

Warren County Public Information and Tourism. (518) 761–6368 or (800) 95–VISIT, ext. 143; www.visitlakegeorge.com.

1000 Islands International Council. (315) 482–2520 or (800) 847–5263; www.visit1000islands.com.

1000 Islands/Jefferson County. (800) 476–5333; www.1000islands.com.

Alexandria Bay Tourism. (315) 482–9531 or (800) 541–2110; www.alexbay.com.

Oswego County Tourism. (315) 349–8322 or (800) 248–4386; www.co.oswego.ny.us.

St. Lawrence County Chamber of Commerce. (315) 386–4000; www.stlawrence county.org.

Seaway Trail Inc. (315) 646–1000 or (800) SEAWAYT; www.seawaytrail.com; e-mail: seaway@northnet.org.

Saranac Lake Area Chamber of Commerce. (518) 891–1990 or (800) 347–1992; www.saranaclake.com.

Lake Luzerne Regional Chamber of Commerce. (518) 696–3500; www.lakeluzernechamber.org.

Tupper Lake Chamber of Commerce. (518) 359–3328 or (888) TUPLAKE; www.tupperlakeinfo.com.

Western New York

G ateway to the Great Lakes, home to the Seneca for centuries, and the last stop on the Underground Railroad, the western frontier of New York is known for its spectacular natural beauty and fertile farmlands, as well as for the unique communities that have flourished within its borders. From the religious idealists of Chautauqua and the free thinkers of Lily Dale to the peaceable Amish in Conewango Valley and the Native Americans in Salamanca, this region is a refuge for a variety of lifestyles.

Water is the theme in the Niagara area, cradled by Lake Erie and Lake Ontario, strung together by the Erie Canal, and crowned by the cascades of Niagara Falls. The forests and lakes in and around the wilderness of Allegany State Park blanket the southern section with thickly wooded hills rimming sparkling sapphire lakes filled with monster-size muskies. From strolling along prehistoric seashores, or cruising the waterways aboard vintage vessels soaking in the beauty of Niagara (literally), to improving your culture quotient at Chautauqua, there is much to see and do here with your family.

Driving Tips

Paralleling the Erie Canal, Route 31 runs east to west from Rochester to Buffalo. I–90 also runs east and west, heading into Buffalo, then winding south along the scenic Seaway Trail following the shores of Lake Erie. In the Allegany region, east and west travel is easiest on Route 17, passing through Allegany State Park, across to Chautauqua Lake. From Niagara Falls north along Lake Ontario is the continuation of the picturesque Seaway Trail. Dozens of country back roads lace through the region's rolling farmlands and offer interesting detours.

WESTERN NEW YORK

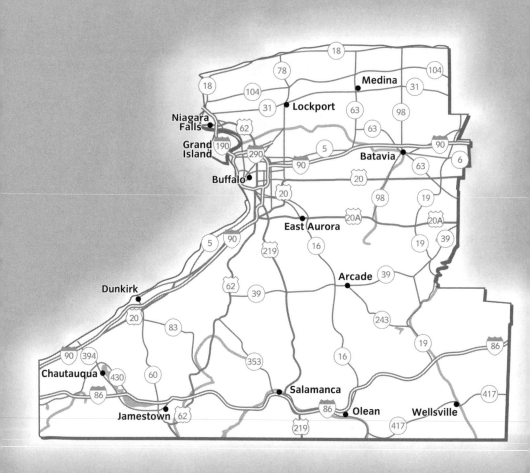

Buffalo

The French were the first to explore this Iroquois land, calling the Niagara River *beau fleuve,* or beautiful river. Somehow that name morphed into the word Buffalo, or so one story goes. After the completion of the Erie Canal in 1825, Buffalo boomed, and railroads, factories, and steel mills multiplied. In 1901, the city proudly hosted the Pan-American Exposition, a spectacular world's fair that was unfortunately the place chosen by Leon Czolgosz to assassinate President William McKinley. Today Buffalo is the second-largest city in the state, offering visitors a variety of activities and attractions, from architectural treasures and great theater to spectacular sports and breathtaking scenery.

Buffalo Niagara Visitor Center (all ages)

Market Arcade, 617 Main Street; (716) 852–BFLO or (800) BUFFALO; www.buffalocvb.org. Call for hours. Free.

Located in the heart of the theater district, this is a good place to get current information about special events and to pick up a map of downtown walking tours.

Buffalo City Hall (all ages)

65 Niagara Square, Observation Tower; (716) 851–4200; observation deck (716) 851–5891. Open year-round Monday through Friday 9:00 A.M. to 4:00 P.M., closed holidays and weekends. Free.

Take the elevator to the twenty-eighth floor of this art deco masterpiece, then walk up three flights to the observation deck overlooking the city, the Niagara River, and Lake Erie.

Buffalo Zoological Gardens (all ages)

300 Parkside Avenue; (716) 837–3900; www.buffalozoo.org. Open year-round, summer 10:00 A.M. to 5:00 P.M., winter 10:00 A.M. to 4:00 P.M. Closed Thanksgiving and Christmas. Adults $$, children $, under 2 free.

More than 1,100 exotic and endangered animals exist in natural habitats at this twenty-three-acre zoo, from rare white tigers and lowland gorillas to, of course, buffalo. The World of Wildlife Discovery Center and the children's zoo and petting area offer families opportunities for up close and personal experiences. Surrounding the zoo is the 350-acre Delaware Park, an emerald oasis designed by Frederick Law Olmstead, where you can rent paddleboats.

Buffalo Museum of Science (all ages)

1020 Humboldt Parkway; (716) 896–5200; www.buffalomuseumofscience.org. Open year-round Thursday through Saturday 10:00 A.M. to 5:00 P.M., Sunday noon to 5:00 P.M. Closed holidays. Adults $$, children $, under 3 free.

From anthropology to zoology, this place has a wide variety of permanent and changing exhibits to explore. The only Tibetan sand mandala in North America is here, along with visiting robotic dinosaurs, Egyptian mummies, and a summer science circus.

Buffalo and Erie County Botanical Gardens (all ages)

2655 South Park Avenue at McKinley Parkway; (716) 827–1584; www.buffalogardens.com. Open daily year-round, weekdays 9:00 A.M. to 4:00 P.M., till 6:00 P.M. on Wednesday, and weekends 9:00 A.M. to 5:00 P.M. Open holidays. Donation.

The eleven glass greenhouses gracing the grounds of this eleven-acre garden are filled with an international array of orchids, fruit trees, palms, and cacti. Built in the 1890s, this Victorian conservatory also offers children's workshops and tours by reservation.

Naval and Military Park (ages 4 and up)

One Naval Park Cove; (716) 847–1773; www.buffalonavalpark.org. Open daily April through October 10:00 A.M. to 5:00 P.M., Saturday and Sunday in November 10:00 A.M. to 5:00 P.M. Open holidays in season. Adults $$, children 6 through 16 $, under 5 free.

Located on six acres of Lake Erie waterfront, this is the largest inland naval park in the country. Board the World War II destroyer USS *Sullivans,* tour the submarine USS *Croaker,* or check out the M41 tank, an F-101 fighter interceptor jet, a guided missile cruiser, or the terrific model-ship collection. For a hands-on approach, try your skill in the British harrier jet or helicopter simulator.

Tifft Nature Preserve (all ages)

1200 Fuhrmann Boulevard; (716) 896–5200 or (716) 825–6397; www.sciencebuff.org. Trails open daily dawn to dusk, visitor center open Wednesday through Saturday 9:00 A.M. to 4:00 P.M. Closed major holidays. Free.

There are 5 miles of nature trails, three boardwalks, and a 75-acre cattail marsh to explore at this 265-acre unique urban sanctuary, operated by the Buffalo Museum of Science. Stop at the Makowski Visitor Center to see exhibits on regional plants and animals and for self-guided trail information.

Buffalo and Erie County Historical Society (ages 5 and up)

25 Nottingham Court; (716) 873–9644; www.bechs.org. Open year-round Monday through Saturday 10:00 A.M. to 5:00 P.M., Sunday noon to 5:00 P.M. Closed holidays. Adults $$, children $, under 7 free.

Housed in the building that was New York's pavilion during the 1901 Pan-American Exposition, this wonderful museum has an interesting exhibit on all the products and inventions that originated in Buffalo, from Cheerios to kazoos. There's also an exhibit highlighting the immigrant heritage of the region, as well as the Native American culture.

New York **Trivia**

There are more than six million apple trees in New York State, producing twenty-five million bushels of apples. For more information log on to www.nyapplecountry.com.

**Theodore Roosevelt Inaugural
National Historic Site** (ages 4 and up)
641 Delaware Avenue; (716) 884–0095; www.nps.gov/thri. Open year-round weekdays 9:00
A.M. to 5:00 P.M., weekends noon to 5:00 P.M. Closed major holidays. $

When President McKinley was assassinated at the Pan-American Exposition in 1901, the library of the Greek Revival Wilcox mansion became the site of Theodore Roosevelt's inauguration. Seasonal activities and events are scheduled throughout the year, but in August be sure to make reservations for your favorite kid and bear to attend the Teddy Bear Picnic.

Buffalo **Performing Arts**

Buffalo has a lot of places to see and hear great theater and music. Here is a partial list, and you can call or visit the Web sites to get current season and schedule information.

Theatre of Youth (TOY). (716) 884–4400; www.buffalo.com/TOY.

UB Center for the Arts. (716) 645–6259 or (716) 645–ARTS; www.arts
.buffalo.edu.

Shea's Performing Arts Center. (716) 847–1410;
www.sheas.org.

Studio Arena Theatre. (716) 856–5650 or (800)
77–STAGE; www.studioarena.org.

Buffalo State Performing Arts Center. (716)
878–3005; www.buffalostate.edu/pac.

Alleyway Theatre. (716) 852–2600; www
.alleyway.com.

Irish Classical Theatre. (716) 853–4282;
www.irishclassicaltheatre.com.

Buffalo Philharmonic Orchestra. (716) 885–5000 or
(800) 699–3168; www.bpo.org.

Paul Robeson Theatre. (716) 884–2013;
www.paulrobesontheatre.com.

HSBC Arena. (716) 855–4100; www.hsbcarena.com.

Buffalo Ensemble Theatre. (716) 855–2225;
www.buffalotheatre.com.

Water **Explorations**

Cruise the Canadian border or the upper Niagara River on scenic, dinner, jazz, or murder mystery excursions from May through October. For more information, call (716) 856–6696 or (800) 244–8684; www.missbuffalo.com.

Miss Buffalo II and *Niagara Clipper.* 79 Marine Drive. Departures from Erie Basin Marina.

QRS Music Rolls Factory (ages 5 and up)

1026 Niagara Street; (716) 885–4600 or (800) 247–6557; www.qrsmusic.com/facilities/ buffalo_factory.htm. Open weekdays year-round 10:00 A.M. to 6:00 P.M.; tours at 10:00 A.M. and 2:00 P.M. Closed holidays. $

Tour the factory of the oldest and largest manufacturer of player piano rolls in the world. Although computers cut the rolls today, at one time it would take an arranger all day to cut out a three-minute master. Vintage and modern player pianos are also on display.

Buffalo **Sports**

Buffalo boasts some of the best professional sports teams in the country, and there's athletic action available year-round. Most events take place at the state-of-the-art HSBC Arena (One Seymour H. Knox III Plaza) or Ralph Wilson Stadium (One Bills Drive). Call ahead for a current season schedule.

Buffalo Bills Football. (716) 648–1800 or (877) BBTICKS; www.buffalobills.com.

Buffalo Bisons Baseball. (716) 843–THE–HERD or (888) 223–6000; www.bisons.com.

Buffalo Sabres Hockey. (716) 855–4100 or (888) GO–SABRES; www.sabres.com.

Buffalo Bandits Lacrosse.(716) 855–4000 or (888) 223–6000; www.bandits.com.

Where to Eat

The Broadway Market.
999 Broadway; (716) 893–0705; www
.broadwaymarket.com. A European ethnic
food market with occasional craft sales. $

Where to Stay

Holiday Inn-Downtown.
620 Delaware Street; (716) 886–2121;
www.harthotels.com. Heated pool and
wading pool, restaurant, coin laundry, and
kids eighteen and under stay **free.** $$

Village Haven Motel. 9370 Main Street,
Clarence; (716) 759–6845; www.newyork
lodging.com. Rooms and kitchenettes,
pool with lifeguard, playground, compli-
mentary continental breakfast, refrigera-
tors, picnic tables, and some whirlpool
suites. $–$$$

East Aurora

Head south on Route 16.

Elbert Hubbard, the charismatic founder of the Arts and Crafts movement in America, created a community of craftspeople and artisans, known as the Roycrofters, in this pastoral
village.

Vidler's 5 & 10 (all ages)

**676–694 Main Street; (716) 652–0481 or (877) VIDLERS; www.vidlers5and10.com. Open
Monday through Saturday 9:00 A.M. to 5:30 P.M., Friday 9:00 A.M. to 9:00 P.M., Sunday noon
to 4:00 P.M. Closed holidays.**

Family owned since 1930, this is a time-travel trip to the premall five-and-dime era. Penny
candy, old-fashioned housewares, and a toy counter make this a unique shopping experience.

Toy Town Museum (all ages)

**636 Girard Avenue; (716) 687–5151; www.toytownusa.com. Open Monday through Saturday
10:00 A.M. to 4:00 P.M. Closed holidays. Donation.**

Rare and one-of-a-kind toys are exhibited at this charming museum, with highlights that
include a fifty-year span of Fisher Price toys, plus Toyworks, an interactive kids' learning
center. Educational programs for ages seven through eleven are offered.

New York **Trivia**

George Washington once remarked to Gen. George Clinton, the state's first governor, that New York might be the "seat of empire," giving it the nickname of the Empire State.

Explore and More . . . A Children's Museum (ages 2 and up)
300 Gleed Avenue; (716) 655–5131; www.exploreandmore.org. Open Wednesday through Saturday 10:00 A.M. to 5:00 P.M., Sunday noon to 5:00 P.M. Closed holidays. $

A variety of interactive exhibits encourage children to explore, experiment, discover, and play at this hands-on museum.

Hawk Creek Wildlife Center (all ages)
655 Luther Road; (716) 652–8646. Walden Galleria Mall, exit 52 off I–90; (716) 681–7600; www.hawkcreek.org. Open Saturday noon to 6:00 P.M., and sometimes Sunday noon to 5:00 P.M. Donation.

Specializing in birds of prey and mammals, this eighty-two-acre wildlife center itself is only open to the public on select weekends in August, but the center staffs a booth with live animals at the Walden Galleria Mall on Saturday and Sunday.

Niagara Hobby and Craft Mart (all ages)
3366 Union Road, Buffalo; (716) 681–1666. Open year-round Monday through Saturday 10:00 A.M. to 9:00 P.M., Sunday 10:00 A.M. to 5:00 P.M.

Near the Buffalo Airport and the Walden Galleria Mall is the biggest hobby store in the country, carrying trains of every type and scale, radio-controlled cars, planes, boats, Estes rockets, dollhouses and furnishings, die-cast miniatures, and arts and crafts supplies.

Reinstein Woods Nature Preserve (all ages)
77 Honorine Drive, Depew; (716) 851–7201. Tours: Wednesday and Saturday 10:00 A.M. Self-guided trail open Tuesday and Thursday 9:00 A.M. to 4:00 P.M. Closed holidays. Free.

Take a ninety-minute guided nature walk through this 289-acre preserve, which harbors one of the largest virgin forests in the state. There are excellent opportunities to spot local wildlife and learn about the unique ecosystem of this ancient forest and wetland.

Where to Eat

Eckl's Beef & Weck Restaurant. 4936 Ellicott Road, Orchard Park; (716) 662–2262. Local cuisine specialties. $–$$$

Old Orchard Inn. 2095 Blakeley Road; (716) 652–4664. Beef, chicken, and fish specialties, with homemade biscuits and desserts, and a children's menu; with fireplaces, outdoor dining, and a duck pond. $$$

Also in **the Area**

Knox Farm State Park. Knox Road, East Aurora; (716) 652–2207 or (716) 655–7200; www.nysparks.com/parks.

Amherst Museum. 3755 Tonawanda Creek Road, Amherst; (716) 689–1440; www.amherstmuseum.org.

Pedaling History Bicycle Museum. 3943 North Buffalo Road, Orchard Park; (716) 662–3853; www.pedalinghistory.com.

Original American Kazoo Museum. 8703 South Main Street, Eden; (716) 992–3960; www.kazooco.com.

Penn Dixie Paleontological and Outdoor Education Center. 4050 North Street, Blasdell; (716) 627–4560; www.penndixie.org.

Woodlawn Beach State Park. S-3585 Lake Shore Road, Blasdell; (716) 827–0293 or (716) 826–1930; www.nysparks.com/parks.

Where to Stay

Orchard Park Inn. 2268 Southwestern Boulevard, West Seneca; (716) 674–6000. Rooms and efficiencies. $

The Roycroft Inn. 40 South Grove Street; (716) 652–5552 or (877) 652–5552; www.roycroftinn.com. Suites have Roycroft furniture and Jacuzzis; complimentary continental breakfast; excellent dining room with children's menu. $$$$

Grand Island

Take Route 16 north to I–190 north.

Nestled between New York and Ontario and caressed by the Niagara River, this is the largest freshwater island in the country.

Martin's Fantasy Island (all ages)

2400 Grand Island Boulevard; (716) 773–7591; www.martinsfantasyisland.com. Open mid-May weekends only 11:30 A.M. to 7:30 P.M., mid-June through Labor Day daily 11:30 A.M. to 8:30 P.M. July and August Saturday to 9:00 P.M. Under 3 free.

Grand Island **Parks**

Located on the north and south sides of the island, these parks offer swimming, hiking, biking, boating, fishing, picnic areas, and a playground, plus cross-country skiing in winter. For more information, call (716) 773–3271 or log on to www.nysparks.com.

Beaver Island State Park. 2136 West Oakfield Road.

Buckhorn Island State Park. 5805 East River Road.

Covering eighty acres, this theme park features more than a hundred wet and dry rides, live stage shows, and a petting zoo.

Herschell Carrousel Factory Museum (all ages)

180 Thompson Street, North Tonawanda; (716) 693–1885; www.carouselmuseum.org. Open April to June Wednesday through Sunday 1:00 to 5:00 P.M., daily June through Labor Day 11:00 A.M. to 5:00 P.M., Labor Day to Christmas Wednesday through Sunday 1:00 to 5:00 P.M. $

Visit the only historic carousel factory in the country and watch artisans craft and carve magical merry-go-round creatures. Afterwards, step outside and have a whirl on an enchanting 1916 classic wooden carousel.

Where to Eat

Mississippi Muds. 313 Niagara Street, Tonawanda; (716) 694–0787. Another kid-friendly place serving eclectic local cuisine on a deck overlooking the water. $

Old Man River. 375 Niagara Street, Tonawanda; (716) 693–5558. Overlooking the Niagara, this fun place serves local favorites and a full seafood bar. The zany decor includes a whale, and there's a pond out back. $

Where to Stay

Cinderella Motel and Campsite. 2797 Grand Island Boulevard; (716) 773–4095. Rooms and efficiencies, playground. $$

Grand Suites Motel. 1725 Grand Island Boulevard; (716) 773–2575. Rooms and efficiencies, with refrigerators and microwave ovens available. $$–$$$$

Niagara Falls

Take I–190 to the Robert Moses Parkway north.

More than ten million people a year come from all over the world to see one of the greatest natural wonders on Earth. Niagara Falls is spectacular. The sheer size of the falls is breathtaking, with more than 0.5 mile of cascades draining four Great Lakes into Lake Erie. As tourist Mark Twain once said, "Niagara Falls is one of the finest structures in the known world."

Niagara Falls State Park (all ages)
Prospect Street, off Robert Moses Parkway; (716) 278–1770 or (716) 278–1796; Viewmobile (716) 278–1730; Observation Tower (716) 278–1762; *Maid of the Mist* (716) 284–8897; Schoellkopf Geological Museum (716) 278–1780; Cave of the Winds (716) 278–1730; Niagara Historic Walking Tours (716) 285–2132; www.niagarafallsstatepark.com and www.nys parks.com/parks. Free, but individual attractions are extra. Ask about Master Pass Book for one-price package discounts within the park. $–$$

This is the first and oldest of New York's state parks. Begin your exploration at the Visitor Center at Prospect Point, where interesting exhibits, displays, and a short film offer a good introduction to this awesome area. It's also a great spot to view the 1,000-foot drop of the American Falls. The Viewmobile, a people-mover operating during the peak season, can be boarded here as well, and for one fee passengers can disembark and reboard at points of interest throughout the park. Head to the nearby Observation Tower for a ride up the glass-enclosed elevator to the 200-foot platform overlooking the gorge. Finally, descend to the base of the falls to board the famous *Maid of the Mist,* a legendary tourist attraction since 1846.

For an up close and wet walk, take the Cave of the Winds trip, a descent down wooden stairs to the base of Bridal Falls. By the way, children must be able to navigate the path themselves, for no back carriers or babes in arms are allowed on this trek.

Rock hounds will enjoy exhibits and multimedia presentations on Niagara's 435 million-year history at the Schoellkopf Geological Museum, which offers self-guided and naturalist-guided walks into the gorge. An excursion of a different type is offered by Niagara Historic Walking Tours, where costumed guides take you on an interactive one-hour outing into the park's interior.

Niagara Falls
Fun Facts

The edge of the falls was originally 7 miles downstream, but erosion continues to cut away the cliff at a rate of about an inch a year, forming the Niagara Gorge.

Niagara Falls
Fun Facts

The average flow of water over the Bridal Veil and American Falls is about 75,000 gallons per second.

Niagara's Wax Museum of History (all ages)

303 Prospect Street; (716) 285–1271. Open year-round 11:00 A.M. to 5:00 P.M. $

Niagara's dramatic history is depicted in forty-six exhibits featuring figures of wax. Other interesting memorabilia is here as well, including several daredevil barrels.

Daredevil Museum (all ages)

303 Rainbow Boulevard; (716) 282–4046; www.niagarafallslive.com. Open daily in summer 9:00 A.M. to 10:00 P.M. Free.

Immortalizing the late and great challengers of Niagara Falls, this museum has a collection of steel-banded, giant rubber balls, barrels, and other containers used by daring adventurers to plunge headlong over the precipice.

Aquarium of Niagara (all ages)

701 Whirlpool Street; (716) 285–3575 or (800) 500–4609; www.aquariumofniagara.org. Open daily year-round 9:00 A.M. to 5:00 P.M. $$, children under 4 free.

Discover denizens of the deep at this terrific aquarium. More than 1,500 aquatic animals live here, from sea lions and sharks to piranhas and Peruvian penguins.

Niagara Power Project's Visitor's Center (all ages)

5777 Lewiston Road, Lewiston; (716) 286–6661 or (866) NYPAFUN; www.nypa.gov. Open daily year-round 9:00 A.M. to 5:00 P.M. Free.

The history of hydroelectricity and other sources of energy is explored through excellent hands-on displays, exhibits, and interactive computer games. The observation deck offers a terrific panorama of the gorge, or cast a line out for salmon, trout, or bass from the fishing platform.

Niagara Falls
Fun Facts

The Niagara River flows north and is 36 miles long.

The falls were formed 12,000 years ago by melting glaciers.

Old Fort Niagara (all ages)

Fort Niagara State Park, Robert Moses Parkway, Youngstown; (716) 745–7611; www.oldfort niagara.org. Open daily year-round 9:00 A.M., call for closing times. Closed Thanksgiving, Christmas, and New Year's Day. Adults $$, children $.

Built by the French in 1726 and later occupied by British and American forces, this strategically important stone fortress controlled access to the Great Lakes for nearly three centuries. That turbulent history is brought to life with costumed interpreters, military reenactments, fife and drum drills, and other special events throughout the year. Surrounding the fort is the state park, offering recreation programs, easy hiking trails, fishing, a swimming pool, playground, and picnic areas, with cross-country skiing and sledding in winter.

Artpark (all ages)

450 South Fourth Street, Lewiston; (716) 754–9000, (716) 754–4375, or (800) 659–7275; www.artpark.net. Open daily 8:00 A.M. to dusk. Some events free, some $–$$, and parking $$.

The only state park in the country dedicated to the visual and performing arts, this 200-

More Niagara Area **State Parks**

For more information, contact the regional office of the NYS Office of Parks, Recreation, and Historic Preservation at (716) 278–1770, check out the Web site www.nysparks.com/parks, or call (800) 456–CAMP for reservations.

Whirlpool State Park. Off Robert Moses Parkway, Niagara Falls, 2 miles north of the falls; (716) 284–4691.

Devil's Hole State Park. Robert Moses Parkway, Niagara Falls, 4 miles north of the falls; (716) 284–4691.

Four Mile Creek State Park. Lake Road, Youngstown; (716) 745–3802.

Wilson-Tuscarora State Park. 3565 Lake Road, Wilson; (716) 751–6361.

Joseph Davis State Park. 4143 Lower River Road, Lewiston; (716) 754–4596.

Reservoir State Park. Military Road, Niagara Falls; (716) 284–4691.

Golden Hill State Park. 9691 Lower Lake Road, Barker; (716) 795–3885 or (716) 795–3117.

Niagara Falls
Fun Facts

Sam Patch was the first daredevil to jump over the falls, in 1829. The first woman to take the plunge was Mrs. Annie Edson Taylor, a sixty-three-year-old schoolteacher, in 1901.

acre muse menage has been hosting world-class theater, dance, and concert events for more than twenty-five years. Also on the grounds is an ancient Hopewell Indian burial mound, as well as hiking and nature trails and a picnic area.

Whirlpool Jet Boat Tours (ages 6 and up)
The Riverside Inn, 115 South Water Street, Lewiston; (905) 468–4800; www.whirlpooljet.com. Operating April through September; times depend on trip type. $$$$+

This is a wild white-water adventure aboard jet boats through the world's most famous rapids.

Where to Eat

The Red Coach Inn Restaurant.
2 Buffalo Avenue; (716) 282–1459; www.redcoach.com. Eighteenth-century English tavern overlooking upper rapids, specializing in prime rib, with a children's menu. $$$$

Top of the Falls Restaurant. Terrapin Point, Goat Island; (716) 278–0340. American cuisine, salads, sandwiches, and dinner specials; live bands weekend nights in the summer. $–$$

Niagara Falls
Fun Facts

Seven-year-old Roger Woodward survived an accidental fall in 1960, when his boat overturned upriver. He was picked up by a *Maid of the Mist* tour boat at the base of the Falls.

Where to Stay

Comfort Inn–The Pointe. 1 Prospect Point; (716) 284–6835 or (800) 284–6835. Rooms and suites, restaurant, game and exercise rooms; near shopping mall and Hard Rock Café; children under eighteen stay **free.** $$$–$$$$

The Red Coach Inn. 2 Buffalo Avenue; (716) 282–1459 or (800) 282–1459; www.redcoach.com. Country inn suites, some with kitchens, overlooking upper rapids. $$$–$$$$

Niagara Falls
Fun Facts

Most fish survive the drop over the falls.

The river rapids speed by at 30 mph.

Lockport

Take Route 31 east.

Located along the Erie Canal, Lockport is the home of the fire hydrant and the birthplace of volleyball.

Niagara County Historical Society

(ages 6 and up)

215 Niagara Street; (716) 434–7433. Open September through June Wednesday through Saturday 1:00 P.M. to 5:00 P.M.; July and August Monday through Saturday 10:00 A.M. to 5:00 P.M., Sunday 1:00 to 5:00 P.M. Closed holidays. $

Housed in five buildings, this eclectic collection includes artifacts and memorabilia from the Native Americans and early pioneers, as well as from the Civil War and Erie Canal eras.

Lockport Lock and Canal Tours (all ages)

210–228 Market Street; (716) 433–6155 or (800) 378–0352. Open May through November daily. May tours at 12:30 and 3:00 P.M. plus 10:00 A.M. on Saturday, June through September 10:00 A.M. and 12:30, 3:00, and 7:00 P.M. $$, children under 4 **free.**

Take a two-hour narrated cruise of the Erie Canal, where you'll see five original 1825 locks. An interpretive center highlights the canal's history.

Niagara & Western New York Railroad (all ages)

Union Street; (716) 434–2400; www.niagaratrain.com. $$$–$$$$, children under 3 **free.**

Ride the rails on a two-hour train trip along the Erie Canal between Lockport and Medina, with special seasonal fall foliage runs and a Polar Express.

Lockport Cave and Underground Boat Ride (all ages)

21 Main Street, Olcott; (716) 438–0174; www.lockportcave.com. Open daily mid-June through Labor Day with departures hourly from 11:00 A.M. to 5:00 P.M., 10:00 A.M. on Saturday and holidays. $$

Cruise the historic caves of Lockport, actually a large water-power tunnel that was blasted out of solid rock during the mid-nineteenth century. Special seasonal events, by reservation only, include a Haunted Cave ride in October and Mystery Tours guided by costumed interpreters.

Where to Eat

Becker Farms. 3760 Quaker Road, Gasport; (716) 772–2211 or (716) 221–7815. Fresh fruits and vegetables, bakery, and ice cream, plus a petting zoo and special family events. Picking tour by reservation. $

Shamus Restaurant. 98 West Avenue; (716) 433–9809. Specializing in steak, seafood, and pasta, plus a children's menu. $$

Where to Stay

Holiday Inn Lockport. 515 South Transit Road (Route 78); (716) 434–6151 or (800) 528–1234. Rooms and efficiencies, restaurant, room service, indoor pool, coin laundry, fitness center, and business center; children under eighteen stay **free.** $$–$$$

Lockport Motel. 315 South Transit Road; (716) 434–5595. Rooms and suites, pool, adjacent restaurant, refrigerators, and some rooms with fireplaces and whirlpools. $$–$$$$

Niagara County Camping Resort. 7369 Wheeler Road; (716) 434–3991; www.niagaracamping.com. Cabin rentals and campsites; with live entertainment, a petting zoo, and **free** mini-golf. $

New York **Trivia**

New York became the eleventh state in the Union on July 26, 1788, and New York City became the first capital of the United States.

Medina

Head east on Route 31, then veer left onto Route 31A.

The fine red sandstone deposits of Medina were prized by architects all over the world, including the builders of Buckingham Palace.

Miss Apple Grove Mule-Drawn Canal Cruise (all ages)

11004 West Center Street Extension, off Route 31E; (585) 798–2323. Departing daily May through November, rain or shine, at 10:00 A.M. and 1:00 P.M. Reservations required, call ahead. $$$$

Cruise the Erie Canal aboard an authentic mule-drawn packet boat, with on-board entertainment and lunch included.

The Erie Canal Culvert (all ages)

Culvert Road, 2 miles east of Medina from Route 31; (585) 798–4287, (585) 589–3230, or (800) 724–0314. Open daily year-round. Free.

Listed in *Ripley's Believe It or Not!*, this engineering marvel is the only tunnel that allows motorists to drive *under* the Erie Canal. Note: No RVs or tour buses due to height limit.

Medina Railroad Exhibit Center (all ages)

530 West Avenue; (585) 798–6106. Open daily year-round Tuesday through Sunday 11:00 A.M. to 5:00 P.M. $

The largest HO-scale model train layout in the eastern United States, covering nearly 2,700 feet, is on display here, along with railroad, fire, and law enforcement history exhibits.

Where to Eat

Tillman's Historic Village Inn. Route 104 west and 98, Albion; (585) 589–9151. Steak, seafood, prime rib, barbecue ribs, roast turkey, and pork chops. $$

Watt Fruit Company. 3121 Oak Orchard Road (Route 98), Albion; (585) 589–8000 or (800) 274–5897; www.wattfarms.com. Thirty-five flavors of homemade fudge, fresh vegetables, bakery, ice cream, you-pick fruit, fall tours, and train rides. $

Also in **the Area**

Cobblestone Museum. Routes 98 and 104 at Childs; mailing address: P.O. Box 363, Albion 14411; (585) 589–9013.

Lakeside Beach State Park. Route 18, Waterport; (585) 682–4888; www.nys parks.com/parks.

Iroquois National Wildlife Refuge. 1101 Casey Road, off Route 63, Basom; (585) 948–5445.

Ridge Road Station. 16131 Ridge Road West, Holley; (585) 638–6000; www.rrstation.com.

Brown's Berry Patch. 14264 Roosevelt Highway, Waterport; (585) 682–5569 or (800) 724–0314; www.brownsberrypatch.com.

Where to Stay

Captain's Cove Resort. 14339 Route 18, Waterport; (585) 682–3316. Rooms with full kitchens; boat and canoe rentals, and fishing tackle. $$

Batavia

Take Route 31A east to Route 98 south.

Built at the crossroad of two Iroquois trails, Batavia is an area of fertile farms, lush orchards, and prosperous dairies.

Holland Land Office
and Museum (ages 4 and up)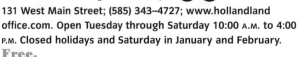
131 West Main Street; (585) 343–4727; www.hollandland office.com. Open Tuesday through Saturday 10:00 A.M. to 4:00 P.M. Closed holidays and Saturday in January and February. Free.

Exhibits housed in the 1815 stone office include Native American and pioneer artifacts, mastodon bones, Civil War memorabilia, and a gallows.

Genesee County Park and
Forest Interpretive Center (all ages)

11095 Bethany Center Road, East Bethany; (585) 344–1122; www.co.genesee.ny.us. Open year-round, dawn to dusk. Interpretive Center open Monday through Friday by appointment, Saturday through Sunday noon to 4:00 P.M. **Free.**

The first and oldest county forest in the state, this popular park contains five small ponds and the headwaters of Black Creek. The self-guided trail system includes a braille and large-print nature path, and there are also ball fields, picnic areas, and a playground.

LeRoy House Museum and Jell-O Gallery (ages 3 and up)

23 East Main Street, LeRoy; (585) 768–7433; www.jellomuseum.com. Open May through October Monday through Saturday 10:00 A.M. to 4:00 P.M., Sunday 1:00 to 4:00 P.M., and weekdays in winter. $

Jell-O jiggled into life in this town, and its history is documented in a gallery with cookbooks, molds, and ad campaigns. Another interesting exhibit inside the mansion focuses on Ingham University, the first women's college in America.

Bergen Swamp (all ages)

6646 Hessenthaler Road, Byron; (585) 548–7304. Call to schedule visit. Donation.

Although you must make advance arrangements with the caretaker to visit this preserve, it's worth the effort, for this unusual 1,900-acre bog, unchanged for 125,000 years, is home to a variety of rare and endangered plants and animals. For more than a hundred years naturalists have been drawn to this unique swamp for nature studies and for its primeval beauty.

Sports and Fun Parks in **Genesee County**

The Gravel Pit Family Entertainment Center. 5158 East Main Road (Route 5), Batavia; (585) 343–4445.

Batavia Muckdogs Baseball at Dwyer Stadium. 299 Bank Street, Batavia; (585) 343–5454; www.muckdogs.com.

Conquest Golf. 10188 Allegheny Road, Darien; (585) 547–9894.

Six Flags Darien Lake Resort. 9993 Allegheny Road (Route 77), Darien Center; (585) 599–4641; www.sixflags.com/darienlake.

Polar Wave Snowtubing. 3500 Harloff Road, Batavia; (585) 345–1630 or (888) 727–2794; www.polarwavesnowtubing.com.

Also in **the Area**

Darien Lakes State Park. 10289 Harlow Road, Darien Center; (585) 547–9242 or (800) 456–CAMP; www.nysparks.com/parks.

Holiday Hollow (all ages)

1410 Main Road, Pembroke; (585) 762–8160; www.holidayhollow.com. Open October weekends and Columbus Day 11:00 A.M. to 5:00 P.M. Adults $$, children $, under 2 free.

Every October weekend, this place is haunted by talking pumpkins, Captain Hook and Mr. Smee, and a band of silly spooks and goofy ghosts. Along with the live stage shows, there is a Halloween Adventure, a haunted forest walk, a haunted hotel, games of skill, and lots of pumpkins looking for a good home.

Where to Eat

D & R Depot. 63 Lake Street, LeRoy; (585) 768–6270; www.dandrdepot.com. Home-cooked specials served in an old depot with a upside-down model train running around. $$–$$$

Miss Batavia Family Restaurant. 566 East Main Street; (585) 343–9786. Excellent home-cooked meals. $

Where to Stay

Darien Lake Lodge on the Lake. 9993 Allegheny Road (Route 77), Darien Center; (585) 599–2211; www.sixflags.com/darien lake. Located on the theme park property, with family-size rooms, heated pool, wading pool, free continental breakfast, and 1,500 campsites. Room rates include theme park admission. $–$$$$

Lei-Ti Campground. 9979 Francis Road; (585) 343–8600 or (800) 445–3484; www.leiti.com. Located on a five-acre lake, this campground has campsites and cabins, a recreation lodge, petting zoo, mini-golf, hiking trails, tennis courts, playgrounds, camp store, snack bar, and a coin laundry. $

Arcade

Take Route 98 south.

Amid rolling pastures dotted with dairy cows lies Arcade, once a very busy cheese and produce shipping center. For a peek at a pastoral paradise, take a drive along nearby Routes 39 and 78.

Arcade and Attica Steam Railroad (all ages)

278 Main Street, Route 39; (585) 496–9877 or (585) 492–3100; www.anarr.com. **Open Memorial Day through October weekdays 10:00 A.M. to 5:00 P.M.; Saturday, Sunday, and holidays 12:30 and 3:00 P.M.; July and August Wednesday, Saturday, and Sunday 12:30 and 3:00 P.M.; Friday 1:00 P.M. Adults $$, children $.**

Ride the rails for a ninety-minute trip back in time aboard the only steam excursion trains in New York. Operating between Arcade and Attica, the train's twenty-minute layover at the Currier Depot allows time to tour the station's mini-museum and model railroad display. Seasonal specialty trips include children's trains with costumed characters, Civil War reenactment excursions, Halloween and fall foliage runs, and a Santa Express.

Beaver Meadow Audubon Center (all ages)

1610 Welch Road, North Java; (585) 457–3228; www.buffaloaudubon.com. **Grounds open year-round; visitor center open Tuesday through Saturday 10:00 A.M. to 5:00 P.M., Sunday 1:00 to 5:00 P.M. Observatory open first and third Saturdays April through October, dusk to 10:00 P.M. Closed holidays. $**

This 324-acre sanctuary offers special programs and activities, nature trails, a discovery room, and a 20-inch telescope for celestial night sights.

Where to Eat

Nellie's Restaurant. 572 West Main Street; (585) 492–9905. Breakfast, lunch, and dinner, with homemade sausage, soups, and pies daily. $

The New Farm. 1990 Route 19, Wyoming; (585) 237–2652; www.home.rochester.rr.com/thenewfarm/thenewfarm.html. A farm and craft market featuring baked goods, fresh produce, and quilts. $

Where to Stay

Arcade Village Motel. West Main Street; (585) 492–3600. Between a restaurant and grocery mart; children stay **free.** $

Jellystone. 5204 Youngers Road, North Java; (585) 457–9644; www.whyjellystone.com. Campsites and chalets, laundry room, miniature golf, playgrounds, two heated swimming pools, stocked fishing pond and store, paddleboats, planned activities, and a game room. $–$$

Also in **the Area**

New York and Lake Erie Railroad. 50 Commercial Street, Gowanda; (716) 532–5716; www.shortlineservices.com.

Wellsville

Head south on Route 98 to Route 243 east, then turn right onto Route 19.

The earth around Allegheny County yielded oil near Wellsville and rich clay for ceramics near Alfred.

Mather Homestead Museum (all ages)
343 North Main Street; (585) 593–1636. Open year-round Wednesday and Saturday 2:00 to 5:00 P.M. Call ahead. Free.

A 1930s room furnished with period furniture, tools, and toys is the focus of this small museum, with planned programs throughout the year. Of special interest is a braille copy of the Constitution, a cardboard clock, and a classic Cord automobile.

Seneca Oil Springs (all ages)
Cuba Lake Road, Oil Spring Indian Reservation, off Route 305, Cuba; (585) 268–9293. Open daily May through October. Free.

Known to the Seneca for centuries, the springs is a favorite fishing spot, where early pioneers first saw petroleum in America in 1627.

Alfred University (ages 4 and up)
26 North Main Street, Route 244, Alfred; (607) 871–2421; Stull Observatory (607) 871–2270; www.alfred.edu. Museum open Wednesday through Friday 10:00 A.M. to 4:00 P.M. Observatory open September through November and February through April, clear Friday evenings from 9:00 to 11:00 P.M. May through July Thursday 10:00 P.M. to midnight. Free.

The home of the International Museum of Ceramic Art opened in 2000, and the collection contains more than 8,000 pieces of beautiful clay creations. Nearby Stull Observatory is open on certain Thursday and Friday evenings for star searching.

Where to Eat

Beef Haus Restaurant. 176 North Main Street; (585) 593–6222. "Best beef on the block." $$

Wellsville Texas Hot. 132 North Main Street; (585) 593–1400. Serving Texas hot dogs since 1921, as well as great chili, meat loaf, and other American favorites. $

Where to Stay

Pollywogg Holler. North Road, off Route 244, Belmont; (585) 268–5819 or (800) 291–9668; www.pollywoggholler.com. Native American tepee, rustic main lodge, lofts, and solar power. $$–$$$$

Willard's Country Place. 7496 Crawford Creek Road, Caneadea; (585) 365–8317. Four rooms at the bed-and-breakfast, recreation room, and cabins and campsites on 150 acres, with trails, woods, and ponds to explore. $–$$

Olean

Take Route 417 west.

Inspired by the "black gold" bonanzas of the area, Olean's name is derived from the Latin word oleum, for oil.

Rock City Park (all ages)

505 Rock City Road, Route 16 south; (585) 372–7790. Open daily May, June, September, and October 9:00 A.M. to 6:00 P.M. $

Once a natural stone fortress for the Seneca, this is the world's largest exposure of quartz conglomerate. More than 300 million years ago, these massive monoliths were the bottom of a prehistoric ocean, but today the giant rocks rest atop the Enchanted Mountains. Trails wind through narrow "streets" and up to panoramic overlooks. A small museum offers a fluorescent mineral room and a video tour for folks preferring not to scramble among the stones.

Bartlett House Museum (ages 4 and up)

302 Laurens Street; (716) 376–5642. Open Wednesday through Saturday 1:00 to 5:00 P.M., extended hours at Christmas season. $

This grand Victorian mansion is lovely to look at any time of year, but it's especially magical during the festive Christmas season.

Allegheny River Valley Trail (all ages)

Access at Gargoyle Park or Henley and Nineteenth Streets, or at the west entrance of Saint Bonaventure University; (716) 372–4433. Open year-round. Free.

This 5.6-mile multiuse recreational loop trail was envisioned and realized by local businessman Joseph Higgins in 1992. Paralleling the Allegheny River, it provides easy paths for hiking, biking, running, and in-line skating.

O'Dea's Recreation Center (all ages)

3329 West River Road; (716) 373–5471 or (716) 372–4559. Open daily 8:00 A.M. to dark. Snowtubing Friday 5:00 to 9:00 P.M.; Saturday and school vacations 11:00 A.M. to 9:00 P.M.; Sunday and Monday holidays 11:00 A.M. to 7:00 P.M. Golf daily 8:00 A.M. to 9:00 P.M. $–$$$

Contoured, sloping greens and a sand trap are the features of this miniature golf course, and there's also a golf driving range. In winter this is a snowtubing paradise, with one of the highest elevations and longest runs of any tubing hill currently in operation. Children must be seven years or older for tube runs, and special tubes, tows, and helmets are available.

Also in **the Area**

Pfeiffer Nature Center. Lillibridge Road, Portville; (716) 933–0187; www.pfeiffernaturecenter.org.

Forness Fun Park. 800 East State Street, Olean; (716) 372–1199.

Where to Eat

Old Library Restaurant. 116 South Union Street; (716) 372–2226. Continental cuisine and a children's menu, served in Andrew Carnegie's former library, a National Historic Landmark. $$–$$$$

Salamanca

Go west on Route 17.

Allegany State Park (all ages)

2373 ASP Route 1, off Route 17; (716) 354–9101 or (716) 354–9121; www.nysparks .com/parks, www.ReserveAmerica.com. Park open year-round, campgrounds open mid-May through Labor Day. $

Covering 97 square miles of wooded wilderness, this is New York's largest state park. With three campgrounds containing a total of 315 sites and 380 cabins, a family can settle in and spend some time enjoying the variety of activities available. Hike or bike more than 90 miles of trails, fish and swim in two blue lakes, or participate in recreation programs. There's a small nature museum and a miniature golf course, and boats and bicycles can be rented at the boathouse. Both the Red House Lake and Quaker Lake have lifeguards, ball fields, playgrounds, and picnic areas. Near the Red House area is a favorite hike for families, the trek to the Three Bears Caves. In the Quaker Lakes vicinity lies the easy Three Sisters Trail.

Seneca-Iroquois National Museum (ages 4 and up)

774–814 Broad Street, off Route 17 exit 20; (716) 945–1738 or (716) 945–1760; www.seneca museum.org. Open April through mid-October Tuesday through Saturday 10:00 A.M. to 5:00 P.M., Sunday noon to 5:00 P.M.; closed Monday. Open mid-October until April Monday through Friday 9:00 A.M. to 5:00 P.M. Closed January and certain holidays. $

The history and heritage of the Seneca Nation, known as the "Keeper of the Western

Suggested **Reading**

The Niagara Falls Mystery by Gertrude Chandler Warner

The Rough-Face Girl by Rafe Martin

Maggie Among the Seneca by Robin Moore

Brother Wolf: A Seneca Tale by Harriet P. Taylor

Journey to Nowhere by Mary Jane Auch

Door," is highlighted at this interesting museum. There are exhibits of Native American traditions, medicine, art, artifacts, and culture, and there's even a life-size bark longhouse to explore.

Salamanca Rail Museum (ages 3 and up)
170 Main Street; (716) 945–3133. Open Monday through Saturday 10:00 A.M. to 5:00 P.M., Sunday noon to 5:00 P.M.; closed Monday October, November, and December. Free.

Flash back eight decades to a time when Salamanca was a major railroad center. This fully restored 1912 passenger depot houses exhibits of artifacts and photographs, with a video recalling the golden age of rail travel.

Holiday Valley Resort (all ages)
Route 219 and Holiday Valley Road, Ellicottville; (716) 699–2345 or (800) 367–9691; www.holidayvalley.com. Open daily year-round. $$$–$$$$

This is the largest public ski area in the state, with fifty-three slopes and trails, twelve lifts, and a ski school. In summer the resort offers eighteen-hole golf, three swimming pools,

Other Ski Spots in **Western New York**

Kissing Bridge. Route 240, Glenwood; (716) 592–4963; www.kissingbridge.com.

Cockaigne. 1493 Thornton Road, Cherry Creek; (716) 287–3223; www.cockaigne.com.

Peek N Peak. 1405 Olde Road, Findley Lake; (716) 355–4141; www.pknpk.com.

Ski Tamarack. Route 240, Colden; (716) 941–6821.

Holimont. 6921 Route 242, Ellicottville; (716) 699–2320; www.holimont.com.

Also in **the Area**

Gentle Thunder Farm. 7067 Hencoop Road, Ellicottville; (716) 699–2940.

R & R Dude Ranch. 8940 Lange Road, Otto; (716) 257–5663; www.rrduderanch.com.

Northeastern Wildlife Company. 4141 Route 242, Ellicottville; (716) 699–8813.

The Crosspatch Horse Ranch. 5281 Baker Road, Ellicottville; (716) 938–6313.

Zaepfel Nature Sanctuary & Research Center. Box 1, Cattaraugus 14719; (716) 257–3237.

on-site accommodations, and a children's learning center, providing day care and outdoor activities for ages two and up.

Nannen Arboretum (all ages)

28 Parkside Drive, off Route 218, Ellicottville; (716) 699–2377 or (800) 897–9189; www.cce.cornell.edu. Open daily year-round dawn to dusk. **Free.**

More than 200 species of rare and unusual trees flourish in this botanical garden. Perennial, herb, and Japanese stone gardens grace the grounds, and special programs are offered at the outdoor Northrup Nature Hall and the Chapman Nature Sanctuary.

Mansfield Coach and Cutter (all ages)

6864 Sodum Road, Little Valley; (716) 938–6315; www.coachandcutter.com. Open year-round. Call for seasonal hours and reservations. $–$$$

Depending on the season, families can ride across fifty acres of woodlands and fields in horse-drawn wagons, coaches, or sleighs. Check out the Carriage House Museum, where custom coaches and antique surreys are available for special outings with advance notice.

Griffis Sculpture Park (all ages)

6902 Mill Valley Road, East Otto; (716) 667–2808. Open May through October 9:00 A.M. to dusk. $, children under 12 **free.**

Similar to a surreal dreamscape, more than 200 magical metal sculptures dot the fields and woods of this 400-acre park, with trails lacing through three different sections.

Where to Eat

Barn Restaurant. 7 Monroe Street, Ellicottville; (716) 699–4600. Buffalo steaks, seafood, prime rib, pasta, local specialties, plus a children's menu. $$

Where to Stay

High Banks Campground. Route 394, West Perimeter Road, Steamburg, about 8 miles west of park; (716) 354–2267. Owned and operated by the Seneca Nation, this campground has winterized cabins, campsites, hot showers, docks, inground pool, laundry, playground, and trading post. $

The Inn at Holiday Valley. Holiday Valley Road and Route 219, about 2 miles south of Ellicottville; (716) 699–2345 or (800) 323–0020; www.holidayvalley.com. Rooms and suites, recreation center, indoor/outdoor pool, continental breakfast, day care, youth day camp, and golf and ski packages. $$$$

Jamestown

Continue west on Route 17.

Lucy & Desi Museum (ages 6 and up)

212 Pine Street; (716) 484–0800; www.lucy-desi.com. **Open May through October Monday through Saturday 10:00 A.M. to 5:30 P.M., Sunday 1:00 to 5:00 P.M.; November through April Saturday 10:00 A.M. to 5:30 P.M., Sunday 1:00 to 5:00 P.M. $**

This museum pays tribute to the town's favorite daughter, Lucille Ball, and there are interesting displays highlighting her illustrious career and that of Desi Arnaz.

Roger Tory Peterson Institute (all ages)

311 Curtis Street; (716) 665–2473 or (800) 758–6841; www.rtpi.org. **Open Tuesday through Saturday year-round 10:00 A.M. to 4:00 P.M., Sunday 1:00 to 5:00 P.M. Closed holidays. Grounds open daily dawn to dusk. $**

Another Jamestown native is the famous ornithologist, artist, and author Roger Tory Peterson. The center has a gallery of wildlife art, nature photography and exhibits, a butterfly garden, and nature trails winding through twenty-seven wooded acres.

Jamestown Audubon Nature Center (all ages)

1600 Riverside Road, off Route 62; (716) 569–2345; www.audubon.org. **Open March through October Monday through Saturday 10:00 A.M. to 4:30 P.M., Sunday 1:00 to 4:30 P.M. Call for hours November through February. Sanctuary open dawn to dusk. Closed holidays. $**

This 600-acre sanctuary of mixed forests and marsh is a favorite stop for multitudes of migrating birds. Five miles of trails wind through the woods and swamps that are home to more than 400 species of plants. At the Peterson Nature Building, you can pick up self-guided trail maps, tour the Butterfly Garden, and check out a variety of hands-on exhibits at the Children's Discovery Center.

Jamestown Jammers (all ages)

Russell E. Dietrick Jr. Park, 485 Falconer Street; (716) 664–0915. Call for ticket and schedule information.

Called "The Greatest Show on Dirt," this Class A affiliate of the 2003 World Series Champion Florida Marlins battles the ball clubs of the New York–Penn League from June through September.

Panama Rocks Scenic Park (all ages)

11 Rock Hill Road (Route 10), Panama; (716) 782–2845; www.panamarocks.com. Open daily early May through mid-October 10:00 A.M. to 5:00 P.M. Adults $$, children $, under 6 free.

Similar to the rock city outside of Olean, this stone citadel of Paleozoic sea islands is surrounded by an old-growth forest. Massive quartz conglomerate towers, boulders, caves, and crevices are the remnants of weathering and glacial erosion and are a lot of fun to explore. It can get muddy, so wear boots if possible.

Where to Eat

Jones Tasty Baking Co. 209 Pine Street; (716) 484–1988. A third-generation family bakery, this is where Lucille Ball bought her bread, having it sent to her in Hollywood years later. $

Where to Stay

Comfort Inn. 2800 North Main Street; (716) 664–5920 or (800) 228–5150. Complimentary continental breakfast; children under eighteen stay **free.** $$$$

Pope Haven Campground. 11948 Pope Road, Randolph; (716) 358–4900. Campsites, cabins, swimming pool, fishing in stocked pond, playgrounds, laundry, game room, hot showers, and planned activities. $

Chautauqua **County Bounty**

The Berry Bush. 2929 Route 39, Forestville; (716) 679–1240.

Busti Cider Mill and Farm Market. 1135 Southwestern Drive, Jamestown; (716) 487–0177.

Sugar Shack Fruit Syrups. 7904 Route 5, Westfield; (716) 326–3351 or (888) 563–4324.

Chadakoin Farms. 1690 King Road, Forestville; (716) 965–2923.

Blueberry Sky Farm Winery. 10243 Northeast Sherman Road, Ripley; (716) 252–6535.

Big Tree Maple. 2040 Holly Lane, Lakewood; (716) 763–5917; www.bigtreemaple.com.

Chautauqua

Take Route 17 west to Route 394.

Home to the world-renowned cultural summer camp for families, the Chautauqua Institution, this area is also known for its vineyards and rolling farmlands.

Chautauqua Institution (all ages)

1 Ames Avenue, Route 394; (716) 357–6200, (716) 357–6250, or (800) 836–ARTS; www .chautauqua-inst.org. Open late June through August. Tours daily. Accommodation and admission packages available. Day pass $$, classes $$–$$$$.

Founded in 1874 as an arts and education summer camp for Sunday school teachers, Chautauqua weaves a magical spell around all who visit. For generations families have returned year after year to participate in the wide variety of more than 300 programs offered for all ages, from the performing arts classes and performances of dance, music, theater, and opera to lectures and courses in literature, philosophy, religion, history, and science. Children have always been welcome here, and there are special programs just for them. Visitors can stay for a day or sign up for the full nine-week season.

Long Point State Park on Lake Chautauqua (all ages)

Off Route 430, Bemus Point; (716) 386–2722; www.nysparks.com/parks. Open daily year-round. **Free.**

Reaching out into Chautauqua's waters, this day park has more than 5 miles of hiking and nature trails running through it, as well as excellent swimming, fishing, boating, and bicycling opportunities.

Traveling by Water **in Chautauqua**

Chautauqua Belle Steamboat Cruises. Lakeside Park, Mayville; (716) 753–2403.

Summer Wind Lake Cruises. Docked at Lucille Ball Memorial Park, Celeron; (716) 763–7447; www.thesummerwind.com.

Chautauqua Marina. Route 394, Mayville; (716) 753–3913; www.chautauqua marina.com.

Midway Park (all ages)
Box E, Route 430, Maple Springs 14756; (716) 386–3165; www.midwaypark.com. Open weekends late May through late June and Tuesday through Sunday July through early September 1:00 P.M. to sunset. Closed Monday except holidays. **Free** parking and beach, with admission charge for rides and games.

For more than a century, families have been coming to this charming amusement park on the shores of Chautauqua Lake. There's no charge for swimming at the sandy beach, and there are sixteen rides to experience, including go-karts, bumper boats, and an antique carousel, plus an outdoor roller rink, miniature golf, a water wars area, and an arcade, with a laser light show August evenings.

McClurg Museum (ages 4 and up)
Village Park, Routes 20 and 394, Westfield; (716) 326–2977. Open 10:00 A.M. to 4:00 P.M. Tuesday through Saturday. $

This restored 1818 mansion houses a collection of Native American, pioneer, and military artifacts. Of special interest is an exhibit on Grace Bedell, an eleven-year-old Westfield girl who wrote a letter to Abraham Lincoln in 1860 suggesting that "he would look a lot better" if he grew a beard. He took her advice, and the rest is history.

Double D.A.B. Riding Stables (ages 6 and up)
5811 Welch Road, Ripley; (716) 736–4418; www.doubledab.com. Open daily 9:00 A.M. to 5:30 P.M. by reservation. $–$$

Day and overnight trail rides as well as pony rides and a petting farm are offered at this family-friendly stable.

Where to Eat

The Italian Fisherman. 61 Lakeside Drive, Bemus Point; (716) 386–7000. Deck dining overlooking Chautauqua Lake. $$–$$$

Where to Stay

Athenaeum Hotel. On western shore of lake at the Chautauqua Institution; (800) 821–1881; www.athenaeum-hotel.com. Built in 1881, this Victorian hotel was once the largest wooden building in the country. There's an excellent restaurant, and package rates are available. $$$$

Hotel Lenhart. 20 Lakeside Drive, Bemus Point; (716) 386–2715. Facing Chautauqua Lake, with rocking chairs on the veranda and a restaurant. $$–$$$$

We Wan Chu Cottages. Route 394, 1 mile south of Chautauqua Institution; (716) 789–3383; www.wewanchu.com. Modern, fully furnished cottages on Chautauqua Lake; with play and picnic areas, recreation room, lawn games, dock, and boat rentals. $$$–$$$$

Dunkirk

Take Route 394 west to Route 5 north (Seaway Trail).

Situated on the shores of Lake Erie, Dunkirk was named after the French harbor of Dunkerque.

Dunkirk Historical Lighthouse and Veterans Park Museum

(all ages)

1 Lighthouse Point Drive; (716) 366–5050; www.netsync.net/users/skipper. Open late April through June and September through October 10:00 A.M. to 2:00 P.M., closed Sunday and Wednesday; July and August 10:00 A.M. to 4:00 P.M., closed Sunday and Wednesday. Closed holidays. $

Tour the tower and eleven rooms of this light-keeper's house, with displays of maritime and military historical artifacts and exhibits.

Where to Eat

Aldrich's Dairy. Route 60 South, Fredonia; (716) 672–5133. Sandwiches, ice cream, and all the milk you can drink. $

The White Inn. 52 East Main Street, Fredonia; (716) 672–2103; www.whiteinn .com. American and continental cuisine; serving breakfast, lunch, and dinner, with buffet specials. $–$$$

Where to Stay

Southshore Motor Lodge. 5040 West Lakeshore Drive; (716) 366–2822. Rooms, efficiencies, and cottages; heated pool, playground, laundry, lawn games, and picnic area. $–$$$$

For More Information

Niagara County Tourism. (716) 439–7300 or (800) 338–7890; www.niagara-usa.com.

Niagara Falls Convention and Visitors Bureau. (716) 285–2400 or (800) 421–5223.

Buffalo Niagara Convention and Visitors Bureau. (716) 852–0511, (888) 228–3369, or (800) BUFFALO; www .buffalocvb.org.

Genesee County Chamber of Commerce. (585) 343–7440 or (800) 622–2686; www.geneseeny.com.

Orleans County Tourism. (800) 724–0314; www.orleansny.com/tourism.

Wyoming County Tourism. (585) 493–3190 or (800) 839–3919; www.wyomingcountyny.com.

Chautauqua-Allegheny Regional Information. (716) 357–4569 or (800) 242–4569; www.chautauqua-allegheny.org.

Chautauqua County Visitors Bureau. (716) 357–4569 or (800) 242–4569; www.tourchautauqua.com.

Allegany County Tourism. (585) 268–7472; www.alleganyco.com.

Cattaraugus County Tourist Bureau. (800) 331–0543; www.co.cattaraugus.ny.us.

Nature **Preserves**

The Nature Conservancy maintains several sites of special significance in this area, each one a unique ecosystem. For more information, write to the Conservancy at 339 East Avenue, Suite 300, Rochester 14604, call (585) 546–8030, or log on to www.tnc.org.

Chaumont Barrens, Lyme and Clayton

El Dorado Beach Preserve, Ellisburg

Thousand Acre Swamp, Penfield

Moss Lake Nature Sanctuary, Caneadea

Deer Lick Sanctuary, Persia

French Creek Watershed, Mina

Canadaway Creek State Wildlife Management Area, Arkwright, New York State Department of Environmental Conservation; (518) 402–8540; www.dec.state.ny.us.

Other Things to See and Do
in Western New York

Albright-Knox Art Gallery. 1285 Elmwood Avenue, Buffalo; (716) 882–8700; www.albrightknox.org.

Millard and Abigail Fillmore Museum. 24 Shearer Avenue, East Aurora; (716) 652–8875.

Lancaster National Speedway. 57 Gunnville Road, Lancaster; (716) 759–6818.

Evangola State Park. Route 5, Old Lake Shore Road, Irving; (716) 549–1802; www.nysparks.com/parks.

Ransomville Speedway. 2315 Braley Road off Ransomville Road, Ransomville; (716) 791–3602; www.ransomvillespeedway.com.

Allenburg Bog. Pigeon Valley Road and Farm Market Road, Little Valley; (716) 938–9111.

Chautauqua Watershed Conservancy. 413 Main Street, Jamestown; (716) 664–2166; www.netsync.net/users/chautwsh.

Lake Erie State Park. 5905 Lake Road, Route 5, Brockton; (716) 792–9214; www.nysparks.com/parks.

Dart Airport Aviation Museum. 6167 Plank Road, Route 430, Mayville; (716) 753–2160.

Delevan Drive-In Theater. Route 16, Delevan; (716) 496–5660.

Kabob Bear Country. 6359 South Stockton–Cassadega Road, Sinclairville; (716) 962–4647; www.kabobbear.com.

Music and Magic Dinner Theatre. 300 Third Street, Niagara Falls; (716) 834–2971; www.vivaniagara.com.

Motherland Connextions. 476 Hyde Park Boulevard, Niagara Falls; (716) 282–1028; www.motherlandconnextions.com.

Becker Farms. 3760 Quaker Road, Gasport; (716) 772–2211; www.becker farms.com.

Long Island

Stretching eastward from New York City for almost 120 miles, Long Island resembles a great whale basking between the Sound and the Atlantic Ocean. This is the largest island adjoining the continental United States, and it was once home to thirteen Algonquin tribes before the arrival of the Europeans in the seventeenth century. The fertile farmlands and abundant fishing encouraged the Dutch and English settlers to stay, and 300 years later Long Island became synonymous with suburbia. But Long Island's heritage has left us with more than sprawling malls and car-choked highways. There is an ageless beauty and rich history to this place the Native Americans called Paumanok. Divided into five distinct regions, each area offers opportunities to experience a surprising variety of natural and historical treasures. Whether you choose to explore the opulent estates of the North Shore, meander for miles along the barrier beaches of the South Shore, watch for wildlife in the pine barrens of Central Suffolk, feast on the fruitful harvest of the North Fork, or bask in the sun and sand of the South Fork, your family will find a wealth of activities and adventures. Once you've paused in Paumanok, it's likely you'll be lured back again by its charms.

Driving Tips

Bisecting the center of Long Island is the Long Island Expressway (I–495), known as the LIE to the multitude of motorists who ply its pavement daily. Don't even think about trying to travel the LIE during rush hour or Friday summer afternoons, unless you enjoy seemingly endless miles of bumper-to-bumper traffic. Along the North Shore, travel along Routes 25 and 25A, or the Northern State Parkway, and along the South Shore follow the Montauk Highway (Routes 27A and 80), the Sunrise Highway (Route 27), or the Southern State Parkway. For north and south travel, there are dozens of roads cutting across the 20-mile-wide girth of Long Island, including the Seaford–Oyster Bay Expressway and the Sunken Meadow, Wantaugh, and Meadowbrook State Parkways.

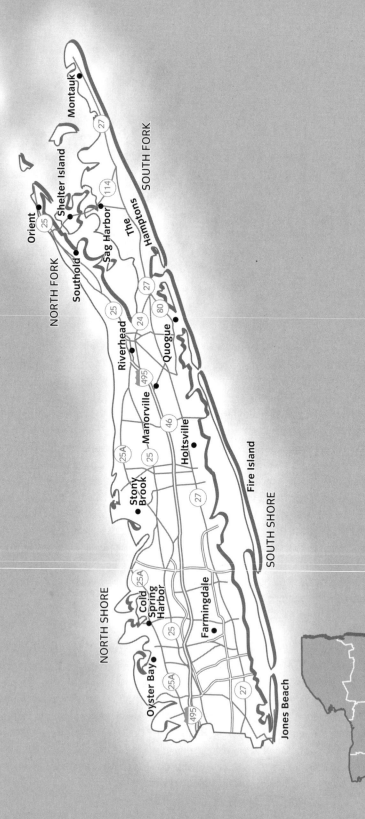

LONG ISLAND

NORTH FORK

SOUTH FORK

Montauk

Shelter Island

Orient

Southold

Sag Harbor

The Hamptons

NORTH FORK

Riverhead

Quogue

Manorville

Holtsville

Fire Island

Stony Brook

NORTH SHORE

Cold Spring Harbor

Farmingdale

Oyster Bay

SOUTH SHORE

Jones Beach

North Shore

Turn-of the-twentieth-century captains of commerce and industry created a fabled land of fabulous mansions and exquisite gardens along the "Gold Coast" of Long Island's North Shore. Many of those extravagant estates no longer exist, but the ones that do are awesome. There are other treasures to be found here, as well. Thousands of years of Native American culture and a rich Revolutionary War heritage offer an interesting counterpoint, and farsighted philanthropy has provided numerous nature preserves to explore.

Vanderbilt Museum & Planetarium (ages 6 and up)

180 Little Neck Road, Centerport; (631) 854–5555; www.vanderbiltmuseum.org. Open late April through late June and September through October Tuesday through Friday noon to 5:00 P.M., Saturday, Sunday, and holidays 11:30 A.M. to 5:00 P.M.; late June through August Tuesday through Saturday 10:00 A.M. to 5:00 P.M., Sunday and holidays noon to 5:00 P.M.; November through April Tuesday through Friday noon to 4:00 P.M., Saturday to 5:00 P.M., Sunday and holidays 11:30 A.M. to 5:00 P.M. Closed Christmas, and New Year's Day. Adults $$, children $.

Called Eagle's Nest, this forty-three-acre estate was once the home of William Kissam Vanderbilt II, great-grandson of Comm. Cornelius Vanderbilt. He filled his mansion with an amazing array of art and artifacts from his family travels around the world, devoting a wing to wildlife dioramas and natural-history exhibits. The Marine Museum, next door, houses more than 2,000 specimens of aquatic interest. Added to the complex in 1971 is the Vanderbilt Planetarium, one of the best equipped in the country, featuring a 60-foot Sky Theatre and a 16-inch telescope open to the public on clear evenings. During the day, sunspot and solar flare activity can be viewed on monitors in the lobby. Special children's programs are offered throughout the year.

Cold Spring Harbor Fish Hatchery & Aquarium (all ages)

Route 25A, Cold Spring Harbor; (516) 692–6768; www.cshfha.org. Open daily year-round 10:00 A.M. to 5:00 P.M. Closed Easter, Thanksgiving, and Christmas. $

Opened in 1883, this is New York's oldest fish hatchery and a National Historic Landmark. Feed the fish at several outdoor trout ponds, then ogle the aquariums that hold the largest collection of native freshwater fish, reptiles, and amphibians in the state.

St. John's Pond Preserve (all ages)

Route 25A, Cold Spring Harbor; (631) 367–3225 or (516) 692–6768; www.nature.org. Open daily 10:00 A.M. to 5:00 P.M. Donation.

While you're at the hatchery, ask for a key to the gate of this Nature Conservancy gem next door. A trail winds through woodlands filled with mountain laurel and moss and past ponds and marsh. Rabbits, red fox, muskrats, and turtles make their home here, and the wildflowers in spring are lovely.

Cold Spring Harbor Whaling Museum (ages 4 and up)

25 Main Street (Route 25A), Cold Spring Harbor; (631) 367–3418; www.cshwhaling museum.org. **Open year-round Tuesday through Sunday 11:00 A.M. to 5:00 P.M. Open Memorial Day and Labor Day and summer Mondays. Closed Christmas and New Year's Day. $**

Most children would probably prefer to see their whales alive, but this interesting museum traces the rich maritime history of Long Island with kid-friendly hands-on exhibits, exquisite scrimshaw, and a fully equipped nineteenth-century whaleboat. Programs for families include sea chantey workshops.

DNA Learning Center (ages 7 and up)

334 Main Street, Cold Spring Harbor; (516) 367–5170; www.dnalc.org. **Open year-round weekdays 10:00 A.M. to 4:00 P.M., Saturday noon to 4:00 P.M. Closed holidays. Free.**

This is the world's first biotechnology museum, a branch of the Cold Springs Harbor Laboratory, with kid-friendly interactive exhibits that explore the brave new world of DNA. Also of interest is the center's multimedia historical presentation, *Long Island Discovery.*

Garvies Point Museum and Preserve (all ages)

50 Barry Drive, Glen Cove; (516) 571–8010 or (516) 571–8011; www.garviespointmuseum.com. **Preserve open daily 8:30 A.M. to dusk; museum open Tuesday through Sunday 10:00 A.M. to 4:00 P.M. Closed winter holidays, open summer holidays. $**

Five miles of nature trails meander through this sixty-two-acre preserve, once the campsite of Matinecock Indians. Exhibits at the museum include animatronic figures demonstrating various aspects of Native American culture, and archaeological and geological displays. Outside there's a tulip tree dugout canoe and a wigwam to explore, as well as the first and only dinosaur footprints found on Long Island.

Sea Cliff Village Museum (ages 6 and up)

95 Tenth Avenue, Sea Cliff; (516) 671–0090; www.seacliff.org. **Open Saturday and Sunday 2:00 to 5:00 P.M., closed mid-July to mid-October. $**

Artifacts and albums of photographs highlight the history of this Victorian resort overlooking Hempstead Harbor.

Cinema Arts Centre (ages 6 and up)

423 Park Avenue, Huntington; (631) 423–7610 or (631) 423–3456. **Call for schedule. Adults $$, children $.**

International and independent films are screened at this theater, along with frequent showings of silent movie classics accompanied by live music.

Walt Whitman Birthplace (all ages)

246 Old Walt Whitman Road, Huntington Station; (631) 427–5240; www.nysparks.com/hist. **Open year-round. Summer: Monday through Friday 11:00 A.M. to 4:00 P.M., Saturday and Sunday noon to 5:00 P.M. Winter: Wednesday through Friday 1:00 to 4:00 P.M., Saturday and Sunday 11:00 A.M. to 4:00 P.M. Closed holidays. $**

In 1819, Walt Whitman, one of America's most beloved poets, was born in this finely crafted farmhouse built by his father. Although his family moved to Brooklyn when he was five, Whitman returned to Long Island to become a schoolteacher at sixteen and founder and editor of a newspaper at nineteen, a period in which he also wrote his classic collection of poems *Leaves of Grass*. Ask about a driving tour map of some of Whitman's favorite places to amuse the muses, including the highest point on the Island, Jayne's Hill.

Governor Alfred E. Smith/Sunken Meadow State Park

(all ages) 🏛 🏊

Route 25A, Kings Park; (631) 269–4333; www.nysparks.com/parks. Open year-round daily sunrise to sunset. $$

Enjoy a mile of beach along Long Island Sound at this popular 1,266-acre park. Swim in Smithtown Bay, hike or bike along nature trails or bridle paths through a salt marsh, have a picnic, and visit the small nature museum for interesting eco-exhibits.

Other Parks and **Nature Preserves**

Uplands Farm Sanctuary. 250 Lawrence Hill Road, Cold Spring Harbor; (631) 367–3225.

Caleb Smith State Park Preserve. Off Jericho Turnpike (Route 25), Smithtown; (631) 265–1054; www.nysparks.com/parks.

David Weld Sanctuary. Boney Lane, Nissequogue (Smithtown); (631) 367–3225.

Muttontown Preserve and Bill Paterson Nature Center. Muttontown Lane, off Route 25A, East Norwich; (516) 571–8500.

Welwyn Preserve and Holocaust Memorial and Educational Center of Nassau County. Crescent Beach Road, Glen Cove; (516) 571–7900; (516) 571–8040 (Holocaust Museum).

North Shore Wildlife Sanctuary. Frost Mill Road, Mill Neck; (516) 671–0283.

Caumsett State Historic Park. West Neck Road, Lloyd Harbor; (631) 423–1770.

Target Rock Wildlife Refuge. Target Rock Road, Lloyd Neck; (631) 271–2409 or (631) 286–0485.

Nissequoque River State Park. St. Johnsland Road, Kings Park; (631) 269–4927; www.nysparks.com/parks.

American Merchant Marine Museum (all ages)

At bottom of Steamboat Road, Kings Point; (516) 773–5391 or (866) 546–4778; www.USMMA.edu. Grounds open year-round, except July, daily 8:00 A.M. to 4:30 P.M. Museum open Tuesday through Friday 10:00 A.M. to 3:00 P.M., Saturday and Sunday 1:00 to 4:30 P.M., except mid-June through August. Free.

Located on the campus of the United States Merchant Marine Academy, this museum has a wonderful collection of model ships, marine artifacts, and maritime art, as well as interesting interactive exhibits.

Joseph Lloyd Manor House (all ages)

Lloyd Lane, Lloyd Harbor; (631) 271–7760. Open Memorial Day through Labor Day Sunday 1:00 to 5:00 P.M. $

Built in 1766, this was the estate of Griselda and James Lloyd, as well as the home and workplace of Jupiter Hammon, a slave and the first published black poet in America. Tour the restored mansion, then step outside and stroll through the fragrant formal gardens overlooking the Sound.

Northport Historical Museum (ages 4 and up)

215 Main Street, Northport; (631) 757–9859. Open year-round Tuesday through Sunday 1:00 to 4:30 P.M. Closed holidays. Donation.

The shipbuilding heritage of this charming village, once known as Cowharbor, is highlighted here with exhibits, artifacts, and memorabilia.

Earle-Wightman House Museum (ages 7 and up)

20 Summit Street, Oyster Bay; (516) 922–5032; www.members.aol.com/obhistory. Open year-round Tuesday through Friday 10:00 A.M. to 2:00 P.M., Saturday 9:00 A.M. to 1:00 P.M., Sunday 1:00 to 4:00 P.M. Free.

Home of the Oyster Bay Historical Society, this 1720 landmark house is filled with authentic eighteenth-century furnishings.

Planting Fields Arboretum State Historic Park (all ages)

Planting Fields Road, Oyster Bay; (516) 922–8600 or (516) 922–9210; www.planting fields.org. Open daily year-round 9:00 A.M. to 5:00 P.M., Coe Hall (1039 Van Buren Street, Oyster Bay) open April to September daily noon to 3:30 P.M., except Christmas. $

Formerly the Gold Coast estate of William Robertson Coe, this 409-acre verdant plantation has spacious lawns, woodlands, cultivated gardens, and an arboretum designed by Frederick Law Olmsted Jr. The sixty-five-room Tudor Revival Coe mansion is an architectural delight, and its restored rooms are filled with beautiful antiques.

New York **Trivia**

The Little Prince, by Antoine de Saint-Exupéry, was written on Long Island.

Raynham Hall (ages 7 and up)

20 West Main Street, Oyster Bay; (516) 922–6808; www.raynhamhallmuseum.org. Open year-round Tuesday through Sunday 1:00 to 5:00 P.M., July through Labor Day noon to 5:00 P.M.; closed major holidays. $

Built in 1738, this was the home of Samuel Townsend, whose son Robert was Gen. George Washington's top spy during the Revolutionary War. The house was occupied by the British Queen's Rangers during the war, and reportedly several ghosts from that era remain.

Sagamore Hill National Historic Site (ages 5 and up)

20 Sagamore Hill Road, Oyster Bay; (516) 922–4788; www.nps.gov/sahi. Visitor's center open May through September daily 9:00 A.M. to 4:50 P.M., closed Monday and Tuesday October through April. Closed major holidays. $

Operated by the National Park Service, this Victorian mansion was the permanent home and summer White House for President Theodore Roosevelt, his wife, and six children. The Old Orchard House contains exhibits and a short documentary highlighting Roosevelt's life and times.

Theodore Roosevelt Sanctuary (all ages)

134 Cove Road, Oyster Bay; (516) 922–3200; www.audubon.org/trsac.htm. Open year-round 9:00 A.M. to 5:00 P.M. Donation.

Despite Roosevelt's passion for hunting, he was a strong supporter of environmental conservation. This twelve-acre sanctuary is the first owned by the National Audubon Society and offers eco-education programs for all ages, such as raptor rehabilitation and flight demonstrations, endangered species survival, and aquatic ecology.

Mount Sinai Marine Sanctuary Nature Center (all ages)

Harbor Beach Road, Mount Sinai; (631) 473–8346. Open daily June through September 10:00 A.M. to 2:00 P.M. Free.

Outdoor touch tanks and indoor aquariums house a variety of local marine life, from fish, turtles, clams, and moon snails to a rare blue lobster.

Christopher Morley Park (all ages)

500 Searington Road, Roslyn Heights; (516) 571–8113. Open daily dawn to dusk year-round. Park free, some facilities $$.

This ninety-eight-acre county park, site of writer Christopher Morley's cabin, offers ball fields and courts, golf, an outdoor ice rink, model boating, and an outdoor swimming pool.

The Science Museum of Long Island (all ages)

1526 North Plandome Road, Manhasset 11030; (516) 627–9400; http://ourworld .compuserve.com/homepages/smli. Call for more information.

Interactive exhibits and hands-on workshops and activities designed to encourage children's curiosity about the physical sciences are offered here.

Sands Point Preserve (all ages)

95 Middleneck Road, Port Washington; (516) 571–7900; www.sandspointpreserve.org. Open year-round Tuesday through Sunday 10:00 A.M. to 5:00 P.M. $

Unfortunately, children under ten are not allowed to tour the mansions, but the grounds will probably be of more interest to kids, anyway. Stop by Castlegould, the Kilkenny Castle knockoff, once the servant quarters and stable and now a visitor center, to see natural history exhibits and to pick up a map of six short nature trails to explore.

Old Westbury Gardens (all ages)

71 Old Westbury Road, Old Westbury; (516) 333–0048; www.oldwestburygardens.org. Open late April through October daily 10:00 A.M. to 5:00 P.M., Sundays in November and holiday celebrations in December, closed Tuesday. Adults $$, children $.

Steel magnate John S. Phipps built this palatial country estate as a wedding present for his heiress wife, Margarita Grace, in 1904. The Charles II manor house and surrounding gardens were patterned after her childhood home in England, and the results are breathtaking. The mansion is filled with beautiful furniture, art, and family mementos, and the formal English gardens surrounding the house are considered to be the best in the country. Children will enjoy exploring playhouses, from a miniature thatched cottage complete with a tiny tea party for dolls inside to three rustic kid-size log cabins.

Museums at Stony Brook (all ages)

1208 Route 25A, Stony Brook; (631) 751–0066; www.fieldtrip.com/ny/67510066.htm. St. James General Store and Post Office, 516 Moriches Road; (631) 862–8333. Deepwells, Route 25A; (631) 862–6080. Open year-round Wednesday through Saturday, Monday, and holidays 10:00 A.M. to 5:00 P.M., and Sunday noon to 5:00 P.M.; daily July and August. Closed Thanksgiving, Christmas, and New Year's Day. Adults $$, children $, under 6 free.

Explore this nine-acre complex of three museums, as well as a blacksmith shop, a one-room schoolhouse, and an 1870 barn, to learn more about the art and history of Long Island. The Melville Carriage House has nearly one hundred vehicles, including ornate European coaches, shiny fire engines, cheery omnibuses, and rare gypsy wagons. The Art Museum's collection of paintings depicts rural Islander life, as well as changing exhibits. The Margaret Blackwell History Museum features a great decoy collection, but children will be drawn to the fifteen miniature furnished sixteenth- to twentieth-century period rooms. With advance reservations, older children and their families may attend a theatrical tea party hosted by historical characters at nearby Deepwells.

Stony Brook Grist Mill (all ages)

Harbor Road, Stony Brook; (631) 751–2244; www.stonybrookvillage.com. Open June through Labor Day Friday through Sunday noon to 4:30 P.M., Saturday and Sunday only May through June and September through early December. $

Built in 1751, this is Long Island's most completely equipped working mill.

Saddle Rock Grist Mill (all ages)

Grist Mill Lane, Great Neck; (516) 572–0257. Open Sunday May through October. Free.

Possibly the oldest tidal gristmill in the country, this restored 1702 mill offers demonstrations; call for a schedule.

Long Island Reptile Museum (all ages)

70 Broadway (Route 107), Hicksville; (516) 931–1500 or (631) REPTILE; www.reptile museum.com. Open daily 10:00 A.M. to 6:00 P.M., Friday until 8:00 P.M. Closed Thanksgiving and Christmas. $$

More than 3,000 reptiles live here, and the live shows, hands-on exhibits, and large pet-

North Shore **Play Places**

Fun 4 All. 200 Wilson Street, Port Jefferson; (631) 331–9000; www.fun4allny .com.

Sports Plus. 110 New Moriches Road, Lake Grove; (631) 737–2100.

The Rinx. 660 Terry Road, Hauppauge; (631) 232–3222.

North Shore **Boats & Ferries**

Port Jefferson Ferry. 102 West Broadway, Port Jefferson; (631) 473–0286.

Thomas Jefferson Paddlesteamer. 128 Shore Road, Glen Cove; (516) 671–5563; www.byy.com.

Liberty Cruises. 377 Jerusalem Avenue, Hempstead; (516) 486–3057.

Discovery Wetlands Cruise. 111 Main Street, P.O. Box 572, Stony Brook 11790; (631) 751–2244.

ting area allow families to get up close and personal with pythons and other slithery creatures.

Where to Eat

Once Upon a Moose. 304 Sea Cliff Avenue, Sea Cliff; (516) 676–9304. Soups, sandwiches, and salads. $

Pier I. 33 Bayville Avenue, Bayville; (516) 628–2153. Seafood, steak, and lobster, with home baking and children's meals. $$$

Three Village Inn. 150 Main Street, Stony Brook; (631) 751–0555; www.three villageinn.com. Colonial homestead serving steak, seafood, regional specialties, and home baking. $$$$

Where to Stay

Chalet on the Pond Motor Inn. 23 Centershore Road and Route 25A, Centerport; (631) 757–4600. Rooms and suites; overlooking pond; children under twelve stay **free.** $$–$$$

East Norwich Inn. 6321 Northern Boulevard, East Norwich; (516) 922–1500 or (800) 334–4798. Rooms, suites, cottages, heated pool, complimentary continental breakfast, and children under twelve stay **free.** $$$$

Other Parks of the **North Shore**

Blydenburgh County Park. Smithtown; (631) 854–3713.

West Hills County Park. Huntington; (631) 854–4423.

Hempstead Harbor Beach Park. Port Washington; (516) 571–7930.

Whitney Pond Park. Manhasset; (516) 571–8300.

Flax Pond Marine Laboratory (all ages)
Shore Drive, off Crane Neck Road, off Route 25A, Old Field; (631) 632–8709; www.sunysb
.edu. Lab is open weekdays 8:00 A.M. to 3:00 P.M.; marsh is open daily. **Free.**

Budding biologists will enjoy touring this research and instructional laboratory, operated
by the State University of New York, where the ecology of crustaceans, fish, mollusks, and
algae is studied. Surrounding the lab is a 150-acre tidal wetlands preserve with an interesting nature trail winding through the marsh.

South Shore

Pristine sugar sand beaches line the southern coastline of Long Island, beckoning beach-
combers, sun worshipers, and sports enthusiasts. There are enough malls in the area to
shop till you drop, but that doesn't usually appeal to the preteen-and-under crowd. What
will impress them are the seemingly endless barrier beaches; the eclectic assortment of
museums, mills, and mansions; and the wide variety of indoor and outdoor playgrounds.

Empire State Carousel (all ages)
Buckley Road, in the Holtsville Ecology Park and Animal Preserve, Holtsville; (631) 277–
6168; www.empirestatecarousel.org. Open every Saturday 10:00 A.M. to 4:00 P.M. and Sunday noon to 4:00 P.M. $

Recalling the history and culture of New York, this full-size, hand-carved merry-go-round
features relief portraits of Captain Kidd, Rip Van Winkle, George Gershwin, Clarissa the
Cow, Daphne Duck, the Montauk Lighthouse, and other people and symbols of the state.

The Hicksville Gregory Museum
and L. I. Earth Science Center (all ages)
Heitz Place and Bay Avenue, Hicksville; (516) 822–7505; www.gregorymuseum.org. Open
Tuesday through Friday 9:30 A.M. to 4:30 P.M., Saturday and Sunday 1:00 to 5:00 P.M. $

The largest collection of rocks and minerals on Long Island is displayed inside this former
historic courthouse, along with interesting plant and animal fossils, a bevy of butterfly
specimens, and a 1915 jail cell.

Heckscher State Park (all ages)
Heckscher Parkway, East Islip; (631) 581–2100; www.nysparks.com/parks. Open year-round
sunrise to sunset; campgrounds open May through September. Parking fee $.

Covering 1,657 acres, this is a great family park, with three sandy beaches, a swimming
pool, hiking trails, ball fields, a playground and picnic area, fishing in Great South Bay and
Nicoll Bay, recreation programs, and campsites. This is also a trailhead where hikers can
enter the Long Island Greenbelt Trail, a path winding past woodlands and wetlands,
stretching 34 miles to Sunken Meadow State Park.

Long Island Children's Museum (ages 2 to 12)

11 Davis Avenue, Garden City; (516) 224–5800; www.licm.org. Open Wednesday through Sunday 10:00 A.M. to 5:00 P.M., July and August Tuesday through Sunday. Closed Christmas and New Year's Day. Strollers must be checked. $$

Multimedia, interactive, and hands-on exhibits in twelve galleries are offered at this learning laboratory recently moved to a new 40,000-square-foot facility. You can blow big bubbles, explore the senses, dance to music from all over the world, or be a TV star at the Communication Station.

Amityville Historical Society–Lauder Museum (ages 5 and up)

170 Broadway, Amityville; (631) 598–1486. Open Sunday, Tuesday, and Friday 2:00 to 4:00 P.M. Closed Easter, Christmas, and New Year's Day. Donation.

Artifacts and memorabilia from Amityville's past include paintings, photographs, carriages, and china, as well as a replica of an old schoolroom.

Sagtikos Manor (ages 4 and up)

Route 27A, West Bay Shore; (631) 661–8348. Open Wednesday, Thursday, and Sunday in July and August 1:00 to 4:00 P.M., Sunday in June 1:00 to 4:00 P.M. $

Other South Shore Indoor Play Spaces, **Laser Parks, and Arcades**

Fun Zone. 229 Route 110, Farmingdale; (631) 847–0100.

Boomers. 655 Long Island Avenue, Medford; (631) 475–1771.

Fun Station USA. 40 Rocklyn Avenue, Lynbrook; (516) 599–7757.

Laser Kingdom. 133 Milbar Boulevard, Farmingdale; (631) 694–6148.

The Looney Bin. 6 Rockaway Avenue, Valley Stream 11580; (516) 593–9121.

Q-Zar. 151 Voice Road, Carle Place; (516) 877–7200.

Jillian's. Airport Plaza, Routello, Farmingdale, and Old Country Road, Westbury; (631) 249–0708 and (516) 542–8501.

Art on **Long Island**

Parrish Art Museum. 25 Job's Lane, Southampton; (631) 283–2118; www.thehamptons.com.

Pollock-Krasner House and Study Center. 830 Fireplace Road, East Hampton; (631) 324–4929.

Heckscher Museum of Art. 2 Prime Avenue, Huntington; (631) 351–3250; www.heckscher.org.

Nassau County Museum of Art. One Museum Drive, Roslyn Harbor; (516) 484–9338; www.nassaumuseum.com.

Built in 1692, this forty-two-room mansion served as headquarters for the British during the Revolutionary War, and in 1790 George Washington really did sleep here.

Clark Botanic Garden (all ages)

193 Willets Road, Albertson; (516) 484–8600. Open daily year-round 10:00 A.M. to 4:00 P.M. Closed Christmas and New Year's Day. **Free.**

Wander through twelve acres of wooded sandy moraine dotted with three ponds and adorned with fragrant wildflower, herb, perennial, annual, rose, and rock gardens.

Bellport-Brookhaven Historical Society Museum (ages 4 and up)

31 Bellport Lane, Bellport; (631) 286–0888. Exchange shop open Memorial Day through Columbus Day Thursday through Saturday 11:00 A.M. to 5:00 P.M., museum open Thursday through Saturday 1:00 to 4:00 P.M. $

Exhibits of Island life are on display at this museum complex, from farm tools and antiques to decoys, vintage toys, and Native American artifacts.

Grist Mill Museum (all ages)

Wood and Atlantic Avenues, Memorial Park, East Rockaway; (516) 887–6300 or (516) 887–6320. Open weekends June until Labor Day 1:00 to 5:00 P.M. **Free.**

Native American, shipping, and century-old artifacts and memorabilia, as well as an old schoolroom exhibit, recall the early days of Long Island.

Adventureland Amusement Park (all ages)

2245 Broadhollow Road (Route 110), Farmingdale; (516) 694–6868; www.adventureland familyfun.com. Open year-round daily; call for hours, as they vary by month. Adults $$$$, children $$$.

Twenty-five rides will rock and roll you, there's a haunted house to spook you, and a mini-golf course for terra-firma types. The arcade features more than 300 games and attractions, and aspiring singers and actors can make a recording and video on-site.

Cradle of Aviation (all ages)

Mitchell Field, Charles Lindbergh Boulevard, Garden City; (516) 572–4111; www.cradleof aviation.org. Open Tuesday 10:00 A.M. to 2:00 P.M., Wednesday through Sunday 10:00 A.M. to 5:00 P.M. $$

Housed in hangars near where Charles Lindbergh in the *Spirit of Saint Louis* took off on his daring trans-Atlantic solo flight is an incredible collection of seventy historical aircraft, from balloons to biplanes to lunar land rovers. Then enjoy the largest domed IMAX theater in the state.

Woodcleft Canal (all ages)

202 Woodcleft Avenue, Freeport; (516) 337–2246; www.freeportny.com. Open Tuesday through Friday 11:00 A.M. to 4:00 P.M., Sunday 1:00 to 5:00 P.M. In summer also open Saturday 1:00 to 5:00 P.M. $

Stroll along the "Nautical Mile," past charter fishing boats, open-air seafood markets, interesting shops, and outdoor cafes. This is also the site of the Long Island Marine Education Center, where interactive exhibits highlight marine ecosystems and the area's history of boat building and commercial fishing.

Bayard-Cutting Arboretum (all ages)

Route 27A, Montauk Highway, Oakdale; (631) 581–1002; www.fieldtrip.com/ny/65811002.htm. Open year-round Wednesday through Sunday 10:00 A.M. to 5:00 P.M. $

Located along the Connetquot River, this 680-acre estate was designed by Frederick Law Olmsted and features five marked trails that wind through gardens, meadows, and marshes and past artistic arrangements of century-old oaks, elms, maples, and conifers. A Tudor mansion houses a small nature museum of mounted birds and other local flora and fauna.

African American Museum (ages 4 and up)

110 North Franklin Street, Hempstead; (516) 572–0730. Open year-round Monday through Saturday 10:00 A.M. to 5:00 P.M., Sunday 1:00 to 5:00 P.M. Donation.

Dedicated to preserving the history and culture of African Americans on Long Island, this small but interesting museum has permanent displays as well as special exhibits from the Smithsonian Institute and the Brooklyn Museum.

Freight House, 1901 Restored Depot (all ages)

South Broadway and South Third Street, Lindenhurst; (631) 226–0133. Open July through August Wednesday, Friday, and Saturday 2:00 to 4:00 P.M. Free.

Artifacts and memorabilia of the railway era are displayed at this restored century-old depot and freight house, including a working telegraph system.

More Area **Parks**

Visit www.licvb.com for more information.

Belmont Lake State Park. North Babylon; (631) 667–5055.

Bethpage State Park. Farmingdale; (516) 249–0701.

Hempstead Lake State Park. West Hempstead; (516) 766–1029.

Long Beach Island Resort. Long Beach; (516) 432–6000.

Bay Park. East Rockaway; (516) 571–7251.

Cantiague Park. Hicksville; (516) 571–7052.

Cedar Creek Park. Seaford; (516) 571–7473.

Cow Meadow Park & Preserve. Freeport; (516) 571–8685.

Eisenhower Park. East Meadow; (516) 572–0348, 572–0218.

Grant Park. Hewlett; (516) 571–7820.

Nassau Beach Park. Lido; (516) 571–7700.

North Woodmere Park. North Woodmere; (516) 571–7800.

Valley Stream State Park. Valley Stream; (516) 825–4128.

Wantagh Park. Wantagh; (516) 571–7460.

Connetquot River State Park Preserve (all ages)

Sunrise Highway, 0.5 mile from Connetquot Avenue, Oakdale; (631) 581–1005 or (631) 581–1072. Open year-round with permit Wednesday through Sunday 8:00 A.M. to 4:30 P.M., plus Tuesday from April through Labor Day. Vehicle fee $$.

Although you must obtain a permit in advance to enter this 3,473-acre preserve, it's worth the effort. The former clubhouse has a small nature exhibit depicting Long Island habitats, a touch tank, and a collection of bird eggs. Miles of trails wind through woods and past the river, and there's a good chance of seeing deer, fox, rabbit, osprey, and wild turkey. Fly-fishing is good here, for the oldest fish hatchery in Long Island is about a mile upstream.

Old Schoolhouse Museum (all ages)
90 Quogue Street East, Quogue; (631) 653–4111. Open July to Labor Day Wednesday and Friday 3:00 to 5:00 P.M., Saturday 10:00 A.M. to noon. Free.

In 1822, this was the biggest and best school in Suffolk County and cost about $350 to build. Today it houses photographs, maps, and memorabilia of the town's early years, as well as a collection of toys, household items, and farm tools.

Quogue Wildlife Refuge (all ages)
3 Old Country Road, Quogue; (631) 653–4771; www.dec.state.ny.us/website/reg1/ quogue.html. Refuge open daily year-round dawn to dusk. Nature center open February through November Tuesday and Thursday 1:00 to 4:00 P.M. Free.

Surrounded by farms and fields, this refuge has 7 miles of trails snaking through 300 acres of swamps, bogs, and pine barrens. Stop at the Charles Banks Belt Nature Center to see habitat displays and visit the Distressed Wildlife Complex, where injured animals are rehabilitated.

Ferry and Cruise Services
of the South Shore

Although the east and west tips of Fire Island are accessible by car, the rest of the island may be reached only by private boat, foot, or ferry. Here are several companies providing regular service. For more information, visit the Web site www.webscope.com/li/ferries.html or www.visitlongisland.com.

Davis Park Ferry Co. Patchogue; (631) 475–1665; www.pagelinx.com.

Fire Island Ferries. Bay Shore; (516) 665–3600 or (516) 666–3601.

Sayville Ferry Service. Sayville; (631) 589–0810 or (631) 589–8980; www.sayvilleferry.com.

Sunken Forest Ferry Co. Sayville; (631) 589–8980.

Captree State Park Ferries. (631) 669–6464; www.captreefleet.com.

***Lauren Kristy* Paddleboat.** Bayshore; (631) 321–9005; www.laurenkristy.com.

Islip Grange (all ages)

10 Broadway Avenue, Sayville; (631) 224–5411. Open daily year-round 9:00 A.M. to 5:00 P.M. **Free.**

Spread over twelve acres, this complex of historic structures saved from demolition includes a water-powered mill, barns, and cottages.

Tackapausha Museum and Preserve (all ages)

Washington Avenue, just north of Merrick Road, Seaford; (516) 571–7443; www.co.nassau .ny.us. Open year-round Tuesday through Saturday 9:30 A.M. to 4:00 P.M., Sunday 1:00 to 4:00 P.M. Closed Monday and holidays. $

Five miles of trails wind through this eighty-acre nature preserve. The museum's wetlands displays include several live snakes and frogs and a nocturnal-animal exhibit.

Jones Beach State Park (all ages)

Ocean State Parkway, Jones Beach; (516) 785–1600; Captree State Park (631) 669–0449; Charter boat information (631) 669–6464; www.jonesbeach.org. Open daily year-round. Vehicle fee $.

Developed by the legendary Robert Moses in 1929, this 2,400-acre barrier beach park stretches for more than 5 miles along the Atlantic. Although it can get very crowded in summer, it's still a great place to catch the rays. Facilities include eight swimming areas with several hundred lifeguards, art deco bathhouses, Olympic-size and toddler-size swimming pools, ball courts, picnic areas, restaurants and refreshment stands, 2 miles of boardwalk, a chip-and-putt golf course, and top-line concerts in summer.

Lakeside Riding Academy (ages 4 and up)

633 Eagle Avenue, West Hempstead; (516) 486–9673; www.licvb.com. Open daily year-round Monday and Friday 3:00 to 5:00 P.M., Tuesday through Thursday 3:00 to 7:00 P.M., Saturday and Sunday 10:00 A.M. to 5:00 P.M. Fee depends on ride.

Equestrian enthusiasts will enjoy trail rides through nearby Hempstead Lake State Park, with English- and Western-style lessons available, as well as pony rides for the younger set.

Long Island Maritime Museum (ages 4 and up)

86 West Avenue, West Sayville; (631) HISTORY; www.limaritime.org. Open year-round Wednesday through Saturday 10:00 A.M. to 4:00 P.M., Sunday noon to 4:00 P.M. Donation.

Highlights of Long Island's maritime heritage are exhibited here, with photographs, small watercraft, and a bayman's cottage to explore.

Fire Island National Seashore (all ages)
Mailing address: 120 Laurel Street, Patchogue 11772; (631) 289–4810; www.nps.gov/fiis.
Robert Moses State Park (631) 669–0449; Fire Island Lighthouse (631) 661–4876. Sailors
Haven (631) 597–6183; Watch Hill (631) 597–6455; Fire Island Wilderness Visitor Center
(Smith Point) (631) 281–3010; Smith Point County Park (631) 852–1313; William Floyd Estate
(631) 399–2030. Park is open year-round sunrise to sunset, and lifeguards are on duty at
main beaches from Memorial Day to Labor Day. Cars not allowed on most of Fire Island.
Parking fee at Robert Moses State Park and Smith Point $.

Running for 32 miles along the Atlantic shore of Long Island, this scenic strip of sand was
established as a National Seashore in 1964 and is the only developed barrier beach in the
country without roads. Numerous ferries ply the waters of Great South Bay between
Robert Moses State Park and Smith Point County Park, providing access to seventeen
resort communities catering to a variety of lifestyles. The Interpretive Centers at Sailors
Haven, Watch Hill, and Smith Point offer excellent maps and information, and nature trails
wind through several diverse habitats. The 875-acre Robert Moses State Park can be
reached by car via the Robert Moses Causeway and offers pristine beaches and a historic
lighthouse to explore. Local legends tell of pirates who lit bonfires on the beach to lure
ships to their doom, thereby giving the island its name. But since 1826, sailors have
looked to the Fire Island Lighthouse for guidance. A small museum is housed in the
keeper's cottage, and tower tours are offered in summer.

Almost 7 miles down the beach is the Sunken Forest at Sailors Haven, a below-sea-
level stunted woodland of century-old holly, sassafras, and shadblow. Farther down the
beach is Watch Hill, a seven-acre area of windswept dunes next to the only National
Wilderness Area in the state. At the eastern end of the park is Smith Point, accessible
from Route 46, offering bathhouses and snack bars, and 146 campsites in the
adjacent Smith Point County Park.

Where to Eat

Chowder Bar. 123 Maple Avenue, Bay
Shore; (631) 665–9859. Casual dining;
offering seafood, chicken, burgers, pasta,
and homemade desserts. $ $

Ehrhardts. 239 Woodcleft Canal, Freeport;
(516) 378–9789. Casual place serving
steamers and fresh clam chowder. $

Raay-Nor's Cabin. 550 Sunrise Highway,
Baldwin; (516) 223–4886. Fried chicken
and other down-home specialties, served
in a big log cabin. $$

Where to Stay

Fire Island Hotel and Resort. 25 Cayuga
Park, Ocean Bay Park, Fire Island; (631)
583–8000. Formerly Coast Guard build-
ings, this place is very popular with fami-
lies and has a restaurant, playground, and
heated pool. $$$$

Nature Preserves of Central Suffolk

The nature preserves below offer a range of hiking and wildlife-viewing opportunities, as well as educational opportunities for families. Call the numbers listed for more information.

Cranberry Bog County Nature Preserve. County Road 63 (Lake Avenue), Riverhead; (631) 854–4951.

Wading River Marsh Preserve. Sound Avenue, Wading River; (631) 367–3225.

Hoyt Farm Park Preserve. New Highway, east of Commack Road, Commack; (631) 543–7804.

Daniel R. Davis Sanctuary. Mt. Sinai–Coram Road, Coram; (631) 367–3225.

David A. Sarnoff Pine Barrens Preserve. County Road 63, south of the Riverhead traffic circle, Riverhead; (631) 369–3300.

East Farm Preserve. Shep Jones Lane, 0.5 mile from Route 25A, Head of the Harbor; (631) 367–3225.

Garden City Hotel. 45 Seventh Street, Garden City; (516) 747–3000. Four-star hotel with rooms and suites, room service, restaurants, indoor pool, whirlpool, and entertainment. $$$$

Lands End Motel and Marina. 70 Browns River Road, Sayville; (631) 589–2040. Rooms and efficiencies; with pool, beach, and marina. $$$

Activities and **Amusements**

When the kids need to work off some energy, try one of these entertainment centers:

Laser Kingdom. 544 Middle Country Road, Coram; (631) 698–0414.

Splish Splash Water Park. 2549 Splish Splash Drive, Riverhead; (631) 727–3600; www.splishsplashlongisland.com.

Central Suffolk

The heart of Long Island is a tapestry of pitch pine and scrub oak forests threaded by the Carmans and Peconic Rivers and hemmed in by sandy Atlantic beaches and the rocky shores of the Sound. Within Central Suffolk's borders lies the Pine Barrens Preserve, a 100,000-acre wilderness area crowning a giant aquifer and providing an Eden for wildlife. Other opportunities for animal observation are available at the numerous zoos, farms, and marine labs in the area, and there's even a ten-ton duck to check out.

Wildwood State Park (all ages)
Off Route 25A, along Hulse Landing Road, Wading River; (631) 929–4314; www.nysparks.com/parks. Open daily sunrise to sunset; campgrounds open April through October. Summer parking fee $.

Although this popular 767-acre park can get a bit crowded in summer, it offers more than 10 miles of hiking trails and more than a mile of beachfront tidal zones to explore. There are campsites, a recreation program, bike paths, ball fields, a playground, picnic area, and swimming and fishing in Long Island Sound.

Peconic River Herb Farm (all ages)
310-C River Road, Calverton; (631) 369–0058; www.prherbfarm.com. Open April through June 9:00 A.M. to 5:00 P.M., July through October 9:00 A.M. to 4:00 P.M. Free.

More than 700 varieties of unusual and unique plants grow at this thirteen-acre working riverfront farm.

The Big Duck (all ages)
Route 24, Flanders; (631) 852–8292. Open May through Labor Day Tuesday through Sunday 10:00 A.M. to 5:00 P.M. Free.

Where does a ten-ton duck sit? Anywhere she wants, and this one sits patiently along Route 24, a tribute to the area's duck farm heritage. Inside is a small museum and gift shop.

Long Island Game Farm Wildlife Park (all ages)

Chapman Boulevard, about 1 mile north of Route 111, Manorville; (631) 878–6670; www.longislandgamefarm.com. Open daily April through October 10:00 A.M. to 5:00 P.M., weekends and Memorial Day through Labor Day to 6:00 P.M., weekends only in April. Adults $$$, children $$, under 2 free.

Kids love the goats, sheep, cows, and pigs at Old MacDonald's Farm; the deer at Bambi-land; and the bottle-fed animal babies at the Nursery. There's also an assortment of amusement rides, slides, an antique carousel, alligator shows, pony rides, and an 1860s vintage Iron Horse train.

The Animal Farm (all ages)

184A Wading River Road, Manorville; (631) 878–1785. Open April through October 10:00 A.M. to 5:00 P.M. on weekdays, to 6:00 P.M. on weekends. $$

Pet and feed barnyard buddies at this family farm, or take a gander at Long Island's largest flock of rare and exotic poultry as well as llamas, burros, monkeys, snakes, and even kangaroos.

Harold Malkmes Wildlife Education and Ecology Center at Holtsville Park (all ages)

249 Buckley Road, Holtsville; (631) 758–9664 or (631) 451–6100. Open daily 9:00 A.M. to dusk; zoo closes at 4:00 P.M. Donation.

Built atop a garbage dump, this scenic park offers swimming pools, a fitness trail, picnic and playground areas, a zoo housing local injured wildlife, and a barnyard of friendly farm animals to pet.

Hallockville Museum Farm (all ages)

6038 Sound Avenue, Riverhead; (631) 298–5292; www.riverheadli.com/hallock.html. Open Tuesday through Saturday 11:00 A.M. to 4:00 P.M. $

Built in 1765, this was home to the Hallock family for five generations. The complex includes the Homestead, a big barn, a smokehouse, cobbler's shop, and a workshop, making this one of the oldest intact farms on the Island.

Atlantis Marine World (ages 4 and up)

469 East Main Street, Riverhead; (631) 208–9200; www.atlantismarineworld.com. Open year-round daily 10:00 A.M. to 5:00 P.M. Closed Christmas. $$, children under 3 free. Explorer cruises 11:30 A.M. and 2:00 P.M. $$$

Atlantis offers more than eighty interesting marine and ecology exhibits, including the Ray Bay touch tanks, a 120,000-gallon shark tank, a sea lion show, nature trails, and the largest live coral reef display in the country. New exhibits include Shark Reef Lagoon, Japanese snow monkeys, and Nemo's Family Fun Center. Docked outside is the *Atlantis Explorer,* offering naturalist-led two-hour voyages on the Peconic River.

New York **Trivia**

The hottest day on record in the state is 108°F, which was recorded on July 22, 1926, in Troy.

Riverhead Foundation for Marine Research and Preservation (all ages)

467 East Main Street, Riverhead; (631) 369–9840 or (631) 208–9200; www.riverhead foundation.org. Open daily 10:00 A.M. to 5:00 P.M., seal watch January through April; call for hours. Closed Christmas. $.

Founded to promote public awareness of Long Island's marine environment, this not-for-profit center, located within Atlantis Marine World, offers touch tanks, aquariums of local and tropical sea creatures, and a rescue and rehabilitation program for stranded sea turtles, harbor seals, and other marine mammals. Educational programs are offered year-round, as well as seasonal seal-watching excursions.

Suffolk Historical Museum (ages 5 and up)

300 West Main Street, Riverhead; (631) 727–2881. Open year-round Tuesday through Saturday 12:30 to 4:30 P.M. Closed holidays. Donation.

The county's colorful history is highlighted here, with exhibits on Native Americans, whaling, transportation, and arts and crafts.

Brookhaven National Laboratory (ages 8 and up)

William Floyd Parkway (County Road 46), Upton; (631) 344–2345; www.bnl.gov. Tours on Sunday in July and August, except holidays, 10:00 A.M. to 3:00 P.M. Free.

An enormous research center covering more than 5,000 acres, this is the habitat of the Scanning Transmission Electron Microscope. Hands-on activities, historic exhibits, multimedia presentations, and guided lab tours explore the wonders of particle physics, nuclear energy, and just about every other field of science.

Colorado Teddy Bear Factory (ages 4 and up)

1070 Route 58, Riverhead; (631) 369–0127; www.coloradoteddybearfactory.com. Open year-round Thursday through Monday 11:00 A.M. to 5:00 P.M., Sunday to 4:00 P.M.; mid-June through December Wednesday also. Free guided tours weekends only, or by appointment. Design-your-own bears $17–$35.

Take a tour of a teddy bear birthplace, then create your own unique ursine from stuffing scratch to furry finish in fifteen minutes.

Silly Lily Fishing Station (ages 4 and up)

99 Adelaide Avenue, East Moriches; (631) 878–0247. March to November 6:00 A.M. to 4:00 P.M. All day rental $93.

Fish for fluke, bluefish, and striped bass in Moriches Bay aboard 16-foot powerboats. Bait, tackle, and poles available. Sailboats and kayaks also available.

Suffolk County Farm and Education Center (all ages)
4600 Yaphank Avenue, Yaphank; (631) 852–4600; www.cce.cornell.edu/suffolk. **Open daily 9:00 A.M. to 3:00 P.M., with weekend programs. Free.**

Workshops and demonstrations at this 300-acre working farm offer families the opportunity to learn about home on the grange. There are sheep, goats, pigs, chickens, and cattle to feed and care for and daily hayrides in summer.

Where to Eat

Jerry & the Mermaid. 469 East Main Street, Riverhead; (631) 727–8489. Casual outdoor dining with a water view; serving fresh seafood, chicken, and steak. $–$$

Spicy's Barbecue. 225 West Main Street, North Suffolk; (631) 727–2781. Great barbecued ribs and fried chicken. $

Where to Stay

Budget Host Inn. 30 East Moriches Road, Riverhead; (631) 727–6200. Rooms and kitchenettes, pool, picnic and grill area, and kids under sixteen stay **free.** $$$–$$$$

Comfort Inn. 2695 Route 112, Medford; (631) 654–3000. Seventy-six rooms and efficiencies, outdoor pool, guest laundry, and complimentary continental breakfast. $$$–$$$$

Wading River Motel. 5890 Middle Country Road, Wading River; (631) 727–8000. Rooms and kitchenettes on five landscaped acres, with heated pool, grill and picnic areas, and lawn games. $$$$

South Fork

Home to the Shinnecock Native Americans, celebrities, and sybarites, the South Fork is an interesting mosaic of farmland, rolling dunes, deep harbors, and sparkling wave-washed beaches. The hamlets of the Hamptons are here, as are one of the oldest lighthouses in the country and possibly the best fishing in the state.

Horsing around
South Fork

Deep Hollow Ranch. Off Montauk Highway, Montauk; (631) 668–2744; www.peconic.net/deephollow.

Rita's Montauk Stable. West Lake Drive, Montauk; (631) 668–5453.

Sears Bellows Stables. Route 24, Hampton Bays; (631) 723–3554.

East Hampton Town Maritime Museum (all ages)
Bluff Road, off Route 27, Amagansett; (631) 324–6850; www.easthamptonhistory.org. Open July and August weekdays 10:00 A.M. to 5:00 P.M., plus weekends in June, September, and October. $

Housed in a former U.S. Coast Guard barracks, this museum contains an interesting collection of maritime memorabilia highlighting the seaworthy history of Amagansett. Explore a trawler and a whaleboat, examine artifacts from shipwrecks, learn a new fishing technique, and then visit the Children's Discovery Room upstairs for hands-on fun.

Mercedes-Benz Polo Challenge (all ages)
Two Trees Farm, Bridgehampton; (212) 421–1367. Events held Saturday at 4:00 P.M. from mid-July to mid-August. $$$$ per car.

Some of the best polo players in the world compete in this very prestigious sporting and social event.

Sagg Swamp Preserve (all ages)
Sagaponack Road, Bridgehampton; (631) 329–7689. Open daily dawn to dusk. Donation.

Stroll through stands of oak, red maple, and Atlantic white cedar; past cattails, arrowhead, and jewelweed; and a dozen species of ferns. A 700-foot boardwalk curves out over the swamp, offering opportunities to spot fourteen species of mammals that live here, including mink, muskrat, and white-tailed deer, and eighty-four species of birds, from hawks to herons.

Home Sweet Home Museum (ages 6 and up) 🏛
14 James Lane, East Hampton; (631) 324–0713. Open year-round Monday through Saturday 10:00 A.M. to 4:00 P.M., Sunday 2:00 to 4:00 P.M.; closed holidays. $

This was the boyhood home of John Howard Payne, best remembered for writing the lyrics to "Home Sweet Home." Explore Payne's extensive china collection, then step outside to see the picturesque 1804 Pantigo windmill.

Old Hook Mill (all ages)

North Main Street, East Hampton; (631) 324–0713. Open June through September 10:00 A.M. to 5:00 P.M., grounds accessible year-round. Short guided tours are given in summer. $

There are more windmills in this town than anywhere else in the country, and this one, built in 1806, was restored to working condition in 1939.

Mulford Farm House (all ages)

10 James Lane, East Hampton; (631) 324–6850. Open July through August Thursday through Monday 11:00 A.M. to 4:00 P.M., weekends September through Columbus Day. Free.

Built in 1680, this restored colonial farm is unique in that it was home to one family for eight generations. All the structures are intact and in their original locations. Farm tools and furnishings tell the tale of seventeenth- and eighteenth-century agrarian activities.

Town House (all ages)

149 Main Street, Route 27, East Hampton; (631) 324–6850. Open Memorial Day through Columbus Day weekends 11:00 A.M. to 2:00 P.M. $

Travel back to the mid-nineteenth century via an interactive history class taught by costumed interpreters at the town's first schoolroom and meetinghouse.

Other Parks of the **South Fork**

Visit www.licvb.com for more information

Cedar Point County Park. East Hampton; (631) 852–7620.

Montauk County Park. Montauk; (631) 852–7878.

Sears Bellows County Park. Hampton Bays; (631) 852–8290.

Shinnecock East County Park. Southampton; (631) 852–8899.

Montauk Mountain Preserve. Montauk; (631) 329–7689.

Wolf Swamp Preserve. North Sea; (631) 329–7689.

Fort Pond. Montauk; (631) 668–4473.

Kirk Park Beach. Montauk; (631) 324–2417.

Meschutt Beach County Park. Hampton Bays; (631) 852–8205.

Theodore Roosevelt County Park. Montauk; (631) 852–7878.

Slo-Jack's Miniature Golf (all ages)

212 West Montauk Highway, Hampton Bays; (631) 728–9601. $

A classic course of sixties-style putt-putt, with windmills, wishing wells, and a great snack bar at the nineteenth hole.

Montauk Point Lighthouse (all ages)

2000 Montauk Highway, Montauk State Park, Montauk; (631) 668–2544 or (888) MTK–POINT; www.montauklighthouse.com. Open March through May Saturday and Sunday, May through September daily; call for schedule November through December. Montauk Point State Park (631) 668–3781; www.nysparks.com/parks. Park open year-round. Adults $$, children $.

Commissioned by George Washington, this is the oldest operating lighthouse in the state. Built on the easternmost tip of the Island where the British Navy set signal bonfires for its ships during the Revolutionary War, this area was heavily fortified during World War II against a possible German U-boat invasion. Tour the small museum next to the lighthouse-keeper's cottage, check out the electrified exhibit of miniature eastern seaboard light-houses, and, unless you are under 41 inches tall, climb the 137 steps to the top.

Viking Fishing Fleet Ferry Service (all ages)

Viking Dock, Montauk Harbor, Montauk; (631) 668–5700; www.vikingfleet.com. Operating daily Memorial Day through Columbus Day 8:00 A.M. to 6:00 P.M. Fee depends on trip.

Choose from naturalist-led whale-watching expeditions, fishing charters, and ferry service to Block Island.

Sag Harbor Whaling and Historical Museum (all ages)

200 Main Street, Sag Harbor; (631) 725–0770. Open May through Labor Day Monday through Saturday 10:00 A.M. to 5:00 P.M., Sunday 1:00 to 5:00 P.M. Open weekends until Thanksgiving. $, children under 12 free.

Housed in the Greek Revival mansion of a nineteenth-century whaling captain, this museum has an eclectic collection of artifacts and memorabilia from Sag Harbor's colorful maritime past.

Custom House (ages 4 and up)

Main and Garden Streets, Sag Harbor; (631) 692–4664 or (631) 725–0250. Open Memorial Day through June and Labor Day through Columbus Day weekends 10:00 A.M. to 5:00 P.M., July through August Tuesday through Sunday. $

Two hundred years ago, when Sag Harbor was one of two official U.S. ports of entry, this was the home office of customs inspector Henry Packer Dering, his wife, and their nine children. It also served as Long Island's first post office.

Elizabeth A. Morton National Wildlife Refuge (all ages)

784 Noyack Road, Sag Harbor; (631) 286–0485; www.refuges.fws.gov. Open daily sunrise to sunset. $ per car or pedestrian/cyclist.

Two-thirds of this sanctuary stretches out between Little Peconic and Noyack Bays like a long sandy finger beckoning birds. More than 220 avian species have been seen here, from osprey to the endangered piping plover, and there are red fox, rabbits, raccoons, weasels, and white-tailed deer, as well.

Halsey Homestead Museum (ages 4 and up)

249 South Main Street, Southampton; (631) 283–2494. Open July through mid-October Friday and Saturday noon to 5:00 P.M., Sunday 1:00 to 5:00 P.M., by appointment October through June. $

Built in 1648 by Southampton's founder, Thomas Halsey, this is the oldest English frame house in New York. Inside are seventeenth- and eighteenth-century furnishings, with a vintage apple orchard and herb garden outside.

Southampton Historical Museum (ages 4 and up)

17 Meeting House Lane, Southampton; (631) 283–2494; www.southamptonhistory museum.com. Open May through December Tuesday through Saturday 11:00 A.M. to 5:00 P.M., Sunday noon to 5:00 P.M.; January through April Thursday through Saturday noon to 5:00 P.M. $

Built by a sea captain in 1843, this Greek Revival home and surrounding grounds feature exhibits in twelve buildings, ranging from displays on Shinnecock and Montauk Native Americans to artifacts from the Revolutionary War. Outside are a one-room schoolhouse, a barn, a carriage house, blacksmith and carpentry shops, a country store, a saloon, and an apothecary shop.

Water Mill Museum (all ages)

41 Old Mill Road, Water Mill; (631) 726–4625. Open mid-May to mid-September Monday and Thursday through Saturday 11:00 A.M. to 5:00 P.M., Sunday 1:00 to 5:00 P.M. $, children free.

For more than 300 years, this wooden water mill has served the community, grinding grain, weaving cloth, spinning yarn, and even manufacturing paper. The small museum has displays of colonial crafts and grinding tools.

Suggested **Reading**

The Wainscott Weasel by Tor Seidler

Eleven Kids, One Summer by Ann M. Martin

Samuel's Choice by Richard J. Berleth

Walt Whitman by Nancy Loewen

My Secret War: The World War II Diary of Madeline Beck by Mary Pope Osborne

Hither Hills State Park (all ages)

50 South Fairview Avenue, Old Montauk Highway, Montauk; (631) 668–2554 or (631) 668–2461; www.nysparks.com/parks. Open year-round daily, with lifeguards on duty in summer. Be aware that hunting is allowed in fall and winter. Summer parking fee $$.

This 1,755-acre state park is adjacent to two large nature preserves, making the area a wonderfully wild place to explore. Hike through pine and oak forests, past a cranberry bog, and around advancing sand dunes dotted with beach plum and rugosa roses. Follow the path to the crest of the dune for panoramic views of Napeague Harbor, Block Island Sound, and the legendary site of Captain Kidd's treasure, Gardiner's Island. For families planning to spend more time in the area, the campground offers recreation programs, ball fields and courts, a general store, bathhouse, playground, and picnic area.

Merrill Lake Sanctuary at Accabonac Harbor (all ages)

Springs Fireplace Road, East Hampton; (631) 329–7689; www.tnc.org. Open daily sunrise to sunset. Free.

A self-guided nature trail winds through woodlands and meadows and leads down to the cordgrass-lined Accabonac Harbor. Depending on the tides, the path can get a bit swampy, so bring your rubber boots.

Where to Eat

Laundry. 31 Race Lane, East Hampton; (631) 324–3199. Seafood specialties served in a former laundry. $$$

The Lobster Roll Restaurant. 1980 Montauk Highway at Napeague Beach Amagansett; (631) 267–3740. Wonderful beach place, specializing in char-grilled fish, chowder, and, of course, lobster rolls. $–$$$

New Moon Cafe. 524 Montauk Highway, East Quogue; (631) 653–4042. Great Tex-Mex and barbecue, plus homemade desserts. $$

Where to Stay

The Bentley. 161 Hill Station Road, Southampton; (631) 283–6100. Kitchen suites, pool, tennis, golf privileges, lawn games, game room, and picnic area. $$$$

Colonial Shores Cottages. 83 West Tiana Road, Hampton Bays; (631) 728–0011; www.colonialshoresny.com. Rooms and suites with full kitchen; private beach, pool, marina, rowboats and paddleboats; children under twelve stay free. $$$–$$$$

East Hampton House Motel. 226 Pantigo Road, East Hampton; (631) 324–4300. Rooms and efficiencies, heated pool, wading pool, tennis courts, patios, and grills. $$$$

North Fork

More rural than the South Fork, this region also has a rich maritime and farming heritage. Colonial saltboxes and a dozen award-winning vineyards grace the historic hamlets settled more than 300 years ago. Shelter Island, nestled between the Forks' prongs, is the jewel of the Peconic, harboring a rare white-pine swamp and a large population of nesting osprey.

Cutchogue Village Green (ages 5 and up)

Route 25 at Cases Lane, Cutchogue; (631) 734–7122. Buildings open late June through September Monday and weekends 1:00 to 4:00 P.M. Donation.

The village green that's the heart of this picturesque hamlet is surrounded by historic wooden buildings dating back to the seventeenth century. The oldest house in New York is here, built in 1649 and named, appropriately, Old House. Next door is the 1740 Wickham Farmhouse, with agrarian artifacts and the earliest school in the area, the 1840 Old Schoolhouse Museum.

East End Seaport Museum (ages 4 and up)

End of Third Street, Greenport; (631) 477–2100; www.eastendseaport.org. HMS Bounty (631) 588–7900; www.tallshipbounty.org. Open mid-May through mid-October daily except Tuesday 11:00 A.M. to 5:00 P.M. Donation.

Exhibits cover the fishing, whaling, shipping, and boatbuilding heritage of the area, and there are several aquariums filled with local marine life. Docked outside are the *Malabar* and the *Mary E.,* available for cruises, and a full-size replica of the crew quarters of the USS *Holland* submarine; there are also seasonal visits from the HMS *Bounty*.

Railroad Museum of Long Island (ages 4 and up)

440 Fourth Street, Greenport; (631) 477–0439 or (631) 727–7920; www.rmli.org. Open Memorial Day through Columbus Day weekends 11:00 A.M. to 4:00 P.M. $

Located inside a former freight station, this museum recalls the railroads of Long Island with artifacts, photographs, and memorabilia.

Orient Beach State Park (all ages)

North Country Road/Route 25, Orient; (631) 323–2440; www.nysparks.com/parks. Orient Point Ferry (860) 443–5281 or (631) 323–2525; www.longisland ferry.com. Open daily sunrise to sunset. Lifeguards on duty in summer. Parking $.

Reaching westward into Gardiners Bay, this 357-acre sliver of sand has miles of polished pebble beach to stroll, a small maritime forest to explore, and

a great sandy swimming spot. Osprey circle overhead, a herd of deer roam the bayberry and beach plum thickets, and endangered piping plovers nest in shallow dimples in the sand. From the tip of the spit you can see the restored Long Beach Bar Lighthouse, better known as "Bug Light." At Orient Point ferries can be boarded for travel to New London, Connecticut, past Plum Island, the site of a top secret U.S. biomedical research center.

Oysterponds Historical Society (ages 4 and up)

1555 Village Lane, Orient; (631) 323–2480. Open Thursday, Saturday, and Sunday 2:00 to 5:00 P.M. Call for exhibition dates. $

An interesting collection of seven buildings traces the history of everyday eighteenth- and nineteenth-century East End life. See Village House, a furnished Victorian boardinghouse; the Hallock Building's maritime collection; the Red Barn's vintage carriage collection; the Webb House, once a tavern; and the two one-room schoolhouses.

Mashomack Preserve (all ages)

79 South Ferry Road, Shelter Island; (631) 749–1001. Open daily 9:00 A.M. to 5:00 P.M., closed Tuesday July through August, open weekends only in January. Donation.

On the southeastern third of Shelter Island, 17 miles of trails lace through 2,000 acres of oak and beech forests, with 10 miles of coastline cut by tidal creeks and a rare 4,000-year-old white-pine swamp. The three main trails originate at the visitor center.

Old Havens House (ages 4 and up)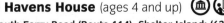

16 South Ferry Road (Route 114), Shelter Island; (631) 749–0025. Open Thursday mornings and Saturday and Sunday noon to 4:00 P.M. in summer. $

Built in 1743, this historic home was also a general store and post office. Several rooms display nineteenth-century furnishings, but children will gravitate to the antique doll and toy collection.

Southold Historical Society Museum Park (ages 3 and up)

54325 Main Road, Prince Building, Southold; (631) 765–5500 or (631) 765–5800. Open July through October on Saturday, Sunday, and Wednesday 1:00 to 4:00 P.M. Donation.

This museum complex chronicles 350 years of Southold's history with a variety of restored buildings filled with period furnishings. Children will enjoy a visit to the Victorian Curie-Bell House, with its collection of antique toys, dolls, and dollhouses made from soap boxes. Other interesting sites to explore here include Thomas Moore House, Pine Neck Barn, Old Bayview Schoolhouse, the Buttery, the blacksmith shop, and the carriage house.

Southold Indian Museum (all ages)

1080 Main Bay View Road, Southold; (631) 765–5577. Open Sunday 1:30 to 4:30 P.M. in summer and by appointment. Donation.

More than 300,000 Algonquin artifacts are housed at this archaeological museum. Permanent exhibits include arrowheads and spears, agricultural displays, and one of the largest collections of Native American pottery in the country.

Custer Institute (ages 6 and up)

Main Bay View Road, Southold; (631) 765–2626 or (631) 722–3850; www.custer
observatory.org. Public observing every Saturday after dusk. Donation.

Stargaze on a Saturday night at this observatory that's usually available for members only.
Equipment includes a 3-meter radio telescope and several refractors, and there's also a
small museum.

Horton Point Lighthouse (all ages)

Lighthouse Road, Southold; (631) 765–5500. Open Memorial Day to Columbus Day on Saturday and Sunday 11:30 A.M. to 4:30 P.M. $

Overlooking Long Island Sound, this nineteenth-century lighthouse offers panoramic vistas, a keeper's cottage, and a nautical museum filled with maritime artifacts.

Suffolk County Marine Environmental Learning Center
(all ages)

3690 Cedar Beach Road, Southold; (631) 852–8660. Open weekdays year-round 8:30 A.M. to
4:30 P.M. Call ahead. Closed holidays. Free.

This is a working shellfish hatchery, with an integrated hydroponics and fish culture system.
Stroll through saltwater wetlands, then check out the touch tanks and aquariums. There
are also displays on marine and wildlife ecosystems, water quality, and fishing techniques.

Where to Eat

Chowder Pot Pub. 104 Third Street,
Greenport; (631) 477–1345. Excellent clam
chowders; with seasonal outdoor dining.
$$$

Claudio's. 111 Main Street, Greenport;
(631) 477–0627. Steak and seafood; with
seasonal outdoor dining, clam bar, and
view of the harbor. $$–$$$

Where to Stay

North Fork Beach Motel. Sound Avenue,
Southold; (631) 765–2080. On the water-
front with beach, terraces, pool, fishing,
and picnic and grill area. $$$–$$$$

Rams Head Inn. 108 Ram Island Drive,
Shelter Island Heights; (631) 749–0811. On
the waterfront with beach, restaurant, ten-
nis, picnic area, playground, and boats
available. $$$–$$$$

Santorini Hotel Resort. 3800 Duck Pond
Road, Cutchoque; (631) 734–6370. Efficien-
cies, pool, beach, free continental break-
fast. $$$$

For More Information

**Long Island Convention and Visitors
Bureau.** (631) 951–3440 or (877)
FUN–ON–LI; www.licvb.com or
www.funonli.com.

Shelter Island Chamber of Commerce.
(631) 749–0399; www.shelter-island.net.

East Hampton Chamber of Commerce.
(631) 324–0362; www.easthampton
chamber.com.

Southampton Chamber of Commerce.
(631) 283–0402; www.southampton
chamber.com.

Sag Harbor Chamber of Commerce.
(631) 725–0011 or 725–2100; www.sag
harborchamber.com

thehamptons.com. (631) 726–5444;
www.thehamptons.com.

Westhampton Chamber of Commerce.
(631) 288–3337; www.whbcc.com.

Long Island Farm Bureau. (631)
727–3777; www.lifb.com.

Long Island Lodging Guide. (631)
293–6600; www.longislandlodging.com.

Montauk Chamber of Commerce. (631)
668–2428; www.montaukchamber.com.

Fire Island Tourism. (631) 563–8448;
www.fireisland.com.

New York City

Friends of mine from out of town always seem amazed I choose to raise my children in New York City. True, it's crowded, expensive, sometimes pretty gritty, and my sons don't have their own tree house or a big dog, but there are other perks. Their backyard playhouse is a castle in Central Park; they're on a first-name basis with the zoo's polar bears; they can see the best of Broadway, Off Broadway, or street performers; there's always a parade, festival, or movie filming around town; they can sample the cuisine of dozens of cultures or get a pizza delivered anytime; and they're ten minutes from the best dinosaurs and mummies in the country. For us, New York City is the original magic kingdom. Anything you want to buy, see, do, or dream is possible here.

Divided into the five boroughs of Manhattan, Brooklyn, Queens, the Bronx, and Staten Island, each section is again divided into a mosaic of unique neighborhoods. This is a city that is constantly reinventing itself and always offering opportunities to see, experience, or understand something new and different. Pick up a MetroCard, your transportation key to the kingdom; a good map of the town; and prepare your family for a wonderful whirlwind adventure in glorious Gotham.

Driving Tips

Don't. Don't drive in Manhattan, at least. New York City is blessed with an arguably efficient subway and bus mass-transit system, accessible by the customized MetroCard, and unless you know the streets, you will spend a lot of boring, exasperating time in traffic jams and a fortune on parking and parking tickets. Leave the driving to the yellow medallion taxis, most operated by knowledgeable drivers; fasten your seat belt; and get a

NEW YORK CITY

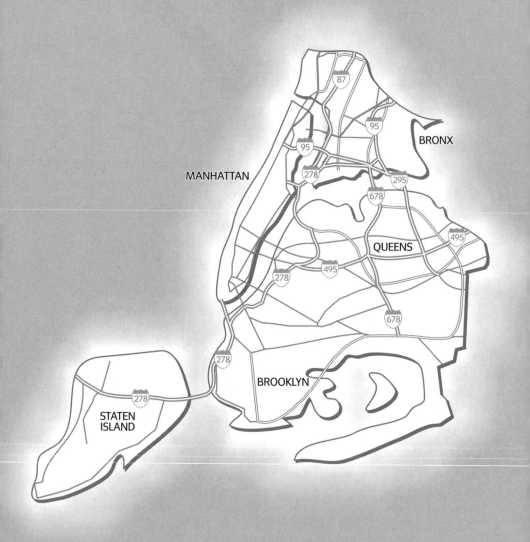

MANHATTAN

BRONX

QUEENS

BROOKLYN

STATEN
ISLAND

receipt. The subway is the fastest way around the boroughs, but the slower buses offer more scenic views. Unless you want to experience the premier thrill ride of this international theme park. For that, board the first subway car on the train, stand in front of the front window, hold on tight, and ride the subterranean city rails through spooky darkened tunnels. Very cool. New front train cars will no longer have this configuration, and older cars will be phased out, so catch this ride while you can. As for the best way to get around town, walking wins. Don't despair on crowded sidewalks, for the pedestrian polka can be mastered with practice.

The Bronx

Once the tribal lands of the Weckquasgeek Indians, the area was settled in the mid-seventeenth century by a Scandinavian sea captain named Jonas Bronck. Remaining rural until the late nineteenth century, the construction of the subway brought waves of new immigrants from Europe, building the borough into a multicultural stew of more than a million people.

International Wildlife Conservation Park (Bronx Zoo) (all ages)
2300 Southern Boulevard; (718) 367–1010 or (718) 220–5100; www.bronxzoo.com or www.wcs.org. Open daily April through October 10:00 A.M. to 5:00 P.M. weekdays, 10:00 A.M. to 5:30 P.M. weekends and holidays; November through March 10:00 A.M. to 4:30 P.M. daily. Adults $$$, children $$. Free for everyone on Wednesday. Additional admissions for rides. Strollers may be rented.

Possibly the country's premier urban zoo, there are more than 6,000 animals of 600 species here, most living in large landscaped natural habitats and environmentally controlled ecosystems. Little feet can get tuckered out traversing the 265 acres of abodes, so pick up a map at the gate and plot your course past the family favorites. Head for the wonderful Children's Zoo, where you can crawl through a prairie dog den, climb a giant spider web, or feed the farm animals. Traipse through a tropical rain forest at JungleWorld, take a ride on a camel, or hop aboard the monorail Bengali Express. Trek across the African Plains, then wander into the World of Darkness for a peek at the largest captive bat colony in the country. Be at the World of Birds by afternoon to experience a daily tropical thunderstorm inside the giant aviary or take a hike to the Himalayan Highlands, home to endangered red pandas and snow leopards. Don't miss the Congo Gorilla Forest, a six-and-a-half-acre fern and waterfall–bedecked primate paradise that's home to twenty-three western lowland gorillas. Tiger Mountain, one of the newest exhibits, re-creates the natural habitat of the Siberian Tiger. To get a bird's-eye view of the park's vast reserve, skim the treetops inside Skyfari "skybuckets." In winter, evening hours are extended during Holiday Lights, a magical display of hundreds of thousands of twinkling lights sculpted into giant animal shapes scattered throughout the park.

New York Botanical Garden (all ages)

Southern Boulevard and 200th Street; (718) 817–8700; www.nybg.org. Open year-round Tuesday through Sunday April through October 10:00 A.M. to 6:00 P.M., November through March and Monday holidays 10:00 A.M. to 4:00 P.M. Adults $$, children 2 to 12 $.

Located next door to the Bronx Zoo, this 250-acre verdant oasis offers twenty-seven out-door gardens to stroll, ranging from rose to rock to rhododendron. The jewel of this horti-cultural haven is the Enid A. Haupt Conservatory, the country's largest Victorian crystal palace, filled with the fragrance of exotic and unusual tropical and desert plants from around the world. In winter this glorious glass house hosts A Victorian Holiday, with G-scale trains running past dozens of miniature replicas of New York's most famous century-old mansions, built entirely from leaves, twigs, and acorns. Outside, trails wind through stands of 300-year-old trees and past the only freshwater river in the city. Discovery carts dot the paths, offering interesting flora facts and hands-on activities. A newer addition is the wonderful Everett Children's Adventure Garden, a twelve-acre discovery zone for fami-lies. When the tootsies get tired, hop aboard the narrated tram traversing the trails of the garden or stop for a snack at the Garden Cafe.

Yankee Stadium (all ages)

East 161st Street at River Avenue, Highbridge; (718) 293–6000 or (212) 307–1212; www.yankees.com. Tours (718) 579–4531. Tours year-round Monday through Friday 10:00 A.M. to 4:00 P.M., Saturday 10:00 A.M. to noon. Tours limited when team is in town. Admission varies with seat location.

Home of the American League New York Yankees, this is "the house that Ruth built." The Bronx Bombers play from mid-April to early October, with special promotional days with hat, bat, and glove giveaways scheduled throughout the season. So take your family out to the ballgame, buy them some peanuts and Cracker Jack, and see the best ballplayers in the business, right here in the Bronx.

Edgar Allan Poe Cottage (ages 7 and up)

East Kingsbridge Road, Grand Concourse; (718) 881–8900; www.bronxhistoricalsociety.org. Open Saturday 10:00 A.M. to 4:00 P.M. and Sunday 1:00 to 5:00 P.M. $

Once surrounded by farmland, this was the home of master writer Edgar Allan Poe and his wife, Virginia, during the 1840s. Poe moved to the Bronx hoping the fresh air would restore Virginia's health, and it was here, "in a kingdom by the sea," that he wrote "Annabel Lee," the haunting poem inspired by his beloved wife.

Bronx Museum of the Arts (all ages)

1040 Grand Concourse at 165th Street; (718) 681–6000. Open year-round Wednesday noon to 9:00 P.M., Thursday through Sunday noon to 6:00 P.M. Adults $, under 12 free.

More than 600 multicultural contemporary and twentieth-century works of art are exhib-ited at this museum, and special programs and workshops are offered for families throughout the year.

Wave Hill (all ages)

675 West 252nd Street, Riverdale; (718) 549–3200; www.wavehill.org. Open mid-April through mid-October Tuesday through Sunday 9:00 A.M. to 5:30 P.M., Wednesday until 9:00 P.M. during June and July; mid-October through mid-April Tuesday through Sunday 9:00 A.M. to 4:30 P.M. $, children under 6 free; Saturday mornings and Tuesdays and all of December through February are free for everybody.

Perched on a bluff overlooking the Hudson River, this twenty-eight-acre estate is a wonderful place to play. With plush rolling lawns, spectacular views of the New Jersey Palisades, and formal gardens and woodland nature trails to explore, Wave Hill is a pastoral place of grace and beauty. The two mansions on the grounds, once a peaceful retreat for Mark Twain, Theodore Roosevelt, and others, serve today as cultural centers, offering workshops, concerts, and art exhibits. An artist-in-residence leads the year-round Family Art Project, a series of creative eco-art explorations, and master storytellers weave their magic into folktales from nature.

Van Cortlandt Park (all ages)

246th Street and Broadway; (718) 430–1890 or (718) 543–3344 (mansion), or (718) 548–0912 for Urban Park Ranger walking tours; www.nyc.gov/parks. Park is open daily year-round. Mansion is open Tuesday through Friday 10:00 A.M. to 3:00 P.M., Saturday and Sunday 11:00 A.M. to 4:00 P.M. Park is free, museum $, separate golf fees.

This 1,146-acre nugget of nature abutting the northern border of the Bronx has a hodgepodge of habitats, ranging from woodland to swamp, and red foxes, bald eagles, and even coyotes have been seen here. Nature trails loop through the woods, past a lake, and along an abandoned railway bed. Stop by the Forest Ecology Center for a map and to see the flora and fauna displays, then head over to the eighteenth-century Van Cortlandt Mansion. Furnished in period antiques, this was another place George Washington slept, as did the Van Cortlandt family slaves. The farmland that surrounded the house has been converted to ball fields, and to the south are the Moshulu and Van Cortlandt golf courses, the latter being the oldest public course in the country.

Pelham Bay Park (all ages)

895 Shore Road, Pelham Bay Park; (718) 885–1461, (718) 430–1890, or (718) 885–3466; www.nyc.gov/parks. Pelham Bay Stables, 9 Shore Road, Bronx 10464; (718) 885–0551. Park is free and open year-round; fees for stables and golf course.

Nestled in the northeast corner of the Bronx and encompassing 2,764 acres, this is New York City's largest park. Once the site of a 1638 settlement founded by liberal religious leader Anne Hutchinson, today the area attracts sun worshipers to the popular "Riviera of New York," Orchard Beach. Nature trails loop through the rocky Hunter Island Zoology and Geology Sanctuary and past a lagoon's green salt marsh that's home to wading birds and osprey. Overlooking the lagoon and Long Island Sound is the nineteenth-century Greek Revival Bartow-Pell Mansion, filled with period antiques and surrounded by formal gardens. For a different perspective, take a trail ride through woods or along the water atop a mount from Pelham Bay Stables.

Brooklyn

This was home to the Lenape and Canarsie Indians until the Dutch arrived and began building Breuckelen and other farming villages in the early seventeenth century. In 1898 Brooklyn became a part of New York City, and today some 2.5 million people of more than a hundred ethnic cultures reside in this 71-square-mile borough. For an awesome view, stroll across the famous Brooklyn Bridge, the unique link between Kings County and Manhattan.

Brooklyn Children's Museum (all ages)

145 Brooklyn Avenue at St. Mark's Avenue; (718) 735–4400; www.bchildmus.org or www.brooklynkids.org. Open July through August Tuesday through Friday 1:00 to 6:00 P.M., weekends 11:00 A.M. to 6:00 P.M. September through June Wednesday through Friday 1:00 to 6:00 P.M., weekends 11:00 A.M. to 6:00 P.M. $

Founded in 1899, this was the country's first children's museum. Housed in an underground four-level maze of interconnecting tubes and tunnels, there are dozens of hands-on and interactive exhibits that will excite and enchant all ages, and the museum's collection of more than 20,000 natural-history specimens and cultural artifacts is fascinating. Family workshops and special performing arts programs, from theater to dance, highlight the multicultural diversity of New York.

New York Aquarium (all ages)

Surf Avenue and West Eighth Street, Coney Island; (718) 265–3400 or (718) 265–FISH; www.nyaquarium.com. Open daily year-round 10:00 A.M. Closing time varies by season. $$$

Birthplace of baby beluga whales, this is one of the best aquariums in the Northeast. Sea and shore creatures here include bottle-nosed dolphins, tiger sharks, huge sea turtles, schools of candy-colored fish, electric eels, and graceful anemones. Alien Stingers, one of the newest exhibits, explores the mysterious sea jellies. Discovery Cove has starfish and crab touch tanks and interactive exhibits; the Sea Cliffs are home to an assortment of penguins, walruses, and otters; and seasonal sea lion and dolphin shows are scheduled at the Aquatheater. Family programs are offered year-round, ranging from seashore crafts to shark and whale talks.

Brooklyn Botanic Garden (all ages)

900 Washington Avenue, between Empire Boulevard and Eastern Parkway; (718) 623–7220; www.bbg.org. Open April through September Tuesday through Friday 8:00 A.M. to 4:30 P.M., Saturday and Sunday and holidays 10:00 A.M. to 6:00 P.M.; October through March Tuesday through Friday 8:00 A.M. to 4:30 P.M., Saturday and Sunday 10:00 A.M. to 4:30 P.M. Closed Monday except holidays, Thanksgiving, Christmas, and New Year's Day. $, under 16 free.

A lot of trees grow in Brooklyn, but perhaps the most beautiful ones grow in this urban oasis. With the finest cherry blossom gardens outside of Japan, a spectacular 5,000-plant rose garden, and the largest collection of bonsai trees in the country, this is a little slice of paradise. The Conservatory encloses a rain forest and a cacti-filled desert, and the Children's Garden is world-class.

Brooklyn Museum of Art (all ages)

200 Eastern Parkway, at Washington Avenue; (718) 638–5000; www.brooklynart.org. Open Wednesday through Friday 10:00 A.M. to 5:00 P.M., Saturday and Sunday 11:00 A.M. to 6:00 P.M. The first Saturday of the month is sometimes free, open 11:00 A.M. to 11:00 P.M. Closed Thanksgiving, Christmas, and New Year's Day. $$, children under 12 free.

More than 1.5 million works of awesome art from all over the world, spanning some 5,000 years of creative expression and culture, are housed inside this 450,000-square-foot Beaux Arts building. The Egyptian Collection, complete with a real mummy, is one of the best in the West, and kids will enjoy exploring the twenty-eight fascinating American-period rooms. This was the first museum to display African objects as art instead of artifacts, and the Native American collection is impressive as well. Curators have amassed one of the best collections of paintings, prints, and sculpture in the country, with the works of Degas, Rodin, Matisse, van Gogh, Picasso, and the Hudson River School represented. Special programs for children ages four through eighteen are offered seasonally, and there are drop-in art projects, performances, and concerts on weekends.

Coney Island Boardwalk (all ages)

Astroland, 1000 Surf Avenue, Coney Island; (718) 372–0275 or (718) 265–2100; www.astroland.com. Deno's Wonderwheel Park, 1025 Boardwalk and West 12th Street, Coney Island; (718) 372–2592; www.wonderwheel.com. "Sideshows by the Seashore," 1208 Surf Avenue, Coney Island; (718) 372–5159; www.coneyisland.com. Open in summer at noon, closing time depends on weather. Fees for individual rides, or get a pay-one-price pass. $–$$

Long before the debut of Disneyland, Coney Island was the apex of the amusement park world. Once, fantasy islands called Luna Park and Dreamland dotted the boardwalk, but today Deno's and Astroland are the sole survivors of that magical era. For a unique aerial perspective of Manhattan, climb into the 1920s Wonder Wheel or brave the wonderfully rickety Cyclone roller coaster. There are dozens of rides for all ages here, as well as an assortment of pinball and video games at the arcade. East of Astroland is "Sideshows by the Seashore," a tribute to the grittier circus-style shows that once graced the boardwalk. And this being the birthplace of the hot dog, you must not leave before stopping at Nathan's Famous for some authentic Coney Island cuisine.

Other Area Fun Centers

Nellie Bly Amusement Park. 1824 Shore Parkway; (718) 996–4002 or (718) 373–0828; www.nellieblypark.com.

Fun Time USA. 2461 Knapp Street; (718) 368–0500.

MetroCard **Magic**

Catch the A train, or any of the other subways or buses in the five boroughs, all day long with the money-saving, unlimited-use, one-day $7.00 MetroCard Fun Pass, or the seven-day MetroCard for $21.00. Available at the New York Transit Museum, subway vending machines, and many subway booths. For more information, call (212) METROCARD, or log on to www.mta.nyc.ny.us.

New York Transit Museum (all ages)

Boerum Place and Schermerhorn Street; (718) 243–8601; www.mta.info, or www.transit museumeducation.org. Open Tuesday through Friday 10:00 A.M. to 4:00 P.M., Saturday and Sunday noon to 5:00 P.M. $

Housed in an authentic 1930s subway station, the newly renovated museum offers a variety of galleries and exhibits. Highlights include the George T. F. Rahilly Trolley and Bus Study Center, with over fifty detailed models of trolleys and work cars; a vintage collection of subway cars and elevated trains; *Clearing the Air,* an interactive segment on the evolution of fuel technologies; and memorabilia on the city's century-old subway system.

Urbanglass (all ages)

647 Fulton Street; (718) 625–3685; www.urbanglass.org. Open year-round Monday through Saturday 10:00 A.M. to 9:00 P.M., Sunday 11:00 A.M. to 6:00 P.M. Free to watch, but fees for projects, some suitable for older children only.

At this glassworks studio, the largest in the world, visitors can watch artisans magically mold hot globs of glass and electric neon into crystalline creations of color and light. Seasonal Sunday Open Houses offer families the opportunity to paint on glass, custom design a sandblasted jar, or step up to the "glory hole" and make a one-of-a-kind paperweight.

Brooklyn Academy of Music (BAM) (ages 4 and up)

30 Lafayette Avenue, between St. Felix Street and Ashland Place; (718) 636–4100; www.bam.org. Box office open Monday through Friday 10:00 A.M. to 6:00 P.M., Saturday noon to 6:00 P.M. Ticket prices vary with event.

As the oldest and possibly the most innovative performing arts center in America, BAM blends the traditional with the contemporary in its presentations of dance, theater, music, opera, and film. The New Wave Festival showcases modern artistic expression every autumn, and spring is celebrated with KaBAM!, the international performing arts festival for families.

Prospect Park (all ages)

95 Prospect Park West and Grand Army Plaza; (718) 965–8999, (718) 965–8951, or (718) 965–8960; wildlife center (718) 399–7339; www.prospectpark.org, www.nyc.gov/parks, or www.prospectparkzoo.com. Park and museum are free and open year-round. Fee for stables. Zoo opens daily at 10:00 A.M., closes at 5:00 P.M. weekdays April through October, 5:30 P.M. weekends and holidays, and at 4:30 P.M. daily November through March. $

Centered around the terminal moraine of a retreating glacier, the 526 acres of this rustic retreat from the Brooklyn streets is like a trip to the country. Enter the park at Grand Army Plaza and pass underneath the striking stone Civil War Soldiers and Sailors Memorial Arch, inspired by Paris's Arc de Triomphe. Head south toward the child-friendly Prospect Park Zoo, home to over eighty species ensconced in natural habitats. Nearby is the 1912 vintage carousel, and the Lefferts Homestead, a children's museum housed in an eighteenth-century Dutch Colonial farmhouse. Stroll over to the boathouse and rent a pedal boat for a cruise around Prospect Lake, spend some time at the Imagination Playground, go ice-skating at Kate Wollman Rink, or ride a horse from Kensington Stables along the bridle paths. When the tots get tuckered out, hop aboard the old-time trolley for a spin around the park.

Plumb Beach (all ages)

Belt Parkway, just after the Knapp Street/Sheepshead Bay exit; (718) 338–3799; www.nps.gov/gate. Open daily year-round. Free.

Another slice of the Gateway National Recreation Area, this shoreline was created by sand fill from Rockaway Channel to ease erosion. Somehow a honeymoon haven for horseshoe crabs was created, and every spring they arrive in droves to lay millions of eggs. So be prepared, and look out for the poison ivy.

Also in **the Area**

Marine Park. Avenue U, off Flatbush Avenue; (718) 965–6551, (718) 421–2021, (718) 338–7113, or (718) 338–7149 for golf; www.nyc.gov/parks.

Floyd Bennett Field. Floyd Bennett Drive, off Flatbush Avenue; (718) 338–3799; www.nps.gov/gate.

Jamaica Bay Riding Academy. 7000 Shore Parkway, between Brooklyn Ridge and 70th Street; (718) 531–8949.

Empire–Fulton Ferry State Park. 26 New Dock Street and East River; (718) 858–4708; www.nysparks.com/parks.

Waterfront Museum. 290 Conover Street at Pier 45; (718) 624–4719; www.waterfrontmuseum.org.

Puppetworks. 338 Sixth Avenue at 4th Street; (718) 965–3391; www.puppetworks.org.

Old Stone House Historic Interpretive Center. 336 Third Street; (718) 768–3195; www.oldstonehouse.org.

Queens

Named for Catherine of Braganza, seventeenth-century Queen of England, this is the biggest borough, encompassing 109 square miles and a rainbow of cultures. From Steinways to stained glass to the silver screen, Queens produced a plethora of products and extended a royal welcome to two World's Fairs.

Alley Pond Park (all ages)

228–06 Northern Boulevard, Douglaston; (718) 229–4000 or (718) 217–6034 (Upper Alley Pond Nature Center); www.alleypond.com. Park open daily year-round. Center open Monday through Saturday 9:00 A.M. to 4:00 P.M., Sunday 9:30 A.M. to 3:30 P.M.; closed Sunday in summer. Free.

Although this 654-acre preserve has been chopped up by several major highways, the resulting mosaic of wetlands, woodlands, and ponds provides a diverse habitat for more than 300 species of birds and wildlife, from fiddler crabs to great blue herons. Begin at the Upper Alley Pond Nature Center, which offers a small petting zoo and eco-exhibits, then follow the Cattail Trail boardwalk that opens onto a viewing platform set over a green salt marsh. To the west is scenic Oakland Lake, a nearby stand of oaks and beeches several centuries old, and a 155-foot tulip tree that's taller than the Statue of Liberty.

American Museum of the Moving Image (all ages)

36–01 35th Avenue at 36th Street, Astoria; (718) 784–0077; www.movingimage.us. Open Wednesday through Thursday noon to 5:00 P.M., Friday to 8:00 P.M., Saturday and Sunday 11:00 A.M. to 6:30 P.M. Adults $$, children $, under 5 free.

Before Hollywood there was Astoria, the birthplace of big-screen entertainment, where stars Rudolph Valentino, the Marx Brothers, and Gloria Swanson got ready for their close-ups. Saved from destruction in the 1970s by concerned film folk, today the Kaufman-Astoria Studios complex includes the largest sound stage outside of Hollywood, as well as seven smaller stages, and film and television production is booming. Sesame Street is taped here, and although studio tours aren't available, there's a wonderful museum next door, including thousands of artifacts from famous films and TV shows. This is an interactive museum, where visitors can try their talent at a dozen hands-on exhibits designed to show how movies are made and marketed.

Isamu Noguchi Garden Museum (all ages)

9–01 33rd Road, Long Island City; (718) 721–2308 or (718) 545–8842; www.noguchi.org. Open April through October Wednesday through Friday 10:00 A.M. to 5:00 P.M., Saturday and Sunday 11:00 A.M. to 6:00 P.M. $

Once the studio of the famed modern sculptor, this tranquil garden and twelve galleries house more than 250 of his works of art.

Socrates Sculpture Park (all ages)

Broadway at Vernon Boulevard, Long Island City; (718) 956–1819; www.socrates sculpturepark.org. Open daily year-round 10:00 A.M. to sunset. Free.

This is a hands-on hodgepodge of fantastical contemporary creations of cement, stone, tile, wire, and whatever. Established by local artist Mark di Suvero and friends on five acres of an abandoned trash-strewn lot in the 1980s, today it's a wonderful place where children are encouraged to touch, climb, and explore.

Museum for African Art (ages 6 and up)

36–01 43rd Avenue at 36th Street, Long Island City; (718) 784–7700; www.africanart.org. Open Monday, Thursday, and Friday 10:00 A.M. to 5:00 pm., Saturday and Sunday 11:00 A.M. to 6:00 P.M. Closed Tuesday and Wednesday. Adults $$, children $, free for children under 6 and for all 10:00 A.M. to 11:00 A.M. weekdays.

This museum features terrific traditional and contemporary art and cultural exhibits from Africa. Family programs are offered year-round and may include playing African music and games, arts and crafts workshops, storytelling, and film screenings.

Shea Stadium (all ages)

123–01 Roosevelt Avenue (126th Street), Flushing; (718) 507–TIXX or (718) 507–METS; www.mets.com. Ticket prices depend on seat location.

This is home plate for the National League's New York Mets, with games from mid-April to October. Tickets are usually available on game day, unless there's a "subway series" with the Yankees.

P.S. 1 Contemporary Art Center (all ages)

22–25 Jackson Avenue at 46th Avenue, Long Island City; (718) 784–2084; www.ps1.org. Open Thursday through Monday noon to 6:00 P.M. Donation.

The center's recent merger with the Museum of Modern Art has created a cultural corridor between boroughs and a closer connection with emerging artists.

Queens County Farm Museum (all ages)

73–50 Little Neck Parkway, Long Island City; (718) 347–3276; www.queensfarm.org. Open year-round weekdays 9:00 A.M. to 5:00 P.M. outdoors only, weekends 10:00 A.M. to 5:00 P.M. Closed major holidays. Free.

The land surrounding this 1772 farmhouse has been cultivated for more than 200 years, and this working farm museum offers opportunities for families to experience a historical home on the grange, Queens-style. There's a barnyard full of chickens, goats, cows, and sheep; vintage artifacts of farm life to see and touch; and nature trails to explore aboard a hay wagon. Next door is the more modern Green Meadows Farm, featuring a plethora of petting animals and pony rides perfect for toddlers.

New York **in Song**

Although the official state song is "I Love New York,"
here are a few more tunes that tout the town:

"New York, New York"

"I'm a Native New Yorker"

"I Happen to Like New York"

"Give My Regards to Broadway"

"The Sidewalks of New York"

"The Only Living Boy in New York"

"Broadway"

"Manhattan"

"New York State of Mind"

"Lullaby of Broadway"

"Autumn in New York"

Flushing Meadows–Corona Park (all ages)

53–51 111th Street, at 54th Avenue, Flushing Meadows–Corona Park, Flushing; (718) 760–6565; www.nyc.gov/parks. Queens Wildlife Center (718) 271–1500; www.wcs.org. Park open year-round. Wildlife center open weekdays 10:00 A.M. to 5:00 P.M., weekends and holidays until 5:30 P.M. $

Once the nineteenth-century dumping grounds for Brooklyn's garbage, this 1,225-acre parkland was created by the legendary Robert Moses in the 1930s. With the world on the brink of war, he envisioned an international exposition proclaiming peace and prosperity, and Flushing Meadows became the site of the 1939 World's Fair. In 1964 the World's Fair made a second appearance here, anchored by the 380-ton gilded globe called the Unisphere. Wonderful remnants of those fairs remain and house museums of art and science today. The Queens Zoo, home to 250 animals, features creatures from North America, both domestic and wild, ranging from bison and bobcats to sheep and rabbits.

Queens Museum of Art (all ages)
New York City Building, Flushing Meadows–Corona Park, Flushing; (718) 592–9700;
www.queensmuseum.org. Open September through June Tuesday through Friday
10:00 A.M. to 5:00 P.M., Saturday and Sunday noon to 5:00 P.M., July and August
Wednesday through Sunday 1:00 to 8:00 P.M. $

Across the plaza from the Unisphere, housed in New York's World's Fair pavilion, is an
excellent collection of twentieth-century art, but what really fascinates families is the
9,500-square-foot panorama of the city of New York. More than 900,000 Lilliputian-scale
buildings and bridges, built of wood and plaster, adorn a giant relief map of all five boroughs, complete with a tiny airplane that departs regularly from La Guardia Airport.
Opportunities to construct a building of your own are available at children's art workshops
throughout the year, offering inspiration to aspiring architects.

New York Hall of Science (ages 4 and up)
47–01 111th Street, at 48th Avenue, Flushing Meadows–Corona Park, Flushing; (718)
699–0005; www.nyhallsci.org. Open July and August Monday 9:30 A.M. to 2:00 P.M.,
Tuesday through Friday 9:30 A.M. to 5:00 P.M., weekends 10:30 A.M. to 6:00 P.M.; September
through June Tuesday through Thursday 9:30 A.M. to 2:00 P.M., and Saturday and Sunday
noon to 5:00 P.M. $$

Explore more than 180 interactive exhibits that investigate the world of color, light, biol-
ogy, optical illusions, physics, energy, and more. The friendly guides perform experiments
and regular demonstrations, and on one visit the staff dissected a cow's eyeball, much to
my sons' fascination. Preschoolers will enjoy explorations and story time at their own Dis-
covery Place. Outside is the Science Playground, the largest physically interactive jungle
gym on this side of the planet.

Also in **the Area**

Bayswater Point State Park. Mott Avenue, Jamaica Bay; (212) 694–3722;
www.nysparks.com/parks.

Forest Park. The Oakridge, 1 Forest Park, Woodhaven; (718) 235–4100 or
(718) 846–2731; (718) 296–0999 for golf; (718) 261–7679 for horseback riding.

Cunningham Park. 196th Place, at Union Turnpike and Francis Lewis Boule-
vard, Fresh Meadows; (718) 217–6452 or (718) 740–6800 (tennis center).

Colden Center for the Performing Arts. 65–30 Kissena Boulevard, Queens
College, Flushing; (718) 793–8080; www.coldencenter.org.

Kingsland Homestead. 143–35 37th Avenue, Flushing; (718) 939–0647;
www.queenshistoricalsociety.org/kingsland.html.

Queens Botanical Garden (all ages)

43–50 Main Street, at Dahlia Avenue, Flushing; (718) 886–3800; www.queensbotanical.org. Open April through October Tuesday through Friday 8:00 A.M. to 6:00 P.M., Saturday and Sunday until 7:00 P.M.; November through March Tuesday through Sunday 8:00 A.M. to 4:30 P.M., closed Monday except for legal holidays. Free.

A thirty-nine-acre oasis of flora, featuring formal gardens of roses, tulips, herbs, and candy-colored perennials and annuals awaits visitors, and special bird and bee flower beds attract flying fauna, as well. Seasonal programs for children include garden projects and nature craft workshops, as well as family-oriented concerts and harvest festivals.

Jamaica Bay Wildlife Refuge (all ages)

253 Beach 116th Street, Rockaway Park; (718) 318–4304; www.nps.gov/gate/. Open daily year-round dawn to dusk; visitor center open 8:30 A.M. to 5:00 P.M. Free.

This refuge is part of the Gateway National Recreation Area and the first national urban park in the country. More than 300 species of birds stop or stay here, despite the proximity of JFK Airport. Pick up a map at the visitor center, then follow the path along the South Marsh and the West Pond toward the Terrapin Trail, a nesting area for diamondback terrapin turtles. Rockaway Peninsula is popular with sunbathers in summer and migrating monarch butterflies in September.

Staten Island

Nestled next to New Jersey, the greenest borough of New York is linked to Manhattan by the scenic Staten Island Ferry and connected to Brooklyn by the graceful sweep of the Verrazano-Narrows Bridge.

Snug Harbor Cultural Center (all ages)

1000 Richmond Terrace; (718) 448–2500; children's museum (718) 273–2060; botanical garden (718) 273–8200; www.snug-harbor.org. Grounds open daily dawn to dusk; visitor center open daily 9:00 A.M. to 5:00 P.M.; museum hours Tuesday through Sunday noon to 5:00 P.M., opening at 10:00 A.M. Tuesday through Sunday and Thursday to 8:00 P.M. in summer. Center and grounds free; museum $.

Established in the early nineteenth century by Revolutionary War maritime magnate and possible pirate Robert Richard Randall as a rest home for ancient mariners, this eighty-six-acre complex encompasses twenty-eight historical buildings in various states of preservation. Surrounding the center is the beautiful Staten Island Botanical Garden, a Victorian landscape of lush lawns, ponds, and fragrant gardens. A new addition, and the first one in this country, is the Chinese Scholar's Garden. Head for the award-winning Staten Island Children's Museum, where the bugs are big, and kids can climb inside a giant anthill or inspect interesting insects up close. At the online studio WKID, children can anchor a news show, operate a camera, or run a radio station. Block Harbor, a builder's paradise, has hundreds of wooden shapes to shore up, a wonderful waterfall water table with smocks provided, and a number of touchable art exhibits.

Staten Island Zoo (all ages)

614 Broadway, between Forest Avenue and Clove Road; (718) 442–3100; www.statenisland zoo.org. **Open daily 10:00 A.M. to 4:45 P.M. Closed Thanksgiving, Christmas, and New Year's Day. $, free for children under 3.**

Eight acres of animals and aquariums attract families at the first educational zoo in America. More than 250 species are represented, in habitats ranging from tropical forests to the African savanna. The reptile collection is rather extensive and impressive, full of venomous snakes and lizards. The Children's Zoo has barnyard animals to feed and pony rides for young rustlers.

Clay Pit Ponds State Park Preserve (all ages)

83 Nielson Avenue, at Sharrots Road and Carlin Street; (718) 967–1976; www.nysparks .com/parks. **Trails open dawn to dusk. Preserve headquarters open 9:00 A.M. to 5:00 P.M. Free.**

A hundred years ago, the bricks that built New York were made from the abundant clay deposits found here. What remains today is a 260-acre sand and swamp preserve of pitch pines and blackjack oaks, dotted with kettle ponds and spring-fed streams. This unique ecosystem was designated New York City's first state park preserve and provides habitat for box turtles, screech owls, raccoons, fence lizards, and a variety of birds. Nature walks, eco-talks, plant and animal identification, and arts and crafts programs are offered year-round for families at the park's headquarters.

Historic Richmond Town (all ages)

441 Clarke Avenue; (718) 351–1611; www.historicrichmondtown.org. **Open year-round Wednesday through Sunday 1:00 to 5:00 P.M., with extended hours June through August. $**

Three hundred years of history are highlighted here, re-created in the twenty-seven buildings of a patchwork historic village set on a hundred acres. Costumed guides demonstrate rural and colonial crafts, from candlemaking to cooking, and the oldest elementary schoolhouse in America is here, as well. Seasonal events are scheduled throughout the year, from Civil War encampments to harvest fairs.

Alice Austen House Museum & Garden (all ages)

2 Hylan Boulevard; (718) 816–4506; www.aliceausten.org. **Open Thursday through Sunday noon to 5:00 P.M.; grounds open daily until dusk. Closed January and February. Donation.**

This charming cottage, trimmed in lacy gingerbread and surrounded by rolling lawns and sweeping views of the harbor, was the home of Victorian photographer Alice Austen. From age ten, Alice documented twentieth-century life with more than 9,000 photographs. She lived here until the stock market crash of 1929 plunged her into the poorhouse at age eighty-four.

Garibaldi-Meucci Museum (ages 5 and up)

420 Tompkins Avenue, at Chestnut Avenue; (718) 442–1608; www.garibaldimuseum.org. Open Tuesday through Sunday 1:00 to 5:00 P.M. $

In the mid-1800s, this was the home of Antonio Meucci and Giuseppe Garibaldi, two extraordinary men who changed the world. Meucci is now credited with inventing the first telephone, long before Alexander Graham Bell, but for lack of the $10 patent fee he lost the rights to his device. Garibaldi, later known as the revolutionary expatriate hero and founder of the nation of Italy, lived here with Meucci. Memorabilia, medals, and military artifacts document the lives of these remarkable roommates.

Jacques Marchais Museum of Tibetan Art (ages 5 and up)

338 Lighthouse Avenue, off Richmond Road; (718) 987–3500; www.tibetanmuseum.com. Open Wednesday through Sunday 1:00 to 5:00 P.M. $

Housing the largest private collection of Tibetan art in America, this stone temple complex is a peaceful place to stroll, with a goldfish pond, a terraced sculpture garden, and scenic water views. Special Sunday programs and performances for families focus on the music, dance, art, and culture of Asia, and children's arts and crafts workshops are offered in July.

Staten Island Institute of Arts and Science (all ages)

75 Stuyvesant Place, at Wall Street; (718) 727–1135; www.siiasmuseum.org. Open year-round Tuesday through Saturday 9:00 A.M. to 5:00 P.M., Sunday 1:00 to 5:00 P.M.; closed major holidays. $

More than two million objects and artifacts of art, history, and science are housed in one of New York's oldest museums. The international array of decorative arts, paintings, clothing, and crafts is impressive, but it's the 500,000 specimens in the bug collection that will excite the emerging entomologists in your entourage. Hands-on displays and projects are offered at the Family Gallery, along with frequent workshops, programs, and festivals for children.

Staten Island Greenbelt and High Rock Park

(all ages)
700 Rockland Avenue; (718) 667–2165, Nature Center (718) 351–3450; www.sigreenbelt.org. Open year-round. Center open April through October Tuesday through Sunday 11:00 A.M. to 5:00 P.M. and November through March Wednesday through Sunday. Free.

This lush patchwork of woodlands, covering 2,800 acres and laced together by over 30 miles of trails, is three times larger than Central Park. Stop at the new Greenbelt Center for a map and for guided nature walks, talks, and family workshops, and see the interactive exhibits.

More Staten **Island Parks**

All of these parks are **free** and open year-round. For more information, log on to www.nyc.gov/parks.

Blue Heron Park. 48 Poillon Avenue, between Hylan Boulevard and Amboy Road; (718) 390–8000; (718) 967–3542 (nature center).

Great Kills Park. Hylan Boulevard; (718) 987–6790.

Wolfe's Pond Park. Cornelia Avenue; (718) 984–8266.

Cloves Lake Park. Clove Road; (718) 390–8000 or (718) 720–1010.

High Rock Park. Richmond Parkway at Rockland Avenue; (718) 667–2165 (nature center).

Manhattan

Purchased, or perhaps rented, for $24 in beads from the Algonquin Indians by Peter Minuit in the early seventeenth century, this was the site of New Amsterdam, the only Dutch colony in America. Today, folks say this fantasy island heart of New York is the capital of the world, drawing in dreamers, seekers, and pretty much everybody else for a closer look.

Times Square (all ages)
42nd Street and Broadway; Times Square Visitor's Center located at 1560 Broadway, between 46th and 47th Streets; (212) 869–1890 or (212) 768–1560; www.times squarebid.org. Open daily 8:00 A.M. to 8:00 P.M. NYC & Company–Convention & Visitors Bureau, 810 Seventh Avenue; (212) 484–1222, (212) 397–8222, or (800) NYC–VISIT; www.nycvisit.com. Open daily 8:30 A.M. to 6:00 P.M. Free.

It's been said that if you stand in Times Square long enough, you'll run into every person you've ever known in your whole life. This truly is the "crossroads of the world," and like the rest of the city, it continues to morph. Encompassing a 30-square-block neighborhood—from 40th to 53rd Streets and between Eighth Avenue and Avenue of the Americas—this is also the heart of the theater district and the location of more than 250 restaurants. Full-price tickets to more than forty Broadway shows and other attractions can be purchased at the visitor center or at theater box offices, or you can stand in line at the TKTS half-price booth for same-day shows either at 47th and Broadway or at the South Street Seaport, 199 Water Street.

But much of Times Square's charm is **free,** with 30-foot flashing neon signs, kinetic billboards, and unique street performers. And of course, this is where the ball drops every New Year's Eve, attracting a half million revelers and two tons of confetti. The crime rates have dropped dramatically in recent years, thanks to increased police patrols, but take common-sense precautions with your family and other valuables, stay off deserted or darkened streets, and you'll have a great time.

American Museum of Natural History (all ages)

Central Park West at 79th Street; (212) 769–5100; www.amnh.org. Open daily year-round 10:00 A.M. to 5:45 P.M.; the Rose Center remains open until 8:45 P.M. on Friday. Museum is closed Thanksgiving and Christmas. Adults $$$, children $$, with separate admissions for Hayden Planetarium Space Theater, Naturemax movies, and special temporary exhibitions.

Founded in 1869, and housing more than thirty-two million anthropological artifacts and scientific specimens, this fabulous museum is one of the reasons I can never leave New York. More than forty exhibition halls explore everything in creation, from world culture to the cosmos, and there are more real dinosaurs here than in Jurassic Park. Since there's too much to see in one visit, stop at the Information Desk for a map, event and film schedules, **free** guided tours, and to inquire about the interactive CD-ROM "Audio Expeditions."

If you entered from Central Park West, begin your tour in the Roosevelt Rotunda, where a rearing Barosaurus towers over an attacking Allosaurus. That should whet your appetite for the six spectacular newly renovated fossil halls on the fourth floor, featuring the largest collection of its kind in the world, so head there first. Or, if you prefer to see the dinos later, walk straight toward the herd of charging elephants attempting to exit the Akeley Hall of African Mammals, illuminated by dozens of exquisitely crafted, lifelike dioramas. Continue your safari on the third floor, then head for the North American Mammals dioramas of grizzly bears, bison, and moose on the first floor. From there bear right to arrive at the museum's Hall of Biodiversity. The centerpiece of this salute to Earth's species is a 2,500-square-foot re-created Central African Rainforest, with computer stations, special lighting and audio effects, a video tour of nine ecosystems, and more than 1,500 specimens, including a giant jellyfish, a dodo bird, and a relative of Captain Nemo's nightmare squid. There's a diorama of another squid gripped in a deadly battle right next door, so descend into the depths of the Hall of Ocean Life, where you'll be greeted by a replica of a 94-foot-long blue whale floating peacefully through the ultramarine air.

Stroll through the wonderful Northwest Coast Indians Hall to the 64-foot Haida war canoe carved from a single cedar tree. To your left are the North American Forests, featuring lifelike dioramas perfect for a game of "I Spy," plus a slice of Sequoia to see. To your right is the Human Biology and Evolution Hall, where you can view a holographic archaeological dig, test your paleontological chops on a computer-simulated expedition, and become acquainted with our ancestors and anatomy.

Walk into the next room, and you'll run into the largest meteorite ever plucked from Earth's surface, the 4.5-billion-year-old Ahnighito. Take a peek in the mirror on the ceiling at the pile of pennies pitched there by wishful visitors. Continue around to your right, and you'll come to the museum's glittering gem and mineral collections, set amid carpeted multitiered platforms.

Rocks of a Richter scale, deep-sea sulfide chimneys, and a floating rear-screen projection Earth globe are displayed at the nearby Hall of Planet Earth, a wonderful home-planet prelude for the newest portal to the universe, the Rose Center for Earth and Space. Housed inside a 95-foot-high clear cube constructed from nearly an acre of glass, the Rose Center contains a variety of exhibits that explain, explore, and enlighten visitors curious about the cosmos. Begin at the Big Bang Theater's baby universe blast, then follow the spiraling timeline of the Heilbrunn Cosmic Pathway past diamond dust and dinosaur teeth into the Cullman Hall of the Universe. Anchored by the legendary Willamette Meteorite, the hall features kinetic models, interactive computer kiosks, video screens with Hubble highlights and NASA news, and a giant glass globe filled with tiny swimming

Boat **Tours**

Sometimes it's easier to get the big picture of the Big Apple from the water. With a breathtaking skyline, twenty-two bridges to sail under, and the Statue of Liberty to marvel at, a mini-voyage around Manhattan is a must. Of course, the best deal in town is still the free Staten Island Ferry ride across New York Harbor and back.

Staten Island Ferry. Battery Park, Staten Island; (718) 815–BOAT.

Circle Line Sightseeing Yachts. Pier 83 at West 42nd Street and 12th Avenue, and at Pier 16, South Street Seaport; (212) 563–3200; www.circle line.com.

The Beast. Pier 16, South Street Seaport and Pier 83, West 42nd Street; (212) 563–3200; www.circleline.com.

World Yacht. Pier 81 at West 41st Street at the Hudson River; (212) 630–8100 or (800) 498–4270; www.worldyacht.com.

Spirit Cruises. Pier 62 at West 23rd Street and 12th Avenue; (212) 727–7735 or (866) 399–8439; www.spiritcruises.com.

Bateaux New York. Pier 62 at Chelsea Piers; (866) 211–3806; www.bateauxnewyork.com.

New York Waterway. Pier 78 at West 38th Street at 12th Avenue; (201) 330–7934 or (800) 533–3779; www.nywaterway.com.

Seaport Liberty Cruises. Pier 16, South Street Seaport; (212) 630–8888; www.newyorkwatertour.com.

New York Water Taxi. (212) 742–1969; www.nywatertaxi.com.

shrimp that explores the possibility of life on other planets. But the pearl-shaped gem of this museum is the state-of-the-art spherical Space Theater, the largest and most powerful virtual-reality simulator on Earth. At its heart is the Zeiss Mark IX Star Projector and the Digital Dome System, an intergalactic transporter worthy of wrinkling time, as it speeds space travelers to the edge of the observable universe and back home via a black hole.

If you have more time, be sure to see the Komodo dragons and Eastern Woodlands and Plains Indians on the third floor and the international anthropology halls on the second floor. Also on the second floor is the Natural Science Center, an introduction to city flora and fauna for younger scientists, with glass cases of live frogs, turtles, and snakes. New temporary exhibits open periodically, there're always exciting IMAX films to see, and special family events, field trips, and workshops are offered year-round.

Carnegie Hall (ages 7 and up)

154 West 57th Street at Seventh Avenue; (212) 247–7800 or (212) 903–9790; www.carnegiehall.org. Admission depends on the program, but public tours are offered Monday through Friday at 11:30 A.M., 2:00 P.M., and 3:00 P.M. No tours offered early July to mid-September. $$ for adults, $ children.

Practice, practice, practice. That's the advice usually given to people asking how to get to "The House That Music Built." If you're not prepared to perform, check the season's schedule of classical and popular music offerings and inquire about the Family Concert Series and CarnegieKids concerts.

Cathedral Church of St. John the Divine (all ages)

1047 Amsterdam Avenue, at 112th Street; (212) 316–7540 or (212) 932–7314; www.stjohn divine.org. Open Monday through Saturday 7:00 A.M. to 6:00 P.M., Sunday 7:00 A.M. to 7:00 P.M., until 6:00 P.M. July and August. Free, with admission charged for some special events and concerts.

This Gothic- and Romanesque-style work in progress was started in 1892 and when finished, some fifty years from now, will be the largest cathedral in the world. Much larger than Notre Dame, with ceilings more than 100 feet high and a capacity for 10,000 people, this is an awe-inspiring place. Along with regular Episcopalian services, the cathedral sponsors classical, New Age, and Native American programs; concerts; and special events year-round. My sons' favorite event occurs in October, on St. Francis of Assisi's feast day. New Yorkers come by the hundreds, clutching their dogs, cats, hamsters, parakeets, boa constrictors, and even elephants, to walk down the aisle and have their beasts blessed.

Central Park (all ages)

Between Central Park West and Fifth Avenue, from 59th Street to 110th Street; (212) 360–3444; Visitors Information Center (212) 794–6564; Urban Park Rangers (212) 427–4040; Central Park Zoo (212) 439–6500; www.nyc.gov/parks or www.centralparknyc.org. Open all year. Free, except for carousel $, zoo adults $$, children $, rowboats $$, and ice rink adults $$–$$$, children $. Free guided walking tours (about one hour).

The most famous park in the country was faceted into a lush emerald jewel from a swampy and desolate diamond in the rough by the architects Frederick Law Olmsted and Calvert Vaux in 1858. Back then, this 843-acre area was in the middle of nowhere, populated by pig farmers and small villages of squatters, Irish immigrants, Native Americans, and free black landowners. Workers took twenty years to carve and sculpt this scenic space, used nearly 20,000 pounds of gunpowder to blast carriage paths and meadows out of Manhattan bedrock, and spread tons of topsoil around half a million trees, shrubs, and flowers. Today, more than sixteen million people come to play here every year, and it's the true heart and soul of the city. With 58 miles of paths, twenty-two playgrounds, and a wide variety of activities available, there's just too much to see and do in one day.

A good place to begin your exploration is the visitor center at the Dairy, located at 65th Street midpark. Once a Victorian refreshment stand for schoolchildren that featured milk from cows grazing in a nearby meadow, this is a good place to pick up a map or schedule of activities, and to ask about walking tours guided by the terrific Urban Park Rangers.

Nearby is the Chess and Checkers House, with **free** use of game pieces, and a 1908 carousel sporting fifty-eight brightly painted horses. In winter, swirling skaters whirl around Wollman Rink, enveloped in a steamy fog. In summer, the rink becomes the Victorian Gardens Amusement Park, featuring rides, games, concessions, and entertainment for the entire family. Nearby is the renovated Central Park Wildlife Center and the Children's Zoo, home to more than 450 animals of one hundred species. If you'd like to feed some animals yourself, head over to the adjacent petting zoo; surrounded by giant acorns, huge lily pads, dino-size eggshells, and a kid-size spider web; where goats, sheep, and pot-bellied pigs jockey for food pellets (bring quarters).

Walking north, you'll pass under the Delacorte Clock, with its whimsically musical bronze animals, then head toward 72nd Street, where the beloved Alice in Wonderland statue sits, overlooking the conservatory water often sailed by radio-controlled model boats. Nearby is the statue of Hans Christian Andersen reading from his children's classic *The Ugly Duckling*. Saturdays, June through September, **free** storytelling, rain or shine, takes place at the statue. For a schedule, check out www.hcastorycenter.org.

To the west is the Boathouse, where rowboats can be rented for a leisurely lake voyage. Also nearby is Strawberry Fields, the teardrop-shaped garden memorial to slain musician John Lennon, anchored by the black-and-white mosaic *Imagine*.

Directly south about 6 blocks lies the fairy-tale Tavern on the Green restaurant, with trees festooned in thousands of tiny white lights and giant topiaries of animals standing guard. On the north side of the lake is a wilder area favored by bird-watchers, known as the Ramble. It's lovely and peaceful to wander through, but it's not a place to linger alone. Perched on a rocky outcrop midpark at 81st Street is Belvedere Castle, site of the city's weather station and the Henry Luce Nature Observatory. Panoramic views of Turtle Pond and the Great Lawn can be seen from the castle, while the main floor houses hands-on exhibits of local animals, plants, and nature art activities. The castle is often lighted as a spectacular backdrop to the adjacent Delacorte Theatre's **free** summer productions of Shakespeare in the Park. On the slopes of the castle's hill is the Shakespeare Garden, featuring flowers and plants immortalized by the Bard's words, and the nearby Marionette Theatre presents puppet performances during the school year. At 96th Street are tennis courts and the North Meadow Recreation Center, offering a variety of outdoor activities, including rock climbing.

On the edge of North Meadow is the seasonal Lasker Pool and Ice Rink. Near the east side at 105th Street is the Conservatory Garden, a trio of formal landscapes, including one inspired by the classic children's book *The Secret Garden.* The wilder north end of the park is best explored in groups and has pretty much been left in a rugged and rustic state, except for the restoration of the Harlem Meer and the opening of the Charles A. Dana Discovery Center.

Theater **Tickets**

Broadway Line. (schedules, plots, prices) (212) 302–4111 or (888) BROADWAY.

Off-Broadway. (212) 244–6667; www.offbroadwayonline.com.

TKTS. (half-price tickets to same-day theater shows) 47th Street & Broadway; (212) 768–1818; timessquare.nyctourist.com/broadway_tkts.

Actors' Fund of America. (212) 221–7300.

Broadway Cares/Equity Fights AIDS. (212) 840–0770.

TheaterMania.com. (212) 352–0255 or (866) 811–4111; www.theatermania.com.

Ticketmaster. (212) 307–4100 or (800) 755–4000.

Telecharge. (212) 239–6200 or (800) 432–7250; www.telecharge.com.

School Theatre Ticket Program. (212) 354–4722; www.schooltix.com.

Bird's-Eye **Views**

The five-minute trip across the East River to Roosevelt Island is fast but fun, while braver aerialists may choose a chopper flight.

Roosevelt Island Tram. Second Avenue and 60th Street; (212) 832–4555.

Liberty Helicopter Tours. West 30th Street and 12th Avenue; (212) 967–6464 or (800) 542–9933; www.libertyhelicopters.com.

Helicopter Flight Services. 250 West 34th Street; (212) 355–0801 or (888) WE–FLY–NY; www.heliny.com.

Chelsea Piers Sports and Entertainment Complex

(ages 4 and up) 🏈 🍴

Between 17th and 23rd Streets on the Hudson River; (212) 336–6666; Sky Rink (212) 336–6100; Golf Club (212) 336–6400; www.chelseapiers.com. Open year-round; hours and admission vary with venue.

Built over the piers where Titanic would have docked had she made it to New York, this huge, thirty-acre, $60 million play space for all ages offers first-class facilities for just about any sport you can think of. The Field House features indoor soccer and lacrosse surfaces, batting cages, basketball courts, the largest gymnastics arena in New York, the biggest rock climbing wall in the Northeast, and the longest indoor running track on Earth. Sky Rink's indoor ice surfaces stretch out into the Hudson River, across from the open-air Roller Rink. Another pier houses the Golf Club, with a four-tiered, state-of-the-art, 200-yard driving range and practice putting green, and the forty-lane Chelsea Piers Bowl, featuring glow-in-the-dark and bumper bowling. There's also a full-service marina with charter yacht cruises, a health spa, several sports shops, restaurants overlooking the water, and a lovely promenade and maritime center, where anyone can learn to sail or kayak, and fishing poles are available for amateur anglers.

Red Double-Decker **Bus Tours**

There are dozens of tours of the town available, but for kids, nothing beats bouncing around the Big Apple on the top level of a bright red double-decker bus. Currently, one company offers hop-on, hop-off options, so you can spend more time at favorite attractions and then catch the next bus that comes along.

Gray Line Tours. (212) 445–0848 or (800) 669–0051; www.graylinenewyork .com.

New York **Trivia**

Besides the Big Apple, other New York City nicknames include the Big Onion, the Big Smear, and, of course, Gotham.

Madison Square Garden (all ages)

4 Penn Plaza, at Seventh Avenue between 31st and 33rd Streets; (212) 465–6080 or (212) 465–6741; tickets (212) 307–7171; www.thegarden.com. Knicks hot line (212) 465–JUMP or (877) NYK–DUNK; www.nyknicks.com. Rangers fan hot line (212) 465–4459; www.newyork rangers.com. New York Liberty (212) 564–WNBA; www.nyliberty.com. Tours (212) 465–5800. **Hours and prices vary with the event.**

Outside of Rome's Coliseum, this is possibly the most famous sports arena in the world, and it's the home turf of the New York Knickerbockers ("Knicks"), the New York Rangers, and the women's NBA team The New York Liberty. Although tickets are sometimes tough to get during peak playoff periods, you can almost always get a peek at their locker rooms during the behind-the-scenes tours or book tickets to any of the other events and concerts offered throughout the year.

Children's Museum of Manhattan (all ages)

212 West 83rd Street; (212) 721–1234; www.cmom.org. **Open Wednesday through Sunday 10:00 A.M. to 5:00 P.M. and Tuesday in summer. Closed major holidays. Strollers must be checked. $$**

With four floors of hands-on exhibits and activities, this is an imaginative and educational interactive place for younger kids to explore. Learn about language at Word Play; create a collage, craft, or painting at the Art Studio; make magic with musical instruments; explore the whimsical world of Dr. Seuss; climb the Urban Treehouse; or produce, write, and direct an original TV show at the Time Warner Center for Media. Special events are scheduled throughout the year.

Jewish Museum (ages 4 and up)

1109 Fifth Avenue at 92nd Street; (212) 423–3200; www .thejewishmuseum.org. **Open year-round Sunday through Wednesday 11:00 A.M. to 5:45 P.M., Thursday until 8:00 P.M., Friday to 3:00 P.M. Closed Saturday. Adults $$, under 12 free, and free to all on Tuesday evening.**

Founded in 1904, and housing a collection of more than 27,000 works of art, artifacts, and objects, this is one of the most important archives of Jewish cultural history in the world. At the Family Activity Center, children can create holiday or historical arts and crafts projects or go on treasure hunts, and performances and workshops are offered year-round.

Ellis Island Immigration Museum (all ages)

Ellis Island, New York Harbor; (212) 363–3200; ferry and ticket info (212) 269–5755; www.nps.gov/elis. Open year-round 9:30 A.M. to 5:00 P.M., weekends 9:00 A.M. to 5:30 P.M. Free, but there's a charge for ferry ride. Adults $$, children $.

Between 1892 and 1954, more than twelve million people passed through the portals of this place, seeking a new life in a new land. Reopened in 1990 after a $150 million restoration, the museum helps visitors to retrace the steps of their ancestors' journeys through films, self-guided audio tours, and exhibits of treasured personal possessions brought from their homelands. Ask about the free self-guided Junior Ranger program for children ages seven to twelve. An electronic "family tree" tracks the world's largest mass migration, and the Immigrant Wall of Honor enshrines the names of many members of America's "melting pot," including my sons' great-grandfather, Anthony Supino.

Suggested **Reading**

My New York by Kathy Jakobsen

Hillary & the Lions by Frank Desaix

Eloise by Kay Thompson

The Nighttime Chauffeur by Carly Simon

Music Over Manhattan by Mark Karlins

The Adventures of Taxi Dog by Debra and Sal Barracca

Miffy Loves New York City by Dick Bruna

How to Take Your Grandmother to the Museum by Lois Wyse and Molly Rose Goldman

You Can't Take a Balloon into the Metropolitan Museum by J. P Weitzman and R. P. Glasser

The Cricket in Times Square by George Selden

Stuart Little by E. B. White

All-of-a-Kind Family by Sydney Taylor

A Tree Grows in Brooklyn by Betsy Smith

Journey Around New York from A to Z by Martha and Heather Z. Schock

More **Manhattan Museums**

Whitney Museum of American Art. 945 Madison Avenue, at 75th Street; (212) 570–3676 or (800) WHITNEY; www.whitney.org.

Guggenheim Museum. 1071 Fifth Avenue, at 89th Street; (212) 423–3500 or (212) 423–3555; www.guggenheim.org.

Guggenheim Soho. 575 Broadway, at Prince Street; (212) 423–3500; www.guggenheim.org.

Museum of Arts and Design. 40 West 53rd Street; (212) 956–3535.

Cooper Hewitt National Design Museum. 2 East 91st Street, at Fifth Avenue; (212) 849–8400; www.si.edu/ndm/.

El Museo Del Barrio. 1230 Fifth Avenue, at 104th Street; (212) 831–7272.

International Center of Photography. 1130 Fifth Avenue, at 94th Street; (212) 857–0000 or (212) 857–0045; www.icp.org.

Museum of Jewish Heritage. 36 Battery Place, at Battery Park City; (646) 437–4200 or (646) 437–4202; www.mjhnyc.org.

Lower East Side Tenement Museum. 90 Orchard Street; (212) 431–0233; www.tenement.org.

American Folk Art Museum. 45 West 53rd Street; (212) 265–1040; www.folkartmuseum.org.

Museum of Chinese in America. 70 Mulberry Street, at Bayard Street; (212) 619–4785; www.moca-nyc.org.

Museum of the City of New York. 1220 Fifth Avenue, at 103rd Street; (212) 534–1672; www.mcny.org.

Museum of Television & Radio. 25 West 52nd Street; (212) 621–6600; www.mtr.org.

National Academy of Design Museum. 1083 Fifth Avenue, at 89th Street; (212) 369–4880; www.nationalacademy.org.

New York City Police Museum. 100 Old Slip; (212) 480–3100; nycpolice museum.org.

New York City Fire Museum. 278 Spring Street, between Hudson and Varick Streets; (212) 691–1303; www.nyfd.com.

Madame Tussaud's Wax Museum. Times Square, 234 West 42nd Street; (800) 246–8872; www.madame-tussauds.com.

FDNY Fire Zone. 34 West 51st Street; (212) 698–4520.

Empire State Building (all ages)

350 Fifth Avenue at 34th Street; (212) 736–3100; www.esbnyc.com. New York Skyride (212) 279–9777. Observatories are open year-round, with tickets sold from 9:30 A.M. to 11:30 P.M. daily. Photo ID required of adults. Observation deck $$$, children 6 to 11 $$; skyride $$$.

Once the tallest building in the world, and once again the tallest building in New York, this art deco skyscraper will always be the most famous. Built during the Depression in only fourteen months, using prefabricated pieces when possible, it towers 1,454 feet into the sky, with observation decks on the 86th and 102nd floors. Take the high-speed elevators to the decks, and on a clear day you can see for miles. Visit at dusk, when the sky glows pink and orange over New Jersey, the lights of the city wink on, and the rivers of tiny cars twinkle along the streets below. For an entirely different aerial experience, older kids and brave parents may want to hop aboard the New York Skyride, a wild motion-simulator ride past the city's landmarks.

Fort Tryon Park and The Cloisters (all ages)

799 Fort Washington Avenue and 193rd Street; (212) 923–3700; www.metmuseum.org. Open March through October Tuesday through Sunday 9:30 A.M. to 5:15 P.M.; November through February 9:30 A.M. to 4:45 P.M. Closed Thanksgiving, Christmas, and New Year's Day. Adults $$$, children $$.

For young knights and fair princesses, this medieval monastery is a time-travel trip to the days of yore. A branch of the Metropolitan Museum of Art reconstructed from parts of four European cloisters, it features the exquisite sixteenth-century Unicorn Tapestries, along with other medieval masterpieces. In September a family festival brings forth jugglers, jesters, and jousting knights on horseback.

New York **Trivia**

The lowest Point in New York is on the Atlantic coast, sea level (1,850 miles of ocean coastline).

CityPass

Score big savings with CityPass, a convenient and economical way to see seven major New York City attractions (*Intrepid* Sea-Air-Space Museum, American Museum of Natural History, Empire State Building Observatory, Guggenheim Museum, Museum of Modern Art, the Circle Line Harbor Cruise, and the Whitney Museum of Natural Art). Buy your CityPass at the first attraction you visit, and you'll have nine days to see the other six at a 50% savings off all admissions . . . with no waiting in ticket lines! Adults $48, youth $34. Call (707) 256–0490, or log on to www.citypass.org.

Fort Washington Park (all ages)

Fort Washington Park at 181st Street; (212) 304–2365, (212) 360–2774, or (800) 201–PARK; www.nyc.gov/parks. Park open year-round, but lighthouse hours vary. Free.

In the shadow of the George Washington Bridge, the 3,500-foot majestic link between New York and New Jersey, is a 146-acre shoreline park that's home to a little red lighthouse. Made famous by the Hildegarde H. Swift and Lynd Ward classic children's book, *The Little Red Lighthouse and the Great Gray Bridge,* the river beacon was falling apart by 1951 and slated for demolition. Young fans launched a letter-writing campaign, and the power of the pen saved the literary light.

Grand Central Terminal (all ages)

42nd Street and Lexington Avenue; (212) 532–4900 or (212) 340–2210; www.mnr.org or www.grandcentralterminal.com. Open year-round, twenty-four hours a day. Free.

After a $200 million renovation, this Beaux Arts titan of travel terminals gleams again, from the fiber optics stars in the ceiling's constellations to the gold-plated melon-shaped chandeliers. Dine fancy or food-court style, browse dozens of shops, then wander downstairs to the Whispering Gallery, where you can stand in a corner and talk softly yet be heard clearly on the other side of the room.

Intrepid Sea-Air-Space Museum (ages 6 and up)

12th Avenue at 46th Street on Pier 86; (212) 245–0072; www.intrepidmuseum.org. Open April through September weekdays 10:00 A.M. to 5:00 P.M., Saturday, Sunday, and holidays until 6:00 P.M.; October through March Tuesday through Sunday 10:00 A.M. to 5:00 P.M. Closed Thanksgiving and Christmas. Adults and children 6 to 17 $$$, 2 to 5 $, under 2 free.

A veteran of World War II, Vietnam, and a prime recovery vessel for NASA, this massive aircraft carrier has been reborn as a terrific museum, housing exhibits of naval, aeronautic, and space exploration history. Test your piloting skills inside an F-18 Navy Flight Simulator or talk to retired crew members manning the bridge. Docked nearby is the USS Growler, a nuclear-guided missile submarine, and the destroyer escort the USS Edson, both open for tours. The Kids' Corner offers activities related to history and technology, Seaworthy Saturdays feature exploration adventures for all ages, and a summer-long Seafest hosts tugboat races, sea stories, and fire department festivities.

Fun **Stores**

New York City is the shopping capital of the world with more than 10,000 stores, but toys are what usually capture my sons' interests. Below are their favorite places to spend their allowance.

FAO Schwarz. 767 Fifth Avenue; (212) 644–9400.

Toys "R" Us Times Square. 1514 Broadway; (800) TOYSRUS.

West Side Kids. 498 Amsterdam Avenue; (212) 496–7282.

Dinosaur Hill. 306 East Ninth Street; (212) 473–5850.

Children's General Store. Grand Central Terminal; (212) 682–0004.

Penny Whistle Toys. 448 Columbus Avenue; (212) 873–9090.

Classic Toys. 218 Sullivan Street; (212) 674–4434.

Kidding Around. 60 West 15th Street; (212) 645–6337.

Tiny Doll House. 1179 Lexington Avenue; (212) 744–3719.

Forbidden Planet. 840 Broadway; (212) 473–1576.

Tannen's Magic. 24 West 25th Street; (212) 929–4500.

The Disney Store. 711 Fifth Avenue; (212) 702–0702.

Geppetto's Toybox. 10 Christopher Street; (212) 620–7511.

Kay Bee Toys. 2411 Broadway; (212) 595–4389.

Pokémon Center. 10 Rockefeller Plaza; (212) 307–0900.

St. Marks Comics. 11 St. Mark's Place; (212) 598–9439.

Performing for **Young Audiences**

New York has dozens of outlets for the arts of music, dance, and theater, and many of them tailor their programs for children. For more information about current cultural events, check out www.nyckidsarts.org.

New Victory Theatre. (646) 223–3020; www.newvictory.org.

Symphony Space. (212) 864–1414; www.symphonyspace.org.

Theatreworks/USA. (212) 647–1100 or (800) 497–5007; www.theatreworks usa.org.

TaDa! (212) 627–1732; www.tadatheater.com.

Paper Bag Players. (212) 663–0390; www.paperbagplayers.org.

Little Orchestra Society. (212) 971–9500.

Theatre for a New Audience. (212) 229–2819.

Joyce Dance Theatre. (212) 242–0800; www.joyce.org.

Lincoln Center for the Performing Arts (ages 4 and up)
165 West 65th Street; (212) 875–5456, (212) 875–5000, or (212) 875–5370; box office (212) 721–6500; tours (212) 875–5350; www.lincolncenter.org. Seasonal schedule, with hours and admissions depending upon performance.

Possibly the finest performing arts complex in the country, this multiarts center is the home of the Metropolitan Opera, the New York City Ballet, the New York Philharmonic Orchestra, the New York City Opera, the Film Society of Lincoln Center, the Vivian Beaumont and Mitzi E. Newhouse Theatres, the School of American Ballet, and the Juilliard School, as well as jazz and chamber music programs. Each offers a full schedule of seasonal performances, several present shorter family versions of their productions, and some dress rehearsals are open to the public. Guided behind-the-scenes tours of the entire complex and of the Met are offered almost every day. Ask about family programs, including the Great Performers series.

Metropolitan Museum of Art (all ages)
1000 Fifth Avenue, at 82nd Street; (212) 535–7710; www.metmuseum.org. Open Tuesday, Wednesday, Thursday, and Sunday 9:30 A.M. to 5:30 P.M.; Friday and Saturday until 9:00 P.M. Closed Monday. Recommended admission adults $$$, children $$, children under 12 free with adult. Guided and recorded tours $. Strollers not allowed on Sunday, but back carriers are available.

Housing more than two million international works of art from prehistory to present day, this is the country's finest and most comprehensive art museum. With so much to see, it can be overwhelming, but if you let your child be your tour guide, go with the flow, and leave before you're worn out, you'll have a great time. First stop should be the gift shop, where you'll find a wonderful children's introductory guide to this place called *Inside the Museum,* by Joy Richardson. Or let your children pick out an assortment of postcards of favorite or intriguing works of art, and together embark on a treasure hunt to find the originals.

Using a map, plan your path past the following family favorites: the real mummies, tomb models, and the Temple of Dendur in the Egyptian wing; the renovated Arms and Armor gallery; the European and American period rooms mentioned in *From the Mixed-up Files of Mrs. Basil E. Frankweiler;* the musical instrument gallery; the Costume Institute; the statues and stained glass of the American Wing; the seasonal rooftop sculpture garden; and the more than 3,000 European master paintings.

Ask about the Family Audio Guide (one-hour tours, $) and special family programs (**free** with museum admission).

Morris-Jumel Mansion (ages 7 and up)

65 Jumel Terrace; (212) 923–8008. Open Wednesday through Sunday 10:00 A.M. to 4:00 P.M. $

Built in 1765, this Georgian-style manor served as the Revolutionary War headquarters of Gen. George Washington, and it is the oldest colonial mansion in Manhattan. It's also reportedly New York's most famous haunted house.

National Museum of the American Indian (all ages)

1 Bowling Green; (212) 514–3700; www.si.edu/nmai. Open daily year-round 10:00 A.M. to 5:00 P.M., Thursday to 8:00 P.M. Closed Christmas. Free.

More than a million artifacts, spanning 10,000 years of Native American culture and history, are housed inside this beautiful Beaux Arts building, but only a small portion are on display. Family programs feature Native dance, music, theater, storytelling, and multimedia presentations.

More **Manhattan Parks**

Riverbank State Park. 679 Riverside Drive, at 145th Street; (212) 694–3600; www.nysparks.com/parks.

Inwood Hill Park and Ecology Center. 218th Street and Indian Road; (212) 304–2365 or (718) 383–6363; www.nyc.gov/parks.

Riverside Park. Between the Hudson River and Riverside Drive, from 72nd Street to 153rd Street; (212) 408–0265; www.nyc.gov/parks.

New-York Historical Society (ages 4 and up)

2 West 77th Street; (212) 873–3400; www.nyhistory.org. Open Tuesday through Saturday 10:00 A.M. to 5:00 P.M., closed Saturday in summer. Free.

For nearly two centuries this museum has been the archival heart of New York, housing an interesting and eclectic collection of art and artifacts of the Empire State. Among the treasures are an original copy of the Declaration of Independence, 431 original watercolors of American birds by John James Audubon, and more than a hundred Louis Comfort Tiffany stained-glass lamps. Downstairs is Kid City, an exhibit where children can learn what life was like on the Upper West Side a hundred years ago.

New York Public Library (all ages)

455 Fifth Avenue at Fortieth Street; (212) 340–0833; www.nypl.org. Open Monday, Wednesday, Thursday 9:00 A.M. to 9:00 P.M., Tuesday 11:00 A.M. to 7:00 P.M., Friday and Saturday 10:00 A.M. to 6:00 P.M. Free.

Guarded by the literary lions Patience and Fortitude, this Beaux Arts building houses one of the finest research libraries in the world. Barrel-vaulted ceilings and cool marble staircases lead to the breathtaking Rose Reading Room, recently renovated for $15 million. Nearly as long as a football field and 52 feet high, the Rose Reading Room is truly one of the great public spaces, with polished oak tables, glowing brass lamps, Tintoretto-type clouds on a gilded ceiling, and free access to the thoughts, ideas, and dreams of great minds and master spirits. Access has improved considerably with the wiring of laptop computer and multimedia workstations into the tables, which can connect with the library's electronic collections, databases, and the Internet.

Rockefeller Center (all ages)

30 Rockefeller Plaza (visitor center); (212) 632–3975 or (212) 632–4041; www.radiocity.com. Radio City Music Hall (212) 307–7171 or (212) 247–4777. NBC Studios (212) 664–7174; www.nbc.com. Open year-round. Visitor center open weekdays 10:00 A.M. to 5:00 P.M. Studio and show admission varies with performance.

An art deco dream city within a city of nineteen buildings, this complex was developed by the visionary millionaire John D. Rockefeller Jr. during the Great Depression. Most famous of these structures is Radio City Music Hall, home of the awesome Rockettes and of the "Mighty Wurlitzer" organ, whose booming notes are noted by subway travelers below. The music hall, housing the biggest indoor stage in the world, offers behind-the-scenes tours daily. Nearby are the Channel Gardens, floral fountains sandwiched between the British and French buildings. Stroll down to the golden Prometheus statue that hovers over a seasonal outdoor cafe or a popular winter ice rink. Ask about a schedule for the NBC Studio Tour and the Rockefeller Center Tour.

Theodore Roosevelt National Historic Site (ages 7 and up)

28 East 20th Street; (212) 260–1616; www.nps.gov/thrb. Open Tuesday through Saturday 9:00 A.M. to 5:00 P.M. $, children under 16 free.

This reconstructed childhood home of our twenty-sixth president houses the largest collection of artifacts and memorabilia about his life in the world.

Sony Wonder Technology Lab (ages 4 and up)

550 Madison Avenue, between 55th and 56th Streets; (212) 833–8100. Open Tuesday through Saturday 10:00 A.M. to 6:00 P.M., Thursday to 8:00 P.M., Sunday noon to 6:00 P.M. Free.

Four floors of cutting-edge communication, industrial, and entertainment technology await visitors at this fascinating electronic play place. Using a personally customized photo ID card, kids can experiment with robots, video games, and even a digital recording console, then get a certificate of their accomplishments printed out at the end. Sometimes there's a bit of a wait, but once inside there are plenty of open stations and a helpful staff to guide you.

South Street Seaport (all ages)

12 Fulton Street; (212) 732–8257 or (212) SEA–PORT; www.southstreetseaport.com. Open year-round Monday through Saturday 10:00 A.M. to 9:00 P.M., Sunday 11:00 A.M. to 8:00 P.M. Closing time varies, call to confirm. Adults $$, children $.

Once scores of sleek clipper ships docked at this busy nineteenth-century port. Today, after an extensive renovation and reinvention as part maritime park and part urban shopping mall, the 11-square-block historic district encompasses a Children's Center, three galleries, a working nineteenth-century printing shop, a Maritime Arts Center, a boat-building shop, an archaeological dig, and one of the largest fleets of historical sailing ships in the country. Begin at the Seaport Museum Visitor's Center, where you can buy tickets to the galleries and boat rides and get a schedule of current family events and workshops. The Children's Center has interesting interactive hands-on exhibits, but kids will taste real adventure when they climb aboard the massive four-masted bark *Peking*, sail New York harbor aboard the 1885 schooner *Pioneer*, or take the early morning Fulton Fish Market tour (212–669–9416).

Statue of Liberty (all ages)

Liberty Island, New York Harbor; (212) 269–5755, (212) 363–3200, or (866) STATUE–4; www.nps.gov/stli or www.statueofliberty.org. Open daily, first guided tour begins at 8:45 A.M., the last is at 3:45 P.M. Call for more details. Closed Christmas Day. Free, but there is a charge for the ferry.

Towering 305 feet over New York's harbor, the Statue of Liberty Enlightening the World, a gift from France, has become New York's most famous figure. Designed by sculptor Frederic-Auguste Bartholdi, who used his mother as a model, Lady Liberty has been welcoming visitors since 1886. Board the Circle Line's Statue of Liberty Ferry, docked in Battery Park, for an exhilarating ride across the harbor to Liberty Island. If time is limited, stay on the ferry for a return trip or continue on to Ellis Island.

The Statue of Liberty reopened to the public in August 2004. If you choose to disembark, there's an interesting museum and observation deck inside the statue's base, but at present, the option of climbing the 354 steps to the crown is not possible because of

In **Memory**

On September 11, 2001, the towers of the World Trade Center collapsed after they were targets of terrorists flying hijacked planes. Future plans for this twenty-acre site include a memorial for the thousands of people who perished, but for the present, there is a viewing area at Liberty Street and Broadway open 9:00 A.M. to 9:00 P.M. Stop by the City Hall Park Visitor Information kiosk at Park Row and Broadway for current info.

post-9/11 security measures. The words of Emma Lazarus's poem, "Give me your tired, your poor, Your huddled masses yearning to breathe free," will take on new meaning for you and your family after a visit here.

Forbes Magazine Galleries (all ages)
62 Fifth Avenue, at 12th Street; (212) 206–5548. Open Tuesday, Wednesday, Friday, and Saturday 10:00 A.M. to 4:00 P.M. Closed major holidays. Free.

Media magnate Malcolm Forbes amassed an amazing collection of thousands of toy figures, toy boats, Monopoly games, historical documents, and trophies.

Riverside Church (ages 4 and up)
490 Riverside Drive, at 122nd Street; (212) 870–6700; www.theriversidechurchny.org. Tower open Tuesday through Saturday 11:00 A.M. to 4:00 P.M. and Sunday 12:30 to 4:00 P.M. Grant's Tomb (212) 666–1640. $

Inside this Gothic cathedral rests the largest carillon in the world, with a twenty-ton Bourdon hour bell, and seventy-three smaller ones, as well as an organ with 22,000 pipes. Climb to the bell tower for panoramic views of Manhattan. Across the street is the elaborate Grant's Tomb and the answer to the riddle of who is buried there.

United Nations (ages 7 and older)
First Avenue, at 46th Street; (212) 963–7713 or (212) 963–TOUR; www.un.org. Call (212) 963–1234 each morning for session agenda. For tours in other languages, call (212) 963–7539. Open daily March through December 9:30 A.M. to 4:45 P.M. Monday to Friday 10:00 A.M. to 4:30 P.M. Saturday through Sunday; Monday through Friday only January through February. Note that children under 5 are not allowed on tours. Adults $$$, children $$.

Technically, this eighteen-acre complex is not part of New York or the United States but is an international zone with its own security force and post office. Founded in 1945, the 185 member nations meet to promote world peace and self-determination and to provide humanitarian, economic, and social aid to the world. Tours are offered daily in several languages. Take a moment to look at the poignant exhibit of artifacts from the nuclear bombing of Hiroshima and Nagasaki. If the General Assembly is in session, you'll be able to listen on headsets as delegates debate and discuss their ideas, while being simultaneously translated from or into English, French, Spanish, Russian, Arabic, and Chinese.

Battery Park City Esplanade and Hudson River Park

(all ages) 🚻 🚶 🍴 🏛

Tip of Manhattan, along the river from First Street to Chambers Street; (212) 267–9700 or (212) 416–5300. Winter Garden (212) 945–0505; www.bpcparks.org, www.worldfinancial center.com, or www.batteryparkcity.org. Open year-round. Free.

Someday plans call for a greenbelt all around Manhattan, but for the moment this narrow promenade hugging Manhattan's lower western coastline is a good beginning. To enjoy

---

Theme **Restaurants**

Personally, I think New York is one giant theme park, but for pockets of pop themes in Manhattan, here's a list:

Hard Rock Cafe. 221 West 57th Street; (212) 489–6565. (rock 'n' roll)

Planet Hollywood. 1540 Broadway; (212) 333–STAR (7827). (movies)

Brooklyn Diner. 212 West 57th Street; (212) 581–8900. (50s diner)

Jekyll and Hyde Club. 1409 Avenue of the Americas; (212) 541–9505. (spooky)

Mars 2112. 1633 Broadway; (212) 582–2112. (space)

Ellen's Stardust Diner. 1650 Broadway; (212) 956–5151. (1950s subway)

ESPN-Zone. 1472 Broadway; (212) 921–3776. (sports)

Mickey Mantle's Restaurant. 42 Central Park South; (212) 688–7777. (baseball)

Cowgirl Hall of Fame. 519 Hudson Street; (212) 633–1133. (western)

B. B. King Blues Club & Grill. 237 West 42nd Street, (212) 997–4144. (blues)

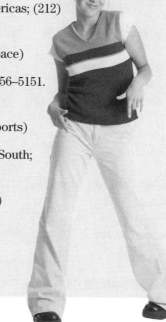

bracing views of New York Harbor, stroll through South Cove and head north along the esplanade. Inside this massive complex is the cavernous glass Winter Palace, with towering palm trees, upscale shops and restaurants, and a regular schedule of **free** live entertainment and family events. About 6 blocks north of Chambers Street, check out the exhibits of the River Project on Pier 26 and the funky miniature golf course farther north. All along the esplanade you'll find open lawns, playgrounds (geared for toddlers as well as older children), gardens, public art pieces, a marina—even a trapeze school.

Where to Eat

New York City has more than 18,000 restaurants, featuring every ethnic cuisine in every price range and nearly 3,000 pizzerias. If the weather permits, pack a picnic with deli delights and head for the nearest park. There are restaurants on every block and a pizza parlor on almost every corner. Below are some of my family's favorite places:

America. 9 East 18th Street; (212) 505–2110. $$–$$$

Boathouse Cafe. 72nd Street, in Central Park; (212) 517–2233. $$$$

Bubby's. 120 Hudson Street; (212) 219–0666. $$

E.J.'s Luncheonette. 477 Amsterdam Avenue; (212) 873–3444. $$$

John's Pizzeria. 278 Bleecker Street; (212) 243–1680. $$

Lombardi's. 32 Spring Street; (212) 941–7994. $$

Mama Mexico. 2672 Broadway; (212) 864–2323. $$

Peanut Butter & Co. 240 Sullivan Street; (212) 677–3995. $

Popover Cafe. 551 Amsterdam Avenue; (212) 595–8555. $$$

Ruby Foo's Times Square. 1626 Broadway; (212) 489–5600. $$–$$$

Serendipity 3. 225 East 60th Street; (212) 838–3531. $$–$$$

Sylvia's. 328 Lenox Avenue; (212) 996–0660. $$–$$$

Tavern on the Green. 67th Street in Central Park; (212) 873–3200. $$$$

Tom's. 782 Washington Avenue, Prospect Heights, Brooklyn; (718) 636–9738. $–$$

Two Boots Restaurant. 37 Avenue A; (212) 505–2276. $

Virgil's Real Barbeque. 152 West 44th Street; (212) 921–9494. $$–$$$$

Where to Stay

There are hundreds of hotels in New York, but they're often heavily booked during peak tourist times, so make reservations in advance. Although accommodations are usually expensive, here are some family-friendly favorites, and NYC & Company can provide many more.

DoubleTree Guest Suites. 1568 Broadway; (212) 719–1600; www.doubletree .com. Theater district. $$$$

Excelsior Hotel. 45 West 81st Street; (212) 362–9200 or (800) 368–4575; www.excelsiorhotelny.com. Upper West Side. $$$$

Le Parker Meridien. 118 West 57th Street; (212) 245–5000 or (800) 543–4300; www.parkermeridien.com. Midtown. $$$$

Quality Hotel on Broadway. 215 West 94th Street; (212) 866–6400; www.bestny hotels.com. $$$$

The Plaza. Fifth Avenue at Central Park South; (212) 759–3000. $$$$

Surrey Hotel. 20 East 76th Street; (212) 288–3700. East Side. $$$$

Washington Square Hotel. 101–105 Waverly Place; (212) 777–9515 or (800) 222–0418. Greenwich Village. $$$$

For More Information

NYC & Company's Visitor Information Center. (212) 484–1222 or (800) NYC–VISIT; www.nycvisit.com.

Times Square Visitors Center. (212) 768–1560; www.timessquarebid.org.

Downtown New York. (212) 509–0300 or (800) 377–1083; www.wallstreetrising.org.

Hotel Reservations. (800) 96–HOTEL; www.hotels.com.

CityPass. (208) 787–4300 or (888) 330–5008; www.citypass.net.

MTA New York City Transit Subway and Bus Information. (718) 330–3322 or (718) 330–1234; www.mta.nyc.ny.us.

MetroCard. (212) METROCARD.

NYC Kids Arts. www.nyckidsarts.org.

New York City Culture Guide & Calendar. www.nyc-arts.org.

Department of Parks and Recreation Special Events. (212) 360–3456, (888) NYPARKS, or (888) 201–PARK; www.nyc parks.com.

Virtual Tour of New York City. www.nyc tourist.com.

The Official New York City Web Site. www.nyc.gov.

Time Out New York. www.timeoutny.com.

Bronx Tourism Council. (718) 590–3518; www.ilovethebronx.com.

Brooklyn Tourism Council. (718) 855–7882; www.brooklynx.org/tourism.

Staten Island Tourism. (718) 816–2000 or (800) 573–SINY; www.statenislandusa.com.

Queens Tourism. (718) 286–2663; www.queensbp.org.

Big Apple Greeter. (212) 669–8159; www.bigapplegreeter.org.

Index

About the Author

An avid explorer and experienced world traveler, Mary Lynn Blanks toured and trekked across almost every continent during her childhood. After attending Florida State University on a theater scholarship, she moved to New York City and joined the casts of ABC's *All My Children* as Tara, and later on CBS's *As the World Turns* as Annie. Fulfilling a lifelong dream, she then ran away with the circus . . . writing and co-producing original television and radio programs and commercials for Ringling Bros. and Barnum & Bailey Circus. Unofficially known as the "Cupcake Queen of MSC," she is also an FAA-licensed pilot, a PADI-certified scuba diver, and the proud soccer mom of sons Christopher and Nicholas.